D1190309

Expressive
Intersections
in Brahms

MUSICAL MEANING AND INTERPRETATION
Robert S. Hatten, editor

EDITED BY
HEATHER PLATT
AND
PETER H. SMITH

Expressive Intersections in Brahms

Essays in Analysis and Meaning

INDIANA UNIVERSITY PRESS

Bloomington and Indianapolis

This book is a publication of

Indiana University Press
601 North Morton Street
Bloomington, Indiana 47404-3797 USA

iupress.indiana.edu

Telephone orders	800-842-6796
Fax orders	812-855-7931

Library of Congress Cataloging-in-Publication Data

Expressive intersections in Brahms : essays in analysis and meaning /
[edited by] Heather Platt and Peter H. Smith.
    p. cm. — (Musical meaning and interpretation)
  Includes bibliographical references and index.
  ISBN 978-0-253-35705-2 (cloth : alk. paper) — ISBN 978-0-253-00525-0
(e-book) 1. Brahms, Johannes, 1833–1897—Criticism and interpretation.
I. Platt, Heather Anne. II. Smith, Peter Howard.
  ML410.B8E77 2012
  780.92—dc23
                        2011031951

1 2 3 4 5 17 16 15 14 13 12

Contents

Acknowledgments

The impetus for a volume of essays exploring intersections of consummate technical craft and profound expressivity in Brahms's music arose from discussions with members of the Board of Directors of the American Brahms Society. We are indebted to the society for its encouragement and for its generous subvention to defray expenses associated with the production of this book. The society has supported five other volumes: *Brahms Studies: Analytical and Historical Perspectives,* ed. George S. Bozarth (Oxford: Clarendon Press, 1990); *Brahms Studies 1–3,* ed. David Brodbeck (Lincoln: University of Nebraska Press in affiliation with the American Brahms Society, 1994, 1998, and 2001); and *On Brahms and His Circle: Essays and Documentary Studies by Karl Geiringer,* ed. George S. Bozarth (Sterling Heights, Mich.: Harmonie Park Press in Association with the American Brahms Society, 2006). *Expressive Intersections in Brahms: Essays in Analysis and Meaning* complements and extends these works by bringing together some of the most recent scholarly approaches to the analysis and hermeneutic interpretation of Brahms's compositions.

From the very early stages of the project, Robert Hatten, series editor, and Jane Behnken, sponsoring editor, at Indiana University Press have demonstrated their unflagging support. We are grateful for their guidance through the various stages of work on this volume and for their assistance in arranging for the illustrations that appear in chapters 3 and 4. Robert gave generously of his time, perceptively reading each of the essays as they were completed; all our authors have benefited from his editorial acumen. A number of other scholars also offered advice at the very earliest stages, when the concept of the volume was only beginning to emerge: we are grateful for the counsel of Richard Cohn, Roe-Min Kok, and Joseph N. Straus. We would also like to acknowledge the constructive criticisms of the anonymous scholars who reviewed our initial proposal for the press; in particular, we greatly appreciate L. Poundie Burstein's advice and encouragement.

We were fortunate to have contributors who immediately recognized the merits of the project. They conceived fascinating essays, each of which brings a unique voice to the volume, and they graciously participated in discussions throughout the editorial process. Aside from the stimulating ideas offered by the authors, both in their essays and in e-mail exchanges, we greatly appreciated their unfailingly prompt responses to our queries and concerns. In particular, we acknowledge Steven Rings, who read and commented on our first chapter,

"'The Wondrous Transformation of Thought into Sound': Some Preliminary Reflections on Musical Meaning in Brahms."

Travis Jeffords set the musical examples in chapters 4, 5, 8, and 9. It was a pleasure to work with an engraver with such a superb eye for detail and who quickly attended to even the slightest correction or alteration. The examples in the other chapters were prepared by the respective authors; their ability to adapt their finely tuned design techniques to a uniform style greatly eased the burdens of production of the final volume.

Finally, we are especially indebted to our families: Peter's wife and son, Lumi and Manny, and Heather's husband, Mark Kaplan. They too gave their love, time, and patience to this project in far too many ways to enumerate here.

Part One

1 "The Wondrous Transformation of Thought into Sound": Some Preliminary Reflections on Musical Meaning in Brahms

Heather Platt and Peter H. Smith

From where he sat, Clive tried to prevent his attention from being drawn into technical detail. For now, it was the music, the wondrous transformation of thought into sound. . . . Sometimes Clive worked so hard on a piece that he could lose sight of his ultimate purpose—to create this pleasure at once so sensual and abstract, to translate into vibrating air this nonlanguage whose meanings were forever just beyond reach, suspended tantalizingly at a point where emotion and intellect fused.

Ian McEwan, Amsterdam

Although the omniscient narrator of Ian McEwan's novel *Amsterdam* attributes these thoughts to a fictional late twentieth-century British composer, Clive Linley, contemplating his own composition, Linley's reflections capture something of the universal mystery of music. The dualities the narrator develops between technical detail and wondrous transformation, between thought and sound, between hard work and sensual pleasure also resonate strongly with the unique musical persona of Johannes Brahms, a composer whose works have long been admired for their highly wrought craftsmanship as well as for their expressive immediacy. So, too, do the narrator's words capture something of the challenge faced by the music scholar dedicated to the close study of Brahms's compositions. How does one remain attuned to Brahms's abundant compositional craft—the fruits of the composer's hard labor and a self-conscious emblem of his works' individuality—without losing sight of the music's sensual beauty? Moreover, how do we engage a musical language that, while not strictly referential, nevertheless possesses deep meaning?

Despite the acuity of McEwan's narrative voice (not to mention the beauty of his prose), the thoughts this voice attributes to the composer Linley remain somewhat marred by an abundance of potentially false dichotomies. Rather than accept the assumption that emotion and intellect stand at odds in Brahms—that we, like Clive Linley, need to avoid being drawn into technical details in order to appreciate the wondrous transformation of thought into sound, to appreciate musical meaning, in other words—the authors in this volume see these characteristics as inextricably linked. Our view and a premise underlying each essay is not that Brahms's music is meaningful in spite of its organizational intricacy but rather that meaning and technical complexity form an intimate bond. These two conceptions of Brahms's music—as a manifestation of powerful intellect and of passionate expressivity—interact dialectically, with meaning poised, as McEwan/Linley would have it, at the intersection of emotion and reason.

Our volume brings together eight perspectives on how meaning may be interpreted in Brahms's compositions, spanning a variety of genres, including works for solo piano, chamber music, and a concerto movement of symphonic proportions, as well as texted works for either solo voice (lieder) or chorus and orchestra. During his lifetime and even throughout much of the twentieth century, Brahms was viewed as a composer of absolute music, that is, music of an abstract or purely formalist character.[1] In more recent decades, historians have uncovered a wealth of documentation demonstrating that neither he nor the members of his circle heard his compositions in this way. Many theorists nevertheless continue to approach his music with something akin to scientific objectivity, apparently, like Linley, finding themselves unable to avoid being drawn into technical detail. *Expressive Intersections in Brahms* argues that a more thorough understanding of Brahms's music emerges when issues of meaning are considered in conjunction with those of structure—indeed, that these aspects of the aesthetic experience are inseparable.

Issues of structure, and the complex ways in which Brahms intertwines all the various musical elements, have been at the heart of the theoretical approaches that have proliferated following Allen Forte's 1983 call for more rigorous analysis of Brahms's music, in his study of the String Quartet in C Minor, op. 51, no. 1.[2] Even now, nearly thirty years later, we find both a steady stream of systematic analyses and a variety of theoretical approaches designed specifically to address the structure of Brahms's music.[3] To a great extent, many of the publications first responding to Forte's challenge focused on technical explanations of motivic, formal, and tonal organization; their positivistic rationality reflected academic culture in many disciplines during, and considerably before, that part of the twentieth century.[4] From an historical perspective, the formalist response to Brahms was in some ways anticipated by Felix Weingartner's 1897 description of the composer's "scientific music" as well as by earlier critics who similarly remarked on this music's technical intricacies.[5] Although works such as Forte's analysis of the C-minor string quartet offered significant new insights, the general trend tended to push the more subjective (or slippery) topic of expressivity to the margin.

The persistence of the image of Brahms as a pure formalist was in part aided by what many have come to understand as a misreading of Eduard Hanslick to the effect that "music was to be understood in exclusively structural terms while issues of meaning were ruled out of court."[6] Aside from the fact that this approach meshed with the pseudoscientific methods of the emerging discipline of music theory, Hanslick had particular relevance because of his friendship with Brahms and his vigorous endorsement of the composer in the nineteenth-century press.[7] Gradually, however, as musicologists sifted through the writings of nineteenth-century critics and documents from Brahms and his circle, it became clear that the formalist label represented an historical distortion. A wide variety of nineteenth-century listeners, including Brahms's closest friends, described his music quite evocatively, and Brahms himself often associated specific instrumental pieces with poems or other extramusical references.

A significant number of recent musicological studies have approached the issue of meaning in Brahms's music through a focus on literary connections or Brahms's habit of alluding in tones to either other composers' works or his own. Other scholars have delved into nineteenth-century German aesthetics, politics, nationalism, and religion to speculate on the degree to which Brahms's music reflects these aspects of his milieu.[8] Despite the insights of these approaches—and they are substantial—there is sometimes a tendency to focus on isolated musical passages, with an emphasis on how such passages may relate provocatively to Brahms's cultural milieu but without a fuller account of how a passage or its cultural references interact with a composition's global organization. For those who hear structurally, these publications, despite their great merits, do not seem to tell the whole story.

By comparison with both the number and prominence of these musicological publications, theorists have seemed somewhat more reluctant to confront questions of Brahmsian meaning. The one major monograph on the topic is Peter H. Smith's *Expressive Forms in Brahms's Instrumental Music*. Smith is nevertheless not the only theorist to discuss Brahmsian expressivity from a technical standpoint. Since the start of the new century, two of our authors—Ryan McClelland and Frank Samarotto—have probed the intersection of structure and expression in Brahms's music.[9] The recent volumes exploring musical meaning by Robert Hatten, Michael Klein, and Kofi Agawu also include interpretations of some of Brahms's instrumental compositions.[10] These interpretations of Hatten, Klein, and Agawu, however, tend to be brief, while the more detailed analyses of McClelland and Samarotto have appeared in such a wide range of international publications that it can be difficult to appreciate the extent to which analytical approaches to Brahms's music have evolved in recent years and, moreover, to grasp the full potential of these approaches to contribute to a deeper intellectual understanding of musical meaning in Brahms. Indeed, the possibilities have scarcely been exhausted. *Expressive Intersections in Brahms: Essays in Analysis and Meaning* aims to build on these theoretical studies, and also on recent musicological work, to place at center stage the interpretation of expressive meaning from the standpoint of close technical analysis.

Aside from their common assumption that structural analysis has the potential to illuminate musical meaning and make it available for reflection, all the essays illustrate that hermeneutic interpretation is inseparable from hearing with one's imagination. Each of the authors draws creative links between a close reading of a composition and aspects of either cultural history or more purely musical traditions—or a combination of the two. The authors' strategies range from references to studies of art and literature to intertextual forays that compare a specific passage or compositional technique with similar ones in other works by Brahms or his predecessors. These comparisons illustrate that meaning may arise when a composition or passage enters into a dialogical relationship—an expressive intersection—with related genres and forms, a theme that unifies the volume. An additional common thread is the recourse, in a number of the analyses, to semiotic concepts such as markedness, developed by Hatten and other theorists of musical meaning, in which a gesture such as a dramatic melodic leap, a rhythmic disruption, or an ambiguous harmonic progression may signal the expressive crux of a piece. A number of our authors also draw on the tradition of topical analysis to facilitate hermeneutic interpretation and on such concepts as "temporal shifting," a term Hatten uses to denote passages in which a "continuous idea is broken off, or its clearly projected goal is evaded, as in certain rhetorical gestures or shifts in level of discourse."[11]

While some of our contributors imply that Brahms intended his pieces to have the meanings they experience, and some build interpretations based on impressions of Brahms's contemporaries, the main thrust is not a concern for authorial intention.[12] Moreover, our argument is not that some pieces of Brahms have extramusical meaning and others do not. Rather, all his compositions have the potential to carry meaning for particular listeners. Inevitably, the techniques for assigning meaning as well as those for parsing the structure of a piece are subjective, and, following Hans-Georg Gadamer in *Truth and Method* (1975), we acknowledge that each author's methods are contingent on his or her background, experience, training, aesthetics, and so forth. Among other consequences, this authorial subjectivity and diversity of background may prove decisive in whether an individual writer engages musical meaning with a greater focus on historical context or more purely technical concerns.

Leo Treitler has argued that "meaning in music is a function of the engagement of codes or orders by the note-complexes of which the music is comprised."[13]

We view these "codes or orders" as deriving from both musical and extramusical realms and believe that an exploration of these realms can only be enriched by a thorough understanding of the technical organization of the "note-complexes." That is to say, like Richard Taruskin, we reject the premise that hermeneutics and a close reading of the score are incompatible, as Gary Tomlinson and other New Musicologists have claimed.[14]

For all our authors, one of the roles of technical analysis—and especially technical analysis based on highly developed theories like those of Schenker, James Hepokoski and Warren Darcy, and recent scholars of musical rhythm—is to provide a basis in musical detail for the intensely personal act of expressive interpretation. Richard Cohn has already demonstrated the advantages of approaching questions of meaning through systematic analysis in his provocative conclusion to an article marshaling Neo-Riemannian techniques to explore the harmonic structure of compositions by Schubert.[15] Systematic analysis not only permits a greater understanding of the technical characteristics of Brahms's music but also creates possibilities for a more thorough and nuanced consideration of its various potential meanings. That is, detailed, theory-based analysis provides the means to make the *subjective* response of a listener *intersubjective*.

Brahms's friends, most notably Clara Schumann and Elisabet von Herzogenberg, and some critics, including Hermann Deiters and Hermann Kretzschmar, often acknowledged the expressive power of his harmony. But despite the acuity of their observations, they did not provide detailed analyses, and their comments are more descriptive than analytical; their evocative metaphors (which still resonate with today's listeners) do not attempt to elucidate how or why the music conveys a given emotion or image. More recent scholars, by contrast, have developed a wide range of approaches to penetrate Brahms's intricate tonal language, including methodologies based on Schenkerian techniques as well as the newer Neo-Riemannian and transformational theories. These methodologies also have the potential to explore the expressive quality that Brahms's colleagues intuited, as essays in this volume demonstrate.[16]

Similarly, whereas nineteenth-century writers often referenced Brahms's harmonies, they usually did not discuss the complexities of his rhythmic invention. It is only in recent decades that theorists such as Carl Schachter, William Rothstein, David Lewin, Harald Krebs, and Richard Cohn have developed techniques for addressing the types of complex rhythmic-metric phenomena that characterize Brahms's music.[17] By extending and adapting these concepts, writers in this volume engage the expressive power of Brahms's rhythmic-metric artistry. And likewise, with the recent reinvigoration of the *Formenlehre* tradition in the work of either William Caplin or Hepokoski and Darcy, theorists are now able to interrogate the intersections of structure and meaning in Brahms's large-scale forms with much greater precision than either the composer's contemporaries or earlier twentieth-century scholars.[18] In all cases, these elements (harmony, rhythm, and form) are not viewed in isolation—it is their interaction with each other and with other musical and extramusical elements that creates the meanings that our authors interpret.

Expressive Intersections in Brahms comprises three sections. Part 1 presents an overview of issues associated with interpretation of meaning in Brahms, part 2 includes analyses of texted works in their cultural context, and part 3 covers explorations of expressive forms in instrumental music. Steven Rings's essay encompasses many of the approaches to interpretation that recur throughout the volume and hence is paired with this introduction as part 1. "The Learned Self: Artifice in Brahms's Late Intermezzi" exhibits rigorous analysis of voice leading and motive, sensitivity to Brahms's rhythmic manipulations, and insight into Brahms's late style and the environment in which it emerged. Like the writers in part 2, Rings draws on the responses of Brahms's circle, but he also emphasizes the experience of the performer through a focus on the meaningfulness that the intermezzi's most intricate moments provide for the pianist who renders them. Whereas analysts occasionally use the image of a composer *staging* a particularly rhetorical gesture, Rings argues that when playing these pieces, a pianist physically *enacts* the types of inwardness and subjectivity that frequently characterize Brahms's piano miniatures, offering a means of interpretation that has rarely been addressed by either Brahms scholars or other students of meaning.[19] In his recent monograph *Music as Discourse,* Agawu recounts the private joy of the individual analyst reveling in the discovery of the distinct threads of an intricate passage.[20] Rings's essay not only exemplifies this wonderment but also derives musical meaning specifically from the personal experience of the solitary performer. It demonstrates, moreover, that Brahms appears to have designed technical aspects of the intermezzi in order to draw the performer bodily into these moments of heightened expressive rapture. The technical and expressive literally work hand in hand through performance in a powerful demonstration of a core thesis of this collection.

In their forays into music with text in part 2, Yonatan Malin, Heather Platt, and Margaret Notley achieve much more than an account of how Brahms's music meshes with, contradicts, or supplements the poetic sources. Malin and Platt engage both the visual and literary arts of Brahms's time, in conjunction with their insights into the tonal and temporal dimensions of Brahms's musical settings, to interpret meaning in his lieder. Notley provides a sympathetic account of Brahms's interpretation of the Goethe text in his *Gesang der Parzen* by drawing on a vast array of sources, encompassing ideas about ancient Greek ode structure, Aristotle's conception of tragedy, the critical reactions of nineteenth-century writers, and discussions of the work in Brahms's correspondence. In so doing, she offers a far more stimulating and novel interpretation of the meaning of this underappreciated composition than either critics of the composer's own time or modern scholars have been able to achieve.

Malin focuses on the five songs that the artist Max Klinger included in his illustrated anthology of compositions by Brahms, the *Brahms Fantasy*. Whereas Rings marshals descriptions by Brahms's colleagues to support his reading of the tactile and intensely introspective quality of the late intermezzi, Malin studies one artist's visual responses to Brahms's songs and allows those responses to influence his own original interpretations of the compositions. In his essay, "'Alte Liebe' and the Birds of Spring: Text, Music, and Image in Max Klinger's *Brahms Fantasy*," Malin begins with a detailed account of relationships among text, music, and image throughout the first of the songs, "Alte Liebe," and illustrates how the three interact to create a pandimensional "structural downbeat" at the climax of the song. This climax arrives at the unique moment in the *Brahms Fantasy* in which Klinger presents an image that literally emerges out of Brahms's musical score, and Malin explores ways in which this text-music-image "blend" affects the interpretation of these domains (both individually and in combination) throughout the remainder of the song. The literal merger of score and image sets the song's poetic persona onto the path of a dream that has taken hold of him while in the throes of an "old love-sorrow," and Malin then traces how this poetic "journey" continues, in text, music, and image, through the other four songs of the cycle.

Platt, in "Brahms's *Mädchenlieder* and Their Cultural Context," develops a still broader context for her interpretation of Brahms's lieder. She accesses the stereotypical portraits of young women in nineteenth-century literature and the visual arts and allows these images to shape her interpretation of three of Brahms's songs depicting similar figures. Platt proposes that the naiveté in these songs should not be taken prima facie but rather as a musical "mask" that is analogous to the poses thrust upon girls by social expectations. This hermeneutic window suggests an ironic reversal: the simplicity of the songs' folk style expresses not a natural truth but rather a socially imposed falseness. What is true about the emotions described in these songs is their heartfelt character, and Brahms depicts this emotional depth with great acuity through ingeniously combining unusual, large-scale tonal structures with a variety of expressive rhythmic dissonances and melodic gestures.

For Platt, the meaning of a piece emerges from the interaction between literary and visual representations of a cultural archetype and the idiosyncratic technical characteristics of Brahms's musical renderings of that archetype. Notley brings a similar historical orientation to bear, although in her study of the *Gesang der Parzen* the relevant context is the nineteenth century's critical reception of Brahms's composition and the work's relationship to the Goethe play from which Brahms took its text. In "Ancient Tragedy and Anachronism: Form as Expression in Brahms's *Gesang der Parzen*," she demonstrates that the *Gesang's* development of its main thematic ideas in a novel musical form reflects the text's shift from a depiction of vengeful gods and mythic suffering in the distant past to personal suffering and a more humanistic perspective on the tragic condition in the present. In addition to the work's formal processes, Brahms's references to conventional genres and topics and his employment of striking harmonic progressions (including both startling third-related progressions and consistent evasions of strong tonic chords) contribute centrally to Notley's interpretation. Indeed, all these elements influence expressive interpretation throughout the volume, but they become especially prominent as hermeneutic tools with the shift in emphasis to instrumental compositions in part 3.

Whereas part 2 investigates ways in which meaning may be constructed through interactions with poetic texts and cultural contexts, the essays in part 3 tend to be more musically self-referential. All the authors nevertheless reach well beyond the single opus to engage meaning through comparisons with related pieces by Brahms and his predecessors or, more broadly, with time-honored compositional traditions.[21] Whereas James Hepokoski and Frank Samarotto infer meaning through reference to formal and generic conventions, and Peter H. Smith similarly explores tonal pairing in movement-length contexts, Ryan McClelland takes one of the most characteristic small-scale elements—the sequence—and demonstrates that, despite its ubiquity, sequential writing may well have a pivotal expressive function. In "Sequence as Expressive Culmination in the Chamber Music of Brahms," he explores the function of sequences in Brahms's final thematic statements or codas as a departure from their traditional deployment in the eighteenth century as agents of transition or development.

These sequences frequently convey a powerfully climactic effect in both tragic and affirmative contexts, but in some cases sequential writing participates in the recessive endings so typical of Brahms's first movements. The structural anomalies and richness of compositional detail in these *innig* sequences contribute to their profound, otherworldly character and suggest a turn inward in contrast to the extroversion of outward expansion in the climactic sequential types. The passages of introversion that McClelland describes are reminiscent of the moments of intimacy that Rings savors in Brahms's late piano pieces, and both authors reveal that these *innig* moments correspond with passages of intense compositional artifice. Indeed, one could say that the "intellectuality" of these moments, far from working against the potential for expressive depth (as

Brahms's critics often assert—here Weingartner's description of "scientific music" comes to mind), contributes centrally to that expression.

In contrast to Rings's and McClelland's concern for interiority, Samarotto's "'Phantasia subitanea': Temporal Caprice in Brahms's op. 116, nos. 1 and 7," draws attention to the remarkable volatility of the first D-minor Capriccio in op. 116 and concludes by noting similarities with the final capriccio of the set, which is also in D minor. Samarotto views the unexpected continuations and outright discontinuities of these late works through the filter of their generic title of "Capriccio" and draws his own self-referentially capricious line from a seventeenth-century theoretical definition through the op. 1 Caprices of Locatelli and a piano fantasy by Haydn to Brahms. The capriciousness of op. 116, no. 1, arises through what Hatten refers to as "confrontational strategies," a compositional approach oriented around "reversals, deferrals, sudden recognitions, redirections, and projections," which may ultimately function in the service of "positive rechargings of expressive energy."[22]

Samarotto's analysis of these confrontational strategies forms an illuminating comparison with Agawu's recent discussion of meaning in another late piano miniature, the Intermezzo op. 119, no. 2. Agawu hears this intermezzo in terms of a contrast between speech and song modes, and he deliberately eschews any attempt to relate the work's meaning to issues of genre or Brahms's late style. Rather, he states that his concern is with meanings that "emerge from 'purely' musical considerations" in an attempt to demonstrate that formalist analyses are themselves "legitimate modes of meaning formation."[23] Samarotto additionally illustrates that penetrating expressive interpretations may arise out of the intersection of explorations of other musical categories (e.g., genre) with in-depth analysis (in his case, Schenkerian analysis) of tonal and metric structures.

In their influential codification of eighteenth-century sonata form, Hepokoski and Darcy repeatedly demonstrate that at every formal juncture a composer makes choices that have both structural and expressive ramifications.[24] Theorists quickly realized that many of the concepts outlined in their *Formenlehre* could also be applied to nineteenth-century sonata forms, but to date most studies have concentrated on sonata "deformations" in composers such as Bruckner and Liszt.[25] Given Brahms's status as the leading proponent of the Viennese sonata tradition in the late nineteenth century, it is surprising that there has not been more of a concerted effort to apply Hepokoski and Darcy's principles to his music. In his essay for this volume, "Monumentality and Formal Processes in the First Movement of Brahms's Piano Concerto No. 1 in D Minor, op. 15," Hepokoski opens this promising avenue.

Not content merely to explore the formal structure of this complex movement, Hepokoski pursues the hermeneutic implications that emanate from its dialogical relationship with sonata conventions. Specifically, he traces how the movement stages an idiosyncratic manifestation of an archetypal form of sonata expression: the confrontation in the minor mode between the negative forces of crisis-ridden primary thematic material and the promise of transcendence offered by contrasting secondary material. More broadly, Hepokoski argues that the monumentality expressed in the movement's highly charged musical narrative intersects with the heated debates about the state of composition in Germany in the 1850s, and in this way, the essay returns to the themes of historical context explored in part 2.

Unlike most other major nineteenth-century figures, Brahms first established himself as a composer through works for chamber ensembles. Chamber genres were not widely associated with progressive compositional trends, and New Germans such as Wagner and Liszt largely eschewed this medium. Furthermore, adherents of the New German School and, perhaps even more significantly, scholars of the first half of the twentieth century associated chamber works, especially those by Brahms, with the designation of "absolute" music. Both Smith and McClelland refute this formalist association and demonstrate that the reputedly abstract intricacies of these works may well be primary carriers of expressive content. Whereas McClelland focuses on the expressive function of sequences that other commentators might regard as insignificant, Smith hones in on dialectical harmonic relationships in his essay "The Drama of Tonal Pairing in Chamber Music of Schumann and Brahms."

Smith explores movements that are organized around pairs of keys related by the interval of a third. Two of the articles in part 2 of the collection, those by Notley and Platt, also describe Brahms's penchant for third relations, and Platt analyzes two songs that also explicitly engage tonal pairing.[26] Numerous analysts have explored the diverse ways in which nineteenth-century composers manipulated keys and chords related by third and the ways these tertian relationships may be understood to have displaced the traditional tonic–dominant polarity.[27] Nevertheless, what is sometimes missed, particularly in studies of instrumental genres, is detailed pursuit of the expressive functions of these structures.[28]

Of course, Brahms was not the only composer to exploit the expressive potential of tonal pairing; it was a favorite technique of Schumann. Whereas Platt mentions this in passing, Smith brings it to the fore and demonstrates the many salient points of comparison between the strategies of the two composers. Smith focuses on the middle movements of three works: Schumann's Violin Sonata in A Minor, op. 105, and Brahms's Violin Sonata in A Major, op. 100, and String Quintet in F Major, op. 88. In all these middle movements, a particularly dramatic perspective emerges from the tension between the unitary demands of tonal centricity and the seemingly contradictory claims for a decentered harmonic rhetoric of tonal pairing. Like Hepokoski, Smith avoids programmatic interpretation or extramusical narratives; rather, he reads technical processes as forms of dramatic development to which various types of expression may correlate. This approach corresponds with the hermeneutic methods of a number of other theorists, including Hatten and Byron Almén. Klein's summary of this school of interpretation could also be applied to Hepokoski's and Smith's essays in that they too eschew "the mapping of a particular story of actors and actions onto the music and, rather, [concern themselves] with describing expressive states evoked by the music and the ways that their unfolding implies a narrative."[29]

*　　*　　*

Taken as a whole, the essays in *Expressive Intersections in Brahms* demonstrate a broad diversity of approaches to meaning in Brahms's music. The analyses draw on some of the most influential constructs developed by music theorists of the last twenty-five years. The authors, moreover, integrate these techniques with interdisciplinary methods, investigations of Brahms's milieu, attention to musical topics, and consideration of the dialogical relationships of Brahms's works with established genres and forms and with the music of his predecessors. The collection also plumbs the depths of Brahmsian expressivity through the sheer variety of works analyzed, from small-scale lieder to compositions for orchestra and chorus; from one of Brahms's first large-scale compositions, the op. 15 piano concerto of 1856–59, to one of the last, the Clarinet Sonata in E♭ Major, op. 120, no. 2, of 1894. Moreover, the volume offers more than a demonstration of the variety of analytic techniques that theorists are currently employing to analyze Brahms's music. The essays underscore the reciprocal role that engagement with Brahms's compositions may play in the further development of those techniques and the direct relevance of those developments to hermeneutic pursuits.

Although only two of the essays (those by Notley and Hepokoski) deal with large-scale works that have traditionally been viewed as dramatic, all the essays reach beyond the technical organization of Brahms's music to highlight its inherent drama and expressivity. This of course will come as no surprise to the current generation of Brahmsians, but it nevertheless vividly contrasts with approaches to Brahms's music during much of the twentieth century. Whether it is lieder in folk-style idiom (such as the songs analyzed by Platt) or ones with the thinnest, simplest textures (such as "Kein Haus, keine Heimat," which Malin discusses), the interaction of Brahms's harmony and phrase rhythm creates compelling dramatic moments that probe the psychological depths of the poetic texts. Much the same applies to the pieces without text—the chamber works and piano solos. In these pieces, the drama extends to such diverse characteristics as the temporal disturbances of idiosyncratic phrase structures, sequences that provide culminations of triumph or transcendence, tonal pairings that express wit or mystery, or canonic textures capable of drawing the performer into solitary moments of rapturous beauty. Even in the discussions of works of an overtly dramatic character—the *Gesang der Parzen* and the first piano concerto—close structural readings reveal expressive intersections that have for too long been overlooked.

NOTES

1. The concept of absolute music has a long and complex history, and the equation of it with notions of abstractness and formalism represents a simplification. For a study that probes the complexities, see Carl Dahlhaus, *The Idea of Absolute Music*, trans. Roger Lustig (Chicago: University of Chicago Press, 1989).

2. Allen Forte, "Motivic Design and Structural Levels in the First Movement of Brahms's String Quartet in C Minor," *Musical Quarterly* 69/4 (1983): 471.

3. Some of the most recent examples of this innovative theorizing explore elements of Brahms's style that had remained elusive, such as his rhythmic invention. Samuel Ng, for instance, has adapted Schoenberg's concept of the *Grundgestalt* to analyze elements of rhythm and meter, including the types of disturbances to temporal norms known as metric dissonances; Brent Auerbach has studied the interrelations of texture, pitch-cell cycles, and metrical dissonances; and Scott Murphy has extended the rhythmic theories pioneered by David Lewin and Richard Cohn. Samuel Ng, "A *Grundgestalt* Interpretation of Metric Dissonance in the Music of Johannes Brahms" (Ph.D. diss., University of Rochester, Eastman School of Music, 2005); Brent Auerbach, "Tiered Polyphony and Its Determinative Role in the Piano Music of Johannes Brahms," *Journal of Music Theory* 52/2 (2008): 273–320; and Scott Murphy, "Metric Cubes in Some Music of Brahms," *Journal of Music Theory* 53/1 (2009): 1–56.

4. This proliferation of analytical approaches to Brahms's music coincided with the blossoming of the discipline of music theory, which followed the founding of the Society for Music Theory in 1977. As Patrick McCreless has noted, the academic machinery required to maintain theory as an independent discipline fostered specific types of theoretical models and working methods. See his "Contemporary Music Theory and the New Musicology: An Introduction," *Journal of Musicology* 15/3 (1997): esp. 292–95.

5. Felix Weingartner, *Die Symphonie nach Beethoven* (1897), trans. Arthur Bles as *The Symphony Writers since Beethoven* (London: William Reeves, 1925), 41–61. Weingartner subsequently wrote more positively about Brahms's music.

6. Nicholas Cook, "Theorizing Musical Meaning," *Music Theory Spectrum* 23/2 (2001): 174. For a brief overview of recent approaches to Hanslick's stand and its relation to discussions of meaning in the late twentieth century, see Robert S. Hatten, *Musical Meaning: Markedness, Correlation, and Interpretation* (Bloomington: Indiana University Press, 1994), 323 n. 5.

7. In recent decades, Hanslick's relationship with Brahms and the degree to which he understood the composer's works has been more closely scrutinized. See, for example, Constantin Floros, "Das Brahms-Bild Eduard Hanslicks," in *Brahms-Kongress Wien 1983: Kongressbericht*, ed. Susanne Antonicek and Otto Biba (Tutzing: Hans Schneider, 1988), 155–66.

8. Among the most recent authors to probe Brahms's deployment of allusions, Paul Berry has proffered some of the most imaginative interpretations of the ways in which these allusions resonated with Brahms's circle of friends and carried emotional significance for the composer. See, for example, his "Old Love: Johannes Brahms, Clara Schumann, and the Poetics of Musical Memory," *Journal of Musicology* 24/1 (2007): 72–111. One important study that contextualizes Brahms's music in relation to his views on religion, nationalism, and contemporary politics is Daniel Beller-McKenna, *Brahms and the German Spirit* (Cambridge, Mass.: Harvard University Press, 2004).

9. Peter H. Smith, *Expressive Forms in Brahms's Instrumental Music: Structure and Meaning in His* Werther *Quartet* (Bloomington: Indiana University Press, 2005); Ryan McClelland, "Discontinuity and Performance: The Allegro appassionato from Brahms's Sonata Op. 120, no. 2," *Dutch Journal of Music Theory/Tijdschrift voor Muziektheorie* 12/2 (2007): 200–214; McClelland, "Tonal and Rhythmic-Metric Process in Brahms's Early C-Minor Scherzos," *Intersections: Canadian Journal of Music* 26/1 (2005): 123–47; McClelland, "Metric Dissonance in Brahms's Piano Trio in C Minor, Op. 101," *Intégral* 20 (2006): 1–42; Frank Samarotto, "Determinism, Prediction, and Inevitability in Brahms's Rhapsody in E♭ Major op. 119, no. 4," *Theory and Practice* 32 (2007): 69–99; Samarotto, "Fluidities of Phrase and Form in the 'Intermezzo' of Brahms's First Symphony," *Intégral* 22 (2008): 117–43; Samarotto, "Against Nature: Interval Cycles and Prolongational Conflict in Brahms's Rhapsody, op. 79, no. 1," in *A Composition as a Problem III: Proceedings of the 3rd International Conference on Music Theory, Tallinn, March 9–10, 2001*, ed. Mart Humal (Tallinn: Estonian Academy of Music, 2003), 93–108.

10. Robert S. Hatten, *Interpreting Musical Gestures, Topics, and Tropes: Mozart, Beethoven, Schubert* (Bloomington: Indiana University Press, 2004), 75–89 (on the Third Symphony); Michael L. Klein, *Intertextuality in Western Art Music* (Bloomington: Indiana University Press, 2005), 98–106 (on the Intermezzo op. 118, no. 1, and the relationship of its harmonic language to the music of Wagner); Kofi Agawu, *Music as Discourse: Semiotic Adventures in Romantic Music* (Oxford: Oxford University Press, 2009), 229–52 (on the Intermezzo op. 119, no. 2, and the second movement of the First Symphony).

11. Robert S. Hatten, "The Troping of Temporality in Music," in *Approaches to Meaning in Music*, ed. Byron Almén and Edward Pearsall (Bloomington: Indiana University Press, 2006), 68. For a summary of Hatten's concepts, see *Interpreting Musical Gestures*, 8–18. That Hatten developed his theories in *Musical Meaning in Beethoven: Markedness, Correlation, and Interpretation* through an exploration of Beethoven's music is significant because this music has been widely acknowledged as exerting considerable influence on Brahms. Moreover, Hatten concentrates on Beethoven's late works—the very pieces that Joachim and Brahms discussed at length during the all-important formative years of the 1850s.

12. Richard Taruskin opines that "any view of hermeneutics that reduces it to intentionalism is a willfully impoverished view." He quotes Mikhail Bakhtin's description of hermeneutics as a process that first understands "the work as the author himself understood it, without exceeding the limits of his understanding," and that second takes "advantage of one's own position of temporal and cultural outsideness" to explore what the work does. Taruskin, *Defining Russia Musically: Historical and Hermeneutical Essays* (Princeton, N.J.: Princeton University Press, 1997), xxvi.

13. Leo Treitler, *Music and the Historical Imagination* (Cambridge, Mass.: Harvard University Press, 1989), 35.

14. In the introductory essay to *Defining Russia Musically*, Taruskin dissects Tomlinson's style of hermeneutics and his negative attitude to close reading of scores as exemplified in such publications as "Musical Pasts and Postmodern Musicologies: Response to Lawrence Kramer," *Current Musicology* 53 (1993): 21–22. Although Carolyn Abbate also concedes that hermeneutics and close reading are not incompatible, as recently as 2004 she

seems to voice a certain discomfort with detailed study of scores, this time claiming that such study is divorced from performance. Not only do we disagree with her belief that the score is an "unper-formed abstraction," we also reject her claim that analyzing "the work's technical features or saying what it represents reflects the wish not to be transported by the state that the performance has engendered in us" ("Music—Drastic or Gnostic," *Critical Inquiry* 30 [2004]: 505–506 and similarly on 530). Aside from our own analytical proclivities, the "retreat" to the score (to use Abbate's unnecessarily pejorative image) is precisely what Brahms's most valued friends did. In her recent monograph on Brahms's lieder, Inge van Rij has cogently argued that this type of intense study was part of the appreciation of the *Witz* of the nineteenth-century writers whom Brahms and Schumann admired (including E. T. A. Hoffmann and Jean Paul) and by extension of the art of Max Klinger and the music of Brahms. Although Van Rij does not mention it, the importance of the eye in studying Brahms's scores was explicitly acknowledged by Elisabet von Herzogenberg during her explication of her study of Brahms's Fourth Symphony (which Rings discusses in his essay following this introduction). Inge Van Rij, *Brahms's Song Collections* (Cambridge: Cambridge University Press, 2006); for a discussion of the importance of score study, see 171–72; on the relationship between Klinger's cycles and Brahms's opus groupings of songs and the role of the viewer/listener's careful study, see 189–211.

15. Richard Cohn, "As Wonderful as Star Clusters: Instruments for Gazing at Tonality in Schubert," *19th-Century Music* 22/3 (1999): 213–32.

16. The Schenkerian literature on Brahms's harmony is far too substantial to list here. In this current collection of essays, Platt, Samarotto, and Smith all employ Schenkerian techniques. Schenker himself published analyses of a number of Brahms's pieces and left unpublished voice-leading graphs of others. Some of this unpublished material has been the basis for subsequent investigations of Brahms's voice leading. See, for example, Allen Cadwallader, "Schenker's Unpublished Graphic Analysis of Brahms's Intermezzo op. 117, no. 2: Tonal Structure and Concealed Motivic Repetition," *Music Theory Spectrum* 6 (1984): 1–13.

In his path-breaking demonstrations of the power of Neo-Riemannian concepts for analysis of tonal music, Richard Cohn has explicated a number of brief passages from Brahms's *German Requiem* and Double Concerto. See "Maximally Smooth Cycles, Hexatonic Systems, and the Analysis of Late-Romantic Triadic Progressions," *Music Analysis* 15/1 (1996): 13–15; "Neo-Riemannian Operations, Parsimonious Trichords, and Their 'Tonnetz' Representations," *Journal of Music Theory* 41/1 (1997): 33–35; and "Square Dances with Cubes," *Journal of Music Theory* 42/2 (1998): 291–92. More recently, Steven Rings has offered a somewhat contrasting approach to transformational analysis in combination with techniques drawn from the methods of Schenker and other theorists. He analyzes Brahms's op. 118, no. 2, op. 119, no. 2, the Adagio of the op. 111 String Quintet, and the opening of the First Piano Concerto in *Tonality and Transformation* (New York: Oxford University Press, 2011), 124-34, 185-220. Both Cohn and Rings were influenced by David Lewin, who briefly discussed passages from the opening of Brahms's G-minor Rhapsody and the last movement of his Horn Trio in *Generalized Musical Intervals and Transformations* (New Haven, Conn.: Yale University Press, 1987), 119–21, 165–69. Among authors in the present volume, Hepokoski further demonstrates the hermeneutic potential of Neo-Riemannian concepts.

Recently, theorists in addition to Rings have begun to explore the extent to which Schenkerian and Neo-Riemannian techniques can be combined. Smith pursues this two-pronged approach in an article concentrating on Brahms's String Sextet in G Major, op. 36, String Quartet in C Minor, op. 51, no. 1, and String Quintet in G Major, op. 111. "Brahms's Motivic Harmonies and Contemporary Tonal Theory: Three Case Studies from the Chamber Music," *Music Analysis* 28/1 (2009): 63–110.

17. Carl Schachter, "A Preliminary Study," "Durational Reduction," and "Aspects of Meter," in *Unfoldings: Essays in Schenkerian Theory and Analysis*, ed. Joseph N. Straus (New York: Oxford University Press, 1999), 17–117; William Rothstein, *Phrase Rhythm in Tonal Music* (New York: Schirmer, 1989); David Lewin, "On Harmony and Meter in Brahms's Opus 76, No. 8," *19th-Century Music* 4 (1981): 261–65; Harald Krebs, *Fantasy Pieces: Metrical Dissonance in the Music of Robert Schumann* (New York: Oxford University Press, 1999); and Richard Cohn, "Complex Hemiolas, Ski-Hill Graphs and Metric Spaces," *Music Analysis* 20/3 (2001): 295–326.

18. William E. Caplin, *Classical Form: A Theory of Formal Functions for the Instrumental Music of Haydn, Mozart, and Beethoven* (New York: Oxford University Press, 1998); James Hepokoski and Warren Darcy, *Elements of Sonata Theory: Norms, Types, and Deformations in the Late-Eighteenth-Century Sonata* (Oxford: Oxford University Press, 2006).

19. This integration of performance and analysis stands in sharp contrast to Abbate's opposition of the two, as described in note 14 above.

20. Agawu, *Music as Discourse*, 252.

21. Although the volume is thus organized by the duality of more overtly historical approaches and more technically focused or intertextual methods (or extroversive and introversive semiotics), we do not mean to imply that these categories are mutually exclusive. Indeed, the first essay, by Steven Rings, eloquently demonstrates that these approaches may be profitably combined. Similarly, although Hepokoski's essay on the first movement of the Piano Concerto in D Minor, op. 15, is primarily concerned with deriving meaning from a dialogue with sonata conventions, it also argues for a wider colloquy with nineteenth-century musical politics and complements existing scholarship concerning the extramusical and autobiographical meanings of the work. One may also observe that the essays invoking the wider artistic and societal conventions of the nineteenth century all concern texted compositions, whereas the essays dealing with instrumental works in part 3 rely far more heavily on technical comparisons either among works or between a work and the traditions of compositional practice it reflects. To be sure, the presence or absence of a text may have a profound impact on expressive interpretation. That historically oriented approaches may be applied to instrumental and vocal works with equal success, however, is evidenced by Notley's pioneering scholarship on Brahms's chamber compositions and by Rings's essay in the current volume.

22. Hatten, *Interpreting Musical Gestures*, 47.

23. Agawu, *Music as Discourse*, 239.

24. Hepokoski and Darcy, *Elements of Sonata Theory*.

25. See, for example, Warren Darcy, "Bruckner's Sonata Deformations," in *Bruckner Studies*, ed. Paul Hawkshaw and Timothy L. Jackson (Cambridge: Cambridge University Press, 1997), 256–77; and Steven Vande Moortele, "Form, Program, and Deformation in Liszt's *Hamlet*," *Dutch Journal of Music Theory/Tijdschrift voor Muziektheorie* 11/2 (2006): 71–82.

26. Robert Bailey coined the term *tonal pairing* and the related term the *double-tonic complex*. For a representative discussion of these concepts, see his "An Analytical Study of the Sketches and Drafts," in *Prelude and Transfiguration from Tristan and Isolde*, ed. Robert Bailey (New York: Norton, 1985), 121–22. Following Bailey, William Kinderman explored the structural and expressive implications of tonal pairing in Wagner's other operas. See, for example, "Dramatic Recapitulation in Wagner's *Götterdämmerung*," *19th-Century Music* 4/2 (1980): 101–12.

27. Given that the emphasis on chords and keys related by thirds was so pervasive during the nineteenth century, there is now an appropriate range of literature on this matter. Research has covered the harmonic practices of composers exhibiting otherwise

contrasting styles; likewise, analysts have developed a wide range of theories to explain these tonal practices. The following publications offer only a tiny sampling of the available studies. Many of the initial investigations focused on forms in which the main keys are related by third rather than fifth. See, for example, Rey Longyear, "Liszt, Mahler and a Remote Tonal Relationship in Sonata Form," in *Studien zur Instrumentalmusik: Lothar Hoffmann-Erbrecht zum 60. Geburtstag,* ed. Anke Bingmann, Klaus Hortschansky, and Winfried Kirsch (Tutzing: Hans Schneider, 1988), 457–68. Many other studies, including Smith's article in the current volume and Bailey's study of *Tristan and Isolde* (see note 26), focus on the potential for tonal ambiguity created by mediant-related tonal areas. David Kopp discusses a wide range of compositions and various types of mediant relationships in his exploration of transformational voice leading in nineteenth-century music. He includes analyses of short passages from the finale of Brahms's Clarinet Sonata in F Minor, op. 120, no. 1, and the opening of the second movement of the Piano Sonata in F Minor, op. 5, in *Chromatic Transformations in Nineteenth-Century Music* (Cambridge: Cambridge University Press, 2002), 186–88 and 198–99.

28. Both Allen Cadwallader and Steven Rings offer insightful analyses of Brahms's Intermezzo in A Major, op. 118, no. 2, which is characterized by the type of tonal pairing that Smith and Platt explore. The former uses Schenkerian analysis and the latter, transformational theory. Neither, however, engages issues of meaning. Cadwallader, "Foreground Motivic Ambiguity: Its Clarification at the Middleground Levels in Selected Late Piano Pieces of Johannes Brahms," *Music Analysis* 7/1 (1988): 64–74; Rings, *Tonality and Transformation,* 185–204. Most of the Neo-Riemannian publications cited in the preceding notes to this chapter are primarily focused on developing aspects of that theory and as a result do not discuss the possible meanings of third-related progressions. Cohn, however, has published two contrasting essays that clearly demonstrate the potential of approaching questions of meaning through transformational theory. Neither of these, however, concerns Brahms's compositions. See his "As Wonderful as Star Clusters," 213–32, and "Uncanny Resemblances: Tonal Signification in the Freudian Age," *Journal of the American Musicological Society* 57/2 (2004): 285–323. Given that cycles of thirds are one of the frequently cited fingerprints of Brahms and that numerous scholars have suggested that these cycles signify topics such as death and despair, it is somewhat surprising that a transformational theorist has not pursued this avenue of research. For an overview of some of the related literature, see Heather Platt, "New Paths to Understanding Brahms's Music: Recent Analytic Studies," *Nineteenth-Century Music Review* 6/2 (2009): 121–22.

29. Klein, *Intertextuality in Western Art Music,* 115. On musical narrative, see Byron Almén, *A Theory of Musical Narrative* (Bloomington: Indiana University Press, 2008).

2 The Learned Self:
Artifice in Brahms's Late Intermezzi

Steven Rings

An Example by Way of Introduction

We begin by exploring aspects of Brahms's Intermezzo in A Major, op. 118, no. 2, focusing on the passages shown in Examples 2.1a and b. Example 2.1a presents the opening theme, while 2.1b shows a later transformation in mm. 34–36. Examples 2.1c and d make the nature of the transformation clear: the melody of mm. 34–36 inverts that of mm. 0–2. The down-stemmed, parenthe-sized eighths in Example 2.1e show a canonic imitation of the inverted theme one octave lower, at a temporal interval of three eighth notes, which creates a subtle hocket effect.

(a) mm. 0^3–2^2

(b) mm. 34^3–36^2

(c)

(d)

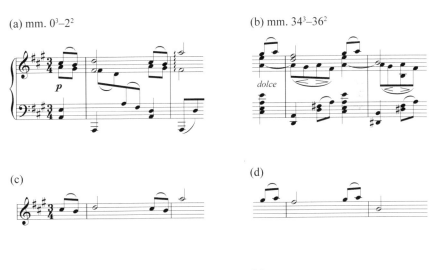

(e)

Example 2.1. The opening theme of the Intermezzo in A Major, op. 118, no. 2, and its later transformation in mm. 34–36.

This already suggests that Example 2.1b is a moment of quiet, composerly achievement. But there is more still to notice. First, observe that the inverted theme in 2.1d occupies the same registral band as does the recto statement in 2.1c: they have the same lower and upper pitch boundaries, B and A. Indeed, the operation that maps the recto theme onto its inversion is the diatonic pitch inversion that maps these outer pitches onto one another.[1] B and A have a highly sensitive character in the opening theme itself. In Example 2.1a, B proves unable to descend to A, instead consistently leaping up across the bar line; these leaps are central to the gestural physiognomy of the piece.[2] They are mirrored by leaps down in the bass. These mirroring outer-voice leaps lend a subtle dialectical energy to the intermezzo's pervasive *auftaktig* gestures: while the bass agrees with the kinetic profile of such an *Auftakt* (up–DOWN), the melody gently contradicts it (down–UP), giving extra poignancy to the local melodic apexes of D (m. 1) and A (m. 2). The B–A leap across the bar line into m. 2 is especially striking, as it is at once an intervallic expansion of the previous B–D leap as well as a paradoxical "resolution": B now proceeds to A, but it is the "wrong" A, one octave too high.[3] As a result, the high A has a curiously unstable quality due to its register, despite its intervallic consonance with the bass.[4] The arpeggiation in the right hand on the downbeat of m. 2 further marks the moment, giving the leap a vocal intensity, as Charles Rosen has noted, by slightly delaying the arrival of the high A in the manner of a singer ascending to that pitch (and belying the ease with which the leap might otherwise be played on the piano).[5] All of these factors combine to make the B–A leap an expressive locus for the piece, a gesture to which the player will return again and again, its harmonic lighting often subtly varied.

The space opened up by the B–A leap serves as the frame for the inversion of the subject in mm. 34–36; upward leaps become downward leaps, A now leaps down to B. The inversion has a striking effect on the motive—the change in direction across the bar lines now has a feeling of *release,* of easing back after the reach up to A, as opposed to the mild infusion of tension projected by the upward leaps of the recto statement. The inverted motives now land on downbeats that have a feeling of relative stability. This change in kinetic profile results not only from the change in intervallic direction but also from an inversion of the motives' patterns of consonance and dissonance. As indicated above the top staff of Example 2.2a, the three notes of the initial motive project the sequence consonant-dissonant-dissonant. These values invert in mm. 34–36 to dissonant-consonant-consonant, as shown in 2.2b.

The hearing of the melodic D on the downbeat of m. 1 as a dissonant fourth over the bass note A agrees with the harmonic reading below the staff of Example 2.2a, which treats the $^6_4$ harmony as an embellishing sonority to the opening $^5_3$.

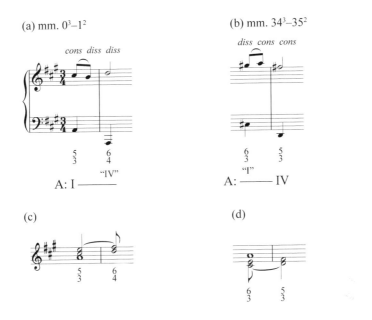

Example 2.2. Harmony in mm. 0–1 and 34–35 of the Intermezzo in A Major, op. 118, no. 2.

Comparison with the harmonic reading in Example 2.2b reveals further manifestations of inversional logic. Note first the figured-bass signatures: the stable $\frac{5}{3}$ sonority sounds on the upbeat in the recto statement but on the downbeat in the inverted statement, realigning the motive's harmonic-metric center of gravity from weak upbeat to strong downbeat. As shown in 2.2c and d, the $\frac{6}{4}$ and $\frac{6}{3}$ sonorities that embellish these $\frac{5}{3}$ chords exhibit an inversional logic of their own: the $\frac{6}{4}$ neighbors its $\frac{5}{3}$ above and after, while the $\frac{6}{3}$ neighbors *its* $\frac{5}{3}$ below and before. All of this inversional symmetry results in a reversal of harmonic priority, as shown in the roman numerals beneath 2.2a and b: the tonic harmony decorated by a putative IV suffix in the recto statement becomes a subdominant harmony decorated by a putative I prefix in the inversion.

The neighboring role of the putative I in the inversional statement is made clear in Example 2.3a. The initial three-note motive appears in the bass at the upbeat to m. 31, with C♯ serving as a neighbor to D in the local harmonic context.[6] The textural inversion—with the motto now sounding in the bass, not in the soprano—is thus paired with an inversion in harmonic priority: the putative I harmonies on the upbeats now neighbor the D-based harmonies on the downbeats. The energy of the motive carries through to the inverted statement in the soprano of mm. 34–35; the $\frac{6}{3}$ chord over C♯ maintains its neighboring role

Example 2.3. Harmony and motive in mm. 30–35
of the Intermezzo in A Major, op. 118, no. 2.

throughout. Example 2.3b isolates further details in the passage. In addition to
the statements of the three-note motive—first in the bass, then inverted in the
soprano—the example summarizes the activity of the right hand in mm. 30–34.
The upper voice in these bars traces two *Septzüge* from A down to B. This linear
span is, of course, a transposition—one octave down—of the crucial A/B minor seventh of the opening. The melodically sensitive pitch classes, A and B, are
fused harmonically in the ii$^6_5$ chord that governs mm. 30–34. They are not only
the end points of the two *Septzüge*, they are also played as a simultaneity by the
pianist's right-hand thumb in mm. 31 and 33 (see the down-stemmed half notes
in 2.3b). Remarkably, the thumb's A/B dyad serves as a *literal axis* of pitch-space
inversion, as the three-note motto travels from the bass to its inverted form in
the soprano. This axial function is shown in Example 2.3c: the parenthesized A/B
dyad is the exact center of pitch-space inversion between minor bass motto and
inverted soprano motto. Unlike the inversion explored in Examples 2.1c and d,

the inversion here is chromatic, or real: the inflection of the bass motive (and the surrounding harmony) to minor in mm. 33–34 alters the motto's intervallic profile to m2↓–m3↑, which inverts exactly to m2↑–m3↓ in the soprano.[7]

The inversion of the theme in mm. 34–36 is thus a moment of quintessentially dense Brahmsian thought: inversional logic abounds, embracing melody, harmony, mode, register, texture, consonance and dissonance, and metric weight. Even more remarkable than all these signs of compositional craft, however, is the way the music here *sounds*: Brahms makes the moment of inversion almost unutterably tender. It is not only a formal nodal point for various technical processes in the music, it is also an expressive nodal point—a moment of *innig* intensity that seems to distill and intensify the particular *Stimmung* of this intermezzo. The moment sounds so extraordinary in part because of the various details we have explored thus far—inversions in harmonic and melodic kinetics and so forth—but this is not the entire story. Brahms *stages* the passage in a way that is independent of these local technical details. The event is spotlighted in advance; we know to expect something special as it approaches. A quick review of the rhetorical preparation will make this clear.

After two statements of the opening period, Brahms begins the contrasting B section of the AABA' song form with the pickup to m. 17, destabilizing both harmony and meter in the process. In the measures that follow, metric and harmonic dissonance work in a characteristically Brahmsian tandem; it is not until the firm arrival on the dominant on the downbeat of m. 25 that the two resolve simultaneously and we regain our harmonic and metric bearings (this after a wonderfully vertiginous mm. 23 and 24). The buildup over the dominant pedal that ensues seems to suggest the imminent return of the A-major tonic and (one presumes) the opening theme. The theme does arrive, but the tonic does not: a harmonic deflection in mm. 28–29 diverts us from A to D, the subdominant, which arrives in m. 30 with the loudest dynamic in the piece thus far (*forte*). That loud dynamic coincides with the high A of the opening theme, now celebratory rather than diffident. The subdominant pull in the theme, evident since the first downbeat, reaches its apotheosis here, forcing a figure-ground reversal that momentarily displaces the A tonic entirely: D becomes the music's momentary center of gravity, pulling all other events into its orbit. The music shown in Example 2.3a follows the subdominant breakthrough. The ruminative iterations of the motive in the bass, the shift to minor in m. 33, the *decrescendo* and *calando* marking in mm. 33–34—all engender expectation as the subdominant climax ebbs. The music stalls out on a ii⁶₅ chord, causing us to wonder how we can possibly emerge from this harmonic cul-de-sac; in the minor-inflected hush of the first two beats of m. 34, there is a gathering together of attention. Then, on beat 3, minor gives way to major, recto bass theme gives way to inverted treble theme, dark trombone voicings give way to the shimmering woodwind clarity of the upper register—and the myriad technical marvels outlined above unfold. As so often in Brahms's late intermezzi, the moment of greatest poetry in the movement is also the moment of greatest artifice.

Late Brahms, Artifice, and the Intermezzi

In a valuable recent study, Margaret Notley has explored the role of artifice in Brahms's late style, arguing that the composer "overtly cultivat[ed] musical artifice in his later music."[8] Christian Martin Schmidt similarly describes Brahms's late style as "characterized by an uncompromising prominence of artifice, by the far-reaching penetration of the musical details."[9] While the word *artifice* carries a potentially negative connotation—suggesting artificiality, undue cleverness, and perhaps even an opposition to "nature"—Schmidt and Notley do not seem to have such connotations in mind. Notley, for one, situates the term within a network of (positive) Viennese Liberal values. She persuasively ties Brahms's emphasis on compositional craft to the ideals of the Viennese *Bürgertum*, then under threat from the ascendant Christian Socialist right. She observes that Brahms's late works embody the Liberal values of intellectual refinement and subtlety, technical achievement, consummate craft, unassailable compositional logic, and hard work (à la Max Weber's Protestant ethic). All of these characteristics were opposed to what the left viewed as the dangerous sensationalism, superficiality, and illogic of Bruckner, the musical hero of the Viennese right. Additionally, Notley argues, Brahms's late works can be heard, in various ways, to enact aspects of an inward, reflective, even ironic consciousness in which rationality nevertheless prevails—a sort of sonic image of the Liberal Viennese self.[10]

Brahms's late intermezzi represent both a vivid manifestation of these ideas and something of a special case.[11] Due to their status as piano miniatures—technically accessible character pieces to be played by an individual—these works engage issues of inwardness, ironic awareness, rational control, and subjectivity in ways that are not merely abstract but instead potentially enacted at the keyboard in the moment of performance. They do not merely signify as sounds taken in by a listener, they also signify as sets of actions—bodily and expressive—to be performed by a pianist. Such meaning emerges in and through first-person action. As we will see, this makes the intermezzi a particularly fruitful site for an exploration of the ways in which Brahms's music—with its conspicuous mix of technical accomplishment and expressive immediacy—can be meaningful for one who plays it.

It is clear that Brahms and Clara Schumann themselves found the act of playing the late piano works deeply meaningful. On receiving the first batch of op. 116 pieces in November 1892, Clara describes them in her diary as "full of poetry, passion, sentiment, emotion, and having the most wonderful effects of tone. . . . In these pieces I at last feel musical life stir once more in my soul, once more I play with real devotion."[12] Clara and Brahms's epistolary exchange about the Intermezzo in B Minor, op. 119, no. 1, is more revealing still. On sending the piece to her in May 1893, Brahms writes:

> It teems with discords. These may be alright and quite explicable, but you may not perhaps like them, in which case I might wish that they were less right but more pleasing and more to your taste. It is exceptionally melancholy, and to say "to be played very slowly" is not sufficient. Every bar and every note must be played as if *ritardando* were indicated, and one wished to draw the melancholy out of each one of them, and voluptuous joy and discomfort out of the discords.[13]

Clara, 8 June:

> You must have known how enthusiastic I should be when you were copying out that bittersweet piece which, for all its discords, is so wonderful. Nay, one actually revels in the discords, and, while playing them, wonders how the composer ever brought them to birth.[14]

Brahms's reply later that month is at once wry and telling:

> I must write a line to tell you how glad I am that my little piece has pleased you. I really had not expected that it would, and now shall be able to enjoy it in peace and calm at my own piano as if I had a license to do so from the head of the police.[15]

The exchange is fascinating on many levels, especially as regards its intertwining themes of license, rule, and private pleasure. It is hard to know just how to read Brahms's final statement, with its characteristic mix of apparent sincerity and distancing humor, but the sense of almost illicit private enjoyment that he describes is highly suggestive of traditional narratives about nineteenth-century *Charakterstücke*, those quintessential vehicles of Romantic interiority, of which Brahms's opp. 76 and 116–19 are the most notable late-century examples. Only here it is not just any bourgeois subject who plays the music alone, "in peace and calm," but the composer himself, presumably drawing out its melancholy dissonances.[16]

Remarkably, Eduard Hanslick employs similar imagery in his 1896 review of opp. 118 and 119, conveying the music's effect (and affect) via a highly vivid description of Brahms at the keyboard:

> One can describe these two volumes as "Monologues at the piano": Monologues that Brahms recites by and for himself during lonely evening hours, defiantly

pessimistic [*in trotzig-pessimistischer Auflehnung*], in brooding contemplation, in Romantic reminiscence, from time to time also in dreamy wistfulness.[17]

Once again, the composer, performing for himself, adopts the role of the solitary subject so familiar from descriptions of the Romantic *Charakterstück,* communing with himself through the medium of the piano piece. Hanslick's suggestive addition is his description of the pieces as monologues. He seems to mean the word in the most literal sense: monologues as *things said to oneself.* Brahms does not deliver these monologues to an audience from a stage, in the manner of a soliloquy; instead, he recites them to himself, over long evenings, as he works through the surfeit of emotions and affective states that Hanslick senses in the music.[18]

Clara, Brahms, and Hanslick all describe Brahms's late pieces as affording an intensely involving personal experience for the solitary performer.[19] But what of the music's pervasive artifice? How does it relate to these images of deeply personal engagement with the music, of emotionally charged performance for oneself as a sort of reflexive monologue? Baldly put, is the music affecting *because* of its artifice or *in spite* of it? Or is the relationship more complex than this? To begin, we should observe that the late piano music rarely wears its learnedness on its sleeve: it is worked deep into the fabric of the compositions. Carl Dahlhaus, in a passage that manages at once to invoke Castiglione and Nietzsche, attributes this to the aesthetic principle of *nascondere l'art:*

> Aristocratic taste objected to an obtrusive use of strict counterpoint, regarding it as music that, to borrow Nietzsche's term, "sweats." The goal instead was an attitude of light-handed geniality, of *nobile sprezzatura;* the exertions of musical artifice, if unavoidable, were at least not to be flaunted.[20]

Those in Brahms's circle occasionally expressed sentiments along these lines. Clara, for example, in a letter to Joachim in 1862, writes of the music that would become the opening allegro of the First Symphony:

> The movement is full of wonderful beauties, with a mastery in the treatment of the motifs which is indeed becoming more and more characteristic of him. Everything is so interestingly interwoven, yet as spirited as a first outburst; one enjoys [it] completely to the full, *without being reminded of the craft.*[21]

Clara thus holds it as a virtue that Brahms's symphony does not make a point of its artifice, or at least does not let that artifice distract the listener from enjoying its many other "wonderful beauties."

There is thus some truth to Dahlhaus's statement, but something about it still falls wide of the mark. For one, attribution of such an aesthetic stance to a proto-

Nietzschean aversion to "music that sweats" rings false. After all, Nietzsche himself very likely felt that Brahms's music *does* sweat, every bit as much as Wagner's and in just the way that Bizet's, for instance, does not.[22] Further, as Notley has noted, there are indeed chamber works by Brahms in which artifice takes on a prominence that shades over into mannerism; not all his artifice is hidden, as Dahlhaus suggests—in many passages compositional exertion is on full display (think of the String Quartet op. 51, no. 1).[23] Nor does it seem right, when confronting works in which artifice is less overt, to attribute its concealment to a sort of aristocratic squeamishness. This ill fits what we know of Brahms's character and is especially inapt when it comes to music as private and inward as the late piano works—here, concern for aristocratic decorum seems misplaced.

I therefore propose that there are other ways to understand the "submerged artifice" in many of Brahms's late intermezzi. Here it will be useful to return to the A-major intermezzo. The discussion above explored ways in which various formal and expressive processes converge on the moment of thematic inversion in mm. 34–36. As I stated there, the poetic effect of that passage cannot be attributed solely, or even primarily, to the technical processes. It is, rather, a product of the piece's rhetoric: the ways in which the moment is carefully prepared and staged. Brahms focuses the player's attention on a nodal point in the music in which a set of highly learned processes comes to a head; he does so, however, *not* by drawing attention to those processes but by making this a moment of potent expressive concentration. As a result, it is not difficult to imagine a player who knows the piece well, and perhaps even cherishes this moment in it above all others, but is not consciously aware of its thematic inversion. Perhaps the expressive impact of the passage occupies the pianist's attention to such a degree that awareness of all formal details recedes from consciousness.[24]

We might thus detect two parallel aesthetic tracks at work in the intermezzo, one concerned with the beauties of sound and expression, the other concerned with the beauties of craft. The two tracks cannot be entirely separated, of course—the sonic beauty of the piece depends to a large degree on its submerged craft, and there is a remarkably seamless fit between technical and expressive contour. As Joachim said in 1877 about the first symphony: "One does not quite know where the enormous virtuosity of workmanship stops and the music begins," words that apply a fortiori to the A-major intermezzo.[25] But artifice and affect nevertheless retain a degree of autonomy in the work, as I have proposed above; the work's *innig* crux did not *need* to be a site of such learned procedure. Further, it can hardly be denied that there is a purely formal beauty at work in the intermezzo: the relationships explored in Examples 2.1–3 can themselves be objects of aesthetic contemplation. They have a certain crystalline perfection that is independent of the sound of the music. But it is precisely the sound that draws the player deeply into the intermezzo. And the fact that both the affective and learned processes in the piece reach fulfillment in the same moment is deeply telling. The affective stratum almost seems to express a stance toward the technical relationships, to *value* them via its expressive contours. It is as though the music sonically interprets its own formal values.

The player, in turn, comes to know these affective and technical strata through a complex mixture of somatic, intellectual, and affective processes. The relative proportions of these processes will vary from individual to individual due to differences in temperament, training, enculturation, and so forth. But for all players, the process of learning to re-create the piece at the instrument will involve, among other things, an act of assimilation—or perhaps even incorporation (in the most literal sense)—in which the boundary between player and piece becomes difficult to fix. The music, when well learned, can seem to become something *of* the player. This idea is reflected in certain familiar locutions, as when we say that a player has made a given piece his or her "own" (one thinks, perhaps, of Glenn Gould and the *Goldberg Variations*). But the very fact that familiar music can continue to move a performer suggests that it in some way maintains its autonomy. That autonomy is physically reified by the score sitting on the piano in front of the player; it is also manifested in the physical sound that surrounds the pianist, sound that the pianist at once produces and reabsorbs in the act of listening. Player and music thus constitute a sort of a dialectical circuit in which "the music" is at once something of the playing subject and simultaneously an object for that subject.

This idea is especially suggestive when we think of Brahms at his keyboard alone, responding to music that he himself composed—music that is "of him" in a very strong sense but that retains the power to move him. Particularly suggestive is the impression Brahms gives of repeatedly playing the B-minor intermezzo: having received Clara's blessing regarding its opening dissonances, he can now "enjoy it in peace and calm at [his] own piano"; the language strongly evokes meditative, repeated playings. This suggests that, even for its composer, the music affords a sort of inexhaustible interaction, existing in a state of continual discovery.[26]

Of course, this "continual discovery" differs in important ways for players who are not the composer. For those players, the density of the music's formal argument abets the process of repeated and varied engagement: there is a persistent gap between what one knows about the work and what one *could* know about it. That gap opens a space in which the player's relationship to the piece can evolve and change.[27] Surely the most vivid contemporary accounts of this kind of engagement with Brahms's music are to be found in Elisabet von Herzogenberg's letters to the composer. She describes a process of coming to know Brahms's works—of playing them, living with them, and experiencing them at various stages of acquaintance—that is at once revealing of the values prized by the Brahms circle and indicative of the sort of interaction with his music that Brahms might have hoped for from an ideal listener or player. None of Herzogenberg's letters are more suggestive in this regard than those regarding the Fourth Symphony. Though these letters concern a symphony and not a short character piece, they are highly apposite to our present discussion, as they reveal Herzogenberg's process of coming to know a piece at the piano.[28] Writing on 8 September 1885, she describes the process of first getting acquainted with the work:

> [The symphony] is becoming ever more alive [*Lebendiger*] and clear to me, and it consistently reveals new mysteries. . . . Your piece affects me curiously: the more penetration I bring to bear on it, the more impenetrable it becomes; the more stars define themselves in the twilight glow, which at first served to hide them; the more distinct sources of joy do I have, some expected, some unexpected; and the more plainly can I trace the great central driving power which gives unity to the complex work. One never wearies of straining eyes and ears to grasp all the clever turns, all the strange illuminating effects of rhythm, harmony, and color, or of admiring your fine chisel for its firm and delicate strokes. Indeed the possibilities are so inexhaustible that one experiences the joys of a discoverer or a naturalist at every new evidence of your creative ingenuity.[29]

Herzogenberg's language is remarkable: the symphony is not only becoming clearer to her, it is also becoming "more alive" (*Lebendiger*). She likens musical details to stars that were only dimly perceived at first but are now seen more clearly; the analogy to the observation of the physical world is made explicit when she compares the process of discovery to that of a naturalist (*Naturforscher*).

As her comments about the piece's persistent impenetrability suggest, however, Herzogenberg was at this point still critical of the work's abundance of artifice. Tellingly, she worries that this technical complexity will work *against* the symphony's expressive directness:

> Yet it seems to me that if its actual appeal proves simple and direct, the effect is only gained *at the cost of* all that tangled overgrowth of ingeniously interwoven detail, which must be overlooked if one would taste and enjoy the fruit itself.[30]

Writing some three weeks later, however, Herzogenberg's relationship to the piece has changed (though one senses that her reservations have not disappeared completely). Enclosing the 8 September note within a longer letter of 31 September, she says:

> How glad I am now that I did not air my half-formed impressions, for I know so much more about it today—the dear E-minor movement—and have played it so

often, inwardly and at the piano, devoting to it practically every free minute . . . that I am now wholly intimate with it, and many of the remarks I made the other day now seem quite inappropriate. If I send the other shred of a letter all the same, it is with the idea that you might be interested in following the workings of a plain person's mind in chronological order.

I can now trace the hills and valleys so clearly that I have lost the impression of its being a complicated movement; or rather I no longer look on the complication as detrimental to its effect in any way. At worst it seems to me as if a great master had made an almost extravagant display of his skill! I was glad to see how great an effect it *could* have when I played it to my sister at Hosterwitz. She was quite carried away by the general sound and character of the movement in spite of the inadequate performance, and she is, I may say, a good example of the intelligent but wholly uninitiated listener. She never noticed the points with which we were chiefly concerned—the ingenious combination of the themes, the massing together of separate links, but simply enjoyed what she heard. And it is the same with me, now that I have heartily absorbed it; my piece [*mein Stück*] makes me immensely happy, and I have a furious longing to *hear* it soon.[31]

The details worthy of mention in the letter are too numerous to address in all. We should simply note Herzogenberg's vivid account of her evolving relationship to the piece, which has developed through her playing it "inwardly and at the piano" (*innerlich und am Klavier*) in "practically every free minute" in the three-plus weeks since the previous note. In the process, she has become "wholly intimate" (*ganz intim*) with the work. Most strikingly, she says she has now absorbed the symphony: "now that I have heartily gulped everything down" (nun ich alles gehörig in mich hineingeschluckt habe); one can hardly imagine a more vivid image of a player assimilating a piece and making it her own—the assimilation in Herzogenberg's language is literally corporeal. She underscores the point by referring to the work now as "my piece" (*mein Stück*).[32] And yet the fact that her relationship to the work continues to evolve and change suggests that the symphony maintains a degree of relative autonomy from her—as a beguiling but occasionally perplexing other.

In a passage that resonates with Herzogenberg's description of her own experience with the symphony, Hanslick discusses the expressive and compositional complexity of the intermezzi. He says that they represent a kind of music that "does not win one over at first glimpse" (die nicht auf den ersten Blick gewinnt) but that instead requires effort to get to know. More cryptically, he states about opp. 118 and 119: "There is much ore [*Eisengehalt*] buried in these pieces, and this ore will long be conserved."[33] Hanslick seems to suggest that the works' technical and expressive details can be mined only with difficulty by the player or interpreter; they are thus not easily exhausted.[34] This meaning becomes explicit a few sentences later. After comparing Brahms's music to that of Spohr, he says: "The new Brahms pieces do not speak immediately to the soul [Gemüt], nor flatteringly to the ear; for that reason, they do not need to fear such early withering [Abwelken]." The contrast between the inorganic Eisengehalt and organic withering is striking; Brahms's works are at once valorized for their durability, yet that durability is purchased at the cost of a certain hardness, even coldness. One might disagree with this assessment—uninitiated listeners (listeners like Elisabet von Herzogenberg's sister) often do react immediately and powerfully to the intermezzi, suggesting that they can speak directly to the Gemüt. But it is clear that, for Hanslick, and likely for other musical Kenner, the music's reticence to disclose all its technical intricacies opens the possibility for a process of continual discovery.

We thus might distinguish two general ways in which artifice, expression, and intense personal engagement can interact as a player comes to know a Brahms intermezzo. On the one hand, the music's expressive contours often correspond with the learned processes occurring beneath the surface—but without drawing attention to those processes. In this way, not only does the music seem sonically to interpret its own formal values, it also draws the player into those very moments at which formal processes are at their richest. This interaction can lead to what we might call a "covert assimilation" of the music's learned features in which the player, though perhaps unaware of the music's artifice, is drawn closest to the work—and identifies with it most deeply—at its moments of greatest technical achievement. Second, the music's submerged formal complexity makes it an inexhaustible source of discovery and consistently renewed interaction, especially for musical Kenner (such as Elisabet von Herzogenberg, Clara Schumann, Eduard Hanslick, or modern players of an analytical bent). For such musicians, the affective physiognomy and learned procedures in Brahms's intermezzi offer quasi-independent modes of aesthetic contemplation, which nevertheless can become entangled in striking and highly variable ways from piece to piece. The dialectical circulation between assimilation and reflective distance can become especially intense for such players.

To further flesh out these ideas, we will now turn to a survey of several additional intermezzi, exploring the pieces' diverse aesthetic affordances—technical and sonic—and tracing their interactions. These analytical vignettes will also bring to light certain striking corporeal aspects of Brahms's music—moments in which the composer asks the player to enact bodily motions that correspond in some way to the music's underlying technical processes, thus constructing a learned self in a quite literal sense.

Intermezzo in E♭ Major, op. 117, no. 1

The Intermezzo in E♭ Major, op. 117, no. 1, at first seems like one of the most artless of the intermezzi: folklike, pastoral, and direct, with a simple homophonic accompaniment at the outset that has been likened to the strum-

Example 2.4. Intermezzo in E♭ Major, op. 117, no. 1, A section (mm. 1–20).

ming of a guitar.[35] The folklike character is reinforced by the piece's epigraph, taken from a Scottish lullaby in Herder's *Stimmen der Völker in Liedern*.[36] Brahms referred to all three pieces of op. 117 as "lullabies of my sorrows" (*Wiegenlieder meiner Schmerzen*), but the E♭ is the most explicit *Wiegenlied* of the set.[37] (We will return to the *Schmerzen* below.) Example 2.4 shows the work's A section (mm. 1–20). A host of musical details signify maternal song: gently rocking ⁶⁄₈ meter, simple diatonic melody, slow harmonic rhythm, and enveloping E♭ octaves tolling in multiple registers. The lulling E♭s create a sonic field that enfolds the melody in tonic security. This sonic image resonates with contemporary German ideas about the lullaby and the mother's voice. As Karen Bottge has observed (drawing on ideas of Friedrich Kittler), the maternal voice was often described in nineteenth-century German writings on parenting as creating an "aural envelope" that surrounds the infant in a field of sensuous pleasure.[38]

But there is a curious textural inversion in the intermezzo: it is the lullaby melody itself that is enveloped by the E♭s. In other words, the melody that would be associated with the mother's voice finds itself in the middle of the texture, comfortably enveloped, in the place reserved for the child. One can thus detect a blurring of identities between mother and child, or a confusion of boundaries.[39] Later events reinforce this understanding, as the melody gradually saturates the texture, further breaking down any clear distinction between enveloper and enveloped. Voices that had been part of the static homophonic field gradually become melodically individuated: with the pickup to m. 5, the right-hand octaves are set in motion melodically (along with the "upper" tenor voice, in sixths below), while the bass and "lower" tenor voice begin to move with the pickup to m. 7. As shown in Example 2.5, the bass octaves present an exact transposition of the opening of the melody in the dominant. The now-mobile upper voices further echo this melody in a free canon, as shown. Thus, each stratum picks up portions of the lullaby melody—each voice at once asserts its own melodic identity and at the same time fails to distinguish itself from the other linear strata, which have the same melodic material. The lullaby

Example 2.5. Free canon in mm. 6–8 of the Intermezzo in E♭ Major, op. 117, no. 1.

resonates in all registers of the sonic envelope, creating a tension between melodic differentiation (or independence) and homogeneity. As suggestive as such ideas are for a Lacanian reading of the piece, such an interpretation would take us too far afield from the present topic. What is most pertinent to our subject is that the idea of *canon* arises very naturally in this expressive context, as a web of melodic lines that are at once independent yet highly similar—one might even say genetically linked.

The canon in Example 2.5 occurs at the first expressive crest in the piece, the music swelling dynamically and reaching an affective peak with the entry of the *comes*. The intersection between expressive apex and learned device recalls the A-major intermezzo. While this initial canon is quite free rhythmically, two later passages show a progression toward increasingly exact canonic activity. Example 2.6 isolates the two passages, which sound at parallel moments in the A and A' sections. As shown in Examples 2.6a and b, the lullaby melody enters into a canon with itself in m. 13 at the temporal interval of two eighths. This two-eighths span sets off a hemiola in the left hand, the first departure from the lulling ♩♪♪♪ rhythm in the piece. The canon grows out of the right hand's E♭ octaves: the *dux*, departing from the upper E♭, seems to peel away the *comes* from the lower E♭, further interlinking melody and homophonic background. The canon is exact until the *comes* begins moving in sixteenths. Examples 2.6c and d show the return of this passage in the A' section in mm. 50–51. Now the resounding E♭ is integrated into the canonic melody itself via oscillating sixteenths. The canon here is entirely literal, extending from m. 50 through the end of m. 51; it further projects vertically through nearly the entire sounding texture. The incursion of the *comes* into the bass clef in m. 51 involves yet another stratum in the canonic activity, mixing melodic tones with the arpeggiated tenor-register harmonies.

Daniel Beller-McKenna hears such learned processes as opening up a distance between the listener or player and the pastoral lullaby:

> With each passing device that Brahms applies to the pastoral opening, the folk character of the initial idea is objectified and thus placed at a distance. . . . The folk quality of the opening is rendered not so much an affectation as a memory of something cherished from afar, something over which the ego can reminisce and contemplate—even brood—but which has become distant.[40]

Though Beller-McKenna does not explicitly mention the canons, they can certainly be heard to contribute to this process, opening up a subtle ironic distance from the simple, folklike homophony of the opening. But there is no crisp separation. The canons at once seem to grow naturally out of the music—as ineluctable products of its descending diatonic lullaby—and at the same time suggest a surfeit of technique that is not in keeping with the piece's initial pastoral premise.[41]

The high register of both canons in Example 2.6 creates the effect of a shimmering cascade, but the canonic activity also gives the passages a subtly mechanical sound, almost like a music box.[42] This suggests a vaguely impersonal character, or perhaps even an affective detachment at these moments. That detachment contrasts strongly with the music that follows—both canons lead into one of the most arresting harmonies in the piece: the vii^{o7}/V in mm. 15 and 52. The re-

Example 2.6. Increasingly exact canons in mm. 13–14 and 50–51 of the Intermezzo in E♭ Major, op. 117, no. 1.

gistral contrast and the A bass note—a tritone away from the still-resounding
E♭ octaves—suggest a subjective presence beneath the pastoral surface (and its
curious canons), a presence that only emerges fully in the minor-key B section.
Dillon Parmer reads this as the subjective presence of the "unhappy mother" in
the lullaby, which Herder titles "Wiegenlied einer unglücklichen Mutter."[43] In
such a reading, the *Schmerzen* of Brahms's description reside in this subject, as
the fourth line of the lullaby suggests:

> Schlaf sanft mein Kind, schlaf sanft und schön!
> Mich dauerts sehr, dich weinen sehn.
> Und schläfst du sanft, bin ich so froh,
> Und wimmerst du—das schmerzt mich so!
> (Sleep softly, my child, sleep softly and sweetly!
> It troubles me so to see you cry.
> And if you slept softly, I would be so happy,
> But your sobbing pains me so!)

However we choose to read the intermezzo—a literal mapping of music onto lullaby text is not the only possible interpretation—the innocent, even mechanical
canons seem to act as a foil for this brooding, subjective presence; they grow out
of the lullaby and reveal it as a repetitive process that covers deeper emotions like
a carapace. As such, and perhaps paradoxically, they are among the intermezzo's
most memorable moments—sonic emblems of its enigmatic expressive world.

Intermezzo in B Minor, op. 119, no. 1

Commentaries on the Intermezzo in B Minor, op. 119, no. 1, almost always begin—and all too often end—with a discussion of the famous opening
arpeggios: the chains of descending thirds that conceal underlying root progressions by fifth.[44] What is rarely observed is that this harmonic mist clears in m.
4 to reveal a canon. Example 2.7a shows the A section and the first measure of
the B section (mm. 1–17). Example 2.7b isolates the canonic passage between
soprano and bass in mm. 4–7, while 2.7c shows a longer canon in mm. 12–16, in
the consequent phrase. Annotations beneath the staves in Examples 2.7b and c
indicate the canonic intervals at which *comes* follows *dux*.

Canon plays a very different expressive role in the B-minor intermezzo
than in the E♭ work. While in the E♭-major intermezzo canon can be heard to
epitomize both the innocence and routine of the lullaby (while also ironically
distancing the playing subject from that innocence), the canons in the B-minor
intermezzo suggest a rational control and purposefulness that contrast with
the hazy harmonic wash of the opening. The strictness of procedure in these

Example 2.7. Intermezzo in B Minor, op. 119, no. 1, mm. 1–17.

Example 2.8. Submerged three-note chromatic canons in mm. 17–20 of the Intermezzo in B Minor, op. 119, no. 1.

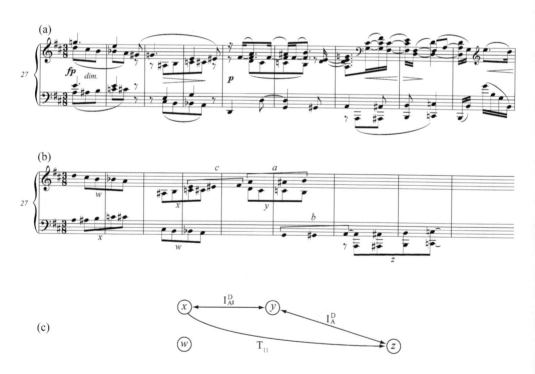

Example 2.9. Canonic activity in mm. 27–35 of the Intermezzo in B Minor, op. 119, no. 1.

bars—the canons are all literal, with the only license being a shift in interval of imitation between phrases—recalls Brahms's comments in his exchange with Clara about compositional license and rule. Following the descending third-chains—with their "teeming discords"—the canons are textbook examples of contrapuntal decorum; one is reminded in this connection of the etymological link between "canon" and "law."

The canons of Examples 2.7b and c coincide with an infusion of harmonic direction and syntactical clarity into the music: they seem to act as engines that drive the work toward cadential fulfillment, as the hazy third-chains give way to purposeful canonic sequences. In the rarefied waltz of the B section, they also drive the intermezzo toward its affective climax. Example 2.8 shows three-note chromatic gestures submerged within the opening of the waltz, labeled *a*, *b*, *b'*, and *c*. The first two, *a* and *b*, project an exact canon at the pitch interval of a ninth and the temporal interval of a quarter note. Segments *b'* and *c* are in a looser canonic relationship as regards rhythm; *b'* is so labeled because it contains the same pitch-class sequence as *b*. At the repeat of the waltz theme in m. 31, canonic activity redoubles and is paired with inversional patterning. As shown in Examples 2.9a and b, the canonic entries now extend to four-note gestures, beamed in 2.9b and labeled *w*, *x*, *y*, and *z*. Of these, *x*, *y*, and *z* are chromatic tetrachords; *w* is almost chromatic. Statements of *c*, *a*, and *b* also sound in mm. 30–33, as shown by the brackets.

The canonic activity rubs ironically against the B section's underlying waltz. As Roger Moseley has observed, the left hand in the opening bars of the B section could easily be recomposed as an oom-pah-pah bass pattern, revealing the closeness of the music's melodic and rhythmic idiom to Brahms's op. 39 and the *Liebeslieder*, opp. 52 and 65.[45] But the chromatically surging canonic voices defamiliarize this waltz, saturating the texture with overdetermined contrapuntal imitation. Here the fact that the artifice is buried deep within the texture seems to be of crucial expressive significance: as the four-note beamed gestures surge upward and downward, the music projects a sense of energy welling up underneath the elegant surface of the dance. That energy breaks the surface with the statement of tetrachord *z* in octaves in mm. 33–34. As in the A-major intermezzo, this is a moment of both technical and expressive fulfillment. Brahms underscores the importance of the passage by repeating it immediately in mm. 37–39, now embellishing the *z* tetrachord with elaborate sixteenth-note triplets. This passage is the movement's dynamic plateau—a sustained *forte* from m. 37 to the *diminuendo* hairpin in m. 39.

What is fulfilled here? Tetrachord *z* can be heard in one sense as a "corrected" version of tetrachord *w*. The latter has the local dominant A as its lowest note, but it is not fully chromatic; it is thus an inexact inversion of *x*, against which it sounds in the liquidation of mm. 27–30. Tetrachord z also has the dominant A as its lowest note, but it *is* a fully chromatic tetrachord. It is an exact inversion of tetrachord *y*, which precedes it canonically in mm. 31–32; *y* is, for its part, an exact inversion of *x*. The transformational network in Example 2.9c summarizes these relationships. As it indicates, *x* inverts into *y* via the inversion that maps A♯ onto D; *y* then inverts into *z* by the inversion that maps A onto D. And *z* is further the T_{11} transposition of *x*. T_{11} moves the A♯ at the bottom of *x* down to the A at the bottom of *z*, presenting a diatonic correction of sorts and providing the first chromatic tetrachord that begins on the local dominant.

But these transformations result in a new chromatic inflection: the C♮ that concludes motive *z*. This note turns back the motive's ascending chromatic energy, bending it now in the direction of the *sub*dominant. This is the first flatward motion in the piece. The A section proceeded from the tonic (two sharps) to the minor dominant (three sharps), while the first phrase of the B section was shot through with ascending chromatics, driven by the three-note motives shown in Example 2.8b. In mm. 21–24, the entire musical texture is draped onto these chromatics, resulting in a metrically unstable passage of ascending parallel ⁶₄ chords: D major, D♯ minor, E minor, E♯ minor(!), F♯ minor, G minor. After this ascent, the tilt in the direction of the subdominant at the end of tetrachord *z* is powerfully affecting: the flatward easing of tension is held in check by the upward thrust of the gesture, the increased dynamics (to the *forte* plateau of mm. 37–39), and the thick, octave-doubled texture. These competing forces at once give the *z* motive a rhetorical heft and a sense of valedictory turning back. As Robert Hatten and Michael Klein have suggested, in much tonal music the dominant can have the quality of pointing to the future ("time as experienced rushes forward," as Klein puts it), while the subdominant can seem instead to gesture toward the past ("time as experienced turns back").[46] Klein's comments seem especially apt for Brahms's subdominant in mm. 34 and 38, as the music here seems to double back on itself, giving this, the emotional apex of the movement, a strongly retrospective charge.

In the retransition (mm. 43–46) Brahms asks the pianist to cross hands repeatedly in executing overlapping four-note descending third-chains. This is merely one vivid instance of a common procedure in the intermezzi, in which the composer asks the performer to execute a motion that in some sense physically manifests the technical idea at work in the music—in this passage, the technique of register transfer through reaching over (loosely in Schenker's sense). Another vivid instance of this phenomenon occurs in the final chord of the intermezzo, shown in Example 2.10. As indicated on the right-hand side of the example, Brahms easily could have notated the chord as two close position B-minor triads, one in each hand. Instead, he chose to notate it as shown on the left-hand

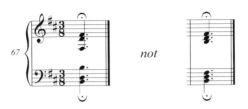

Example 2.10. The final chord of op. 119, no. 1.

side of the example, with each hand playing characteristically Brahmsian gapped sonorities. This not only causes the pianist's thumbs to overlap but places the hands in an explicitly inversional configuration. Thus, the inversional patterning evident at the work's climax (Example 2.9 and following) finds its way into the pianist's hands for the final sonority.

Intermezzi in E Minor, op. 116, no. 5, and B♭ Minor, op. 117, no. 2

The concluding observations about op. 119, no. 1, reveal an additional way in which Brahms constructs the experience of the playing subject in his late intermezzi: the artifice embedded within certain passages is made physically palpable by being mapped into the performer's hands. Through fingerings, voicings, and patterns of figuration, Brahms choreographs the player's movements in ways that interact with and project the work's learned processes. Most notably, he often exploits the natural inversional relationship of the pianist's hands at the keyboard, with each hand presenting a mirror image of the other as regards the ordering of thumb and fingers. By exploiting this somatic configuration, Brahms can map inversional activity in the music directly onto the performer's body.[47]

Such a mapping is especially evident in the inversional patterning of the Intermezzi in E Minor, op. 116, no. 5, and B♭ Minor, op. 117, no. 2. In the former piece, the pianist's hands overlap while executing mirroring inversional gestures. Example 2.11 shows bars 1–2. The voicing of the first sonority matches that of the concluding sonority of op. 119, no. 1. The fingerings, which are present in the original 1892 Simrock edition, make the mirroring relationship of the hands explicit. In a letter dated 13 October 1892, Clara commented on this very aspect of the piece:

> I should never like to hear the E minor with the single notes only, because it is just the position of the hands, one on top of the other, that has a peculiar charm and sounds quite different.[48]

Andante con grazia ed intimissimo sentimento

Example 2.11. Intermezzo in E Minor, op. 116, no. 5, mm. 1–2.

(a) Gestures x and x^{-1}

(b) mm. 0–1

(c) mm. 39–44

Example 2.12. Gestures x and x^{-1} in the Intermezzo in B♭ Minor, op. 117, no. 2.

The Intermezzo in B♭ Minor, op. 117, no. 2, exhibits equally pervasive inversional structuring in the gestures given to the pianist's hands. Example 2.12 explores the interaction of two gestures in the piece: the persistent four-note descending figure played by the right hand, labeled x, and its inversion, played by the left, x^{-1}. Example 2.12a isolates these gestures in a staffless space. The slurs in both gestures project a melodic dyad, usually a diatonic or chromatic step. The beamed thirty-second notes that follow are a gapped arpeggio. Example 2.12b shows the configuration of x and x^{-1} in the piece's opening measures. Here the gestural rhythm x–x–x^{-1} or rh–rh–lh is established.

Throughout the A section of the piece, the right hand leads with two or sometimes three statements of x, while the left hand responds with one statement of x^{-1}. In the retransition, however—shown in 2.12c—the left hand leads. It begins with two statements of x^{-1}, which are imitated canonically by x in the right hand, leading to a stretto pile-up in mm. 40–42. In mm. 43–44 (and 45–46, not shown) the tight alternation and overlap of the two motives is liquidated by extended, single-direction arpeggios: x–x–x followed by x^{-1}–x^{-1}–x^{-1}. Here, however, the hands for the first time abandon their allegiance to a single x-form: Brahms's stemming suggests an alternation of hands within each arpeggio. This new pattern leads to a larger-scale inversional symmetry, as the middle x-form in each unidirectional arpeggio is played by the "wrong" hand. As indicated on the example, the descending x–x–x arpeggio is performed rh–lh–rh, while the ascending x^{-1}–x^{-1}–x^{-1} is realized by the *inverse* pattern lh–rh–lh. Though such relationships appear recondite on paper, they have a somatic immediacy for the player, who bodily manifests the music's inversional structures.

Intermezzo in F Minor, op. 118, no. 4

The Intermezzo in F Minor, op. 118, no. 4, initially seems as though it will be concerned with the same issues of inversional patterning between the hands. Example 2.13a shows mm. 1–14. The triplet figures in the hands present an exact inversional relationship in their initial gestures, suggesting that the piece might be an essay on canon in inversion. But the inversions soon become increasingly free, until they are seemingly displaced by an explicit (and exact) *non*inverted canon at the cadence in mm. 7 (beat 2) through 12. The replacement of inverted with noninverted canon is only "seeming" because this noninverted canon has in fact been sounding all along, as shown in Example 2.13b. It begins with the accented long notes at the work's opening. The player's (and listener's) attention is not drawn to these notes at the outset, however, as the triplet activity occupies center stage. But the gradual emergence of the canon into the sonic foreground reveals a process that has already been under way.

Example 2.13. Intermezzo in F Minor, op. 118, no. 4, mm. 1–14.

Example 2.14. Intermezzo in F Minor, op. 118, no. 4, mm. 52–67.

The submerged nature of the canon in mm. 1–11 seems bound up with the piece's agitated *Stimmung*. It is as if the canonic activity is suppressed in these bars, or kept under a lid. It is only when that "lid" is removed, and the canon can emerge clearly in mm. 7–12, that the pressure in the piece eases slightly and the music is able to cadence. This sense of release is even more evident in the work's B section: here all noncanonic material disappears, and the hands alternate serenely in A♭ major. Example 2.14 shows the first two systems of this section (mm. 52–67). As in the A section, the canon is at the octave, and the temporal interval is one quarter note. While it is the mirror symmetry of the player's hands that Brahms exploits in the E-minor and B♭-minor intermezzi, here it is the translational symmetry of the player's arms—their role in moving the hands right and left along the horizontal plane of the keyboard. As in the A-major intermezzo, there is a remarkable congruence in Example 2.14 between technical process and affect, both of which exhibit a placid simplicity. This congruence is matched by the serene process of the player's hands in the F-minor intermezzo—indeed, the canon is even more evident to the player's body than it is to the listener's ear.

The Learned Self as Modern Analyst

I have proposed that artifice and affect interact in telling ways in Brahms's intermezzi, with the music's affective stratum seeming to *value* its technical processes sonically. I have also proposed that these works engender certain modes of musical engagement, in which the music's learned values are assimilated by the player—to varying degrees and in diverse ways—through affective identification, cognitive reflection, somatic enactment, or (most likely) some combination of the three. Though my focus has been on the experience of the performing subject, these observations also have much to tell us about the perennial appeal of these works to music analysts.

The habitus of the professional music analyst has its historical, modernist roots in a tradition that leads directly back to Brahms via Schoenberg. It thus makes sense that the way of being with music encouraged by Brahms's works—and by Brahms's circle—would transfer, through a sort of historical transitivity, to the practices of the modern analyst. Though published analyses and conference papers have a decidedly social aspect, the analytical act itself is often a highly solitary pursuit, and a deeply inward one. Modern music theory as a research discipline is thus closely bound up with the *innig* musical behavior that we witness in the descriptions of Elisabet von Herzogenberg and Clara Schumann as they come to know, and assimilate, Brahms's music.

While the solitary pursuit of analysis has come in for much criticism of late, the central place of Brahms's intermezzi in the analytical tradition might help us better understand its attractions. For it is not that analysts keep returning to these pieces *solely* because of their elegant formal properties. It is also surely because of the captivating sound of this music, and the special ways in which that sound seems to move in similar motion with those properties. The pleasures of the analytical act reside not only in the elegance of the relationships discovered or in the personal satisfaction one has in discovering them—though those are undoubtedly important—but also in the ways in which formal relationships emerge into consciousness when one is in direct contact with the music's sonic materiality. Contra Vladimir Jankélévitch, Carolyn Abbate, and others, there can be something deeply hedonistic about this pursuit.[49] Analysis entices in part because of the diversity of aesthetic engagements it affords—from the formal to the physically sensuous—and the potential that it holds for illuminating their myriad interactions. To judge from the intermezzi, such interactions seem to have fascinated Brahms as well.

NOTES

1. The diatonic inversion takes place within an A-major gamut. While the inversion here is diatonic (or tonal), we will soon observe instances of chromatic (or real) inversion in the vicinity of Example 2.1b. For a different technical perspective on these inversions—and on other aspects of this intermezzo—see Steven Rings, *Tonality and Transformation* (New York: Oxford University Press, 2011), 185–202.

2. Schenker hears the B in the upbeat to the first measure as an incomplete passing tone within an implicit third progression C♯–B–(A), a hearing that I find persuasive. As he notes, in each statement the motive consistently "leaps off" (*springt ab*) of this *Zug* as it crosses the bar line. See Schenker's unpublished comments on the piece (from 1914) in the Ernst Oster Collection (New York Public Library), folder 34, item 29. Folder 34 has been called the "Brahms folder" by researchers. For a general discussion of its contents, see Allen Cadwallader and William Pastille, "Schenker's Unpublished Work with the Music of Johannes Brahms," in *Schenker Studies* 2, ed. Carl Schachter and Hedi Siegel (Cambridge: Cambridge University Press, 1999), 26–46.

3. As Schenker notes, this seventh leap (*Septsprung*) yields the tone A, the tone that "had to come" after B according to the "law of the passing tone" (*Durchgangsgesetz*). Nevertheless, the passing B is not resolved "in the strict sense" (*im strengen Sinne*) due to the registral displacement of the leap. Oster Collection, folder 34, item 29.

4. The high A becomes harmonically dissonant as well when the leap reappears in the parallel consequent phrase: the A of m. 6 sits atop a B⁷ chord in first inversion, forming a tritone with the D♯ bass.

5. Charles Rosen, *Piano Notes: The World of the Pianist* (New York: Simon and Schuster, 2004), 9.

6. A massive subdominant arrival, discussed below, precedes the music shown in Example 2.3a, reinforcing the sense of bass-note D as structural in these measures, with C♯ as its neighbor. For a detailed Schenkerian reading along these lines, see Rings, *Tonality and Transformation*, 200, Fig. 6.13. For alternative Schenkerian readings, see Allen Cadwallader, "Foreground Motivic Ambiguity: Its Clarification at Middleground Levels in Selected Late Piano Pieces of Johannes Brahms," *Music Analysis* 7/1 (1988): 70, Ex. 9; and Eric Wen, "Bass-line Articulations of the *Urlinie*," in Schachter and Siegel, *Schenker Studies* 2, 294–97, Ex. 21.

7. The local harmonies accompanying the chromatic (real) inversion in mm. 33–34 have a suggestive dualist character: minor subdominant inverts to major tonic. This delivers on a dualist implication already evident in Examples 2.2c and d. The inversional sketches of those examples have a mildly dualist appearance on the page, with the neighboring third motions surrounding a central A above and below. Appropriately, the "under thirds" of 2.2d align with the heavily subdominant transformation of the inverted motive. The harmonic context of 2.2d is not properly dualist, of course, as the D harmony is major, not minor. But in mm. 33–34 the true minor subdominant does sound, setting up a genuine dualist flip around A, in concert with the flurry of other inversional activity already explored.

8. Margaret Notley, *Lateness and Brahms: Music and Culture in the Twilight of Viennese Liberalism* (Oxford: Oxford University Press, 2007), 34.

9. Christian Martin Schmidt, *Brahms und seine Zeit* (Laaber: Laaber Verlag, 1998), 89, cited and translated in Notley, *Lateness and Brahms*, 40–41. See also Carl Dahlhaus, *Nineteenth-Century Music*, trans. J. Bradford Robinson (Berkeley: University of California Press, 1989), 258–61.

10. See Notley, *Lateness and Brahms*, 2ff. David S. Luft offers a particularly cogent discussion of the constitutive roles of concepts such as rationality, individuality, inwardness, reflexivity, and so on in Viennese Liberalism in his book *Eros and Inwardness in Vienna: Weininger, Musil, Doderer* (Chicago: University of Chicago Press, 2003), see esp. 14–22. The classic accounts of the decline of Viennese Liberalism in the decades leading up to the fin de siècle are Carl Schorske, *Fin-de-siècle Vienna: Politics and Culture* (New York: Knopf, 1980); and John Boyer, *Political Radicalism in Late Imperial Vienna: Origins of the Christian Social Movement, 1848–1897* (Chicago: University of Chicago Press, 1981). For a collection of recent historical essays that challenge the

accounts of Schorske and Boyer, see Steven Beller, ed., *Rethinking Vienna 1900* (New York: Berghahn, 2001).

11. Notley primarily explores chamber music in her discussion of Brahmsian artifice; she only mentions two intermezzi in passing (op. 116, no. 5, and op. 118, no. 4; see *Lateness in Brahms*, 59). Though in this chapter I focus on the works that Brahms titled "Intermezzo," my comments will be generally applicable to all Brahms's late piano works in opp. 116–19 as well as the earlier set of op. 76. As Elisabet von Herzogenberg noted in an 1880 letter to Brahms, the titles for such small pieces—Intermezzo, Romance, Capriccio, Ballade, Rhapsody—were largely arbitrary: "It is practically a characteristic of these various designations that they have lost their true characteristics through application, so that they can be used for this or that at will." Max Kalbeck, ed., and Hannah Bryant, trans., *Johannes Brahms: The Herzogenberg Correspondence* (New York: E. P. Dutton, 1909), 99.

12. Berthold Litzmann, *Clara Schumann: Ein Künstlerleben* (Leipzig: Breitkopf und Härtel, 1923), 3:563, my translation. Jan Swafford speculates that Brahms may have composed the late piano pieces "to sustain Clara" in her declining health. See his *Johannes Brahms: A Biography* (New York: Vintage, 1997), 602.

13. Berthold Litzmann, ed., *Letters of Clara Schumann and Johannes Brahms, 1853–1896* (London: Edward Arnold, 1927), 2:228.

14. Litzmann, *Letters*, 2:229.

15. Litzmann, *Letters*, 2:229.

16. In an extended discussion of the idea of melancholy in Brahms's music, Reinhold Brinkmann draws attention to the curious mixture of the words "melancholy" and "delight" (*Wollust*) in the May 1893 letter. See Brinkmann, *Late Idyll: The Second Symphony of Johannes Brahms*, trans. Peter Palmer (Cambridge, Mass.: Harvard University Press, 1995), 131. See also Jan Brachmann's discussion of Brahmsian melancholy in *Kunst, Religion, Krise: Der Fall Brahms* (Kassel: Bärenreiter, 2003), 264ff. Daniel Beller-McKenna explores the idea of melancholy in the intermezzi in "Reminiscence in Brahms's Late Intermezzi," *American Brahms Society Newsletter* 22/2 (2004): 6–9.

17. Eduard Hanslick, *Fünf Jahre Musik [1891–1895]* (Berlin: Allgemeiner Verein für deutschen Literatur, 1896), 258–59, my translation.

18. It is apposite in this connection to note that Brahms only once performed any of the late piano pieces in a semiformal concert: at the *Tonkünstlerverein* on 31 October 1893. All other known performances were in the homes of friends (at the Fellingers' in Vienna and the Villa of Miller zu Aichholz in Gmunden). See Renate and Kurt Hoffman, *Johannes Brahms als Pianist und Dirigent: Chronologie seines Werkes als Interpret* (Tutzing: Hans Schneider, 2006). For a brief description of the *Tonkünstlerverein* event—at which Brahms evidently first played op. 118, no. 2, very poorly and then returned to play it much better—see Richard Heuberger, *Erinnerungen an Johannes Brahms* (Tutzing: Hans Schneider, 1971), 62. The first significant public performances of the works were those of Ignaz Brüll (reviewed by Hanslick) and Ilona Eibenschütz.

19. For further accounts of the reception of the late piano works, see Imogen Fellinger, "Brahms' Klavierstücke op. 116–119: Kompositorische Bedeutung und zeitgenössische Rezeption," in *Johannes Brahms: Quellen—Text—Rezeption—Interpretation: Internationaler Brahms-Kongreß, Hamburg 1997*, ed. Friedrich Krummacher and Michael Struck (Munich: Henle, 1999), 199–210.

20. Dahlhaus, *Nineteenth-Century Music*, 260. The passage follows an analytical discussion of Brahms's Capriccio in G Minor, op. 116, no. 3.

21. Litzmann, *Clara Schumann*, 3:123, emphasis added. Translation from David Brodbeck, *Brahms: Symphony No. 1* (Cambridge: Cambridge University Press, 1997), 10.

22. Nietzsche asserts that Brahms's music differs from Wagner's music in degree, not in kind: "Fifty steps beyond Brahms you encounter Wagner." Friedrich Nietzsche, *The*

Case of Wagner, in *Basic Writings of Nietzsche,* ed. and trans. Walter Kaufmann (New York: Modern Library, 2000), 643.

23. Notley, *Lateness and Brahms,* 57–62. See also Richard Taruskin, *The Nineteenth Century,* vol. 3 of *The Oxford History of Western Music* (Oxford: Oxford University Press, 2005), 732.

24. Anecdotal evidence that I have collected indeed confirms that even highly trained musicians who know the piece well may be unaware of the inversion here.

25. Ernst Rudorff, "Johannes Brahms: Erinnerungen und Betrachtungen," *Schweizerische Musikzeitung* 97 (1957): 83. Cited in Brodbeck, *Brahms: Symphony No. 1,* 31.

26. These ideas engage what Leonard Meyer calls the "rehearing problem" in music cognition: the listener's ability to encounter the same musical work repeatedly and continue to find it deeply engaging. We are concerned here with the matter not only of rehearing but also, we might say, of "replaying." See Meyer's *Music, the Arts, and Ideas: Patterns and Predictions in Twentieth-Century Culture* (Chicago: University of Chicago Press, 1967), 42–53. See also Edward T. Cone, "Three Ways of Reading a Detective Story—or a Brahms Intermezzo," in *Music: A View from Delft,* ed. Robert Morgan (Chicago: University of Chicago Press, 1989), 77–93.

27. Of course, a composer's relationship to his or her music also evolves and changes. Brahms's own comments about the B-minor intermezzo suggest as much: after Clara has "approved" the melancholy dissonances, he can now enjoy the piece without reservation.

28. Sadly, Elisabet von Herzogenberg died before Brahms completed the late piano works, so we have no record of her getting to know them at the keyboard.

29. Kalbeck, *The Herzogenberg Correspondence,* 249. I have altered Bryant's translation of the first sentence in the block quote to make it more faithful to the original German. See Max Kalbeck, ed., *Johannes Brahms in Briefwechsel mit Heinrich und Elisabet von Herzogenberg* (Berlin: Deutschen Brahms-Gesellschaft, 1921), 2:85.

30. Kalbeck, *The Herzogenberg Correspondence,* 250, emphasis original.

31. Kalbeck, *The Herzogenberg Correspondence,* 243–44, emphasis original. I have again altered portions of Bryant's translation. For the original, see Kalbeck, *Brahms in Briefwechsel,* 2:80–81.

32. Also fascinating is the contrast between Elisabet's experience of the piece and that of her sister in a passage that has echoes of Mozart's famous comments to his father about *Kenner* and *Nichtkenner.* Elisabet's sister "simply enjoys what she hears," unaware of the music's technical complexities. Elisabet, however, needs to work to arrive at a similar stage of easy enjoyment. Emily Anderson, ed. and trans., *The Letters of Mozart and His Family,* 3rd ed., rev. Stanley Sadie and Fiona Smart (London: Macmillan, 1985), 833, letter 476.

33. Hanslick, *Fünf Jahre Musik,* 259, my translation.

34. Other readings are possible, however, as a result of the potential cultural resonances of the mysterious word *Eisengehalt* (literally, "iron content"). Berthold Hoeckner, in private communication, has suggested that the term might even refer to iron in the human blood or the bones, thus carrying connotations of healthiness and long life.

35. Daniel Beller-McKenna, *Brahms and the German Spirit* (Cambridge, Mass.: Harvard University Press, 2004), 168.

36. Johann Gottfried von Herder, *Stimmen der Völker in Liedern* (Stuttgart and Berlin: Cotta'sche Buchhandlung Nachfolger, 1903), 37–39. George Bozarth and Dillon Parmer both advance interpretations of the intermezzo based on close readings of the lullaby text. See George Bozarth, "Brahms's *Lieder ohne Worte:* The 'Poetic' Andantes of the Piano Sonatas," in *Brahms Studies: Analytical and Historical Perspectives,* ed. George Bozarth (Oxford: Oxford University Press, 1990), 345–78; and Dillon Parmer, "Brahms and the Poetic Motto: A Hermeneutic Aid?," *Journal of Musicology* 15/3 (1997): 353–89.

37. Rudolf von der Leyen, *Johannes Brahms als Mensch und Freund* (Düsseldorf: Karl Robert Langeweische, 1905), 82–83. See also Max Kalbeck, *Johannes Brahms* (Tutzing: Hans Schneider, 1976), 4:277.

38. Karen Bottge, "Brahms's 'Wiegenlied' and the Maternal Voice," *19th-Century Music* 28/3 (2005): 186–87.

39. Bottge offers a highly apposite discussion of the blurring of boundaries in the mother/child dyad in "Brahms's 'Wiegenlied,'" 187–89.

40. Beller-McKenna, *Brahms and the German Spirit,* 169–70.

41. The canons also distance the playing subject from the pastoral naiveté of the *Wiegenlied* in a rather literal sense. Measures 13–14 and especially 50–51 contain the only passages in an easy piece that require careful fingering and some practice to realize in tempo, forcing the pianist to step out of musical time, plan carefully, and rehearse.

42. Michael Vidmar-McEwen has presented a highly suggestive account of such "music-box passages" in nineteenth-century works in his paper "Franz Schubert and the Etherealized Mechanical," presented at the 2008 annual meeting of Music Theory Midwest, Bowling Green, Ohio, 17 May 2008.

43. Parmer, "Brahms and the Poetic Motto," 367–75. The original English title of the lullaby is "Lady Anne Bothwell's Lament," published in Thomas Percey's *Reliques of Ancient English Poetry.*

44. One also presumes that Brahms was talking about these arpeggios—in the opening bars and in later occurrences—when he wrote Clara that the movement "teems with discords."

45. Roger Moseley, personal communication.

46. Michael Klein, "Chopin's Fourth Ballade as Musical Narrative," *Music Theory Spectrum* 26/1 (2004): 39; Robert S. Hatten, *Musical Meaning in Beethoven: Markedness, Correlation, and Interpretation* (Bloomington: Indiana University Press, 1994), 43; and Hatten, "Music and Tense," in *Semiotics around the World: Synthesis in Diversity,* ed. Irmengard Rauch and Gerald F. Carr (Berlin: Mouton de Gruyter, 1996), 1:628.

47. These ideas mark out a potentially fruitful point of contact and further exploration between Brahms studies and Elizabeth Le Guin's concept of "carnal musicology," as elaborated in *Boccherini's Body: An Essay in Carnal Musicology* (Berkeley: University of California Press, 2006).

48. Litzmann, *Letters,* 2:213.

49. Vladimir Jankélévitch and Carolyn Abbate both detect in analysis a desire to flee music's pleasures. See Vladimir Jankélévitch, *Music and the Ineffable,* trans. Carolyn Abbate (Princeton, N.J.: Princeton University Press, 2003); and Carolyn Abbate, "Music— Drastic or Gnostic?," *Critical Inquiry* 30 (2004): 505–36. For further discussion, see Steven Rings, "*Mystères limpides:* Time and Transformation in Debussy's *Des pas sur la neige,*" *19th-Century Music* 32/2 (2008): 178–208.

Part Two

3 "Alte Liebe" and the Birds of Spring: Text, Music, and Image in Max Klinger's *Brahms Fantasy*

Yonatan Malin

The *Brahms Fantasy* is a bound volume, completed in 1894, with musical scores by Brahms (five songs and the *Schicksalslied,* op. 54) and original etchings, engravings, and lithographs by Max Klinger (1857–1920). Klinger, a generation younger than Brahms, was a painter, sculptor, and printmaker, renowned as one of the premier German artists of his day. He was also a devoted amateur pianist; he kept a piano in his studio, was a great admirer of the music of Beethoven, Schumann, and Brahms, and incorporated musical themes in many of his works. The *Brahms Fantasy* is unique, however, in that the musical scores form an integral part of the graphic work.

Klinger's volume is of interest for Brahms scholars as a form of reception history.[1] Klinger chose five songs from four different published collections by Brahms, determined their arrangement, and juxtaposed them with a myriad of images ranging from relatively literal illustrations to surreal fantasies. Klinger presented the songs as one part in a larger work; following the songs there is a series of images on the Prometheus story and the piano-vocal score for Brahms's *Schicksalslied,* op. 54.[2] Klinger's volume thus situates the songs in new and sometimes unexpected relationships with each other and with mythological representations of human fate and the divine. Brahms received Klinger's work with great enthusiasm; he wrote to Klinger of his pleasure in the interaction of words, music, and images, shared the volume with friends, and dedicated his own *Four Serious Songs,* op. 121, to Klinger two years later.[3]

In the present chapter, I provide an analytical and interpretive reading of the first song in the *Brahms Fantasy,* "Alte Liebe" (op. 72, no. 1), in dialogue with an image that Klinger placed at the end of the score. Many scholars have commented on this image and its relation to individual details in Brahms's song, but its relation to the song as a whole has not been adequately understood.[4] I also explore the image on its own—its play of light and dark, fantasy and realism, public gaze and private intimacy—and discover expressive tensions between the song and image. Finally, I draw on insights gained in the study of

"Alte Liebe" and Klinger's image to explore narrative threads, musical links, and radical juxtapositions in the cycle of images and songs that make up the first part of Klinger's album. Klinger's cycle of Brahms songs begins with "Alte Liebe"; continues with "Sehnsucht" (op. 49, no. 3), "Am Sonntag Morgen" (op. 49, no. 1), and "Feldeinsamkeit" (op. 86, no. 2); and concludes with "Kein Haus, keine Heimat" (op. 94, no. 5).

The analysis will show that the subject matter, gestural features, framing, and composition of Klinger's graphic images respond to the songs at many levels and to the songs as words and music, not just to the scores as visual images. External evidence for Klinger's musical engagement can be found in a letter that he wrote to Brahms in December 1893 to accompany proofs of the work. Klinger wrote that he had doubts about the sequence of musical works and had considered turning to Brahms earlier for advice. He then writes, however, "I finally decided to rely on myself alone, on the way your works as writing and sound at the piano affected me on my own."[5] The intensely personal character of this engagement is further reflected in Klinger's portraits of himself at the piano in "Accorde" and "Evocation," two images that frame the five songs, and in a portrait of himself as the lyric persona of "Alte Liebe" at the beginning of the song.[6]

In certain respects, Klinger's graphic settings of musical scores are analogous to Brahms's musical settings of poetic texts. In both cases, the artist/composer takes completed works and provides "readings" of them in a new medium. Brahms discussed the importance of reading poems aloud before setting them to music; and, as we have just seen, Klinger described his private performance of Brahms's songs.[7] There are also differences, however. The elements of fantasy and surreal juxtaposition are more pronounced in Klinger's work; the images extend beyond illustration or interpretation.[8] Klinger described the intended relationship of image to song in his 1893 letter to Brahms: "Above all, I had no thought of making 'illustrations' with these things. Rather, I wanted to move outward from the judgments into which we are led—led blindly—by poetry and above all music; I wanted to cast a glance over the range of feeling, and from there look around, continue, connect, or complete."[9] The idea of moving outward is crucial: many of the images extend to subject matter that is not in the songs. And yet Klinger also talks about "continuing" and "connecting," and where the subject matter is distinct, images can be seen to respond to aspects of style and expression in the songs.

I have collaborated with colleagues in music, art history, and the New Media Lab at Wesleyan University to produce an online digital version of the entire *Brahms Fantasy* with recordings of the songs (http://www.wesleyan.edu/dac/view/brahmsphantasie/). The online version is a reproduction; viewing it does not capture the experience of the physical object, but it is an essential resource for this chapter in lieu of access to Klinger's volume.[10] Passages from the songs will be referenced by measure numbers in the usual way but also by page and system in the *Brahms Fantasy*. (Page numbers can be found at the top of the pages starting on page 3, the second page of "Alte Liebe.") A click on the score will zoom in; the circular arrow below returns the image to the full page. Note that whereas each image in the online reproduction captures a single page, the physical volume opens to a spread of two pages. The margins of the online images, with thin lines of the maroon cover visible on three sides, may be used to determine whether one is looking at a left or right page—and thus to envision a spread with the corresponding right or left page.[11]

I shall begin the analysis of "Alte Liebe" with an overview of the poem by Karl Candidus and Brahms's setting. Klinger's image at the end of the song will lead to a presentation of the remarkable circular pathway of images, words, and music; to an exploration of tonal and then metric links between the song's denouement and an earlier moment of crisis and climax; and to a consideration of the combined "resonances" of the piano postlude and Klinger's image. I shall then explore features of the image on its own, expressive tensions between the image and song, and analogies based on the notion of darkness and light in the visual and tonal domains. The theme of circular temporality that emerges will lead us to consider an image that accompanies the first page of "Alte Liebe." I conclude with two complementary readings of structure and expression in the cycle of songs and images that form the first part of Klinger's volume. Both readings demonstrate the remarkable depth and acuity of Klinger's artistic response to Brahms's songs.

Psychological Contours in the Poem and Song

"Alte Liebe" (Old love) is a song of nostalgia and longing. Table 3.1 provides the poem with a translation.[12] Observations about swallows and storks returning from a distant land in stanza 1 lead to memories of an old "love-sorrow" in stanza 2. A series of memory-induced perceptions then builds through stanzas 3 and 4 and the beginning of stanza 5, and a reflection on the old dream in the final couplet brings the poem to a close. Whereas the two statements in stanza 1 are declarative, in stanza 2 the poet describes his experience in the subjunctive mode. Nothing is certain—the poet does not himself know for sure what he feels or remembers. In stanza 3 the memory-induced perceptions are still framed in the subjunctive, with the key phrase "als ob" (as though). The poet still sides—at least in his conscious discourse—with present reality. In stanza 4 the poet drops the subjunctive and describes conflicts between perception and reality: there is a knock at the door but no one outside, a jasmine scent but no bouquet. The first

Table 3.1. "Alte Liebe" (Candidus)

1.	Es kehrt die dunkle Schwalbe	The dark swallow returns
	Aus fernem Land zurück,	From a distant land,
	Die frommen Störche kehren	The faithful storks return
	Und bringen neues Glück.	And bring new happiness.
2.	An diesem Frühlingsmorgen,	On this spring morning,
	So trüb', verhängt und warm,	So dull, overcast and warm,
	Ist mir, als fänd' ich wieder	It seems as though I find again
	Den alten Liebesharm.	The old love-sorrow.
3.	Es ist als ob mich leise	It seems as though someone
	Wer auf die Schulter schlug,	Lightly touched my shoulder,
	Als ob ich säuseln hörte,	As though I heard a rustle,
	Wie einer Taube Flug.	Like that of a dove's flight.
4.	Es klopft an meine Türe	There is a knock at my door,
	Und ist doch niemand draus;	But no one is outside;
	Ich atme Jasmindüfte	I breathe a jasmine scent,
	Und habe keinen Strauß.	Yet have no bouquet.
5.	Es ruft mir aus der Ferne,	There is a call to me from the distance,
	Ein Auge sieht mich an,	An eye gazes at me,
	Ein alter Traum erfaßt mich	An old dream takes hold of me
	Und führt mich seine Bahn.	And leads me on its path.

couplet of stanza 5 is climactic; there are two memory-induced perceptions and no reality to rein them in. Up to this point, each perception had been given in a full couplet; here, the two perceptions are given in successive poetic lines. The perceptions themselves also are more vivid: a call, perhaps the beloved's voice, and a gaze from the other for the first time.

The final couplet is thematic for the entire poem. It is the only declarative statement that does not describe nature or memory-induced perceptions. It explains the earlier contradiction between perception and reality, for the poet now understands his perceptions to be part of an old dream. The poet, however, does not say, "An old dream *took* hold of me and *led* me on its path"; he says, "An old dream *takes* hold of me and *leads* me on its path." The dream remains in force, the poet remains on its path even as he reflects on it, and this path may be understood to lead to further poems and songs in Klinger's cycle.

Brahms's through-composed setting responds beautifully to the psychological trajectory of the poem. Brief piano interludes, elided with vocal cadences, mark the main divisions of the song. Interludes occur between stanzas 1 and 2

Example 3.1. "Alte Liebe," mm. 11–14.

and 2 and 3 and the two couplets of stanza 5. Text repetition and augmentation of declamatory rhythm also mark the ends of sections. By exploring this structural rhythm in detail, we will gain an understanding of Brahms's reading of the poem, and especially how he frames the series of memory-induced perceptions.

Brahms sets the first stanza in an eight-measure span (mm. 2–9), but he then repeats "neues Glück" and extends the stanza for two additional measures. The words "neues Glück" (new happiness) cadence first in C major and then in G minor; we hear the hopefulness of springtime and then its melancholic reflection in the lyric persona's psyche. (I use "lyric persona" to reference the persona of the song, which includes but is not limited to the "poetic persona.")[13] The setting of stanza 2 begins anew, after the first interlude, with the lyric persona's reflection on spring weather and the memory of his old love-sorrow. Note, however, that motion increases through this interlude, which is given in Example 3.1. There is eighth-note motion in the piano through the entirety of each dotted half beat, and octave doublings intensify the final eighth. This interlude, furthermore, re-calls the vocal melody from the setting of the first line; see the circled pitches in Example 3.1 at the top of the piano arpeggios with octave doublings in the left hand.[14] Brahms's interlude thus provides a musical link between stanzas 1 and 2; observations about the returning swallows and storks lead directly to the thoughts of the old love, renewal leads to recollection.

There is a more significant break between stanzas 2 and 3, and with this break Brahms dramatizes a shift from present reality to memory and the ineffable. Brahms repeats the final line of stanza 2, "den alten Liebesharm," ending the first statement with an evaded cadence and the second with a perfect authentic cadence in E♭ (see mm. 19–22; systems 2–3 on page 3). Piano arpeggios rise to sustained dotted halves in the interlude—the only other occurrence of this rhythm is in the song's postlude—and the harmony shifts from E♭ major to E♭ minor. Stanza 3 then begins with a fully diminished seventh chord, and the piano's arpeggios are in a new, higher register. Also, whereas the singer reaches up briefly to E♭ in stanza 2, he or she sustains the upper register with the line C–D–E♭ at the beginning of stanza 3. (The ascending vocal line forms a voice-exchange with the bass E♭–D–C, prolonging the diminished seventh harmony.) The strong cadence on E♭ major, the pause and shift from major to minor in the interlude, the diminished seventh harmony, and the new ethereal piano and vocal registers all dramatize the shift from present reality to memory and fantasy. The new declamatory rhythm for "wer auf die Schulter schlug" and "wie einer Taube Flug" also creates contrast (this is the only time it is used in the song), and chromatic lower neighbor motion in the vocal line adds to the feeling of mystery and unreality.

Brahms then dramatizes the conflict between memory-induced perceptions and reality in his setting of stanza 4. The conflict plays out first of all as the jagged vocal line of "Es klopft an meine Türe," prolonging the dominant with E♭–D bass motion, yields to the G-minor tonic and a recollection of the opening vocal melody for "und ist doch niemand draus" (mm. 32–35; systems 1–2 on page 4). There is a psychological paradox in this setting: the identifiable musical memory and harmonic resolution are associated not with a recovery of past experience but with disillusion, the realization that there is no one outside knocking at the door. Notice also that the vocal melody is cut short; it is left hanging on the A of "draus" because the line, which is the second in its couplet, has six syllables, not seven. (By contrast, the melody descends from A to D in the setting of "Schwalbe" at the beginning of the song.) The conflict between perception and reality plays out again, a step higher, with the setting of "ich atme Jasmindüfte, / und habe keinen Strauss," and a recollection of the opening vocal melody is again associated with disillusion. A tonicization of C major with "ich atme Jasmindüfte" conveys the idea of a sweet smell and foreshadows a later resolution to C major. (A literal transposition of the previous couplet setting would have set this line with ii°⁶₅–V in A minor.)

A direct linear ascent links the perceptual conflicts of stanza 4 to a climactic setting of the stanza 5 hallucinations. There is a stepwise melodic ascent from the Cs of "*Es* klopft an meine *Türe*" to the Ds of "*Ich* atme Jasmin*düfte*," then to

E of "Es *ruft* mir," and finally to the high F of "ein *Auge*." This high F is the vocal highpoint and crux, the moment of greatest rhythmic and emotional intensity in the song. A *crescendo*, textural thickening, and increased dissonance lead into the high E of "Es *ruft*," and a rhythmic conflict propels the vocal line to its climax on F. The $\frac{12}{8}$ groupings of the right-hand arpeggios with "(Es) ruft mir aus der Ferne" conflict with the notated $\frac{6}{8}$, and the ♩♩♪ patterns of the left hand complement the ♩♩ rhythms of the vocal line. The high F itself grates against the E♭ of the piano; this clash provides yet more intensity to the climactic moment. Recall the place of "Es ruft mir aus der Ferne, / Ein Auge sieht mich an" in the trajectory of the poem: these are the two climactic perception-statements, each in a single line, each with no reality-based counterstatement. The point is not only that Brahms leads into these statements with a process of musical intensification; it is also that there is no break, no piano interlude, between stanzas 3 and 4 or stanzas 4 and 5. Brahms thus reads against the poetic structure: on the one hand, he links separate stanzas to create a continuous musical flow, while on the other, he provides a caesura within the final quatrain (mm. 44–45; systems 3–4 on page 4) to dramatize the psychological shift from internal conflict and hallucination back to reflection and reality.[15]

The Circularity of Words, Music, and Image

It is intriguing that Klinger does not provide images for any of the lyric persona's perceptions; there is no engraving or etching for the tap on the shoulder, the rustling of the dove, the knock at the door, the jasmine-scented bouquet, the call from the distance, or the gazing eye. These remain ineffable, precisely as in the poem and in Brahms's song.[16] The two images on the inner borders of pages 4 and 5 are generally taken to represent the energies of female and male sexuality—they thus extend beyond the song's immediate themes.[17] What Klinger does provide, however, is striking: on the final page of this song, birds fly directly out from the score to a tower in the distance, as may be observed in Example 3.2. Klinger's birds may remind us of the birds from the beginning of the poem and song, but Klinger inverts the direction of flight. In the first stanza, swallows and storks *return* from a distant land, bringing new happiness; here they fly out into the distance. Klinger's birds embody the lyric persona's longing for the distant time and place associated with his "old love." And as our eyes descend in Klinger's image, we find a man and woman walking together on a path between the dark foliage and rock or ancient city wall. The birds may be associated quite directly with the old dream and its path of yearning; they fly out with the second iteration of the final couplet, "ein alter Traum erfaßt mich und führt mich seine Bahn."

Example 3.2. *Brahms Fantasy*, p. 5.

Swallows and storks in the poem and song are harbingers of something ineffable, a memory that cannot quite be captured. Recall the precise wording in the second stanza—"it seems *as though* I find again the old love-sorrow"—and the series of not-quite-real perceptions in stanzas 3–5. Brahms inscribes this ineffable feeling in the opening vocal melody, the melody of "Es kehrt die dunkle Schwalbe." As we have observed already, this melody returns hidden in the piano texture of the first interlude to motivate the reflections of the second stanza, and it returns in the fourth stanza with the moments of disillusion. In other words, the melodic gesture becomes a musical memory, but the precise feelings associated with it remain beyond the grasp of consciousness. The melody returns again during the last couplet, where it sets "ein alter Traum erfaßt mich" in its first iteration (mm. 46–47; system 4 on page 4). The melody's function as a motto for the song supports and is supported by the thematic function of the poetic line "ein alter Traum erfaßt mich." The melody is hidden again in the piano texture of mm. 49–50, between the two iterations of the final couplet; see the circled pitches in Example 3.3. In a music-text blend, the old-dream-melody literally takes hold of the singer-as-lyric-persona; the singer is carried on a wave of 7–6 appoggiaturas that begins with the piano's G–F♯ in m. 49 and continues with the

Example 3.3. "Alte Liebe," mm. 49–52.

piano and vocal A–G, B♭–A, and C–B♮ in mm. 50–51 (Example 3.3).[18] Finally, whereas Brahms inscribes ineffable feelings associated with the returning birds in musical melody, Klinger takes the climax of this melody—as it develops in the song's denouement—and sets it in flight. The circularity is complete: returning birds evoke ineffable memories, which are inscribed in the musical melody, which then becomes a flock of birds flying out to a tower, emblematic of longing and memory.

Examples 3.1 and 3.3 provide critical musical links in this circular pathway. Example 3.1, discussed above, presents the interlude between stanzas 1 and 2 and the beginning of stanza 2. Notice that the poetic stanzas themselves are distinct. The first stanza has an introductory function; it provides context that is separate from the main development of the poem. Brahms's interlude provides a link: it is the (musical) thought that connects returning birds to thoughts of the old love, and it is also the first hidden recollection of what will become the song's signature motive (see the circled pitches in mm. 11–12). The musical thought (i.e., the signature motive) persists as the lyric persona reflects on the spring morning in the first couplet of stanza 2 (see the circled pitches in mm. 13–14), but it disappears as the lyric persona provides words for his experience in the second couplet. The feeling is lost as words try to capture it, much as in the second strophe of Brahms's "Wie Melodien zieht es mir," op. 105, no. 1.[19] Example 3.3 then provides the link between iterations of the final couplet. The piano figuration from the first interlude thus returns to link the "old dream" with Klinger's birds in flight.

The High E♭ as Resolution and Denouement

The figurations of Examples 3.1 and 3.3 begin almost identically (there is a slight difference in voicing), but they develop in very different ways. The figuration in Example 3.1 provides an initial energetic impulse, linking stanzas 1 and 2, but A then falls to D in the second measure (as in the original vocal melody), and the music relaxes into E♭ major. The figuration in Example 3.3 latches on to the 7–6 appoggiatura of G–F♯ in the first measure and sequences it upward in a continuous process of intensification. The singer joins in this process straightaway, in the second measure, and he or she is carried away on the path of the old dream. The continuous *crescendo* of Example 3.3 also contrasts with the hairpin dynamics of Example 3.1. What would motivate this new response to the ineffable? What provides the psychological energy for the melodic ascent that sets the birds in flight?

A simple answer can be found via the poetic text. Whereas in stanza 2 the poet observes that it seems as if he has found an old love-sorrow, in the final couplet he observes that an old dream *takes hold* of him and *leads* him on its path. The final couplet, in other words, is inherently more dynamic. One might also observe that with this rising sequence Brahms combines reflection and yearning, which provides for an effective conclusion in conjunction with the poem. The poet describes his dream and its hold on him in the present tense, not the past tense; it remains in force even as he reflects on it.

There is another possible rationale, however. An earlier unresolved moment might be heard to motivate the rising sequence in the final vocal phrase. The climactic F of "ein *Auge* sieht mich an" is the seventh of a V⁷ in C major. This dominant is sustained as the vocal line and piano descend, and F resolves to E♮ at the end of the phrase but in a lower register (see mm. 43–44; system 3 on page 4). The piano returns to the high F in m. 51 (Example 3.3), precisely at the end of the rising vocal sequence, and the F of m. 51 is coupled with D and B♮ as in the V⁷/C from the earlier climax. This high F then resolves to the E♭ of the singer's "führt" in the measure that sets Klinger's birds in flight. In other words, the rising sequence may be heard as an attempt to reach up again and resolve, in its register, the high F from the earlier climax—the high F that had been abandoned so quickly as the lyric persona fell from his hallucinatory perceptions to a reflection on the old dream. In poetic terms, the sequence reaches up to resolve the emotional turmoil of the earlier crisis, the experience of an eye that gazes at the lyric persona and reminds him of the old love-sorrow. It also is striking that the declamatory rhythm expands to one foot per measure precisely at the climax and fall of "ein Auge sieht mich an" and then again at the resolution of "und führt mich seine, seine Bahn."

The high E♭ of "führt" is supported by a Neapolitan harmony, which in turn leads to the structural cadence in G minor. The two "neues Glück" cadences at the end of the first stanza thus foreshadow the events of the song's climax and denouement—the lower register resolution to E♮ in C major and the upper register resolution to E♭ that leads to a cadence in G minor. In the first "neues Glück" cadence, the vocal line arrives on E♮, and the bass then picks up this E♮ and descends chromatically to E♭ and D. Similarly, there is an E♮–E♭ descent in the piano interlude before the final couplet, and the singer brings E♭ down to D with "ein al(ter Traum)." It is E♭, of course, that provides the resolution of the climactic F finally in its own register. The piano arpeggio in m. 51 (Example 3.3) seems to be designed specifically to remind us of this.

Metric Dissonance and Resolution

Broad quarter-note arpeggios are introduced for the first time in the piano with the high E♭ of "führt," and it is the first of these arpeggios that returns ineffable longing and musical melody to an image of birds in flight. The quarter-note arpeggios may be heard to resolve the metric dissonance of the climax, just as the high E♭ resolves the tonal dissonance of the climactic F.[20] The song's fundamental metric dissonance, which emerges intermittently from the second stanza onward and comes to a head at the climax, is between duple groupings of eighths that support the notated ⁶₈ meter and triple groupings of eighths that imply an alternative ¹²₈ meter. The broad arpeggios in the right hand of mm. 52–54 confirm the quarter-note pulse, denying the dotted quarter pulse and ¹²₈ meter.

Let us trace the sources of this metric dissonance and its poetic associations back through the song; the significance of the resolution in the denouement will then become clearer. The dissonance appears first in the second stanza; see mm. 14, 16, and especially 19–21 (page 3: last measure of system 1, second measure of system 2, and the end of system 2 to the beginning of system 3). In the last passage, it underlies "den alten Liebesharm"; we may thus hear it as a form of emotional disturbance associated specifically with the old love-sorrow. It occurs again in the fourth stanza with "Es klopft an meine Türe" and "Ich atme Jasmindüfte," where the perceptions are no longer qualified with the phrase "als ob."

Leading into the climax, with "Es ruft mir aus der Ferne," Brahms reiterates rising three-eighth-note groups in the right hand and conflicting quarter-note motion in the left hand. The $\frac{12}{8}$ meter then becomes strongest at the climax and subsequent descent (mm. 42–43; system 3 on page 4), since there is no regular quarter-note pulse. In a music-text blend, the singer-as-lyric-persona enters into the $\frac{12}{8}$ experience of memories and illusions. (A subtle conflict remains, since vocal quarter notes at the end of each measure imply a continuation of $\frac{6}{4}$.) It is here, as we recall, that reality-based observations no longer contradict the hallucinatory perceptions.

The interlude combines triple groupings of eighths and of quarters in reiterative rising figures. It thus functions as a transition between the (almost) pure $\frac{12}{8}$ meter of the climactic memory/illusion and the $\frac{6}{4}$ return to present reality. The setting of "ein alter Traum erfaßt mich" in mm. 46–47 (the first time) then may be heard as a triple return: $\frac{6}{4}$ is reestablished together with G minor and the opening melody. The broad arpeggios subsequently introduced with the high E♭ (m. 52) provide unambiguous confirmation of the quarter-note pulse and $\frac{6}{4}$ meter.

There are also eighth-note arpeggios in the left hand in mm. 52–54, but these drop out in the latter half of each measure, and the singer joins the quarter-note arpeggios. This particular figuration, with both kinds of motion superimposed in the first half of the measure but only the slower motion in the second half, is especially appropriate in relation to the birds in flight. When a flock of birds is close by, we see both motion and multiplicity; as the flock becomes more distant, the motion appears less obvious, slower, and more unified.

The quarter-note arpeggios link in yet another way with earlier rhythms in the song: they may be heard as a rhythmic augmentation of the eighth-note arpeggios that accompany the singer from the beginning. Heard in this way, however, the triple grouping of quarters in $\frac{6}{4}$ augments the triple grouping of eighths in $\frac{12}{8}$, *not* the duple grouping of eighths in $\frac{6}{4}$! Brahms presents this augmentation directly: pitch-class parallelism implies a triple grouping of eighths in the descending arpeggio of m. 51, and pitch-class parallelism combines with the established $\frac{6}{4}$ meter to convey a triple grouping of quarters in the descending arpeggio of m. 52 (see the brackets in Example 3.3).[21] The transition to the final couplet in mm. 44–45 is the only other passage in which the piano has arpeggios in triple groupings of quarters, and it may be heard to foreshadow the transformation of mm. 51–52. The conjunction of tonal and rhythmic events is remarkable. In m. 51 the piano returns to the high F of "ein Auge" and hints at the $\frac{12}{8}$ meter associated with it as the lyric persona recalls his hallucinations. In m. 52 the singer and piano resolve the high F to E♭ and augment the triple grouping of eighths to a triple grouping of quarters, confirming the $\frac{6}{4}$ meter. Pitch-class parallelisms in the eighth-note arpeggios continue to hint at the $\frac{12}{8}$ meter, however (see brackets in Example 3.3, m. 52), and the lyric persona continues to feel the psychological force of his dream as birds fly out from the score.

The analysis thus far leads to a greater appreciation of Klinger's graphic design in its particular relation to Brahms's musical design and Candidus's poetic design. Klinger chooses this particular moment—the moment of the active verb "führt" (leads), of the combined reflection and yearning, of the precadential Neapolitan harmony realized in a broad descending arpeggio, of resolution of tonal and metric dissonances from the earlier climax—for the birds to fly out. He arranges the score in such a way that this measure is at the top of the page at the end of the system, immediately adjacent to the image. This is the first of five large images that Klinger sets next to the scores of Brahms's songs. (There is also a large image on the first page of "Alte Liebe," but it is above the score, not next to it.) In this context, the moment of musical arrival becomes a moment of graphic departure, a kind of "structural downbeat" in the combination of poem, music, and image.

Klinger's Birds and the Piano Postlude

The high E♭ arrival is, of course, not yet a complete resolution; the singer's structural cadence follows the Neapolitan, and this vocal cadence elides with the piano postlude. The gesture of yearning thus flows into absolute music and graphic image, while words are left behind. The piano postlude itself is highly suggestive in relation to Klinger's image. In the postlude, the piano returns to the song's signature motive, the motive of birds ("Es kehrt die dunkle Schwalbe") and ineffable memory/dream ("ein alter Traum erfaßt mich") and transforms it into flowing dotted halves (mm. 55–58, from "Bahn" in Example 3.2). There are, in fact, four transformations: *rhythmic augmentation*—the pitches D–E♭–G–F♯ are set in two bars rather than one; *loss of rhythmic differentiation*—each pitch is a dotted half; *new harmonization*—a more dissonant and mysterious ii°7 replaces iv with the melodic G; and *repetition and extension*—the concluding A–D descent repeats, extending the gesture to its lower-octave cadence. The augmentation and loss of differentiation may once again be linked with visual experience—with the reduced differentiation and apparently slower motion of birds in the distance. The descending repetition of the A–D figure suggests that outward yearning associated with upward melodic striving gives way to its opposite, melodic descent and a retreat to the interiority of the self.[22] Finally, while tonic resolution arrives with the final chord, the melody does not reach î. There is no answering phrase, as in the vocal settings of the motive at the beginning and end of the song; the concluding tonic simply retains D in the top voice.

Paul Berry provides compelling evidence that the piano postlude, with its prominent presentation of the motive in even dotted halves, is a conscious compositional allusion to Brahms's Capriccio in F♯ Minor, op. 76, no. 1, a work that he had sent to Clara Schumann as a private gift in the spring of 1871. (The piano work sent to Schumann differs in certain details from the later published capriccio.) Berry further argues that Brahms intended this private allusion for Schumann to recall Brahms's prior springtime musical gift and to engage her musical and affective memory in a way that would mirror the experience of the song's protagonist.[23] There is no evidence that Klinger knew about the allusion or its intended effect. Nonetheless, it is intriguing that this postlude reaches out to another work and other memories, just as Klinger's birds reach out to the tower in the distance.

Realism and Fantasy in the Tower Image

What of Klinger's image on its own? The image divides into two parts by shading: in the upper part (nearly half), we see the bright sky and tower with the birds flying around it; in the lower part (slightly more than half), we see the walled city, barren landscape, foreground foliage, and a man and woman walking together.[24] The brightest part of the sky is at the horizon; this strengthens the contrast, but it is paradoxical from a realist point of view. This would seem to be an evening image—morning is also possible but less likely as the time for a lovers' tryst—and the darker shading of city, landscape, and foliage may be understood as a consequence of the setting sun. A few buildings in the more distant part of the city still catch the evening sun. The horizon should then be darker, since the sun is behind us, to the west. The subtle undermining of realism is precisely the point; Klinger is interested in fantasy and feeling, not in the representation of reality. The graphic arts differ from painting in this regard, according to Klinger: whereas painting deals with the material nature of its objects, the objects of drawing may take on qualities that are less associated with the eye and more associated with poetic understanding.[25] Here the bright horizon may represent a distant place of hope or renewed happiness, perhaps the "neues Glück" of the song's first stanza, and the symbolic or mystical associations are strengthened, since the source of light is unclear.

The darkest area of the picture is in the foliage in front of the city, just beyond an angled wall or rock to the left and foliage to the right. This place of darker trees separates the couple from city and tower, and they walk toward it, or rather into it, perhaps to be hidden in the dark undergrowth. There is depth in the image; the tower is distant not only from our point of view and not only from Brahms's score (whence the birds fly) but also from the couple. While Klinger's birds fly to the tower and light, the couple follows a path into darkness, away from all windows and gazing eyes. Windows in the city in fact take the shape of eyes; notice especially the "eyebrows" on the pair of small circular windows just above the foliage. Several of the windows are in pairs, but in the tower there are single windows—one halfway up and one at the top—like the eye that the lyric persona perceives gazing at him at the song's climax.

Expressive tensions emerge if we attempt to relate the image more closely to the song. In the song, an eye gazes at the lyric persona, and this would seem to be the eye of the beloved; in Klinger's image, the couple avoids the windows of the city and tower, the eyes of society. Is there then a painful psychological fusing of the lover's eye and the public eye of the tower window? Does the eye in fact belong to the lover, or is it an eye of public humiliation? The latter interpretation is suggestive in relation to the third and fifth songs of Klinger's cycle, "Am Sonntag Morgen" and "Kein Haus, keine Heimat." Many people in the poem witness the infidelity of the beloved in "Am Sonntag Morgen," and the lyric persona puts on a public show of gaiety to hide his private pain. He is then completely alienated from society in "Kein Haus, keine Heimat," rejecting the world that does not care for him. Also, we may imagine from "Alte Liebe" that the "old dream" leads the lyric persona on a path to his old love, and that might seem at first to be the implication of Klinger's image. The birds fly past the tower and to the sky beyond, however, to a place of freedom and light, not to the couple. Perhaps the yearning for freedom, which the birds symbolize, exists in an uneasy relationship to the memories of old love, including its moments of sexual fulfillment and public shame.[26] Here again, thematic links with the remainder of the *Brahms Fantasy* come to mind. In the *Schicksalslied,* the light and eternal clarity of the gods contrast with the suffering of humanity, falling "blindly from one hour to another . . . many years down into the unknown." There is light and clarity, on the one hand, suffering and obscurity, on the other. The two domains coexist uneasily in the lyric persona's mind in "Alte Liebe" and are then set apart in the *Schicksalslied.*

Keys of Darkness and Light

In relation to the music of Brahms's setting, the tower and bright horizon may be heard as "C-major domains," the darker foliage and couple below as "G-minor domains." The contrast of C major and G minor is fundamental to the song, as we have observed. The tower with its "eye" then links even more closely with the V^7/C harmony of "ein Auge sieht mich an." Similarly, the final G-minor chord is immediately adjacent to the couple in Klinger's image, and the chord and couple are of comparable size.

There are other important major harmonies and keys in the song, however, in addition to C: B♭ (III), E♭ (VI), and A♭ (♭II). The song's first tonal move is a tonicization of B♭ at the end of the first vocal phrase. The second stanza then establishes E♭ major as an alternative key, associated with the overcast spring morning and thoughts of the old love-sorrow. A♭, the Neapolitan, is the predominant harmony in both iterations of the final couplet, the second time with the climactic high vocal E♭. Do these major keys also relate to the tower and birds in Klinger's image, or is it only C major that is the key of light? On an immediate "syntactic" level, it is the "dark" ♭II, not the "bright" C major, that sets the birds in flight, and this is a striking expressive juxtaposition. "Darkness" and "light" are fused in the combination of music and image. B♭ relates naturally to the distant land, since it sets the text "aus fernem Land zurück" in stanza 1. Descending from there in fifths to E♭, we reach the first mention of the old love-sorrow and a spring morning that is overcast, not bright. A♭ is then one fifth farther "down," away from the bright C major.

The flight from a "dark" Neapolitan to the bright tower and sky may itself be understood as a transformative journey. It is intriguing in this regard that the horizon is unnaturally bright; the horizon thereby becomes a mystical goal, a place of light where there should be darkness. The birds fly around the tower and then continue on to the cloudy sky; they fly toward but do not reach the place of light—or at least we are not able to see them arriving there. There are analogous tensions in the two musical progressions to the Neapolitan. In the first (mm. 47–48), the Neapolitan follows directly after the G-minor tonic and leads directly to the dominant (see system 4 on page 4). In the second, it follows a B diminished triad and the ascent to high F, both of which remind us of G⁷, the climactic phrase "ein Auge sieht mich an," and its C major resolution. In other words, the "darkness" of the Neapolitan replaces the "brightness" of C major.

A similar expressive tension occurs at an earlier pivotal moment in the song. A♭ major is tonicized twice as the subdominant of E♭ in the second stanza, with both iterations of "den *alten* Liebesharm" (mm. 18–21; systems 2–3 on page 3). In both instances, the E♭ chord includes a raised fifth, B, which is also the leading tone to C. There is a simultaneous ascent to C and settling on A♭; ambiguity of direction is inherent in the augmented triad. (In the second half of m. 18, the augmented triad is embedded in an E♭⁷ chord with a raised fifth.) The sense of an upward reach is especially notable in the rising chromatic line of "ist mir, als fänd ich wieder den alten," doubled in octaves and thirds below in the piano. The expressive analogy is strong: Brahms provides yearnings for the bright C major in progressions to the dark A♭; Klinger's image provides a bright horizon where there should be relative darkness, away from the setting sun. In both media, there is separation of darkness and light and a subtle undermining of that separation.

There is one element in the poem's final couplet that does not seem, at first glance, to be present in Klinger's image: a reflexive awareness of the old dream and its effect on the self. The image seems to exist entirely in the realm of memory and fantasy; the walled city and tower are from a distant time, and the composition is balanced in a way that suggests fantasy, not realism. We might say that the image is without a qualifying "als ob." And yet, while the contents and composition of the image exist within a domain of memory and fantasy, the perspective and framing highlight that domain in a way that may be understood as self-conscious and reflexive. The man and woman are in the foreground, but they are still distant from us, the viewers. The entire image thus seems to be distant, and the frame has a strong effect. If the image were the scene from a window, one would be standing back, able to see only a portion of the view. It becomes like a glimpse into another world, and as observers we may become aware that we are distant from the dream-memory-fantasy world, the world of the old love-sorrow.

Klinger's Wheel of Time

One of the themes in my analysis of Klinger's "performance" of "Alte Liebe" has been the notion of circularity. Returning birds in the poem and song bring forth memories that are instantiated in the ineffable medium of musical melody. That melody, in turn, builds in the denouement to a point of climax and resolution, at which point both melody and ineffable memory take flight as birds. Klinger also presents the idea of circularity in an image accompanying the first page of "Alte Liebe," reproduced in Example 3.4. To the right of the score there is an ornate wheel on an upward-sloping and partially wooded landscape; Hans Wolfgang Singer refers to this as a "wheel of time."[27] On top of the wheel is an old bearded face, at the bottom is the darker face of a young satyr, a lustful woodland god. There is no overlap with the score, as in the tower image, but it seems significant that this wheel is positioned at a page break precisely between the C-major and G-minor cadences of "neues Glück." The upward slope of the hillside matches the upward contour of the piano arpeggios precisely, and this parallelism contributes to the feeling of a direct link between the music and image. The wheel is positioned in such a way that the bearded face overlaps with the image across the top of the page; given the virtuosity of Klinger's technique, one may assume that the overlap is intentional.[28] The relatively young man stretched out on a balcony (a self-portrait of Klinger on his balcony in Rome) thus seems to be inflected by the concerns of old age.[29]

Example 3.4. *Brahms Fantasy,* p. 2.

There is also tension in the "wheel of time" with implications for the larger cycle of songs and images. On the one hand, the curved "spokes" that radiate out from the center create an impression of movement. On the other hand, all we see is the top, middle, and bottom of the wheel against a cross section of landscape: the wheel is caught at a particular moment. The satyr belongs uniquely to the earthly domain, and the old man gazes appropriately upward; it is hard to imagine them reversed as the wheel turns. Also, a special effort would be required to turn the wheel in the uphill (clockwise) direction of the piano arpeggios. The song's lyric persona is caught in an analogous temporal situation; he experiences the return of spring, but melancholy self-absorption disables the potential experience of cyclic return and the "neues Glück" that might have accompanied it. Cyclic return for the song's protagonist is always a return to a particular moment of trauma, the time of his old love-sorrow. The remaining songs in the *Brahms Fantasy* can be understood as attempts to overcome this "tender, too tender, reflection on what is past and what is lost" through a "powerful, energetic, pulling together of oneself," as Klinger himself put it in his letter to Brahms.[30]

Narrative Structure in Klinger's Cycle

The study of narrative links in the cycle of five songs in the *Brahms Fantasy* takes us yet another step away from Brahms because the volume presents Klinger's selection and arrangement of songs with accompanying images, not a collection that Brahms himself arranged. Klinger's cycle is nonetheless intriguing as reception history and creative analysis: it reveals ways in which songs can be linked across Brahms's published collections. And whereas Brahms objected to singers' arbitrary selection of songs from his collections, he did not object to Klinger's selection and arrangement.[31] It is not only narrative links in the poems that will be of interest here; there are also tonal links and a distinct logic in the arrangement of keys. Therefore, as with my exploration of "Alte Liebe," this discussion will be facilitated by accessing the online version of the *Brahms Fantasy*. (Note that the online version includes complete song texts and translations via links at the bottom-right corner.)

How specifically can the songs that Klinger chose be understood to form a narrative, and how do his images relate to that narrative? My first interpretation of the cycle will depart from the denouement of "Alte Liebe"—from the moment that I earlier referred to as a "structural downbeat" in the combination of poem, music, and image. Klinger's "Neapolitan" birds (i.e., the birds that take flight with the Neapolitan harmony toward the end of the song) can be heard and seen to set the subsequent songs in motion on the path of the lyric persona's old dream. The keys of the first four songs form a pair of Neapolitan relationships: G minor to A♭ major (songs 1–2, "Alte Liebe" to "Sehnsucht") and E minor to F major (songs 3–4, "Am Sonntag Morgen" to "Feldeinsamkeit"). As we shall see, Klinger's images subtly reinforce these pairings, and Neapolitan harmonies are also significant within songs 2, 3, and 4.[32]

In recent years, scholars have taken a variety of approaches to tonal links in Romantic song cycles and collections. On the one hand, David Ferris and Beate Julia Perrey argue for the importance of the fragment in Romantic aesthetics and against claims for organic unity based on key sequence. On the other hand, Berthold Hoeckner traces compelling tonal and narrative paths through Schumann's *Dichterliebe,* and Inge Van Rij argues for the significance of key relations in Brahms's song collections.[33] Brahms himself sanctioned published transpositions of his songs, but he requested that the transposed versions be distinguished from the originals; the original keys thus seem to have been significant for him.[34] In the present context, one may ask not about Brahms's intentions but about Klinger's. Was Klinger aware of the key relations that I shall explore? Did he intend them to be a part of the design? We cannot know for sure, but it is certainly possible that he did. He describes playing the songs himself as he sought to determine the sequence of works (see the letter quoted above).[35] Finally, the kinds of relations that I outline here would have been available for Brahms and those in his circle.[36] As Jan Brachmann observes, the work demanded private, intimate engagement by an elite group of friends and connoisseurs because of its format as a book (which cannot be effectively displayed in a museum), because of the limited printing of 5 and then 150 copies, and because of its cost.[37]

In Klinger's cycle, the Neapolitan of "Alte Liebe" (A♭ major) is the harmony that leads the lyric persona on the path of his old dream, and this harmony then becomes the key of "Sehnsucht" (Longing) as he returns to the time of his dream. The recalled time of "Sehnsucht" is one of active yearning for the beloved; the poem, song, and images are all more dynamic than anything we have experienced thus far in "Alte Liebe." In the poem, a translation by Josef Wenzig of a Bohemian folksong, the protagonist actively yearns for the beloved, who tarries far away "beyond dense forests." A sudden acceleration of poetic rhythm expresses the urgency of this desire: the lines shift from measured trochaic tetrameter, "Hínter jénen díchten Wáldern, / Wéilst du, méine Süßgelíebte" (Behind those thick woods / You tarry, my sweet love), to emphatic dimeter lines with dactylic feet, "Bérstet ihr Félsen, / Ébnet euch Táler" (Crack, you cliffs / Flatten yourselves, valleys). Brahms conveys the effect of this shift musically with a burst of pulsating triplet chords, dominant and fully diminished sevenths, and continuous waves of textural expansion and contraction, the singer and piano moving in contrary motion (mm. 16–23; bottom system on page 7 and first two measures on page 8). There are likewise highly dynamic images on pages 6 and 7, the first two pages of the song. To the left of the score on page 6 we see a full-sized naked female figure; her gaze is intent, her posture is both defensive and alluring. Her face is in profile, and we see a single eye, recalling the vocal highpoint on F of "Alte Liebe." A clothed man reaches awkwardly in her direction from page 7, on the opposite side of the same spread. His entire body stretches dynamically along a line that matches the descending gestures of the singer's melody, especially the descending minor sixth and tritone of "Weit, ach weit!" (Far, oh far!) that we see next to the image (mm. 14–15). The Neapolitan harmony continues to signify yearning and distance in this song: "Sehnsucht" tonicizes its own Neapolitan, A major, with the second iteration of "meine ferne, meine süße [Maid]" (my distant, my sweet [maiden]) in mm. 35–36 (last two measures on page 8).

Klinger then creates a narrative break with the image at the end of "Sehnsucht" (page 9). A woman sits passively on a bed, hunched over and engrossed in thought; the shading is lighter and more uniform than in previous images; and the space is inside, not outside. This image has little or nothing to

72 *Yonatan Malin*

do with the energetic yearning of the song, and certainly nothing to do with the triumphant plagal progressions of the piano postlude. There is something at the woman's feet and to her left; Singer identifies it as a man sitting on the floor with his back to us.[38] One can indeed see a companion figure by visualizing the V-shaped folds extending upward from below her knees as externalized representations of back muscles. The black silhouette next to her head becomes the back of his head; the hand on her cheek is his hand. Viewed this way, there is an Escher-like interlocking of figures, and the man sits on the floor in a submissive posture. He is intertwined with her, and yet she seems to be oblivious of him. The image thus thematizes interiority and a paradoxical form of solitude. Interiority and solitude then continue to be thematic for the next pair of songs, "Am Sonntag Morgen" and "Feldeinsamkeit."

"Am Sonntag Morgen" (On Sunday morning) is a song of betrayal, jealousy, public humiliation, and private torment, as we observed earlier. This E-minor song is in two halves; each half sets four lines of the poem (a translation from Italian by Paul Heyse). In the first half (mm. 1–13; page 10) the lyric persona projects self-control as he reports his awareness of his beloved's infidelity. The pentameter lines are set with even declamation in three-bar phrases, and the piano has "controlled" staccato rhythms. In the second half (mm. 14–27; page 11), public demonstrations of gaiety alternate with private grief, and the irregular phrase rhythms reflect these shifts.[39] The two border images for "Am Sonntag Morgen" reflect and support the two modes of musical expression. The female figure on page 10 stands poised on a classical chariot. There is a dark faun's face below, and envy might be read into the dark striations, but there is no movement. In contrast with this image, the man on page 11 strains upward out of a pool of water, or he may be about to drown. Flowers and butterflies suggest a world of beauty and light, but they are mostly beyond his reach. The man's upward reach parallels the singer's, first to F♯ ("*laut* gelacht"), then G ("*an* zu singen"), and finally to A ("*Hände* wund"). The singer-as-lyric-persona reaches with these high notes for a world of social joviality (perhaps with flowers and butterflies) that he cannot maintain in private. In the music, the F-major Neapolitan chord emerges for this private expression of grief and pain, and it underscores "ge*weint* zur Nacht" (cried at night) and "Hände *wund* zu ringen" (wrung [my] hands soar) in mm. 17–18 and 22–23 (systems 1–2 and 2–3 on page 11). This Neapolitan chord returns in the postlude, three measures from the end, and "Feldeinsamkeit" (The loneliness of the field) then transforms this harmony of private pain into a key of individual transcendence.

In "Feldeinsamkeit" the lyric persona describes his feelings as he rests in a field, surrounded by the sounds and sights of nature. During stanza 2 he experiences a mystical dissolution of the self—"mir ist, als ob ich längst gestorben bin"

(I feel as though I have long been dead)—and imagines himself drifting bliss-fully through eternal space. Klinger's image to the left of the score on page 12 illustrates the song in a relatively straightforward manner. A man lies in the open field, gazing upward, and the texture of his clothes blends seamlessly with the field to convey the dissolution of the self in nature.

The twofold pairing of songs in Neapolitan-related keys and the narra-tive break of Klinger's image at the end of "Sehnsucht" suggest a structural and expressive interpretation. In each pairing, there is a progression from realism to fantasy and from a minor key to its Neapolitan. The realism of "Alte Liebe" (song 1) is apparent in the lyric persona's reflexive statements—he is aware of the dream nature of his sensations at the outset and end of the song—and this leads to the fantastical yearnings of "Sehnsucht" (song 2). In "Am Sonntag Morgen" (song 3) the lyric persona experiences the reality of betrayal and can only express his emotions in private; this leads to the fantasy of transcendence in "Feldeinsamkeit" (song 4). In this way, Klinger's volume highlights a dichotomy between reality and fantasy in his selection of Brahms songs, a dichotomy that is also already present within the psychological contour of "Alte Liebe."

The final stage in this thread of Neapolitan associations occurs in "Feld-einsamkeit" at the famous setting of "mir ist, als ob ich längst gestorben bin" (mm. 26–28; systems 3–4 on page 13). Stark octave D♭s reverberate in m. 26 directly after a cadence in C major, momentarily implying ♭II of the dominant, and "gestorben bin" goes on to outline an inverted German augmented sixth, enharmonically equivalent to V⁷/♭II (and a half-step above the subsequent V⁷). The descending diminished third and upward half-step resolution of "gestor*ben bin*" may remind one of "*wund zu ringen*" at the end of "Am Sonntag Morgen."

A painful undercurrent is also revealed in the remarkable border image that accompanies this page of Brahms's score (page 13). Two faces appear directly next to each other; clasped hands and a bit of a shoulder can be seen against a background of "formless darkness."[40] Tears can be seen on at least one and perhaps both faces. Klinger seems to suggest that the blissful communion of the individual lyric persona with nature is associated not only with the thought of death, as in Brahms's song, but also with a deeply tragic experience of intimacy. This failure of intimacy, which remains unexplained, is finally where the "old dream" of the first song leads. It is the core memory that is revealed precisely as the lyric persona experiences a dissolution of the self.

The couple in darkness is the last image that directly accompanies one of Brahms's songs, and it may remind us of the man and woman walking together toward dark foliage at the end of "Alte Liebe." The last song, "Kein Haus, keine Heimat," is then a "brutally terse" rejection of intimacy, and Klinger fittingly leaves the space above the score empty.[41] "Kein Haus, keine Heimat" breaks the series of Neapolitan pairings; it is in the key of D minor, a fifth above the G minor of "Alte Liebe" and a third below—or the relative minor of—the F major of "Feldeinsamkeit." If the Neapolitan is a harmony of yearning, fantasy, private pain, and imagined transcendence in the Brahms songs that Klinger has chosen, then the move to the dominant of the original key is an appropriate metaphor for the "powerful, energetic, pulling together of oneself" that Klinger described in his letter to Brahms. The relative minor relationship with "Feldeinsamkeit" in turn suggests the disillusion that would lead to an angry rejection of society. "Kein Haus, keine Heimat" ends in a defiant D major (more on this below).

Circularity, Eternity, and Rupture

I offer one more reading of the cycle that complements the reading I have developed thus far. "Sehnsucht" and "Am Sonntag Morgen" (songs 2 and 3) may be understood to occur within the narrative frame of "Alte Liebe" as memories that the lyric persona finds on the path of his "old dream." "Feldeinsamkeit" (song 4), on the other hand, may be understood to be at the same narrative level as "Alte Liebe." It has a duration and musical weight equivalent to "Alte Liebe," it returns to an experience of nature and dreams as in "Alte Liebe," and it once again presents feelings in the subjunctive mode. There is even a conflict between the imaginary and the real in "Feldeinsamkeit" as in "Alte Liebe." The final couplet of "Feldeinsamkeit" combines a subjunctive "als ob" phrase with indicative verb forms: "Mir ist, *als ob* ich längst gestorben *bin* / Und *ziehe* selig mit durch ew'ge Räume" (I feel *as though* I *have* long been dead / And *am drifting* blissfully with them through eternal space). The indicative verb forms grammatically reify death and the infinite expansion of the self against the grain of the subjunctive "als ob." Brahms seems to have valued the existential contradiction; he defended the grammatical "error" in his correspondence with Klaus Groth.[42] What is real, what is imagined? Both "Alte Liebe" and "Feldeinsamkeit" pose this question. ("Feldeinsamkeit" nevertheless can still be understood as an escape into fantasy in relation to "Am Sonntag Morgen," and "Alte Liebe" still functions as a "realist" song before the fantastical yearnings of "Sehnsucht," as described in my first interpretation.)

Ultimately, the significance of the "Alte Liebe"–"Feldeinsamkeit" link lies in the fact that "Feldeinsamkeit" counters the movement and cyclic return from "Alte Liebe" with an expansion of the present moment into eternity. The lyric persona rests quietly in the beginning of the song and imagines himself drifting like clouds "through eternal space" at the end. Musically, the modified strophic form combines with a slow tempo, gently pulsating chords, tonic pedals, and an expansively lyrical vocal line to convey the flow of musical time in an eternal present.

"Kein Haus, keine Heimat" then responds by presenting a radical compression and rupture of time, precisely the opposite of "Feldeinsamkeit." The song is extremely short, and Brahms composes a form of rhythmic acceleration into the end of each strophe. Chords arrive on the third beat with "*so wirbl' ich, ein Strohhalm, in . . .*" (mm. 6–8), and the piano then completes a hemiolic cycle with arrivals on beats 2 and 1, each chord arriving two beats after the last (mm. 9–10; top system on page 14).[43] The same rhythm occurs with the second stanza (mm. 15–19; second system on page 14), but there the vocal line ascends to $\hat{5}$ with a plagal cadence to D major, and the piano continues "in $\frac{2}{4}$" with its final chords.[44] The pianist-as-lyric-persona refuses to comply with the primary meter, as if to say, "World (in $\frac{3}{4}$), if you don't ask about me (in $\frac{2}{4}$), why should I ask about you? (And why in $\frac{3}{4}$?!)" The willful separation of self and society is performed as a rupture in musical time.

* * *

The two interpretations of Klinger's cycle sketched here extend beyond the simple idea that the cycle relates the events or memories of an old love. We have found song pairings, a rupture at the end, and a multilayered narrative analogous to the layered structures that Jan Brachmann finds in the volume as a whole.[45] The dichotomy between fantasy and reality is a recurrent feature in Klinger's work and an element that he underscores in his graphic "performance" of Brahms's songs. The contrasting representations of temporal experience are as significant for Klinger as they are for Brahms. We may return to the image of faces in darkness with "Feldeinsamkeit" and interpret them as a projection of the love-sorrow memory into eternity. We may go on to become aware of the themes of eternity and time-bound fate in Brahms's *Schicksalslied,* featured in the last part of Klinger's album. Klinger's goal, as we recall, was not to illustrate but to "continue" and "connect." We can likewise continue and connect, and we can interpret Klinger's work with sensitivity to the full range of possible interactions among text, music, and image.

ACKNOWLEDGMENTS

I would like to thank Katherine Kuenzli of the Art History Department at Wesleyan University for our discussions and joint presentations on Klinger and his work and for her comments on this chapter. I also thank Neely Bruce, Melissa Datre, Christopher Grundy, Philip Isaacs, Mariah Klaneski, Robert Lancefield, Clare Rogan, and John Wareham for their contributions to the online reproduction of the *Brahms Fantasy*. The digital presentation was generously supported by the Lemberg Fund and a project grant at Wesleyan University.

NOTES

1. See Inge Van Rij, *Brahms's Song Collections* (Cambridge: Cambridge University Press, 2006), 200–211; and Thomas K. Nelson, "Klinger's *Brahmsphantasie* and the Cultural Politics of Absolute Music," *Art History* 19/1 (1996): 26–43.

2. Wagnerian influence is evident in the idea of combining the arts and in the aesthetic program of Klinger's treatise *Malerei und Zeichnung* (Painting and drawing), written during the years of his work on the *Brahms Fantasy*. The *Brahms Fantasy*, however, can also be seen as a critique of Wagner's *Gesamtkunstwerk*; see Kevin C. Karnes, "Brahms, Max Klinger, and the Promise of the *Gesamtkunstwerk*: Revisiting the *Brahms-Phantasie* (1894)," in *Brahms and His World*, 2nd ed., ed. Walter Frisch and Kevin C. Karnes (Princeton, N.J.: Princeton University Press, 2009), 167–91.

3. See Jan Brachmann, *"Ins Ungewisse hinauf . . .": Johannes Brahms und Max Klinger im Zwiespalt von Kunst und Kommunikation* (Kassel: Bärenreiter, 1999), chap. 1.

4. Significant prior studies of the *Brahms Fantasy* include Brachmann, *"Ins Ungewisse hinauf . . ."*; Walter Frisch, *German Modernism: Music and the Arts* (Berkeley: University of California Press, 2005), 93–106; Karnes, "Brahms, Max Klinger, and the Promise"; Ursula Kersten, *Max Klinger und die Musik* (Frankfurt am Main: Lang, 1993), 1:59–88; Karin Mayer-Pasinski, *Max Klingers* Brahmsphantasie (Frankfurt: Rita G. Fischer, 1982); and Van Rij, *Brahms's Song Collections*, 200–211.

5. The letter is reproduced in Kersten, *Max Klinger und die Musik*, 1:166–67.

6. For further background on Klinger's musical training and interaction with Brahms's music, see Brachmann, *"Ins Ungewisse hinauf . . .*," 24–27, 98–99.

7. Gustav Jenner recalls Brahms's instruction to read poems aloud before setting them; see Jenner, "Johannes Brahms as Man, Teacher, and Artist," in *Brahms and His World*, ed. Walter Frisch (Princeton, N.J.: Princeton University Press, 1990), 197–98.

8. J. Kirk T. Varnedoe and Elizabeth Streicher comment on the "disjunctive unity" and dichotomy between fantasy and reality in Klinger's works; see Varnedoe and Streicher, introduction to *Graphic Works of Max Klinger* (New York: Dover, 1977), xxiii–xxiv.

9. Quoted with this translation in Frisch, *German Modernism*, 96. Klinger goes on to express discomfort with the word "complete"; see Kersten, *Max Klinger und die Musik*, 166.

10. The copy used for this study and for the digital reproduction is in the print collection at the Davison Art Center at Wesleyan University. The volume is fairly large; an individual page was measured at 363 mm high and 423 mm wide (14.29 by 16.65 in.).

11. See also the complete listing of contents with indication of left- and right-page placement in Brachmann, *"Ins Ungewisse hinauf . . .*," 132–33.

12. This translation includes elements from translations by Lucien Stark and Bea Brewster; see Stark, *A Guide to the Solo Songs of Johannes Brahms* (Bloomington: Indiana University Press, 1995), 234, and Brewster's translation on *The Lied and Art Song Texts Page*, http://www.recmusic.org/lieder/intro.html.

13. For discussions of the personae of song, see Edward T. Cone, "Poet's Love or Composer's Love?," in *Music and Text: Critical Inquiries*, ed. Steven Paul Scher (Cambridge:

Cambridge University Press, 1992), 177–92; and Berthold Hoeckner, "Poet's Love and Composer's Love," *Music Theory Online* 7/5 (2001).

14. Paul Berry identifies occurrences of this motive throughout the song; see Berry, "Old Love: Johannes Brahms, Clara Schumann, and the Poetics of Musical Memory," *Journal of Musicology* 24/1 (2007): 90–95.

15. Lucien Stark also comments on the continuity of the setting from stanza 3 to the middle of stanza 5; see Stark, *A Guide to the Solo Songs*, 234.

16. A gazing eye does appear in Klinger's image with the beginning of "Sehnsucht," the second song; I return to this in the latter part of the chapter.

17. Brachmann, *"Ins Ungewisse hinauf...,"* 167–69.

18. I borrow implicitly here from the theory of conceptual blending; see Lawrence M. Zbikowski, *Conceptualizing Music: Cognitive Structure, Theory, and Analysis* (New York: Oxford University Press, 2002), 77–95.

19. For a discussion of the ways in which metric displacements combine with tonal ambiguities to evoke a situation of blurred perception in "Wie Melodien zieht es mir," see Yonatan Malin, "Metric Dissonance and Music-Text Relations in the German Lied" (Ph.D. diss., University of Chicago, 2003), 101–106.

20. The concept of metric dissonance has been developed most extensively by Harald Krebs; see Krebs, *Fantasy Pieces: Metrical Dissonance in the Music of Robert Schumann* (New York: Oxford University Press, 1999). Studies of metric dissonance in Brahms's music include Peter H. Smith, "Brahms and the Shifting Barline: Metric Displacement and Formal Process in the Trios with Wind Instruments," in *Brahms Studies* 3, ed. David Brodbeck (Lincoln: University of Nebraska Press, 2001), 191–229; Richard Cohn, "Complex Hemiolas, Ski-Hill Graphs and Metric Spaces," *Music Analysis* 20/3 (2001): 295–326; Yonatan Malin, "Metric Displacement Dissonance and Romantic Longing in the German Lied," *Music Analysis* 25/3 (2006): 267–73; and Scott Murphy, "On Metre in the Rondo of Brahms's Op. 25," *Music Analysis* 26/3 (2007): 323–53.

21. For a further discussion of metric augmentation and examples from other songs by Brahms, see Malin, "Metric Dissonance," 183–202.

22. I explore this feature of Romantic longing in Brahms's "Immer leiser wird mein Schlummer," op. 105, no. 2; see Malin, "Metric Displacement Dissonance," 267–72.

23. Berry, "Old Love," 96–100.

24. The image is a lithograph from a black-and-iris plate; see Hans Wolfgang Singer, *Max Klinger: Radierungen, Stiche, und Steindrucke 1873–1903* (Berlin: Amsler und Ruthardt, 1909), 246.

25. Max Klinger, *Malerei und Zeichnung*, 3rd ed. (Leipzig: Arthur Georgi, 1899), 29–30. Also relevant to my analysis is Klinger's discussion of the importance of darkness and light and their poetic associations in graphic arts (35–36).

26. Karin Mayer-Pasinski observes that the combination of the couple and lush vegetation represents erotic happiness in Klinger's imagery. See Mayer-Pasinski, *Max Klingers Brahmsphantasie*, 53.

27. Singer, *Max Klinger*, 245–46.

28. Varnedoe and Streicher, introduction, xix.

29. Van Rij explores the blurring of narrative levels and reflexivity generated by this and other self-portraits; see *Brahms's Song Cycles*, 16–18, 107–15, and 208–209.

30. Kersten, *Max Klinger und die Musik*, 166. The translation of these phrases is from Frisch, *German Modernism*, 99.

31. See Van Rij, *Brahms's Song Collections*, 2, 210. There would have been plenty of opportunity for Brahms to object to Klinger's arrangement, if not in his response to Klinger, then in his letters and conversations with friends about the volume. Van Rij quotes from letters to Clara Schumann and Viktor Widmann (210). A letter to Helene

Freifrau von Heldburg and Eduard Hanslick's report of a conversation with Brahms about the volume are quoted in Brachmann, "Ins Ungewisse hinauf . . . ," 177–79.

32. John Daverio traces Neapolitan harmonies and key relations through Brahms's op. 32 songs; see Daverio (revised and with an afterword by David Ferris), "The Song Cycle: Journeys through a Romantic Landscape," in *German Lieder in the Nineteenth Century,* ed. Rufus Hallmark, 2nd ed. (New York: Routledge, 2010), 378–79.

33. David Ferris, *Schumann's Eichendorff Liederkreis and the Genre of the Romantic Cycle* (New York: Oxford University Press, 2000), chaps. 2, 3; Beate Julia Perrey, *Schumann's Dichterliebe and Early Romantic Poetics: Fragmentation of Desire* (Cambridge: Cambridge University Press, 2002); Berthold Hoeckner, "Paths through *Dichterliebe*," *19th-Century Music* 30/1 (2006): 65–80; Van Rij, *Brahms's Song Collections,* 30–37. Van Rij addresses arguments by Ferris (30–34), and Hoeckner addresses arguments by Ferris and Perrey (67–70). See also Yonatan Malin, "Review of Beate Julia Perrey, Schumann's *Dichterliebe and Early Romantic Poetics: Fragmentation of Desire*," *Music Theory Spectrum* 28/2 (2006): 299–310.

34. See Van Rij, *Brahms's Song Collections,* 157–62.

35. The graphic detail of a falling glove in the second etching of Klinger's cycle "Ein Handschuh" (A glove) becomes thematic—obsessively so—in the remainder of the cycle. One might hear the Neapolitan relationships within and between Klinger's selection of songs in the *Brahms Fantasy* as a similar compositional device.

36. Brahms's own extremely detailed engagement with the volume is described in Max Kalbeck, *Johannes Brahms* (Tutzing: Hans Schneider, 1976), 4:335–36. See also Brahms's letter to Clara Schumann in *Letters of Clara Schumann and Johannes Brahms, 1853–1896,* ed. Berthold Litzmann (London: Edward Arnold, 1927), 2:245, and background on the close reading of Brahms's friends in Van Rij, *Brahms's Song Collections,* 169–71.

37. Brachmann, "Ins Ungewisse hinauf . . . ," 127–31.

38. Singer, *Max Klinger,* 248.

39. Deborah Adams Rohr discusses the pentameter lines and musical phrase rhythm in "Am Sonntag Morgen"; see Rohr, "Brahms's Metrical Dramas: Rhythm, Text Expression, and Form in the Solo Lieder" (Ph.D. diss., University of Rochester, 1997), 148–53. For further discussion of pentameter line settings in lieder, see Rufus Hallmark and Ann C. Fehn, "Text and Music in Schubert's Setting of Pentameter Poetry," in *Of Poetry and Song: Approaches to the Nineteenth-Century Lied,* ed. Jürgen Thym (Rochester: University of Rochester Press, 2010), 155–219; and Yonatan Malin, *Songs in Motion: Rhythm and Meter in the German Lied* (New York: Oxford University Press, 2010), 25–27, 188–94.

40. Singer, *Max Klinger,* 250.

41. The phrase "brutally terse" is from Craig Bell, *The Lieder of Brahms* (Darley: Grain-Aig Press, 1979), 112.

42. See Peter Russell, *Johannes Brahms and Klaus Groth: The Biography of a Friendship* (Aldershot, England: Ashgate, 2006), 153.

43. See Samuel Ng, "The Hemiolic Cycle and Metric Dissonance in the First Movement of Brahms's Cello Sonata in F Major, Op. 99," *Theory and Practice* 31 (2006): 65–95.

44. As Heather Platt observes, plagal cadences at the end of Brahms's songs are typically used in conjunction with authentic cadences; the procedure here is more radical, since the plagal cadence replaces the final authentic cadence. See Platt, "Unrequited Love and Unrealized Dominants," *Intégral* 7 (1993): 122–23.

45. Brachmann, "Ins Ungewisse hinauf . . . ," 121–24.

4 Brahms's *Mädchenlieder* and Their Cultural Context

Heather Platt

Brahms's attitude toward women has attracted the attention of writers since the nineteenth century.[1] But although a number of scholars have convincingly demonstrated some of the ways in which women such as Clara Schumann and Elisabet von Herzogenberg influenced his works, the more general topic of the ways in which Brahms portrays the female characters in his lieder has been in large part neglected. More than twenty percent of his lieder have texts with a female narrative voice, including "Mädchenlied" ("Am jüngsten Tag," op. 95, no. 6), "Klage" (op. 105, no. 3), and "Mädchenlied" ("Ach, und du mein kühles Wasser!," op. 85, no. 3).[2] I will explore the ways in which these three songs intertwine, in paradoxical and subtle ways, musical portrayals of nineteenth-century societal expectations for women and the emotions of the songs' female characters. While on one level Brahms coordinates sophisticated tonal structures with a panoply of other musical elements to convey the genuinely troubled emotions of the young women, on another he deploys stylistic elements associated with folksong (such as transparent textures, triadic melodies, and diatonic harmonies). These folk elements should not, however, be taken prima facie as traces of the Romantic veneration of folk traditions; rather, they are a musical analogue for the country settings that contemporary illustrations and literature employed to symbolize society's understanding of the innocent, pure "fairer sex."

The female characters who "speak" in Brahms's songs range from innocent young girls to wise women and mothers; from happy maidens full of hopeful dreams to lonely, dying invalids.[3] Following Roland Barthes—and in acknowledgment of the nineteenth-century custom that lieder were performed by both male and female singers regardless of the character the music portrayed—many commentators interpret songs like these as expressions of universal ideas and emotions.[4] But nineteenth-century documents, including letters by Brahms and his friends, clearly show that, irrespective of who performed them, his settings of poems with a female narrative voice were thought to represent a distinctly female mind-set. The clearest evidence of this female perspective appears in letters concerning Brahms's op. 69 lieder. Seven of the nine songs in this collection have texts presenting a young woman's point of view. While preparing these works for publication, Brahms told Fritz Simrock that he considered naming the collection *Mädchenlieder*, and he suggested this term should be used in the related advertising.[5] Although Brahms subsequently stepped away from these ideas, a letter from Theodor Billroth to the critic Eduard Hanslick demonstrates that this is precisely how the composer's friends interpreted these songs. Billroth wrote:

> No. 4, an eighteen-year-old girl, blonde, finding the sensual note unconsciously through the necessity of nature. . . . No. 8, a rather original sixteen-year-old, black-eyed little girl, full of fun, full of spirits, very quick, with natural grace, and singing out with an overwhelming joviality. No. 9 . . . is a tremendously sensuous and passionate song; it must be sung with all that feeling, the czardas getting wilder and wilder. When that girl, after that song, meets her [man] she embraces him as if she would crack all his ribs![6]

The texts of the three songs I discuss in this essay portray maidens of a similar age to those Billroth describes, but, unlike their passionate sisters, these young women lament their loneliness without a loved one. Along with the words of most of Brahms's other songs employing a female narrative voice (including those of op. 69), these texts originated in folksongs: Siegfried Kapper translated the text of "Ach, und du mein kühles Wasser!" from a Serbian folksong; Paul Heyse translated "Am jüngsten Tag" from an Italian folksong; and the text of "Klage" was published as a folksong from the lower Rhine, even though it was probably written by Anton Zuccalmaglio, who was known for his ability to replicate texts in folk style. Brahms acknowledged the folk heritage of each of these songs through a musical setting comprising various combinations of triadic or stepwise melodies, predominantly diatonic harmonies, regular phrase structures, and relatively transparent textures. These folklike gestures are far more pronounced than those in op. 69, and the textures are simpler. Nevertheless, just as Billroth heard the female characters (and Brahms's music) in the op. 69 songs as embodying passion and sensuality, so too I will argue that these three later songs likewise portray genuine emotions. In all three, sophisticated tonal structures, coordinated with other expressive elements such as rhythmic dissonances, asymmetrical phrase structures, and dynamic nuances, trace the respective maiden's emotional trajectory.

In order to sample the ways in which Brahms mediates folklike stereotypes and the psychological plight of a specific female character, I begin by exploring the relationship between the text and music in "Am jüngsten Tag." I will then demonstrate the ways in which depictions of similar female characters in contemporary German visual arts and literature represented the lives of young women and society's expectations for them. These social mores infiltrated both high and low arts, but the higher art forms, like Brahms's songs, offered far more sensitive portrayals of the women's emotions. The hermeneutic perspective that emerges from this interdisciplinary foray will then provide an interpretive context for my analysis of "Klage" and "Ach, und du mein kühles Wasser!"

"Am jüngsten Tag" (op. 95, no. 6)

Brahms took the text of "Am jüngsten Tag," which is given in Table 4.1, from a translation of an Italian folksong that had appeared in Heyse's *Gedichte* (1872) and his *Skizzenbuch: Lieder und Bilder* (1877).[7] Heyse was an acquaintance of Brahms and an admirer of his music, and he sent a warmly inscribed copy of the *Skizzenbuch* to the composer.[8] This particular text is just one of Heyse's many portrayals of women; female characters populate his poems, aphorisms, and stories as well as his translations of the texts of Spanish and Italian folksongs. His success with these genres was so great that he was often described as a woman's writer, and Laura Mohr Hansson included a laudatory chapter devoted to him in her 1896 book *Wir Frauen und unsere Dichter* (We women and our poets).[9] Aside from "Am jüngsten Tag," Brahms's "Spanisches Lied" (op. 6, no. 1) and "Mädchenlied" (op. 107, no. 5) also set Heyse's renderings of young women's voices. The text of the former is a translation of a Spanish folksong, while that of the latter is an original poem.

Just as Heyse did not fashion a literal translation of the original Italian folk text of "Am jüngsten Tag," so too Brahms did not simply mimic the style of folksong.[10] Although the diatonic harmonies, modal mixture, and strophic framework recall the style of folk music, the subtle enmeshing of F-major and D-minor harmonies (which characterizes the beginnings of each stanza), the dissonances and irregular phrase structure of the central sections of each stanza, and the un-

Table 4.1. "Am jüngsten Tag," op. 95, no. 6

Am jüngsten Tag ich aufersteh'	On Judgment Day I'll rise up
Und gleich nach meinem Liebsten seh',	And immediately I'll go looking for my beloved,
Und wenn ich ihn nicht finden kann,	And if I can't find him,
Leg' wieder mich zum Schlafen dann.	I'll lie down and go to sleep again.
O Herzeleid, du Ewigkeit!	Oh heartache, you're eternal!
Selbander nur ist Seligkeit!	To be with another is the only bliss!
Und kommt mein Liebster nicht hinein,	So if my beloved doesn't arrive,
Mag nicht im Paradiese sein!	I'd rather not be in paradise!

usual concluding cadences are more readily associated with the domain of art music.

Brahms begins his song with a somewhat unconventional anacrusis. The piano begins on a high F and descends through the F tonic triad as the dynamic level recedes to *piano*.[11] The singer enters on the last eighth of the anacrusis and continues with an unusually jagged melody. Its C♯–D ascent suggests the tonic might be D minor rather than F major. However, the melody leaps down to a sustained G as the underlying harmonies resolve to a dominant seventh of F. The second measure is a sequential repetition of the first with the motive ending on a B♭ chord—a chord that will become important at the end of each stanza. The rhythmic and metric patterns of these measures are similarly unsteady: although notated in ¾, the piano's figuration sounds more like ⁶⁄₈; and the vocal line is syncopated with its longest (and lowest) notes falling on the second beats of mm. 1 and 2. Even the right hand of the piano does not behave as one might expect: the initial three eighths should flow directly into the downbeat of m. 1, but instead there is an unexpected rest. By contrast, the second half of the first phrase (mm. 3–4), when the girl concentrates on her sweetheart, is much more stable. The metrical ambiguities are resolved, as the voice and piano clearly articulate the notated ¾ meter, and the harmonies steer a conventional path to a half cadence in F major. This progression from initial uneasiness to more clearly directed rhythms and tonal motions loosely maps the girl's experiences: it is as though she gradually awakens or regains full consciousness and then, after finding a firm footing, focuses on her beloved.

The first phrase, its varied repeat at the start of stanza 2 (mm. 15–18), and the last phrase of stanza 2 are the only four-measure phrases in the song. Given the regular structure of the poem, with its four feet in each of its four lines, Brahms's asymmetric phrase structure is somewhat unexpected. Indeed, he could have set the remaining two lines of the first stanza to a four-measure version of mm. 8–12 with only slight changes to the original. Instead, he created an asymmetrical eight-measure unit, comprising a three-measure prefix followed by a five-measure phrase setting the last line of text and its repeat. During the prefix, the right hand repeats and varies a pattern of unresolved dissonances above the bass's detached, repeated Cs, with the B♭ and C♯ of the diminished sevenths clashing against this dominant pedal. A six-measure version of this suspenseful passage recurs in stanza 2, and in both stanzas, the dissonances and unusual length convey the girl's suspicion that she will not be reunited with her loved one. In addition to her disquietude, the combination of the repeated dissonances, pedal point, and momentary delay in starting the last line of each stanza suggest the type of passivity and hesitancy that were routinely associated with women during the nineteenth century and that contrasted with the assertive stereotypes associated with men. This particular girl's reliance on her idealized man is further suggested by aspects of register and duration, as the highest and longest note of the melodic line in this apprehensive passage sets "ihn" in the first stanza and "Lieb(ster)" in the second.

The final phrase of stanza 1, when the maiden acknowledges she might not find her loved one, is filled with borrowings from the minor mode. Both hands of the piano descend, and the tempo and dynamics similarly recede as she considers lying down to sleep. After a half cadence in the subdominant (B♭, mm. 9–10), the final melodic segment ascends twice to the high F, first via a B♭-major triad and then via a B♭-minor triad. These rising gestures, which gradually taper out, imply continuity rather than closure, suggesting that the maiden continues to daydream. Nineteenth-century composers frequently called on ♭6̂ and the minor subdominant to imply melancholy, and in this instance the emphasis on iv shades the girl's dreams, giving them a bittersweet tinge.[12] Moreover, the harmonic progression and the melody's avoidance of a 2̂–1̂ or 7̂–8̂ motion prevents this first stanza (and, later, the second) from ending with a definitive cadence. Brahms's melody does provide an opportunity for a conventional cadential ⁶₄ chord leading to an authentic cadence in F major. The first high F (m. 11), however, is actually harmonized by a root-position tonic. Such a strong tonic in the penultimate measure is unexpected. Indeed, on first hearing one might suppose that this F chord will function as a dominant and lead to a close in B♭ major. But the F chord does not progress to a B♭ tonic or to a C dominant; rather, two diminished sevenths lead to another F chord, which now functions as the final tonic of the stanza. (The second diminished seventh functions as a dominant. It had been used three times with the C pedal in mm. 5–7, though with the D♭ spelled as C♯.)

The second stanza is essentially a repetition of the first, but there are some changes in nuance. Although the stanza opens with the same melody, the harmonies are different, and the ⁶₄ figuration is absent. Since stanza 1 ends with a clear presentation of F major as tonic, an exact repetition of the opening measures would not have the same tonal uncertainty. To re-create the tension of the opening and its trace of an F/d tonal pairing, Brahms harmonizes the initial upbeat with a D-minor chord, reinforcing the D-minor tendencies of the subsequent two notes.[13] Nevertheless, D minor's status as a possible tonic is immediately undercut because the harmonies lead to the dominant of F, as they did in m. 1. The opening measures of this second stanza are the only ones in the song with a chordal texture and *forte* dynamic level, and these elements give emphasis to the maiden's frustrated cry of eternal heartache. Although some of the rhythmic dissonances from m. 1 are absent, the almost flat-footed weighting of the second beats and the placement of the lowest notes in the piano on the second half of these beats reinstate an air of uncertainty. The melodic sequence perfectly fits the two-part structure of the poetic line, and the descending leaps graphically depict the girl's lack of optimism. It is almost as if Brahms wrote this melody with the second stanza in mind. In the first stanza, by contrast, these descending leaps, although anticipating the mood of the entire poem, do not provide an obvious image of a girl rising on Judgment Day and looking for her beloved.

The remainder of the second stanza repeats the material of the first until the final two-measure segment, which is rhythmically augmented to span four measures (mm. 25–28). Once again, B♭ major threatens to displace F major as tonic, and the final high F arrives via an arpeggiation rather than through more conclusive stepwise motion. The instability of these melodic and harmonic gestures is further heightened by the rhythmic dissonances. While the durations of the vocal line are augmented, those of the piano are not, and in order to keep the two parts synchronized, Brahms inserts rests between the piano's chords. As a result, the piano's two-beat, chord-rest groupings contradict the melody's adherence to the triple meter, and they also contribute to a disturbance of the conventional weighting within the four-measure phrase. Whereas rests (rather than strong bass notes) fall on the downbeats of the first and third measures (mm. 25 and 27), the melody and bass stress the downbeats of the second and fourth measures—normally the weaker hypermetric measures. On both of these downbeats, the melody returns to its initial high F accompanied by the piano's bass F, four octaves lower. The rhythmic dissonances, the great gulf between the bass and the melody's high Fs, the *diminuendo,* and the absence of a perfect authentic cadence all work together to convey the maiden's uneasy musings that she will not be reunited with her sweetheart—even in Paradise.

In both stanzas, the melody's final ascent traverses D♭, a pitch that the piano introduced in m. 8 and restated in stanza 2, in m. 22. This note is the enharmonic equivalent of the C♯ that played such an important role in the dissonant central phrase of both stanzas (mm. 5–7 and 19–21), where it conflicted with the C pedal. While the C♯ alludes to D minor, a key often associated with tragedy and death, the C is associated with F major and its traditional pastoral connotations. Just as the competing tonal centers contribute to the tensions of this passage, so too these key characteristics allude to the opposing scenarios the maiden contemplates—either a reunion with her man or eternal loneliness. Although the C prevails during the subsequent final phrase of each stanza, its victory is nevertheless somewhat clouded by the appearance of the melancholy, flattened $\hat{6}$ (D♭).

Resigned longing is the theme of many nineteenth-century lieder, and composers, including Brahms, often portrayed this topic by avoiding a $\hat{2}$–$\hat{1}$ or $\hat{7}$–$\hat{8}$ motion at the final cadence and by breaking their melodies off on a high pitch that does not resolve to the tonic. Several of Brahms's lieder further underscore such yearning emotions by avoiding the expected concluding perfect authentic cadence.[14] "Am jüngsten Tag" is somewhat different because it conceals the $\hat{2}$–$\hat{1}$ and $\hat{7}$–$\hat{8}$ motions in its inner voices and ends with a rising arpeggiation to the tonic. The maiden in this song does not seem to have resigned herself to eternal longing; rather, she is still hoping for a reunion. Nevertheless, the D♭ and the rhythmic dissonances in the final measures imply that she realizes—at least subconsciously—that her sweetheart will not be returning.

As the maiden continues to daydream, the piano and voice return to the same pitch (the high F) that they started on, and the postlude employs music formerly used as the interlude between stanzas 1 and 2. These recurring gestures provide the potential for the song to endlessly repeat. Lawrence Kramer notes that this type of circularity is ubiquitous in the nineteenth century and can represent different ideas depending on the context in which it occurs. In this song (as well as in "Klage," to be discussed shortly) the circularity is paired with feminine topics, a combination that Kramer interprets as projecting "an image of self-enfoldedness."[15] As Lisbeth Hock notes, in literature of the time, "female protagonists tend to turn inward, focusing not on clearly marked external events and actions (as in the male-oriented *Bildungsroman*) but rather on their subjective responses to a world whose boundaries are much narrower than those of their male counterparts."[16]

The unusual opening and concluding passages of this song have significant ramifications for interpreting the large-scale tonal structure. Both of these passages negate the normal tonal functions of opening and concluding measures by avoiding conventional harmonies that strongly assert the tonic. As the graph in Example 4.1 demonstrates, the initial deemphasis of the tonic and the avoidance of the dominant in the concluding cadences of both stanzas reverberate through to the deep middleground level. Rather than a structural I, the first upbeat, tonic arpeggio functions as part of the dominant prolongation that extends through the first two phrases. (This emphasis on the dominant might in part explain why Brahms did not provide a strong dominant bass note at the concluding cadence of each stanza.) Brahms uses similar deep-level auxiliary cadences in a number of his other songs, and most of these, like "Am jüngsten Tag," depict a dreaming protagonist.[17]

Although Example 4.1 focuses on the first stanza, all its significant details are also present in stanza 2; only the harmonies of the initial measure of this stanza are different. Both stanzas are characterized by an unusual structural line that both begins and ends on $\hat{8}$. At the same time as the upper structural line descends from the initial high F, an inner voice rises, and the two lines converge on the *Kopfton* C on the last beat of m. 4. The structural line then descends from this C to the A in m. 11 of stanza 1 (m. 26 in stanza 2). In this way, the piano's initial anacrusis figure is expanded across each stanza.[18] Once $\hat{3}$ is attained, the

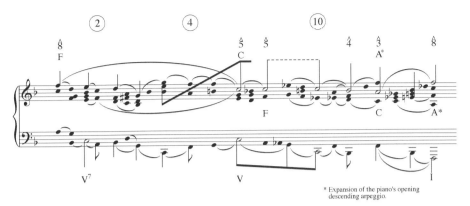

Example 4.1. Middleground graph of "Am jüngsten Tag," stanza 1 (stanza 2 concludes with the same harmonies as shown here).

two melodic lines diverge. As the voice returns to the high F, the piano continues the descent. This final falling third, A–F, is buried in an inner voice, though some astute listeners might be aware of it because this motive is expanded twice in the first phrase's inner voices. It is as though the piano is trying to conform to structural norms, but the voice will not be contained.[19] This conflict is a metaphor for the young woman's behavior and thoughts: although she knows somewhere deep inside herself that her sweetheart will not return, she chooses to ignore this reality and continues to dream of him. The postlude's contrasting registers, with its descent into the tenor and bass ranges followed by two higher final chords, also suggest this quandary.[20]

In "Am jüngsten Tag," the hint of an F/d tonal pairing in the opening measures of both stanzas and the unconventional final cadence allude both to the girl's quiet dismay that she could be alone even in eternity and to her choice to continue to dream of her sweetheart's return. Although this character shares many traits with stereotypical dreaming maidens, she is not the usual forlorn, lamenting type: if her sweetheart does not meet her on Judgment Day, she will simply sleep. Brahms's music shrewdly captures this nonchalance: it carries the unusual tempo marking of *Behaglich* (comfortable); much of the song is pervaded by light, almost dancelike staccato figures in the piano; the melody refuses to acquiesce to a conventional descent to $\hat{1}$; and the final cadence, with its variation of the music from the end of the first stanza, pairs the girl's notion of rejecting Paradise with that of lying down to sleep.

Directing a spotlight on the structural intricacies of Brahms's song might lead to charges that I am attributing to it a complexity that its folklike text and surface elements do not warrant.[21] But a thorough analysis of the meaning of this song (and others of the same genre) should take into account both the folk style *and* the elements of sophisticated compositional technique, which Rings, in chapter 2 of this volume, refers to as artifice. The following survey of contemporary literature and visual arts suggests ways in which these seemingly contradictory elements may be reconciled and how, through this mediation, songs such as "Am jüngsten Tag" take on new levels of meaning.

Mädchen in Nineteenth-Century Literature and Visual Arts

When Brahms set Heyse's version of "Am jüngsten Tag," he omitted the poet's title, "In der Bucht," and the first two stanzas. He probably excised the stanzas so he could begin his song with the maiden in the midst of her reverie. By contrast, Heyse's poem opens in the voice of a narrator who sets the early morning shoreline scene and introduces the protagonist as a fifteen-year-old, sleepy-eyed girl, washing clothes. Similar depictions of adolescents in rural settings, engaged in a domestic chore such as sewing or washing, abound in contemporary German literature and art: Adrian Ludwig Richter (1803–84) was among the most popular and influential of the numerous painters who created such rustic scenes. He clothed the people who populate his canvases in peasant dress and in so doing perpetuated the idealized view that country life was simpler and less troubled than modern urban life. But these works should not be interpreted as merely nostalgic representations of a lifestyle that even in the mid-nineteenth century was on the decline; they also reflected contemporary values.[22] The scenes in which young women happily interacted with children unambiguously inscribe the role women were expected to play in society; the pastoral surroundings had similar implications. Ironically, these types of artworks served not merely to extol the beauty of nature (which inspired many Romantic artists); rather, they reinforced a variety of attitudes that society had traditionally associated with the female sex. These types of outdoor settings underscored a network of widely held perceptions and assumptions that women's assumed innocence and lack of ingenuity resulted from their purported closeness to nature. (To be sure, such feminine, natural purity was venerated and at times prized by the male hegemony.)

Like Brahms's and Heyse's "Am jüngsten Tag," many other works of art portray daydreaming maidens singing or gazing over the countryside. Mathilde Coester's 1889 montage of sketches, titled *Unsere Backfischlein,* depicts representative episodes in the lives of young women, and it includes a particularly common stereotypical maiden, "Die Traum-Lise," wistfully scanning the outside world through a window—that is, from the safety (or confines) of her home.[23] As the following overview demonstrates, these types of societally sanctioned images of young women as demure dreamers whose fate was inextricably bound to a man permeated both high and low art forms and were well known to contemporary musicians, including Brahms.

From at least as far back as the sixteenth century, the term *Backfisch* was coined to denote girls between the ages of fourteen and seventeen (i.e., the type of girl depicted in the works of art described above).[24] These were the transitional years between the relative freedoms of childhood and the more constrained roles of wife and mother. During the nineteenth century, characters in novels and magazine stories modeled appropriate behaviors and dress for such adolescents. These characters sang, played the piano, refined their manners, danced at balls, attended the theater, and yearned to be acknowledged by a man. In sum, they successfully reinforced societal expectations for young women while also intimating youthful sexual awakenings.[25]

Despite their all too often poor literary quality, these stories were extremely popular, especially with female readers. Clementine Helm's *Backfischens Leiden und Freuden* (1863) was so successful that it was reprinted numerous times and translated into other languages, including English.[26] This story traces the life of a young woman from her adolescence through marriage and motherhood. Its appeal can in part be attributed to the fact that the main character was understood as exhibiting all the traits society (including women) expected of a respectable young woman. Further underscoring the heroine's status as a representative of an archetype, Helm gave her maiden the same name as the most famous exemplar of the *Backfisch* topos—Goethe's Gretchen.[27] To be sure, as Hermann Glaser and others have observed, there is a significant disparity between the character in *Faust* and such popular, chaste stereotypes. Nevertheless, the linkage was part of the nineteenth century's image of young German women.[28]

Backfische, similar to Helm's Gretchen, also populate the writings of Elise Polko (1822–99). Polko, a friend of Felix and Fanny Mendelssohn, initially trained as a singer, but when she married she relinquished her aspirations for a musical career. Later, as a widow she relied on writing women's literature to make a living. Two issues of the 1883 *Neue Zeitschrift für Musik* carried an advertisement for her collection of poems, *Blumen und Lieder: Eine musikalisches Blumen-Sprache* (1881), which was specifically addressed to young women. (In addition, this volume was widely advertised and cited in other music journals, including the 1881 *Musikalisches Wochenblatt* and the *Neue Berliner Musikzeitung*.) Moreover, her collection of short stories portraying fictional incidents in the lives of famous composers also includes female characters exhibiting the traits that nineteenth-century culture expected of both mature women and *Backfische*.[29]

To be sure, readers of scholarly publications in the twenty-first century will not be as familiar with the type of literature written by Polko and Helm as readers in their own time. Today, aside from Schubert's "Gretchen am Spinnrade," the

Backfisch most familiar to musicians is the woman Adelbert von Chamisso portrayed in his 1830 cycle of poems, *Frauenliebe und Leben*. These poems were so popular that they were published in a number of editions, and before Schumann's 1840 songs, Carl Loewe set the cycle to music in 1836. In 1879 the artist Paul Thumann (1834–1908) further contributed to the dissemination of Chamisso's poems by producing an illustrated edition, which was subsequently reprinted a number of times. Thumann placed the sketch reproduced as Figure 4.1 before Chamisso's first poem "Seit ich ihn gesehen" (Since I first saw him).[30] This song depicts the young woman in the excited first stages of her romance, describing the dreamlike state in which images of her beloved appear before her.

Thumann's illustrations of similar young women were so ubiquitous—they appeared "on boxes of detergent, cigarette boxes, and popular prints"—that the writer Otto Julius Bierbaum (1865–1910) satirically quipped that Thumann had painted this figure "into the soul of the German bourgeoisie."[31] But Thumann's images were far from unique; similar naive maidens, dressed simply or as peasants, pervaded the contemporary arts. The maiden in Figure 4.1 is very similar to the one adorning the frontispiece of Georg Wigand's 1881 edition of Helm's *Backfischens Leiden und Freuden*. Both employ well-known symbols to represent characteristics that society viewed as feminine: the girl is surrounded by foliage, and her head is slightly bowed in a humble, introspective manner.

In drawings in mass-produced periodicals, such as the family magazine *Die Gartenlaube,* these images took on a triteness, but in high art forms, the placement of the women's bodies and their posture, facial expressions, and gestures create more authentic emotional depth. The artists whom Brahms most admired—Arnold Böcklin, Anselm Feuerbach, and Max Klinger—were among those noted for portraying women in poignant or heart-wrenching moments, and many of their works convey a type of emotional intensity that goes well beyond the mass-produced illustrations of the *Backfisch*. Although these maidens are usually not in peasant costume, their clothing—often a white dress symbolizing purity—and their poses nevertheless reinforce society's expectations of women. Likewise, the pastoral settings of unmanicured foliage are not as rustic as those of Richter, but, being unspoiled by man, they nevertheless carry the same connotations of innocence. Moreover, many of these paintings convey an introspective mood, a feminine type of *Innerlichkeit,* by positioning the woman near a small body of reflective, quiet water. Böcklin's widely reproduced *Herbstgedanken,* shown in Plate 4.1, is a particularly beautiful example of a painting that employs such traditional symbols of the female sex at the same time that it communicates the pensive yearning of the particular woman who is the focus of the canvas. The lack of motion in this scene is also an important attribute of other contemporary depictions of such women, and already ear-

Figure 4.1. Thumann's illustration of Chamisso's maiden in *Frauenliebe und Leben*.

lier nineteenth-century encyclopedists had observed that the type of stillness demonstrated by this figure was a well-established marker of female behavior.[32] Feuerbach explicitly associated this passivity with the emotion of yearning, writing: "The emotional state which we call longing requires physical repose. It entails turning one's self inward."[33]

Literary critics and art historians have explored the manner in which images of young women, either wittingly or not, perpetuated the prevailing male hegemony and underscored "desirable attributes" for young women. Although Ruth Solie has discussed the ways in which Schumann's *Frauenliebe und Leben* does similar cultural work, scholars of the lied have not fully explored this topic.[34] Nevertheless, there are numerous other lieder with texts that similarly model the emotions usually attributed to young females and the roles they were expected to assume within families: Peter Cornelius's cycle *Brautlieder* (1856–58) is just one such example. (Cornelius wrote both the words and music of these songs.) During much of the nineteenth century, such lieder were written for domestic consumption, and stories of *Backfische* often include scenes in which young women perform such songs to entertain themselves, their families, and their suitors. Friedrich Heinrich Himmel's 1803 setting of Karl Friedrich Müchler's poem "Zueignung an Deutschlands Töchter" (Dedication to Germany's daughters) offers just one example of a lied with a text extolling feminine virtues that could be performed by amateurs. This song is the first in a cycle, *Die Blumen und der Schmetterling,* in which each of the subsequent songs embellishes upon the same themes. While the text of "Zueignung an Deutschlands Töchter" employs various flowers to represent traditional prized values of young womanhood, including demure humility and chasteness, Himmel's music is appropriately charming, with delicate ornaments and a softly supporting piano part. Although this song is not of the same artistic quality as subsequent lieder, its regular periodicity, simple harmonies, strophic form, and unassuming piano part are the same characteristic folk elements that, in varying combinations, permeate Brahms's songs depicting young women.

Due in large part to the substantial changes in the status of women that took place during the twentieth century, the various connections between maidens surrounded by nature, folklike poetry and music, and societal expectations are no longer common; moreover, they may seem to have little relevance to twenty-first-century sensibilities. Nevertheless, in order to fully understand the young women depicted in nineteenth-century art forms, one must realize that not all these images are trivial stereotypes. Rather, many represented the roles and predicaments of real women. Furthermore, these characters model the types of emotions society considered acceptable for young women and the appropriate (restrained) manner in which these emotions were to be displayed. In high art forms, including the paintings of Böcklin and Feuerbach, images of women who embodied societal values nevertheless conveyed emotional depth.

It is this mixture of seemingly contradictory ideas—socially imposed expectations for women generally, on the one hand, and an appreciation of an individual female character's unique psychology, on the other—that characterizes

Brahms's "Am jüngsten Tag." The folk elements in this lied function in the same ironic ways as either the peasant garb and country settings in contemporary popular illustrations or the demure white clothing in higher art forms: they represent innocence and nature and also reinforce the attributes that society viewed as feminine. By contrast, the song's unusual tonal structure, coordinated with its rhythmic dissonances and departures from a regular four-measure periodicity, imbue the young woman's reveries with an underlying nervousness. That this combination of stylized simplicity and technical ingenuity is not unique in Brahms's output will be demonstrated by analyses of two other songs depicting similar maidens, "Klage" and "Ach, und du mein kühles Wasser!"[35]

"Klage" (op. 105, no. 3)

In some ways, "Klage" resembles the more tragic D-minor "Kein Haus, keine Heimat" (op. 94, no. 5), which is a dispirited lament issued by a man without a wife or home. Both songs are deceptive in that their brevity and thin textures have caused most scholars to overlook their unusual tonal structures.[36] Almost all commentators attribute the surface simplicity of "Klage" to the influence of folk music—an assessment that seems to be supported by the folk origins of the text. As a result, they also attribute the modally tinged swings between F major and D minor to this folk heritage and fail to examine either how these harmonies actually function or what their interaction might express. The song

Table 4.2. "Klage," op. 105, no. 3

Feins Liebchen, trau' du nicht,	Dear girl, don't trust him;
Daß er dein Herz nicht bricht!	Then he won't break your heart.
Schön' Worte will er geben,	He'll give you fine words,
Es kostet dein jung' Leben,	But they'll cost your young life,
Glaub's sicherlich!	Never doubt it!
Ich werde nimmer froh,	I'll never be happy again,
Denn mir ging es also:	The same fate befell me:
Die Blätter vom Baum gefallen	The leaves have fallen from the tree
Mit den schönen Worten allen,	With all the fine words,
Ist Winterzeit!	It's wintertime!
Es ist jetzt Winterzeit,	Now it's wintertime,
Die Vögelein sind weit,	The birds are far away
Die mir im Lenz gesungen,	That sang to me in the spring,
Mein Herz ist mir gesprungen	My heart is broken
Vor Liebesleid.	With the sorrow of love.

begins and ends in F major, but the last phrase of the vocal line (the penultimate phrase of the song) is set in D minor—a key that had been hinted at during the end of the first phrase (m. 4). As we have seen, the opening measures of both stanzas in "Am jüngsten Tag" also intertwine these third-related keys. "Klage," however, employs them in a much more striking manner, and D minor emerges as a stronger challenger to the overarching tonality of F major.

The female persona in "Klage" warns her less experienced female companion of the dangers of love (see Table 4.2).[37] She herself has been hurt, and the unconventional tonal structure follows the text in suggesting her pain has not entirely dissipated. Feminine friendships of this intimate kind were often depicted in art and literature. Gretchen in Helm's *Backfischens Leiden und Freuden* shares confidences with her girlfriends, and four of the sketches in Coester's *Unsere Backfischlein* portray young women engaged in conversation. Similar intimate pairings appear in higher art forms as well; Caspar David Friedrich's *Die Schwestern auf dem Söller am Hafen* (The sisters on the balcony at the harbor, ca. 1820) offers just one such example. Facing away from the viewer, Friedrich's two young women look out from a balcony at a Gothic cityscape bathed in a sunset's evocative colors. Dwarfed by their surroundings and dressed in black, these poignant figures stand close to one another, and one gently touches the other's shoulder. Closer to the topic of this essay, a somewhat similar intimate, though less pensive, mood informs Wilhelm Hensel's drawing of Josephine von Siebold and her sister Agathe, who would become Brahms's fiancée.[38]

As in "Am jüngsten Tag," "Klage" begins with a tonic chord as an anacrusis. But here the chord is in root position, and the F root receives further emphasis through its registral depth relative to the bass pitches in m. 1. Although this harmony could have continued through to the downbeat of m. 2, Brahms moves the bass to form a dominant pedal, and the upper voices alternate between A-minor and F-major harmonies until the phrase ends deceptively on a D-minor chord (m. 4). This ending, which is rendered somewhat unstable by the piano's neighbor motions, prepares for the prominence of D in the subsequent phrases. Although the second phrase begins with the D chord as an anacrusis and then pivots toward G minor, the key of G is not established, and the phrase ends on the dominant of D minor (m. 8).

"Klage" is a strophic setting, and in all three stanzas, these first two phrases accompany the poetic lines describing false promises. In stanza 1 "fine words" will cost the young girl her life; in stanza 2 "fine words" fall away like leaves on a tree; and in stanza 3 the singing birds of spring fly away in the wintertime, leaving a broken heart. The deceitful nature of these utterances is echoed by the deceptive cadence at m. 4, the conflicting structure of the piano and voice, and the instability of the phrases' tonal centers. Whereas the voice's phrases fall into two

two-measure segments, the piano has one-measure units that do not coordinate with the ends of the voice's segments. The tension created by these conflicts is intensified by the displacement dissonances during the second phrase, when the piano's three-beat pattern begins on the second beat of each measure rather than following the notated meter and the vocal line.

The beginning of the final phrase is somewhat similar to the opening of stanza 2 (m. 15) of "Am jüngsten Tag." The melody's C♯–D motion could lead one to expect a D-minor harmonization, especially since the preceding phrase ended on the dominant of D and the melody places D on the downbeat. But as in "Am jüngsten Tag," the voice's D is harmonized by a B♭ chord, and it proceeds to a half cadence in F major (the tonic) at m. 10. This F tonal center, however, is not maintained; rather, these measures are subjected to a transposed variation, resulting in a perfect authentic cadence in D minor (m. 12). The piano part in this phrase returns to the notated meter, and, unlike the first phrase, it observes the break between the two melodic segments. With both the voice and piano clearly marking the downbeats of each measure, this phrase is more declarative than the preceding ones. Likewise, the repeated falling-third motive in the piano's right hand, which ends with a firm dotted quarter note in mm. 9 and 10, mimics the stress the speaker would use for the final point of each stanza. But despite this new metrical certainty, the phrase has an increased level of harmonic dissonance that musically dramatizes the woman's emotional pain.

The second segment, starting with the upbeat to m. 11, is even more dissonant than the first. Like the preceding segment, this one begins with an augmented triad. But, whereas the upbeat to m. 9 leads to a consonant triad on the downbeat of m. 10, in this second segment, the augmented triad is followed by other dissonances. The melody's downbeat A (m. 11) could have been harmonized with a ⁶₄ chord in F major. Brahms does choose an F chord, but he augments the fifth (to form the same chord as the upbeat to the preceding segment, m. 8), and the resulting C♯ abruptly turns away from F as tonic to prepare a D-minor cadence. This final segment has a denser texture and a more continuous linear trajectory, with the eighth-note motion of the preceding two measures now constant instead of halting. Together with the dissonant harmonies, these elements imply a change in the level of consciousness; the speaker moves from advising her friend to reliving her own pain. These four measures represent an especially understated example of temporal shifting.[39] Contrasting temporal modes are far from unusual in nineteenth-century lieder; however, the more typical scenario is characterized by an expressive, chromatic progression accompanied by an abrupt change in pacing, as is evident in mm. 11–13 of Brahms's "O kühler Wald" (op. 72, no. 3).[40] Strategically marked segments such as these occur more frequently in songs by Brahms that do not employ folk-style music or texts, and most of

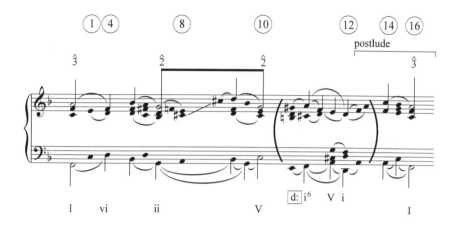

Example 4.2. Middleground graph of "Klage."

these pieces are usually interpreted as portraying a male persona. By contrast, "Klage" is characterized by folk elements, and the narrative voice is clearly that of a woman. These features perhaps prompted Brahms to employ less emphatic contrasts to set off the moment of introspection rather than the type of more overtly dramatic gesture used in "O kühler Wald." (Hock's observations regarding the differences between male and female forms of contemplation, quoted earlier, resonate with these comparisons of Brahms's lieder.)

The postlude has the function of restoring the tonic following the interior emphasis on D minor. It begins with a pedal on A that at first functions as the dominant of D minor; but then the harmonies proceed to form a I⁶ in F major, and an authentic cadence in F follows. At the same time as F major reemerges as tonic, the melody sounds a rhythmically augmented and transposed version of the voice's final descending third motive (C–B♭–A), which contributes to the cadence's conclusive feeling. Without this postlude one would probably hear the song in D minor, but when considering the postlude as an integral part of the structure, it becomes clear that the D-minor phrase ending in m. 12 is best understood as a parenthetical gesture, as shown by the graph in Example 4.2.

To be sure, this is an extremely unconventional structure. Although the half cadence in m. 10 clearly prepares an F-major close, the augmented triad on the upbeat to the following segment wrenches the harmonies off track and onward toward the cadence in D minor. By slightly rewriting the postlude it is possible to show how Brahms could have ended the vocal line in F (Example 4.3), but such a conclusion obviously does not have the same emotional impact, nor does it create the same sense of distance. The lines that Brahms sets in D minor stand apart from the preceding lines of each stanza: they are the fifth in each stanza; they

Example 4.3. Hypothetical conclusion to "Klage."

are distinctly shorter than the preceding lines; and they do not participate in the rhyming scheme of the preceding quatrains. While Brahms avoids a corresponding asymmetrical musical structure, by stating the fifth lines of each stanza twice within a four-measure phrase, his unusual harmonies evoke the poem's change in mood. His subsequent postlude reins in the aberrant harmonies and creates a transition from D minor back to F major. Nevertheless, the final cadence in F does not provide the strongest possible conclusion: the melody ends on $\hat{3}$, not $\hat{1}$, and the chord in the right hand of the piano is arranged in exactly the same manner as that of the song's initial anacrusis. This enables the song to wrap around on itself in the same (feminine) manner as "Am jüngsten Tag." Moreover, the transition back to F major follows the woman's change in mood and the corresponding change in the level of discourse: she gradually gathers her thoughts and returns to the present for the start of the next stanza. This regaining of composure is precisely the way in which women of the nineteenth century were expected to control their emotions.

The interaction between third-related keys in "Klage" is hardly unique in Brahms's oeuvre; he, like many nineteenth-century composers, was fond of tonal dialectics, a compositional strategy he may have inherited from Schumann, among others.[41] As Peter Smith's article in this volume demonstrates, the pairing of the keys of D and F also occurs in Brahms's large-scale instrumental compositions. Moreover, various combinations of D and F harmonies permeate chorales and folksongs, including the folksongs that Brahms arranged, though the combination of D minor with F major inflections is more common than the reverse. Nevertheless, the competing D-minor and F-major cadences in "Klage" are atypical. This is Brahms's only song in which the vocal line concludes on a note that does not belong to the tonic triad, and the accompanying tonicization of a key other than the one concluding the subsequent postlude is also exceedingly rare in the composer's output.[42] This highly unusual ending mirrors the text's rhetorical nuance. Despite the folklike elements (and Brahms's related choice of strophic form), the last line of each stanza is characterized by a change in the level of discourse as the speaker moves from warning her companion of the pain of love to reliving her own heartbreak. Brahms's nontonic conclusion of the melody emphasizes this point. His subsequent return to the tonic, which facilitates the start of each new stanza, depicts the woman regaining her composure as she returns from a vivid recollection of past pain to her present state of emotional equilibrium.[43]

"Ach, und du mein kühles Wasser!" (op. 85, no. 3)

"Ach, und du mein kühles Wasser!" ends with an introverted turn like the one in "Klage," though here a maiden yearns for her far-off sweetheart rather than dwelling on the pain he has inflicted (see Table 4.3).[44] As we have seen in the discussions of "Am jüngsten Tag" and of characters in nineteenth-century literature and art, a young woman was often depicted daydreaming about her sweetheart or, in some cases, longing for a man who has already abandoned her. The text of Brahms's op. 85, no. 3, begins with just such a lonely girl addressing a cool river. Numerous paintings, poems, and lieder, including Brahms's "Sehnsucht" (op. 14, no. 8), similarly position a lamenting woman near a body of water. In Böcklin's *Herbstgedanken* (Plate 4.1), for example, the water visually represents the woman's contemplative mood by its reflection of her (innocent) white dress; the limp yellow flowers floating in the water and the off-white yellowish tinges of the tree trunks further infuse the scene with a melancholy aura. Yellow flowers also dot the grass, and the same hue appears in the motives on the woman's cloak, reinforcing the nineteenth-century belief in women's close relationship with nature. Lost in her thoughts, the woman in Böcklin's painting wraps herself in a cloak, an enfolding feminine gesture that we have already observed in relation to Brahms's setting of "Am jüngsten Tag." Böcklin created similar "shielding" postures for the abandoned women in his darker, more threatening canvases titled *Einsamkeit* (1875) and *Villa am Meer* (1878).[45] The poignancy of the moments captured in *Herbstgedanken* and *Villa am Meer* is in part achieved by the manner in which the women's clasped hands reach up to touch or support their faces. Likewise in Thumann's sketch in Figure 4.1 (p. 91), the young woman's clasped hands are placed in a protective gesture, enclosing her chest and reaching up toward her bowed head. Given the ubiquity of such characterizations, it is not difficult to imagine the character in "Ach, und du mein kühles Wasser!" assuming a similar pose.

Like "Klage," "Ach, und du mein kühles Wasser!" has a recurring piano interlude between its stanzas, but, unlike "Klage," it is not strictly strophic. After the third and final strophe, an expanded version of the prelude's material accompanies the singer's final phrase. Whereas Brahms placed the first and second quatrains of text in a repeated strophe of music, he wrote out the repeated music

Plate 4.1. Arnold Böcklin (1827–1901), *Herbstgedanken*, 1886. Oil on panel; 80.5 × 64 cm. Private collection.

Table 4.3. "Ach, und du mein kühles Wasser!" op. 85, no. 3

Ach, und du mein kühles Wasser!	Alas, and you my cool river!
Ach, und du mein rotes Röslein!	Alas, and you my red rose!
Was erblühst du mir so frühe?	Why do you bloom so early?
Hab' ja nicht, für wen dich pflücken!	I have no one to pluck you for!
Pflück' ich dich für meine Mutter?	Shall I pluck you for my mother?
Keine Mutter hab' ich, Waise!	I the orphan have no mother!
Pflück' ich dich für meine Schwester?	Shall I pluck you for my sister?
Ei doch, längst vermählet ist sie!	But no, she has long since married!
Pflück' ich dich für meinen Brüder?	Shall I pluck you for my brother?
Ist gezogen in die Feldschlacht!	He has gone to the battlefield!
Pflück' ich dich für den Geliebten?	Shall I pluck you for my beloved?
Fern, ach, weilet der Geliebte!	Alas, my beloved tarries far away!
Jenseit dreier grünen Berge,	Across three green mountains,
Jenseit dreier kühlen Wasser!	Across three cool rivers!

for the third quatrain, which describes the lost loved one. The only variants to the music, however, are the accents added under the words "Pflück'" and "Fern" in mm. 11–12. The former gives rhetorical weight to the last statement of this word, which had recurred throughout the poem; the latter emphasizes the unrecoverable distance between the maiden and her beloved. During the first two quatrains, the girl makes simple declarative statements about her lack of family, but at the end of the third, she describes the true object of her affection. Significantly, she does not speak of his return but only confesses that he is far away, across mountains and rivers. That these last two lines of the text both begin with the words "Jenseit dreier" may have prompted Brahms to treat them like a refrain. In the poem, these lines are supplementary, occurring after all the questions and with incomplete syntax.[46] Brahms sets them to a restatement of the two-measure interlude (which is a slightly altered version of the prelude). Then he repeats the last line in a *pianissimo* $\frac{6}{4}$ meter, with the melody in rhythmic augmentation so that it stretches across two measures instead of one. The resulting echo effect enacts the reverberating emotions in the maiden's heart and mind as well as the more literal fading repetition of her words between the mountains' valleys, which in turn represents the unreclaimable physical and emotional distances between the girl and her man. Each measure of this last refrain (mm. 13–14) starts on a successively higher note (C, D, E), musically dramatizing the absent sweetheart as being across *three* successively distant mountains. In mm. 13–14 the melody doubles the right hand of the piano, but in the final segment it is higher and abruptly breaks off on $\hat{3}$ rather than descending to a sustained $\hat{1}$. Despite the rhythmic augmentation of the melody and the new $\frac{6}{4}$ meter, the piano's figuration remains the same as in the prelude. In order to fill out each measure, Brahms inserts a rest after each of the original ⅜ patterns. This rhythmic adjustment results in the singer completing each of the last two measures unaccompanied, aurally symbolizing the maiden's loneliness and isolation. The song ends in the next measure with a tonic arpeggiation in the piano's lower register. From a rhetorical point of view, the last three measures slacken the pace and bring the song to a close. But, as Otto Dessoff, one of Brahms's colleagues, opined, this is far from a convincing ending; rather, one is left hanging in midair.[47] The accuracy of his observation notwithstanding, Dessoff failed to recognize that the rhythmic and melodic figurations aptly capture the maiden's despair.

At first glance, "Ach, und du mein kühles Wasser!" seems to create a more regular tonal space than "Klage" in that the prelude, interlude, and concluding phrase (mm. 13–17) establish A minor as the tonic through slight variants of the same prolonged i–iv–i progression. But Brahms rarely ended a prelude with a plagal cadence; it was far more common for him to end with an authentic cadence. The weaker plagal motion combined with the vacillating, awkwardly halting melody suggests indecision or hesitancy but ultimately also stasis. The rhythms of the ⅜ measures are just as important in conveying this mood as the melodic line and harmonies. Rather than continual, evenly paced durational patterns, Brahms writes three beats of eighth notes followed by two halting quarters. In this way, the song constantly jerks between flowing motions and uneasy pauses. These eighths and quarters are combined with triplets in the bass, which abruptly cease on the last beat of each measure. The resulting two-against-three patterns during the first three beats and the surprising cessation of the triplets on the fifth beat underscore the self-defeating motions of the melody, which oscillates around C but ends each measure by falling dejectedly to A.

After the prelude (and the interludes), the main part of the song begins with an abrupt shift in temporal and tonal worlds (mm. 3–6, repeated in mm. 9–12). The vacillating melody is replaced by repeated descents in each measure in the main strophe. In addition, the prelude's agitated triplet-rest patterns cease, and the bass moves regularly on every beat. Nevertheless, the dissonant harmonies and rhythms do not entirely dissipate; instead, they reverberate throughout the main strophe. Most commentators follow Max Kalbeck in attributing the ⅜ meter to the influence of Serbian folk music, the meter forming a corollary to the Serbian folk origins of the text.[48] But because the lines of the German text each have only four feet, they cannot be evenly spread across the five beats of each measure. Drawing on the rhythm of the prelude's melody, Brahms sets each of the first three poetic feet to one beat, but he elongates the fourth foot across two. In many cases, this lopsided weighting is appropriate because the last word is the most important in the line, as, for instance, "Geliebten" (beloved) in line 11.

Nevertheless, the lines of text are not end-stopped, and the faltering feeling that Brahms's rhythm creates extends beyond the rhetorical emphasis the poem warrants. In addition to these rhythmic characteristics, the main part of the song is also harmonically unsettling, with each of its four measures beginning on a dissonance. Measure 3 establishes the pattern for each of the subsequent measures; it starts on a ii°7 and then proceeds to a half cadence. Measure 4 is a varied repeat of this progression, but this time it ends with a (weak) authentic cadence in G major (♭VII)—a type of modal inflection that perhaps reflects the influence of folk music but might also be a way of avoiding the more strongly directed home dominant. Despite the diatonic melody, the chromatic harmonies in m. 5 feint toward D minor before returning to G via a diminished seventh. Then at the start of m. 6, multiple neighbor tones ornamenting an F chord undermine the G tonality and facilitate the arrival of the tonic, A minor.

While the dissonances in every measure of the strophe convey the pain of the maiden's loneliness, the harmony's journey to the tonic is a musical representation of her search for companionship (see Example 4.4). The tonic arrives with a perfect authentic cadence at the end of the first quatrain (mm. 5–6), and, when repeated at the end of the third quatrain, this cadence functions as the song's structural close (m. 12). But any conclusiveness proffered by this final cadence—from the point of view of either the music's structure or its relation to the woman's psychological plight—is negated by the return of the variation of the prelude, which now forms the concluding refrain. Setting the final lines describing the distance between the girl and her sweetheart, it reinstates 3̂ and reiterates the static tonic harmonies and uneasy rhythms of the opening.

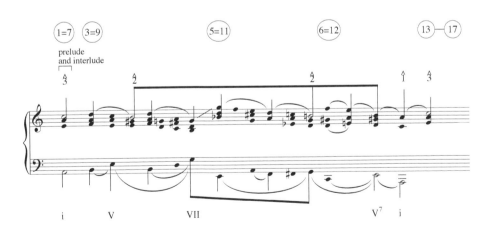

Example 4.4. Middleground graph of "Ach, und du mein kühles Wasser!"

In his codification of middleground structures of art songs, Walter Everett maintains that the voice typically governs the *Urlinie,* but this is not entirely the case in either "Klage" or "Ach, und du mein kühles Wasser!"[49] To exclude either the piano's postlude in "Klage" or the prelude in "Ach, und du mein kühles Wasser!" from the middleground would be to deny a vital part of each composition's structure and an essential element of its meaning. As shown by the graphs in Examples 4.2 and 4.4, these passages contribute crucial structural elements to the songs' tonal worlds.

The piano's A-minor measures in "Ach, und du mein kühles Wasser!" function as frames for vignettes that only regain the A-minor tonic chord in their final measures. Whereas "Klage" is noteworthy because its melodic line ends out of key, this song is unusual because there is a disjunction between the end of the prelude and the entry of the singer. Owing to the strophic structure of the song and the prelude's varied return as the interludes, this disjunction recurs at the start of each strophe. There are somewhat similar disjunctions at the ends of the strophes as well, though these breaks are somewhat less obvious, because each strophe ends with a tonic chord and the refrain then commences with the same tonic harmony. Nevertheless, the return of the two-against-three patterns in the piano and the late entrance of the bass note at the start of the interludes and the last phrase (m. 13) provide enough contrast to mark a change in psychological state.[50] It is as though the maiden lives in a dream world, yearning for the man she cherishes most, but every now and then she returns to physical reality (the water and the rose) and sees her situation for what it is. This dream world is not only signified by the disjunction between the prelude/interludes and the main strophes but also by the prelude/interludes' concluding plagal cadences. As Margaret Notley has observed, passages in a minor key that suppress dominant functions in favor of the subdominant (especially when combined with modal shadings) may connote "otherworldliness, distance, timelessness, possibly even alienation."[51] In varying degrees, all these affects are in play in "Ach, und du mein kühles Wasser!," and they are particularly pronounced during the concluding measures.

Framing devices occur in numerous nineteenth-century lieder and can involve the large-scale structure of a song or a small section within a stanza. In many cases, however, the frame represents reality, and the material it encloses portrays a character's deepest emotions or the memory of a crucial event or former loving relationship. For example, in Brahms's "Regenlied" (op. 59, no. 3) the central section represents the memory of the innocence of childhood, while the outer sections portray a protagonist yearning for this past time. In "Ach, und du mein kühles Wasser!," the framing structure functions in the opposite way: the main strophes of the song depict the lonely maiden's present existence. The repeated descents in every measure, which occur even when the corresponding text poses a question, illustrate both her physical posture and her psychological state. She has passively accepted her companionless state. By contrast, the prelude and interludes, with their wavering melodic contours, conflicted rhythmic patterns, and tonic prolongation that does not include V, depict her wistful dreams of her lost sweetheart. Like the memories of Schubert's and Goethe's Gretchen, this maiden's recollections of her beloved are tinged by her present state of abandonment, and the sting of rejection is suggested not only by the late entrance of the bass but also by the dissonant G♯, which does not immediately resolve in its own register (mm. 7 and 13). This meaning for the framing device, however, only becomes clear at the end of the song, where the A-minor measures accompany the girl's description of her distant loved one.

*　*　*

Surveys of Brahms's lieder, which group "Am jüngsten Tag," "Klage," and "Ach, und du mein kühles Wasser!" with other songs exhibiting folklike elements, typically conclude that these works represent Brahms's somewhat naive (and perhaps overly sentimental) longing for a simpler past.[52] Other than a few tentative suggestions that Brahms's preference for folk texts may be linked to Romantic aesthetics, the wider cultural context for such works has been ignored. Scholars have failed to scrutinize the preponderance of female characters in these types of lieder, let alone the degree to which they mirror the contemporary society's view of womanhood. Furthermore, all too often the music's subtle, unconventional tonal structures and their expressive power have been marginalized in favor of the folk elements. Brahms's recourse to folk style was sharply rebuked by nineteenth-century critics like Hugo Wolf and similarly minded early twentieth-century writers such as Ernest Newman. Both of these men linked their criticisms to assertions that Brahms paid little attention to his texts. I have argued elsewhere that the influence of these critics significantly shaped the negative view of Brahms's lieder that pervaded the first half of the twentieth century.[53] These same writers frequently castigated Brahms for his depictions of tearful maidens and in so doing perhaps deterred analysts from looking more closely at these songs.

Further evidence that the folk elements of these songs should not be emphasized to such a degree that their emotional or psychological aspects are ignored comes from Brahms's courtship of Agathe von Siebold. During 1858, when Brahms had to be absent from Agathe's hometown of Göttingen, he sent her settings of folksong texts speaking of love and absence (op. 14, nos. 1, 4, and 7). Numerous scholars have followed Agathe in interpreting these songs as constituting sincere love letters.[54] Moreover, Matthias Schmidt has suggested that in some lieder, including those associated with Agathe, references to folk style may have been a way for Brahms to conceal autobiographical experiences; John MacAuslan has ventured even further and interpreted Brahms's last collection of folksong arrangements (WoO 33) as recollections of his relationships with Robert and Clara Schumann as well as with Agathe.[55]

The folklike gestures in the songs I discuss, however, function in a different way. The light textures, diatonic melodies, regular phrase structures, and other folk idioms are part of an ironic reversal that is also prevalent in other art forms of the nineteenth century: rather than depicting a natural truth, they represent socially imposed views of womanhood. A chromatically saturated song with a complex accompanying figuration could portray a person overwhelmed by the pain of hopeless love, but it would not reflect the demure comportment expected of a nineteenth-century young woman as effectively as the folksong elements that Brahms employs.

In contrast to these folk elements, Brahms's artful tonal structures, in concert with his deft handling of other musical elements such as rhythm, texture, and dynamics, convey the specific emotional plight of the maiden in each song. It is these subtleties that propel the songs away from mere reflections of nineteenth-century female stereotypes to sensitive interpretations of the emotions of the individual protagonists—much in the same way that visual artists such as Böcklin rendered more plausible and sympathetic images of individual women in contrast to the caricatures of the *Backfisch* in mass-produced media.[56]

"Am jüngsten Tag," "Klage," and "Ach, und du mein kühles Wasser!" are not merely pseudo folksongs, nor are they dramas writ large; that is, they are not Wertherian—male—*Sturm und Drang* suicidal dilemmas. They are internal vignettes, dramas within the confines of the minds of young, daydreaming women, and their pervasive soft dynamic levels underscore this intimacy. It is only by studying the music's structure in coordination with the customs and arts of Brahms's milieu that we can draw nearer to understanding the full meaning of such lieder.

ACKNOWLEDGMENTS

I would like to thank Peter H. Smith, Yonatan Malin, and Robert S. Hatten for their insightful critiques of this chapter. In addition, the observations of one of the anonymous reviewers for Indiana University Press led me to a clearer formulation of the ironic aspects of these lieder, and David Stern generously contributed to an earlier analysis of "Am jüngsten Tag." I am also grateful to Cécile Brunner, Image Resources and Copyright Management, Kunsthaus Zürich, for her assistance in obtaining the image of the Böcklin painting reproduced in Plate 4.1. The preparation of this chapter was facilitated by Special

Assigned Leave during the spring of 2009, which was granted by the Provost of Ball State University, and by a grant for materials from the University's Office of Academic Research and Sponsored Programs. I am extremely grateful to Robert Kvam, Dean of the College of Fine Arts, Ball State University, who strongly supported my applications for these awards and approved release time during the fall of 2010.

NOTES

1. Konrad Huschke completed one of the earliest studies of Brahms's relationships with women, *Frauen um Brahms* (Karlsruhe: Friedrich Gutsch, [1936]). He reports on Brahms's friendships with over thirty women but offers very little in the way of an analysis of the type and complexity of these relationships. By contrast, Eduard Hitschmann does attempt to explore the psychological aspects of Brahms's failed liaisons. See his "Johannes Brahms und die Frauen," *Psychoanalytische Bewegung* 5/2 (1933): 97–129. For a more recent publication discussing just one instance of one of Brahms's close female friends influencing his compositions, see Antje Ruhbaum's article on Elisabet von Herzogenberg's influence on his opp. 69–71 lieder: "Von Eisbergen und Unterwasserlandschaften: Elisabeth und Heinrich von Herzogenberg und der Brahmskreis," in *Musik Netz Werke: Konturen der neuen Musikkultur—Dokumentation des 16. Internationalen Studentischen Symposiums für Musikwissenschaft in Berlin 2001,* ed. Lydia Grün and Frank Wiegand (Bielefeld: Transcript, 2002), 140–64.

2. In order to avoid confusion, op. 95, no. 6, and op. 85, no. 3, will be referred to by their opening lines rather than by their titles.

3. In addition to songs with a female narrative voice, there are numerous others in which women are described in both positive and negative terms. In many of these cases, the narrative voice is male.

4. Barthes states that lieder are "unisexual" insofar as their topic of romantic love "is no respecter of sexes or of social roles." "The Romantic Song," in *The Responsibility of Forms,* trans. Richard Howard (New York: Hill and Wang, 1985), 287.

5. Brahms to Fritz Simrock, 18 April 1877, in *Johannes Brahms Briefe an P. J. Simrock und Fritz Simrock,* ed. Max Kalbeck (1917; repr., Tutzing: Hans Schneider, 1974), 27. For a discussion of other instances in which Brahms's friends (Spitta, Kalbeck, and Billroth) applied the terms *Mädchenlieder* and *Männerlieder* to his lieder, see Otto Gottlieb-Billroth, ed., *Billroth und Brahms im Briefwechsel: Mit Einleitung, Anmerkungen und 4 Bildtafeln* (Berlin and Vienna: Urban & Schwarzenberg, 1935), 238–39 n. 8.

6. The letter is published in Eduard Hanslick's *Aus meinem Leben* (1894; repr., Farnborough: Gregg, 1971), 381. English translation by Hans Barkan in *Johannes Brahms and Theodor Billroth: Letters from a Musical Friendship* (Norman: University of Oklahoma Press, 1957), 50–51.

7. English translation in Table 4.1 after Eric Sams, *The Songs of Johannes Brahms* (New Haven, Conn.: Yale University Press, 2000), 286.

8. Kurt Hofmann, *Die Bibliothek von Johannes Brahms* (Hamburg: Wagner, 1974), 53.

9. Laura Mohr Hansson, *Wir Frauen und unsere Dichter,* 2nd ed. (Berlin: Duncker, 1896), chap. 3.

10. In relation to the translations in Heyse's *Italienisches Liederbuch,* Frank Walker notes that Heyse's German versions are more serious in tone than the original Italian texts. See his *Hugo Wolf, a Biography,* 2nd ed. (Princeton, N.J.: Princeton University Press,

1968), 296. Susan Youens further explores these differences in *Hugo Wolf: The Vocal Music* (Princeton, N.J.: Princeton University Press, 1992), 114–19.

11. I discuss this song in relation to Hugo Wolf's setting of a similar Heyse text in "Brahms, Wolf, and the Girls," *Musicologica Austriaca* 26 (2007): 113–24.

12. For a discussion of the response of nineteenth-century theorists to the use of ♭$\hat{6}$ and the minor subdominant in major-key pieces, see Matthew Riley, "The 'Harmonic Major' Mode in Nineteenth-Century Theory and Practice," *Music Analysis* 23/1 (2004): 1–26. Given the technical focus of this article, issues of interpretation and meaning are of peripheral concern, and Riley does not engage issues of gender and the common practice of interpreting the subdominant as "feminine." In exploring the female voices in "Am jüngsten Tag" and "Ach, und du mein kühles Wasser!," which I discuss in the last section of this chapter, it may be tempting to draw on this tradition. In both songs the subdominant, in combination with other expressive elements such as rhythmic dissonances, contributes to the portrayal of a young woman's wistful mood, but this harmony is also important in many other songs by Brahms that do not explicitly deal with a woman or a feminine trait or emotion. "Es schauen die Blumen alle" (op. 96, no. 3), for example, ends with a prominent plagal cadence, but its text employs the lyrical "ich." Raymond Knapp offers a convincing interpretation of the subdominant as representing the feminine in Beethoven's *An die ferne Geliebte* but also cautions that this trope may not be operative in all situations. "Reading Gender in Late Beethoven: *An die Freude* and *An die ferne Geliebte*," *Acta Musicologica* 75/1 (2003): 55–57 n. 13.

13. Robert Bailey employs the term *tonal pairing* to denote a major triad and a minor triad a third apart (e.g., A minor and C major) that are combined in such a way that either triad can potentially serve as a local tonic. "An Analytical Study of the Sketches and Drafts," in *Prelude and Transfiguration from Tristan and Isolde*, ed. Robert Bailey (New York: Norton, 1985), 121–22. Although many of the subsequent studies discussing the expressive potential of tonal pairing have focused on opera, Harald Krebs has shown that, prior to Wagner, Schubert exploited this potential in his lieder. See "Some Early Examples of Tonal Pairing: Schubert's 'Meeres Stille' and 'Der Wanderer,'" in *The Second Practice of Nineteenth-Century Tonality*, ed. William Kinderman and Harald Krebs (Lincoln: University of Nebraska Press, 1996), 17–33.

14. Songs exhibiting these characteristics include "In Waldeseinsamkeit" (op. 85, no. 6), "Es schauen die Blumen alle" (op. 96, no. 3), and "Kein Haus, keine Heimat" (op. 94, no. 5). These songs employ unusual tonal structures in which the expected concluding authentic cadence is replaced by a plagal cadence, and a conventional structural close is subverted. In contrast to the songs discussed in this chapter, these works do not have texts with a female narrative voice, and the first two do not employ folklike stylistic elements. I analyze these songs in "Unrequited Love and Unrealized Dominants," *Intégral* 7 (1993): 119–48.

15. Lawrence Kramer, "*Carnaval*, Cross-Dressing, and the Woman in the Mirror," in *Musicology and Difference: Gender and Sexuality in Music Scholarship*, ed. Ruth A. Solie (Berkeley: University of California Press, 1993), 307.

16. Lisabeth M. Hock, *Replicas of a Female Prometheus: The Textual Personae of Bettina von Arnim* (New York: Lang, 2000), 14.

17. For analyses of some of the songs by Brahms that are structured on a large-scale auxiliary cadence, see chapter 6 of my "Text-Music Relationships in the Lieder of Johannes Brahms" (Ph.D. diss., Graduate Center of the City University of New York, 1992).

18. As Example 4.1 shows, with annotations between the staves, this triadic figure (F–C–A) is also prolonged in the middle voices of the second half of each stanza.

19. Walter Everett interprets this song in relation to a more conventional *Ursatz* and reads the final cadence as implying a root-position dominant. He hears the descent of the structural line in the piano's tenor register, even though it is buried beneath "covering"

voices. Although he acknowledges that the voice's "refusal to traverse the fundamental line" is a reflection of the girl's thoughts, his graph does not represent the conflicting ideas of the text. "Deep-Level Portrayal of Directed and Misdirected Motions in Nineteenth-Century Lyric Song," *Journal of Music Theory* 48/1 (2004): 42–43.

20. An alternative way to interpret the conflicts between voice and piano is to hear the piano as representing the more pessimistic views and experiences of Brahms himself. The presence of the composer's "voice" has been heard in similar ways in some of his other songs about love, including "Von ewiger Liebe" (op. 43, no. 1). See Richard Cohn, "Complex Hemiolas, Ski-Hill Graphs and Metric Spaces," *Music Analysis* 20/3 (2001): 316–18. See also Natasha Loges, "The Notion of Personae in Brahms's 'Bitteres zu sagen denkst du,' op. 32, no. 7: A Literary Key to Musical Performance?," in *Music and Literature in German Romanticism,* ed. Siobhán Donovan and Robin Elliott (Rochester, N.Y.: Camden House, 2004), 183–99.

21. This was the response of some of the conference attendees when I presented an earlier version of my analysis of "Am jüngsten Tag" at the "Hugo Wolf Internationales Symposium," Graz/Slovenj Gradec, 3–7 November 2003.

22. By the end of the nineteenth century, when greater industrialization and a concomitant rise in urban populations were resulting in profound changes to society, the innocent young maiden associated with rural life came to represent traditional values and an opposition to the emerging modern era. David Ehrenpreis compares such images with more avant-garde, sensual representations of women of the same age in "The Figure of the *Backfisch:* Representing Puberty in Wilhelmine Germany," *Zeitschrift für Kunstgeschichte* 67/4 (2004): 479–508.

23. This sketch was published in an 1889 issue of the popular magazine *Über Land und Meer.* See Ingrid Otto, *Bürgerliche Töchtererziehung im Spiegel illustrierter Zeitschriften von 1865 bis 1915* (Hildesheim: August Lax, 1990), 58.

24. David Ehrenpreis further explores the depiction of this type of female character in "Beyond the Femme Fatale: Female Types in Wilhelmine Visual Culture" (Ph.D. diss., Boston University, 1998), 58, chap. 4. The term *Backfisch* (literally "baked fish") refers to fish that are large enough to be caught but so small that they need to be baked rather than fried.

25. Susanne Zahn discusses the sexual aspects of such fictional characters in *Töchterleben: Studien zur Sozialgeschichte der Mädchenliteratur* (Frankfurt am Main: dipa-Verlag, 1983), 132–33.

26. Clementine Helm wrote twenty such novels, including *Von Backfisch zur Matron* (1889). *Backfischens Leiden und Freuden* was translated as *Gretchen's Joys and Sorrows* by Helen M. Dunbar Slack (Boston: A. Williams & Co., 1877). Other women who wrote in this genre include Rosalie Koch, Lina Morgenstern, Thekla von Gumpert, and A. Stein. See Zahn, *Töchterleben,* 128.

27. Otto Julius Bierbaum's satirical novel *Stilpe* also references the connection between the stereotypical *Backfisch* and Goethe's Gretchen. Bierbaum describes the young girl whom the character Stilpe falls in love with as looking "like all *Backfische*" and that to comprehend this girl one should "imagine Faust's Gretchen." Ehrenpreis, "Beyond the Femme Fatale," 198, 199.

28. Glaser also notes that this idealization of "Gretchen" types was not always driven by women themselves and that the century "did not honor purity per se, but rather the purity of the maiden coveted by the male." Hermann Glaser, *The Cultural Roots of National Socialism* (Austin: University of Texas Press, 1978), 179. The aspects of sensuality that pervaded many of the widely propagated images of young women in all the arts, as well as the concomitant topic of the male gaze, has still not been studied in relation to either Brahms's lieder or his alleged misogyny, and they fall beyond the scope of this chapter.

Nevertheless, one should pause to consider that the second stanza of Heyse's version of "Am jüngsten Tag" began with the phrase "O blush of youth" and went on to describe the girl's shabby little frock "tucked up high." Lucien Stark provides a translation of Heyse's first two stanzas in *A Guide to the Solo Songs of Johannes Brahms* (Bloomington: Indiana University Press, 1995), 294. A few scholars have begun to examine such sensual aspects of lieder by composers other than Brahms, most notably Susan Youens in her study of the over four hundred settings of Heine's "Du bist wie eine Blume," in chapter 4 of her *Heinrich Heine and the Lied* (Cambridge: Cambridge University Press, 2007).

29. Fanny Fuller translated the sixth German edition of this book into English; see *Musical Sketches* (Boston: Ditson, 1863).

30. Adelbert von Chamisso, *Frauen-Liebe und Leben: Lieder-Cyclus,* illustrations by Paul Thumann, 15th ed. (Leipzig: Adolf Titze, 1879). Figure 4.1 is reproduced from this edition.

31. Ehrenpreis, "Beyond the Femme Fatale," 198.

32. Ehrenpreis cites the 1824 *Allgemeine deutsche Real-Encyclopädie für die gebildeten Stände* in "Beyond the Femme Fatale," 125–26.

33. As quoted in Ehrenpreis, "Beyond the Femme Fatale," 123–24. Feuerbach's depictions of Iphigenie are characterized by this same emotional state. Although Iphigenie is a character from an ancient Greek myth, Feuerbach's renditions of her influenced paintings of modern women, possibly including Böcklin's *Herbstgedanken* (see Plate 4.1).

34. Ruth Solie, "Whose Life? The Gendered Self in Schumann's *Frauenliebe* Songs," in *Music and Text: Critical Inquiries,* ed. Steven Paul Scher (Cambridge: Cambridge University Press, 1992), 219–40. Through a series of questions beginning with "how did men control women by means of sentimental symbols?," Youens demonstrates that the issues Solie raises concerning the connections between lieder, the male hegemonic society, and the maturation process of young women in the nineteenth century have still not been thoroughly addressed. *Heinrich Heine and the Lied,* 270.

35. Similar combinations of folk elements and intricate tonal structures characterize many of Brahms's other songs portraying young women. Elsewhere I have discussed the expressive function of the unusual harmonic designs of "Anklänge" (op. 7, no. 3) and "Vorschneller Schwur" (op. 95, no. 5), both of which depict *Backfisch* characters who are similar to those portrayed in the songs I analyze in this chapter. "'Anklänge' as Brahms's Lied Manifesto," *American Brahms Society Newsletter* 28/1 (2010): 6–9; and "Dramatic Turning Points in Brahms Lieder," *Indiana Theory Review* 15/1 (1994): 75–87.

36. I discuss the unusual tonal structure of "Kein Haus, keine Heimat" in "Unrequited Love and Unrealized Dominants," 121–25. By contrast, Yonatan Malin analyzes the song's striking rhythmic dissonances in his chapter in the current volume.

37. English translation by Sams, *The Songs of Johannes Brahms,* 303.

38. This portrait dates from 1855, some three years prior to Brahms's brief engagement to Agathe. It is reproduced in Hans Küntzel's *"Aber Fesseln tragen kann ich nicht": Johannes Brahms und Agathe von Siebold* (Göttingen: Steidl, 2003), 63.

39. Robert S. Hatten states: "When a presumably continuous idea is broken off, or its clearly projected goal is evaded, as in certain rhetorical gestures or shifts in level of discourse, then there is also a sense of shift in temporality." Hatten discusses examples of such shifting in piano sonatas by Schubert. "The Troping of Temporality in Music," in *Approaches to Meaning in Music,* ed. Byron Almén and Edward Pearsall (Bloomington: Indiana University Press, 2006), 68–72.

40. Frank Samarotto refers to such moments as a change in temporal plane. See "A Theory of Temporal Plasticity in Tonal Music: An Extension of the Schenkerian Approach to Rhythm with Special Reference to Beethoven's Late Music" (Ph.D. diss., Graduate Center of the City University of New York, 1999), 129–70. I explored instances of tem-

poral planes in Brahms's songs in my presentation "Rhythm and Phrase as Expressive Gestures in Brahms's Lieder" at the conference "Brahms the Contemporary: Perspectives on Two Centuries," Harvard University, 17–20 April 1997.

41. Schumann's "Der Einsiedler" (op. 83, no. 3) is somewhat like "Am jüngsten Tag" and "Klage" in that it contrasts F major with D minor. Its first phrase emphasizes D minor, but F major is stronger in the second phrase. The melody of each stanza ends with an A accompanied by a first-inversion F-major chord. In the first two stanzas, the piano then confirms the F tonality with an authentic cadence, but the third stanza employs a weaker plagal cadence. Along somewhat similar lines, Schumann alternates D-minor and F-major phrases in "Das ist ein Flöten und Geigen" (*Dichterliebe,* no. 9). Emphasizing the protagonist's pain and yearning, the vocal line draws to a final cadence in F but without a raised leading tone. The piano's lengthy postlude restores the overriding tonic of D minor. (This type of ending, in which the voice concludes on a chord other than the main tonic, is not as unusual in Schumann as it is in Brahms.)

42. In a handful of cases, Brahms ends the melody on $\hat{3}$ or $\hat{5}$ with the piano forming either an inversion of the tonic or the submediant chord; alternatively $\hat{1}$ is harmonized by the subdominant. These chords, however, merely delay the root-position tonic, which the piano provides in a brief postlude. The following songs end with this type of procedure: "Trennung" (op. 14, no. 5), "Gang zur Liebsten" (op. 14, no. 6), "An die Nachtigall" (op. 46, no. 4), "Die Liebende schreibt" (op. 47, no. 5), "Während des Regens" (op. 58, no. 2), "Auf dem See" (op. 59, no. 2), and "Mein wundes Herz" (op. 59, no. 7). In almost every case, the melody's conclusion and the delay in reaching a firm tonic chord are associated with the unremitting yearning described in the text. The unusually dissonant, tonally wandering "Liebesklage des Mädchens" (op. 48, no. 3) is a particularly strange case because the concluding notes of the vocal line, E♯–F♯, and the associated arrival of the dominant via a diminished seventh suggest a possible continuation in the key of F-sharp major. But the postlude quickly slides back to the weakly articulated B-major tonic.

43. The second version of Schubert's "Meeres Stille" (D. 216) exhibits a somewhat similar tonal pairing in that its opening and closing phrases are in C major, whereas the inner phrases are more tonally fluid and emphasize E major. While the outer C-major phrases set lines describing the stillness of the sea, the internal chromatic phrases evoke the sailor's anxiety and the sea's deathly, threatening aspects. The brevity of this song, its sparse texture, and its regular four-measure phrases are similarly important elements in Brahms's "Klage." Krebs explores the tonal pairing in Schubert's song and emphasizes the problematic nature of the closing measures in C major. Like my graph of "Klage," his graph of "Meeres Stille" interprets the *Kopfton* ($\hat{3}$) as prolonged throughout the song, without a stepwise descent to $\hat{1}$. Schubert's melodic line, however, does end with a descending leap to the tonic. See "Some Early Examples of Tonal Pairing," 26–30.

44. English translation after Sams, *The Songs of Johannes Brahms,* 256.

45. In the same somber tones of his better-known *Toteninsel,* both of these canvases portray a tiny, lonely woman who enfolds her head and upper torso in a shawl. She is cut off from the rest of the world by a rugged landscape that surrounds her as if it were a shroud. In *Villa am Meer,* the woman's anguish is underscored by a gray-green sea and by the deserted building she leans against for support or shelter.

46. I am grateful to Yonatan Malin for bringing this element of the text to my attention.

47. Otto Dessoff to Brahms, 7 July 1878, in *Johannes Brahms im Briefwechsel mit Otto Dessoff,* ed. Carl Krebs (1922; repr., Tutzing: Hans Schneider, 1974), 195.

48. Max Kalbeck, *Johannes Brahms* (Tutzing: Hans Schneider, 1976), 3:329.

49. Everett, "Deep-Level Portrayal," 29, 35.

50. For a discussion of the ways in which musical oppositions or contrasts may represent changes in temporal realms and psychological states, see Robert S. Hatten, *Interpreting*

Musical Gestures, Topics, and Tropes: Mozart, Beethoven, Schubert (Bloomington: Indiana University Press, 2004), 55. Along somewhat similar lines, Raymond Monelle notes that a refrain in a rondo "is a change, not only of temporality, but also of ontology, a change of nature and of utterance." *The Sense of Music: Semiotic Essays* (Princeton, N.J.: Princeton University Press, 2000), 137. An analogous change occurs in the prelude, interlude, and mm. 13–17 of "Ach, und du mein kühles Wasser!"

51. Margaret Notley, "Plagal Harmony as Other: Asymmetrical Dualism and Instrumental Music by Brahms," *Journal of Musicology* 22/1 (2005): 95.

52. In his survey of Brahms's lieder, Michael Musgrave spares little time for these types of works. He concludes that Brahms venerated folksongs because they "represented a romantic ideal, songs whose very simplicity and stylization embodied a quality of perfection." Although he acknowledges some of the ways in which Brahms departs from the pure folk style, like most other commentators he does not discuss the sophisticated or unusual tonal structures that underpin some of the most folklike works. "Words for Music: The Songs for Solo Voice and Piano," in *The Cambridge Companion to Brahms*, ed. Michael Musgrave (Cambridge: Cambridge University Press, 1999), 197–98.

53. Heather Platt, "Jenner versus Wolf: The Critical Reception of Brahms's Songs," *Journal of Musicology* 13/3 (1995): 377–403; and "Hugo Wolf and the Reception of Brahms's Lieder," in *Brahms Studies 2*, ed. David Brodbeck (Lincoln: University of Nebraska Press, 1998), 91–111.

54. Agathe describes these songs in her autobiographical sketch "Allerlei aus meinem Leben." Her interpretation is cited by numerous later scholars, including, most recently, Inge Van Rij, in *Brahms's Song Collections* (Cambridge: Cambridge University Press, 2006), 181.

55. Matthias Schmidt, "Volkslied und Allusionstechnik bei Brahms: Beobachtungen an 'Sonntag,' op. 47/3," *Musikforschung* 54/1 (2001): 24–46; John MacAuslan, "'The Artist in Love' in Brahms's Life and in His German Folksongs," *Music & Letters* 88/1 (2007): 78–106.

56. One might speculate that Brahms was able to create such credible representations of the young women's emotions because their loneliness and longing were akin (even if not identical) to his own emotions. In this way, Brahms perhaps approached his art in a manner similar to some of the most famous Romantic literary figures, including Blake, Shelley, and Goethe, who based their heroines as well as their heroes on themselves. This in no way negates the reputed misogyny of these writers or of Brahms. Moreover, these female characters nevertheless reflected the divergent worldviews of men and women, which Hock describes in *Replicas of a Female Prometheus*, and society's understanding of the character and role of women. In any case, conjectures of autobiographical traces in Brahms's songs extend well beyond the scope of this chapter and should be considered in the context of a broader examination of this repertory, which would encompass lieder with texts that describe women as well as those that, like the three in this chapter, set poems with a female narrative voice. For discussions of the relationships between male writers and their female characters, see Lawrence Lipking, *Abandoned Women and Poetic Tradition* (Chicago: University of Chicago Press, 1988), 149; and Irene Tayler and Gina Luria, "Gender and Genre: Women in British Romantic Literature," in *What Manner of Woman: Essays on English and American Life and Literature*, ed. Marlene Springer (New York: New York University Press, 1977), 116–19.

5 Ancient Tragedy and Anachronism: Form as Expression in Brahms's *Gesang der Parzen*

Margaret Notley

Gesang der Parzen (Song of the Fates, op. 89) has always been one of Brahms's least understood compositions. Few recent critics have given close consideration to the poetic text, known as the *Parzenlied*, or its source, the play *Iphigenie auf Tauris* by Goethe.[1] In Brahms's day, many listeners, in contrast, were thoroughly familiar with Goethe's play, and at times this paradoxically also proved to be an obstacle to their understanding of Brahms's setting, as the composer himself had anticipated. Well before the first Viennese performance in February 1883, Brahms wrote to a friend, Theodor Billroth, about the response that he expected from the critic Ludwig Speidel: "I already hear Speidel saying that it is not Goethe's Iphigenie, and of course the Song of the Fates isn't Iphigenie."[2]

Like other documentary evidence related to Brahms's setting, this passage has rarely received the careful attention that might enable insights into his compositional choices. Those writing about the music have erred in other ways as well, often either by trying to force the setting into an existing formal schema or, as I have already implied, by underestimating his grasp of the poetic text. If we assume Brahms's sophistication regarding both the poem's subtleties and the consequences of removing it from Goethe's play, to which he obliquely refers in the letter quoted above, it becomes possible to arrive at a more convincing account of the work.

Although I have stressed the text, I shall delay addressing it more closely for the moment. I ask the reader to consider instead a short instrumental passage for a compelling example of the interrelated formal idiosyncrasies and peculiar expressivity of *Gesang der Parzen*. This passage (mm. 100–103; see Example 5.1) enters after a long development section (not shown) culminates in a prolonged G♯ dominant that arouses overwhelming expectations of resolution to C♯ minor. The subsequent deceptive progression to an A–C♯ dyad in m. 100 is startling indeed, despite the many, at times unusual, semitone resolutions that precede it. Although it appears in a composition in D minor, the dyad enters as the submediant of C♯. Only in retrospect, with the return in m. 104 of one of the main

Example 5.1. *Gesang der Parzen*, mm. 100–103 (contrabasses' *pizzicato* quarter note A on downbeats not shown).

themes, which I shall call the refrain, does the dominant function of A emerge with clarity. The large-scale significance of this thematic return as a recapitulation (rather than a simple restatement) of opening material—and thus of the retransitional function of the A dominant expansion—also requires a more synoptic perspective. As experienced in the moment, the resolution in m. 100 and the three measures that follow are not easily reconciled with a retransitional formal function.

Measures 100–103 also constitute one of the most evocative passages in a composition remarkable for its extremes of expression. When the prolonged G♯ dominant resolves abruptly in m. 100, the bassoons begin to play a mournful descending line in A-Phrygian, all the more striking because Brahms places it within a spare texture otherwise comprising ostinato patterns in the D horns, timpani, cellos, and contrabasses. (These patterns derive from the refrain's accompaniment; see m. 20ff.) The placement of the semitones in the bassoons' line gives a distinctly archaic coloring to the A octave that it traces, whose larger harmonic meaning, like the formal meaning of the measures, remains obscure until the refrain reenters at m. 104. Only when we recognize A as the dominant of D minor does the significance of the equivalence between the lower four notes in A-Phrygian (D–C–B♭–A) and the initial notes in the descending D natural minor (D-Aeolian) scale become clear. A-Phrygian has given way to D-Aeolian.

The modal basis along with the ostinati, moderate tempo, duple meter, and combination of percussion and bassoons create the effect of an ancient processional. This may seem fitting, given the play's basis in a myth that Euripides had dramatized more than two millennia before Goethe; Goethe, however, had reimagined the story within the worldview of late eighteenth-century humanism. The tension between the two textual sources underlies much of the misunderstanding of *Gesang der Parzen*. In the letter to Billroth cited above, Brahms must be referring in part to Goethe's reworking of the myth and his own decision to reinterpret some—but by no means all—of the implications of that reworking in his musical setting. By reimagining the poem outside Goethe's play, Brahms could portray ancient mythic tragedy. Yet in his setting this eventually leads to anachronistic emphasis on human suffering and remorse.

Goethe's Poem in and out of Context

Table 5.1 gives the words of the poem as they appear in the play.[3] My annotations "strophe" and "antistrophe" highlight Goethe's adoption of the classical choric ode structure in lines 9–28, an indication of the poet's own circumscribed embrace of his ancient Greek models. (I will further elucidate this structure below in the section of this chapter titled "Spatial Imagery and Developmental Cycles as Tragic Expression.") The words given in the table are also as they appear in Brahms's composition, with two exceptions: the quotation marks that enclose the first five stanzas do not appear, and the first stanza returns between the fourth and fifth ones. Brahms's omission of the quotation marks may be inconsequential, since the discursive identifier in the final stanza ("Thus sang the Fates") sets it apart from the rest of the poem. The return of the first stanza, in contrast, further articulates a preexisting turning point in the poem. Stanzas 2–4 depict the spatial distance between the gods on high and those whom they have banished to neverending darkness below. By treating the first stanza as a refrain at this point, the poem returns from the mythic past to its present (another kind of distance): in the later age implied by the first and fifth stanzas, rulers continue to exact revenge on the descendants even of those they once favored. In the final stanza, a narrator attributes the warnings of the previous stanzas to a song of the Fates and then refers to an event ostensibly happening in the present: an old man hears the Fates, thinks of his children and grandchildren, and shakes his head, one assumes in despair.

When Iphigenie recites the poem, she is recalling her nurse singing a song in which the Fates sing about the gods, and a narrator—possibly Iphigenie herself—concludes by commenting on the Fates' song and on the aged exile listening to it. Goethe's poem thus hinges on three types of distance: spatial distance between the gods and the banished ones, temporal distance between the original events and the poem's present, and narrative distance between the events and the telling of them.[4] Even more important than the concept of distance in Brahms's setting, however, is the shift from the mythic struggles depicted in stanzas 1–4 to the personal suffering expressed in stanzas 5 and 6.

Table 5.1. The Song (*Parzenlied*) That Concludes Iphigenie's Soliloquy in Act 4, Scene 5 of Goethe's Play

1	1 "Es fürchte die Götter		1	1 "Let the human race	
	2 Das Menschengeschlecht!			2 Fear the gods!	
	3 Sie halten die Herrschaft			3 They hold power	
	4 In ewigen Händen,			4 In eternal hands	
	5 Und können sie brauchen,			5 And can use it	
	6 Wie's ihnen gefällt.			6 As they like.	
2	7 Der fürchte sie doppelt,		2	7 Let he fear them doubly	
	8 Den je sie erheben!			8 Whom once they have elevated!	
	[STROPHE]				
	9 Auf Klippen und Wolken			9 On precipices and clouds	
	10 Sind Stühle bereitet			10 The chairs are prepared	
	11 Um goldene Tische.			11 Around golden tables.	
3	12 Erhebet ein Zwist sich:		3	12 If a quarrel arises,	
	13 So stürzen die Gäste			13 The guests topple,	
	14 Geschmäht und geschändet			14 Reviled and dishonored,	
	15 In nächtliche Tiefen,			15 Into the depths of night	
	16 Und harren vergebens,			16 And wait in vain,	
	17 Im Finstern gebunden,			17 Bound in the dark,	
	18 Gerechten Gerichtes.			18 Fair judgment.	
	[ANTISTROPHE]				
4	19 Sie aber, sie bleiben		4	19 They, however, they remain	
	20 In ewigen Festen,			20 At eternal feasts	
	21 An goldenen Tischen.			21 At golden tables.	
	22 Sie schreiten vom Berg			22 They stride from one mountain	
	23 Zu Bergen hinüber:			23 Over to others:	
	24 Aus Schlünden der Tiefe			24 From the gorges of the deep	
	25 Dampft ihnen der Atem			25 Steams upward to them the breath	
	26 Erstickter Titanen,			26 Of stifled Titans	
	27 Gleich Opfergerüchen,			27 Like the smells of sacrifices,	
	28 Ein leichtes Gewölke.			28 A thin cloud.	
5	29 Es wenden die Herrscher		5	29 The rulers turn	
	30 Ihr segnendes Auge			30 Their blessing-granting gaze	
	31 Von ganzen Geschlechtern,			31 From entire families,	
	32 Und meiden, im Enkel			32 And avoid seeing in the grandson	
	33 Die ehmals geliebten			33 The once-loved,	
	34 Still redenden Züge			34 Quietly eloquent features	
	35 Des Ahnherrn zu sehn."			35 Of the ancestor."	
6	36 So sangen die Parzen;		6	36 Thus sang the Fates;	
	37 Es horcht der Verbannte			37 The exile listens secretly	
	38 In nächtlichen Höhlen,			38 In nocturnal caverns,	
	39 Der Alte, die Lieder,			39 The old man, to the songs,	
	40 Denkt Kinder und Enkel			40 Recalls children and grandchildren	
	41 Und schüttelt das Haupt.			41 And shakes his head.	

Table 5.2. Iphigenie's Lines 1,718–25, Immediately before Her Song in Act 4, Scene 5

Vor meinen Ohren tönt das alte Lied—	In my ears sounds the old song—
Vergessen hatt' ich's und vergaß es gern—	I had forgotten it and forgotten it gladly—
Das Lied der Parzen, das sie grausend sangen,	The song of the Fates that they gruesomely sang
Als Tantalus vom goldnen Stuhle fiel.	As Tantalus fell from the golden chair.
Sie litten mit dem edeln Freunde; grimmig	They suffered with their noble friend, grim
War ihre Brust, und furchtbar ihr Gesang.	Were their souls and horrifying their song.
In unsrer Jugend sang's die Amme mir	In our youth our nurse sang it to me
Und den Geschwistern vor, ich merkt' es wohl.	And my brother and sister: I marked it well.

The *Parzenlied* does not resemble the other monologues in the play: all the monologues depart from the prevailing blank verse, but the others are pure first-person lyrics. Günther Müller, one of the few critics to focus specifically on the poem, notes this distinction and the context. He writes, "It is not Iphigenie's song; it is 'The song of the Fates that they gruesomely sang / As Tantalus fell from the golden chair,' and Iphigenie did not hear it from them but rather from her nurse, who sang it to her and her brother and sister."[5] Both of these points are made clear by Iphigenie herself in a soliloquy right before her recitation of the song (see Table 5.2). Taken on its own terms, however—which is how Brahms presents it—the poem fails to name characters other than the collective Fates, gods, and Titans as it moves from mythic vengeance and suffering in the distant past to individual suffering in the present.

Brahms insisted to Billroth that he had read the entire play while he composed his work, but he did this after asserting that *Gesang der Parzen* was no longer related to Goethe's characterization of Iphigenie. He went so far as to state that he would prefer to suppress any reference to Iphigenie on the title page.[6] By extracting the poem from the play, he had turned it into the song of the Fates as transmitted by a narrator, and it lost any necessary connection to *Iphigenie auf Tauris*. Understandably, some of Brahms's contemporaries persisted in viewing the *Parzenlied* and therefore *Gesang der Parzen* as the song of either Iphigenie or the nurse. Billroth assumed that the *Parzenlied* was the nurse's song and thus that in Goethe's time a composer would have been obliged to set it for an alto soloist. He speculated that Goethe "conceived 'nurse' as perhaps only the personified aging and already more reflective folk imagination," arguing that "Iphigenie's nurse could not possibly have thought and sung in such a way."[7]

Speidel, in contrast, understood the *Parzenlied* to be Iphigenie's song. Three years after Brahms's death, Speidel decried a theatrical practice according to which the actress playing Iphigenie steps out of character and "declaims the song with the force with which, according to theatrical ideas, the Fates may have sung it."[8] This suggests a context for Brahms's comment about Speidel that I cited at the beginning as well as for remarks by his biographer Max Kalbeck. In Vienna the tradition in question was most associated with the performance style of the actress Charlotte Wolter (1834–97), and Kalbeck connected Brahms's setting to his having attended a Viennese performance of the play with Wolter playing the lead role. Kalbeck's description of the actress's manner of reciting the song offers an opposing, positive perspective on the object of Speidel's criticism: "The tragic chorus, banished from the modern stage, seemed to have returned."[9] If we trust Kalbeck's judgment—and in this instance I believe we can—then the actress's performance was a factor in Brahms's inspired decision to remove the poem from the Enlightenment world of the play.

Brahms was not the first composer to set the poem in isolation; he himself owned copies of settings by Friedrich Reichardt (1804) and Ferdinand Hiller (1881).[10] Reichardt in fact called his piece *Lied der Parcen,* a variant of "Gesang der Parzen." But unlike Brahms, both Reichardt and Hiller omitted the final stanza and based their works solely on the Fates' perspective. Reichardt's setting is for a cappella four-part chorus in E minor, with strictly syllabic declamation, unvarying homophonic texture, and no added repetition of words. Within these self-imposed restrictions, he managed to convey the poem's extremes of imagery and affect through his use of harmony, key changes, and differentiation in dynamics. Conceiving the poem along similar lines but without limiting himself so strictly, Hiller took as his title the poem's opening warning: "Es fürchte die Götter das Menschengeschlecht!" (Let the human race fear the gods!) In contrast to Reichardt's setting, this is a large-scale composition for four-part chorus and orchestra, in which the extended setting of stanza 1 returns once and the opening two lines that provide the title recur a number of times. The work is again conceived exclusively as the song of the Fates, as in Reichardt's setting, without the interpretive complications that arise from Brahms's inclusion of the final stanza.

That Brahms commented on Hiller's setting in the spring of 1881 has gone unnoticed in the literature on *Gesang der Parzen.* In a letter to Hiller of 6 June that year, he acknowledged that he could not "do justice right away" to the other composer's chorus. Brahms added, "I myself have repeatedly worked on it and now it is with a peculiarly uneasy feeling that I read [Hiller's score] and cannot let go of ideas of my own."[11] Because earlier writers overlooked Brahms's letter to Hiller, they placed the origin of his chorus in the spring and summer of 1882.[12] The letter suggests, however, that Brahms had struggled with setting the poem well before 1881.

Since we do not have much more than Brahms's final composition to work with, we can only surmise that among the most significant of Brahms's "ideas of my own" would have been his decision to set the final stanza. The other documentary evidence regarding Brahms's choices—Kalbeck's remarks about Wolter's performance as a source of inspiration and the composer's own comments asserting that the work had little to do with *Iphigenie auf Tauris*—imply that he was deliberately going against the late eighteenth-century grain of Goethe's play. And, indeed, Brahms did draw on a wide range of musical signifiers to reinterpret the poem in line with his understanding of the spirit of classical Greek tragedy. Yet by including the last stanza, he not only turned the Fates' song into an embedded narrative, a story within a story, but also introduced an anachronistic psychological perspective at odds with the ancient tragedy that he was otherwise trying to evoke.

The Shape of Tragedy

When Aristotle discussed Euripides's *Iphigeneia in Tauris* as an exemplary tragedy in the *Poetics,* his viewpoint necessarily reflected ideas of his own time. Euripides's dramatization of the myth does not accord any better with modern ideas of tragedy than does Goethe's rendering of the story.[13] The versions by Euripides and Goethe differ in other respects, but in both plays Iphigenie removes the curse on the house of Atreus by avoiding the consecration of her brother, Orestes, for ritual sacrifice by the Taurians, and brother and sister eventually manage to leave Tauris. Because of this happy ending, one twentieth-century critic, while qualifying it as "a close-run thing," writes of the near-cliché of the "avoidance of tragedy" in Goethe's play, just as a number of modern critics decline to categorize Euripides's play as a tragedy.[14]

Goethe's *Parzenlied* has no counterpart in Euripides. Within the context of *Iphigenie auf Tauris,* it resembles, as Müller expresses it, "an erratic boulder," a seeming remnant of another era that protrudes because of its meter, subject matter, and tone.[15] Stated differently, the poem is already out of context in *Iphigenie auf Tauris,* which may account for Wolter's manner of declaiming it as if she were a one-person Greek chorus. On a more detailed level, recent critics consider the last stanza to fall beyond the confines of the poem. Even though the final stanza continues the meter of the earlier stanzas, these critics interpret it as no longer belonging to the song that the nurse used to sing but rather coming directly from Iphigenie.[16] Brahms's inclusion of it also puzzled music critics at the time.[17] But as his comments to Billroth suggest, Brahms did not view his decision to set the sixth stanza as creating a link between the poem and either the play or its title character. For the composer, it seems that the stanza fit within the poem conceived as a discrete text.

The tenor of the poem is undeniably tragic, with images of suffering and retribution and with no hint of the salvation that ameliorates the various dramatizations of the myth, including the one by Goethe. More specifically, we can assume that Brahms shared Aristotle's widely disseminated conception of tragedy.[18] Representation and response are coextensive in Aristotle's *Poetics:* tragic events are described as "fearful and pitiful" in themselves as well as capable of arousing fear and pity and then relieving those feelings.[19] Although Goethe's poem does not suggest catharsis, Hermann Kretzschmar's 1884 commentary on *Gesang der Parzen* supports a hypothesis that Brahms was attempting effects similar to those that Aristotle described:

> The impression of the whole comes as close as possible to the model that we have formed of the effect of ancient music. A somber character dominates the principal part of the work: it begins in an apprehensive tone and rises to ominous significance. At the end, with the entrance of the a cappella passage, terror and anxious wonder dissolve into a plaintive, resigned lament.[20]

Beyond eliciting effects that Kretzschmar describes in general terms, Brahms's *Gesang* pointedly alludes to two musical topoi to suggest ritual performance.[21] The forceful gestures of the opening recall a Baroque ritornello, a specifically instrumental and highly stylized theme type used in opera seria and related vocal genres. The chorus then enters at m. 20 singing the first stanza set by another theme, which I label the refrain and whose duple meter, repetitive rhythmic patterns, and prominent percussion create a processional character that evokes ritual. Because the stanza is a general warning, the setting of it can return as a refrain, as the setting of it and its first two lines did in Hiller's work.

Brahms's large-scale formal strategies were surely crucial in his efforts to maximize the expressive impact of *Gesang der Parzen*. Recognizing the importance of recurring themes, Malcolm MacDonald and Karl Geiringer consider the work to be a rondo, whereas both Christian Martin Schmidt and, with more reservations, Janina Klassen construe it as a series of free variations, thereby acknowledging a degree of motivic concentration unusual even for Brahms.[22] Tracing themes and interpreting motivic transformations will help us understand the work's shape and its affective range. But neither thematic recurrence nor motivic transformation adequately explains the various distinctions in formal function—including thematic statement, development, retransition, and recapitulation—that give the composition its power. Brahms's work invites an approach that takes all these formal processes into account without restricting the piece to a traditional schema, since he himself did not do so.

The terms *development, retransition,* and *recapitulation* are usually linked with sonata form, of course; here, however, I am referring to their functions apart from that formal schema. Moreover, as Table 5.3 shows, these formal processes are integrated into two large-scale sections or "phases" plus a postlude.

Table 5.3. Formal Phases, Formal Functions, and Topical Allusions in Brahms's Setting*

Phase	Measures	Stanza(s)	Formal Function	Topical Allusion
Introduction	1–19		Thematic Statement	Ritornello (Extended)
I	20–31	1	Thematic Statement (Refrain)	Processional
	31–35		Thematic Statement	Ritornello
	36–100	2–4	Development	
	100–103		Retransition	Processional
II	104–11	1	Recapitulation (Refrain)	Processional
	112–15		Cadential Extension of Refrain	
	116–61	5	Major-Mode Thematic Statement**	
Postlude	162–76	6	"Coda"	Ritornello (Transformed)

*As will become clear, Brahms uses some of these formal functions with considerable freedom. As will also emerge when I treat the sections in greater detail, he alludes to the ritornello topos—more precisely, he recalls the ritornello of this piece—in the development.
**This statement is audibly related to the refrain.

Following the first statement of the instrumental ritornello, each section of this basically binary organization begins with a statement of the refrain. The marked style and harmonic structure of this refrain help to underscore each of its entrances as significant. Brahms further emphasizes the binary division by postponing the arrival of a structural tonic—that is, a metrically strong, root-position tonic chord—in both phases. Indeed, the first such tonic does not appear until m. 31, when, as Table 5.3 shows, the refrain ends and the ritornello returns. He similarly delays the second structural tonic (m. 115) and also thoroughly undercuts its effect to the point that "structural" seems a misnomer.[23] This notably weak tonic provides the belated resolution for the A dominant of the unusual retransitional passage I described earlier. Recall that this retransition leads to the return of the refrain at m. 104. The dominant, however, remains the prolonged harmony beyond the thematic return, in one kind of Brahmsian recapitulatory overlap, and yields to the tonic only when the extension to the refrain's second statement ends.[24]

As my qualification of the second "structural" tonic implies, a table cannot convey much about the relative weight of the sections. My broader argument in brief is that Brahms responded to an expressive transformation in the poem and that this transformation inspired the formal approach in his setting. I understand form to be a matter of both the creation and perception of an ongoing process that encompasses themes, functions, cadences, and other markers of change. Here, the opening creates an aura of ancient theater by introducing strongly characterized themes (the ritornello and refrain) evocative of ritual, after which an adaptation of developmental procedures conveys mythic injustice. Emphatic gestures dissipate and the ceremonial themes are altered as the mythic tragedy eventually becomes personal in the closing stanzas.

Ritornello, Refrain, and Ceremonial Formalization

In calling the opening instrumental theme a "ritornello," I am invoking aria and choral types associated with opera seria and other Baroque vocal genres such as certain kinds of cantatas. Along with establishing the requisite elevated style through features such as dotted rhythms, a ritornello provides a frame through its placement at strategic formal junctures. A frame fulfills an articulative but also a distancing role, punctuating (in this case) the music and at the same time suggesting another point of view at the most basic narrative level.[25] Brahms's ritornello creates such a frame, appearing at the beginning, before stanza 2, and twice—albeit in two different keys and initially rhythmically altered—near the close of stanza 4 (in mm. 84–90, not shown in Table 5.3). When a version of the ritornello reappears at the end, the radical changes it has undergone do not cancel its identity as a frame. Indeed, further transformation of the ritornello begins as the narrator is revealed ("Thus sang the Fates"): frame-as-narrator becomes explicit as the frame starts to dissolve, and this dissolution supports the larger expressive trajectory of *Gesang der Parzen*.

The ritornello and refrain sound distinct in most respects. In contrast with the ritornello, the refrain as a processional is both balanced in its phrase structure and tonally closed; indeed, the work's only perfect authentic cadence in D appears as the refrain's conclusion overlaps with the ritornello's return in m. 31, at the first of the aforementioned structural tonics. Despite such distinctions, both themes convey a sense of ceremony, and, indeed, they share melodic motives, which the brackets in Examples 5.2 and 5.3 highlight. Motive x, a rising perfect-fourth anacrusis, initiates both themes and is followed by two versions of a lengthier second motive, labeled y in the ritornello and y^1 in the refrain. Despite its extreme brevity, motive x stands out as an entity and always signals a beginning when it returns. Motives y and y^1 appear many more times than motive x and are subjected to techniques of variation and development, with those applied to the ritornello's motive y playing a central role in the affective transformation that shapes *Gesang der Parzen*. In their initial forms, motives y and y^1 differ considerably not only in their rhythms—those of the ritornello's y form being suitable only for an instrumental theme—but also in their pitches. The chromaticism that distinguishes the pitch content of the ritornello's y from that of the refrain's y^1 requires two additional notes to return the theme to the D tonic. Motive x and the initial notes of y also appear in the phrase linking the ritornello and the refrain. After the half cadence in m. 11, the music begins to sound transitional

Example 5.2. *Gesang der Parzen,* mm. 1–5, opening ritornello.

Example 5.3. *Gesang der Parzen,* mm. 19–21, beginning of refrain.

as motives enter with the telltale anacrusis rhythm derived from the head motive of the ritornello (*x*). The motivic signals in mm. 12–19 forge a link between the ritornello and the refrain soon to enter, and other features further prepare the chorus's entrance. Measure 14 more explicitly recalls the beginning notes of the ritornello, and the motives cohere into a brief theme (mm. 15–19), after which the theme's head motive portentously expands from a major third to a perfect fourth to set the stage for the tragedy to follow.

The harmonic idioms in the ritornello seem extreme, even harsh, especially this early in a work, but they help to establish the desired tragic atmosphere. Particularly noteworthy is the stressed F♯-minor triad within the key of D minor. After a D-minor opening, the treble line in mm. 1–2 traces a D dominant seventh that resolves directly to the F♯-minor triad as a common-tone German augmented sixth (D–C♯/B♯–A–F♯) and then returns as quickly to D minor.[26] Vehement descending lines repeatedly stress B♭ as $\hat{6}$ and C♯ as $\sharp\hat{7}$, the two leading tones in D minor, to counteract the effect of the F♯-minor triad and the preceding chromatic notes.

Unlike the traditional models to which it refers, the ritornello in *Gesang der Parzen* is not tonally closed. In its basic form, it consists of four and a half measures that culminate in a strong half cadence (m. 5). To give the opening a scale and grandeur suitable for the subject matter, Brahms extends the first statement, eliding the half cadence by adding six measures, aided by a motive (z) that will later assume greater prominence (see Example 5.2, m. 5). Throughout mm. 6–11, he places extraordinary emphasis in the violins and violas on the $\hat{6}$–$\hat{5}$ (B♭–A) motion, another motive of great significance for the work as a whole.

In this initial extension, Brahms harmonizes $\hat{6}$ in a number of different ways, but at various other times in the piece, he focuses more narrowly on the ability of $\hat{6}$ to function in the minor mode as $\hat{7}$ does in the major mode. Here I am invoking the revived modal dualism formulated by Daniel Harrison to explain aspects of highly chromatic music from the late nineteenth century. Harrison's system depends on a cleaner separation of the two modes than in most theories of tonal music—hence the dualism. His theory opposes the major-mode authentic system with its dominant harmony, authentic cadences, and $\hat{7}$–$\hat{8}$ motion to the minor-mode plagal system with its subdominant harmony, plagal cadences, and $\hat{6}$–$\hat{5}$ motion.[27] Applying Harrison's ideas to a restricted repertory, I elsewhere described one type of minor-mode plagal harmony as "semi-autonomous," meaning that the dominant with its leading tone is temporarily absent and that the minor subdominant and $\hat{6}$ can therefore assume a cadential function.[28] Drawing also on Robert Hatten's application of the semiotic concept of markedness to music, I pointed out the pronounced sense of otherness conjured by this type of plagal harmony because of the conditions that severely limit its use.[29] In particular, the suppression of dominant function endows it with a striking ability to suggest states not easily conveyed in tonal music through harmonic means. In the *Gesang*'s ritornello, Brahms draws on semi-autonomous plagal harmony, which, with other instantiations of subdominant function, creates a pattern of clear and increasing importance across the work. Measures 18–20 provide a first, brief instance of semi-autonomous plagal harmony: the suppression of $\sharp\hat{7}$ after m.

16 prepares for the new harmonic style of the refrain, leaving only 6̂ to situate the key (see the B♭ in m. 19 of Example 5.3).

Both the ritornello and the refrain enhance the sense of ritual already present in Goethe's poem. More precisely, these recurring themes underscore similarities between the music and typologies of other highly formalized texts: the succession of processionals, choruses, and episodes in an entire Greek tragedy, on the one hand, and the sections of a single choric ode, on the other. I thus conjecture that Brahms interpreted Goethe's poem with both global—Greek tragedy—and local—choric quasi ode—formal strategies in mind.

Unlike Euripides's play, *Iphigenie auf Tauris* does not include a chorus; the poetic monologues instead fulfill two of the traditional choric functions: reflecting upon the dramatic action and thus momentarily halting it. Indeed, a recent biographer of Goethe, Nicholas Boyle, sees the *Parzenlied* and the other monologues as apparently "patterned either on operatic arias or on the choric elements in Greek drama." Drawing on the work of several other scholars, Boyle also stresses connections between *Iphigenie auf Tauris* as a whole and both eighteenth-century opera and the thoroughly stylized, faux-Greek traditions of French classical drama.[30] Because Boyle focuses on the play's publication in 1787 rather than its first performance in 1802, he underscores enthusiastic comments about the supposed similarity of *Iphigenie auf Tauris* to Euripides's version. Perceptions of this aspect of the play changed radically after the premiere.[31]

Without adhering in all respects to Goethe's text, Brahms devised musical correlatives—including the two opening themes—to qualities of the *Parzenlied* that isolate it and bring it closer than the rest of the play to being a simulacrum of ancient tragedy. His opening themes, the ritornello and refrain, are ceremonial, and as such they evoke the idea of music for a community. When they reappear after the central stanzas, both will undergo alteration in a pattern of ever less emphatic musical gestures. The process will entail a number of unusual, at times thwarted, cadences as the music carries out the transference from the mythic and thus communal to the personal ethos expressed in the poem. But first the music becomes more emphatic in stanzas 2–4 as a corollary to the intensifying poetic expression of the disparate conditions of the gods and their victims.

Spatial Imagery and Developmental Cycles as Tragic Expression

The absence of a hero in the *Parzenlied* restricted Brahms's approach in *Gesang der Parzen*. Specifically, this feature prevented him from developing a musical argument in which a theme and its elaboration encourage connections to the character and destiny of a tragic hero.[32] In setting stanzas 2–4, he instead responded to Goethe's depiction of the gods' misuse of their power by suggesting the course of a tragedy. The first two lines of these stanzas recall lines 1–2, "Let the human race / Fear the gods!" In contrast to this general warning, the variant in lines 7–8 prepares the specific situation of the central stanzas: "Let he fear them doubly / Whom once they have elevated!" To my knowledge, no one has noted in print that Goethe modeled the remaining lines of stanzas 2–4 on the structure of Greek choric odes, which typically consist of paired strophes and antistrophes, each antistrophe "echoing" but also qualifying the preceding strophe.[33] Emulating a classical strophe and antistrophe, the *Parzenlied* moves twice in ten-line segments (9–18, 19–28) from the gods' eternal feasts to those whom they have condemned to unending torment (see Table 5.1). Goethe expresses the separation between the two worlds through stark spatial images, images that he subsequently intensifies in the antistrophe.

Several decades before he composed *Gesang der Parzen,* Brahms acquired an edition of Sophocles's tragedies.[34] If for no other reasons than that this edition marks each "Strophe" and "Gegenstrophe" in Sophocles's choric odes and that he was an alert and sensitive reader, Brahms would likely have been aware that Goethe pairs lines 9–18 and 19–28 in the same way. Self-evidently, he also would have observed that Goethe separates lines 7–8 from the following lines. Yet Brahms did not adhere either to Goethe's punctuation at the end of line 8 or to his strophe-antistrophe organization of the rest of stanzas 2–4. Instead he redivided those stanzas in their entirety into two cycles of eleven lines: lines 7–17 and 18–28 (see Table 5.4).[35] A comparison of Tables 5.1 and 5.4 reveals this fundamental difference between the approaches of poet and composer. Whereas

Table 5.4. Brahms's Reorganization of Stanzas 2–4: Compare with Table 5.1

Cycle I	*Cycle II*
Transition/Introduction (mm. 36–39)	**Transition/Introduction (mm. 69–71)**
7 Der fürchte sie doppelt,	18 Gerechten Gerichtes.
8 Den je sie erheben!	**Realm of the gods (mm. 72–83)**
Realm of the gods (mm. 40–47)	19 Sie aber, sie bleiben
9 Auf Klippen und Wolken	20 In ewigen Festen
10 Sind Stühle bereitet	21 An goldenen Tischen.
11 Um goldene Tische.	22 Sie schreiten vom Berge
Those banished to the depths (mm. 48–68)	23 Zu Bergen hinüber:
12 Erhebet ein Zwist sich:	**Those banished to the depths (mm. 84–100)**
13 So stürzen die Gäste	24 Aus Schlünden der Tiefe
14 Geschmäht und geschändet	25 Dampft ihnen der Atem
15 In nächtliche Tiefen,	26 Erstickter Titanen,
16 Und harren vergebens,	27 Gleich Opfergerüchen,
17 Im Finstern gebunden,	28 Ein leichtes Gewölke.

Goethe adopted a symmetrical Greek model in lines 9–28 of his poem, itself part of a larger drama, Brahms molded all of stanzas 2–4 into an alternative textual symmetry to make his setting of the poem stand for a tragic whole.

Ignoring the sense and structure of this text—in a manner anomalous within his secular choral works—allowed Brahms to achieve the sense of tremendous import that comes from overriding expected musical phrase-endings.[36] Thus, whereas Goethe's punctuation segregates lines 7–8 from the rest of the stanza, Brahms's dotted figuration overflows the measure, linking line 8 with the images of godly grandeur to follow (see mm. 38–40)—to great effect but in violation of both syntax and semantics. Brahms likewise worked against the contextual meaning of "Fair judgment" (line 18). Rather than attaching this phrase, which ends stanza 3, to those waiting for justice in lines 16–17, as the poem does, he connected it (m. 69ff.) to the gods in the following stanza (lines 19–21), in large part to avoid closure.

Brahms does respond to the rich density of the images provided by Goethe's poem in lines 9–28 with suitable musical correlatives, using the resources of tone painting: changes in register, mode, texture, and figuration as well as transformation of motives. Kalbeck singled out Brahms's setting of the gods' striding between mountains giving way to his setting of the oppression of those below (lines 22–26), at the end of which (mm. 88–90) a "colossal bass motive [from mm. 3–5] rises like the shadow of a giant."[37] Here and elsewhere in his commentary, Kalbeck remained at the level of individual images rendered in sound. Techniques of development such as fragmentation, sequential patterning, and "roving harmony," however, unite the diverse musical images and emphasize the overarching textual image of spatial distance that conceptually unifies these lines.[38] The distance represents the difference in power between the gods and those whom they oppress: this is the apparent source of the tragedy expressed here, and the cyclic form suggests that the suffering will not end.

Brahms set his two-part arrangement of lines 7–28 (see Table 5.4) to related sections of music. To initiate this musical double cycle, he set line 7 (m. 36) so as to resemble the refrain while also audibly differing from it, as the text here does from that of the refrain. He reduced the opening of the refrain to the first measure, replaced the ascending fourth in motive x with a descending third, and made an open fifth the final interval (compare Examples 5.4 and 5.3). This variant enters after the half cadence of the second ritornello (m. 35, not shown),

Example 5.4. *Gesang der Parzen*, mm. 36–39, soprano line only.

also altered in that F replaces E in the A dominant, weakening the sense of half closure and thereby helping to set the developmental process in motion.

A tercet that includes a reference to the gods' golden tables occurs once in each cycle (lines 9–11 and 19–21). (Here I understand a tercet to be a grammatically self-sufficient unit of three lines rather than a three-line stanza.) Table 5.1 seems to attribute a different poetic function to each of these units, since the first tercet concludes stanza 2 and the second begins stanza 4. In Goethe's symmetrical pairing, however, the first tercet begins the strophe and the second, the antistrophe. And Brahms's redivision of the poem, given in Table 5.4, causes each tercet to appear as the second section in each cycle (beginning at mm. 40 and 72, respectively). Each time, the musical setting of the "golden tables" tercet (mm. 40–47 and 72–78) is based on a leisurely chord progression in C major that moves from an F-major triad to an imperfect authentic cadence; only the type of figuration differs. After each statement of this progression, the music moves upward from the cadential C triad to its Neapolitan, Dâ™. At this point, events in the two cycles begin to diverge.

In Cycle I, an abrupt shift to Dâ™ octaves in m. 48 leads to faster moving, chromatic, rising sequences of fragments from motive y^1 at a sudden *fortissimo*. This intensification corresponds to the affective change in the text, "If a quarrel arises / The guests topple / Reviled and dishonored," which Brahms set twice (in mm. 48–52 and 55–56).[39] Each time, the quicker development slows on the words "Into the depths of night" (in mm. 53–54 and mm. 57–60) to stress Dâ™ as â™$\hat{2}$, with its long-standing connotations of pathos, within an abandoned cadence and then a perfect authentic cadence in C minor.[40] At the cadence of m. 60, motive z, which resembles a linear dominant ninth chord without the leading tone, reappears in the bassoons as an outgrowth of the local C tonic to undermine the resolution, just as in m. 5 it elided the attempted half cadence (see Example 5.5a). Now motive z also becomes the source of a set of three-note motives (see Example 5.5b as well as the bracketed three-note motives in Example 5.5a). The new motives both effect momentary modulations and, through their fragmented nature, convey the powerlessness of those who "wait in vain."

At a subsequent cadence in Bâ™ minor in m. 65, the upper strings introduce a descending variant of motive z. Because of the higher register, this motive, z^1, is more prominent than z was. Furthermore, the haunting manner in which it is altered serves to emphasize the sighing F–E half step, as the depiction of powerlessness deepens with the setting of "Bound in the dark" (mm. 66–68; see Examples 5.5a and 5.5b). Like motive z, z^1 weakens the effect of the cadence, and it is the source of the same three-note motives, which now appear in a different order. C-major and E-minor triads emerge from the harmonic reinterpretation of these motives and lead to one of the most extraordinary effects in *Gesang*

Example 5.5a. *Gesang der Parzen,* mm. 60–68, with motives z and z^1 and two three-note motives derived from them indicated with brackets.

Motive z (m. 60): C–B♭–G–C–D♭

Motive z^1 (m. 65): F–G–B♭–F–E

Derived three-note motives in mm. 60–61 and mm. 65–66:

B♭–C–D♭ (m. 61, soprano and mm. 65.4–66.2, tenor)

D♭–C–B♭ (m. 61, tenor and mm. 65.4–66.3, bass)

E–F–G (mm. 60.4–61.3, bass and m. 66, tenor)

G–F–E (mm. 60.4–61.2, alto and m. 66, soprano)

Example 5.5b. Motives z and z^1 and three-note derived motives in mm. 60–61 and 65–66.

der Parzen. Brahms ostentatiously uses a *Leittonwechsel* to connect the E-minor triad to a C-major triad—the dynamics change from *pianissimo* to *forte* as the musical line rises to begin the new cycle (mm. 69–71)—while defying both sense and syntax in placing "Fair judgment" on high with the gods. His primary objective in doing this appears not to have been irony. Evidently, he sought instead to maintain in the music the continuity that he fashioned in the text and at the same time to underscore the increasing disparity between the images of the gods above and the condemned ones below.

Semitone substitutions and semitone motion preoccupy Brahms through-out his setting of stanzas 2–4. The semitone motions, especially those that descend, connect motivically to the repeated B♭–A figures observed earlier in the first ritornello and simultaneously call up the traditional connotations of sorrow or lamentation held by those figures. This preoccupation with half-step motion—although here it involves raised or rising semitones—is evident already in the initial progression from the altered half cadence on A at the end of the second ritornello (m. 35) to the B♭ triad that begins the setting of these stanzas (m. 36).[41] Along with the descending sighing motives and the rising *Leittonwechsel*, half-step relationships in Cycle I arise from quasi-Neapolitan (e.g., mm. 53–54 and 58–60), augmented sixth (e.g., m. 63), and diminished seventh chords (e.g., mm. 61 and 66) and their resolutions.

Half-step relationships also resonate on larger structural levels: Brahms presents first C major and C minor and then D♭ major and C♯ minor as local keys. Drawing on the traditional major-minor opposition—and in particular C major's connotations of splendor and purity—he associates C major and D♭ major with the gods and C minor and C♯ minor with those imprisoned below. Despite the rapid rate of surface harmonic change, all of Cycle I and almost half of Cycle II (mm. 69–79) prolong C major/minor. Together with the assertion of C major in mm. 69–71, the cadences in C major and C minor in mm. 47, 60, and 79 strongly establish C. At the same time, however, cadential closure is weakened because of overlaps with subsequent phrases within a cyclical musical form.

Even more than the text of Cycle I, that of Cycle II emphasizes the gap between might on high and misery below. After another sudden semitone shift in m. 80, Brahms expresses the gods' striding between mountains through a slow-moving, rising sequence of major triads a major third apart—D♭–F–A (mm. 80–83)—that almost succeeds in symmetrically dividing a D♭ octave. Instead, the A in the bass sinks to G♯ at m. 84, and a return of the ritornello heralds the beginning of Brahms's setting of "From the gorges of the deep / Steams upward to them the breath / Of stifled Titans," a stronger statement of the plight of the gods' victims. And in contrast to the treatment of C in Cycle I, Cycle II more decisively tonicizes D♭/C♯, as the cycle begins to uncoil and the music starts to follow a straightforward linear course. This new turn of events places in greater relief the conflict between the major-mode (now D♭) world of the gods and the newly revealed C♯ minor as key for the realm of the reviled ones, and it will end in a tragic climax.

First the ritornello begins to return. Measures 84–85 recall the harmonies and treble line (motive *y*) from mm. 1–2 but transposed to G♯. Example 5.6 highlights this connection as well as a connection to the succeeding transposition to C♯, the entire passage (mm. 84–87) prolonging the G♯ dominant. The harmonies

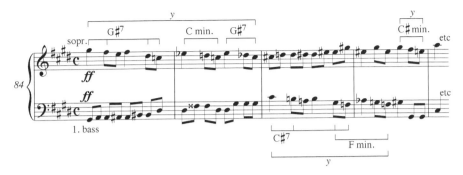

Example 5.6. *Gesang der Parzen,* m. 84–downbeat of m. 88, soprano and first bass lines (the entire passage prolongs the G♯ dominant).

and melodic intervals derive from the ritornello, but the source of the rhythmic pattern is the refrain: since Brahms sets poetic text here, he needs a more vocal style than appeared in the original ritornello. In mm. 86–87 the sopranos and basses reverse their roles in invertible counterpoint at the octave, replicating the same harmonies. At the end of m. 87, the erstwhile bass line returns to the treble to set in motion an exact recollection of mm. 3–5, the ritornello's conclusion, in C♯ minor (mm. 88–90). Recalling the ritornello's first two measures twice should have prepared this moment. It is nevertheless shocking because of the sudden rhythmic exactness, the vehemence (as in the first ritornello), and the fact that until now we have heard the material performed only by the orchestra.

When motive *z* reappears in m. 90 and is immediately imitated in inversion from the C♯ above (*z*[1]), as highlighted by brackets in Example 5.7, it again produces the sighing motive, here C♯–B♯. Otherwise, however, it creates a different effect. Rather than fragmenting into three-note motives, motive *z* leads in Cycle II to extended variants of the entire motive as dominant sevenths, half-dimin-

Example 5.7. *Gesang der Parzen,* m. 90–beat 3 of m. 92.

ished sevenths, or triads, presented in both angular instrumental and smoother vocal styles. That they are extended rather than fragmented is due to the slower surface harmonic motion. All of the momentary applied chords associated with the motive forms as well as the chords to which they are applied in mm. 92–97—involving more semitone resolutions—further underscore the G♯ dominant. A sustained prolongation of this dominant, especially after the assertion of its major-mode tonic in mm. 80–83, proves to be more powerful than the intermittent insistence on C earlier in the double cycle. Indeed, as mentioned at the beginning of this essay, the prolonged G♯ dominant creates strong anticipation of a resolution to C♯, hence the shattering effect of the deceptive resolution in m. 100 (see Example 5.1). The tragedy has culminated in the required catastrophe.[42]

Plagal Harmony and Anachronistic Humanism

Gesang der Parzen never fully recovers from the curtailed conclusion of stanza 4. Brahms has heavily weighted the first one hundred measures and weakened the rest of the work in pursuit of a larger effect. Although the initial two passages that follow the climactic deceptive resolution in m. 100 are undoubtedly a retransition and a recapitulation, Brahms deliberately undermines their effectiveness in fulfilling these roles. It is true that the key of D minor returns with the refrain; indeed, D is indisputably the foreground tonic throughout *Gesang der Parzen,* except in the developmental setting of stanzas 2–4 (mm. 36–100). Yet when the refrain reenters in m. 104, it does so in a restrained manner, *sotto voce*; the dynamics never rise above *mezzo forte* after m. 100, and the music reaches *mf* itself only once and briefly in mm. 109–10. Moreover, after m. 103, the altered refrain, the major-mode theme with which Brahms sets the fifth stanza, and the transformed ritornello involve three new perspectives on D-ness that both demonstrate his characteristic finesse in key articulation and support his conception of musical tragedy.[43]

Each interpretation of D-ness also engages plagal harmony in a different way. I am construing *plagal harmony* to include subdominant function in both major and minor keys.[44] Here as before, the beginning of the refrain—like the retransition that precedes it and the lead-in to the original statement (mm. 18–19)—relies on intimations of plagal-modal harmony to evoke antiquity. But now the refrain ends with a distinctly nonmodal plagal cadence. Brahms replaces the final four measures with a new conclusion based on the transitional motives that first entered in mm. 12–13. This time, however, the conclusion leads to a cadential motive in mm. 114–15. F♯ replaces F in these measures, making the harmony in m. 114 a D dominant seventh, a harmony also found in mm. 1–2. Now, however, this dominant progresses to a G-major rather than an F♯-minor triad.

The subsequent plagal cadence in m. 115 concludes the refrain with the second "structural" tonic I described previously, the decided weakness of which is thoroughly in keeping with the general tapering-off in the composition after m. 100.

Stanzas 1–4 had concerned grandly mythic situations; in line with the new focus on humans in stanzas 5–6, the nature of the poetic discourse changes. The final stanzas make more pronounced use of "shifters," a category that Jonathan Culler defines as "'orientational' features of language which relate to the situation of an utterance." As examples of such "deictic" words, he notes "first and second person pronouns . . . , anaphoric articles and demonstratives which refer to an external context rather than to other elements in the discourse [and] adverbials of place and time whose reference depends on the situation of utterance."[45] The implied speaker ("I") throughout and the addressee ("you") in the opening stanza and lines 7–8, for example, are left open. Shifters in the fifth stanza include "The rulers," "the grandson," "the once-loved," and "the ancestor" and, in the sixth stanza, "The exile" and "The old man." When the poem appears in the play, the deictic features imply the story of Iphigenie's family; removed from the play, the poem requires that readers construct a context, which need not be as specific as the situation in the play. Although Brahms would not have framed his views in these terms, the referents' open-endedness likely formed part of the appeal of these last two stanzas.

When the instrumental extension (mm. 112–15) enters to conclude the abbreviated refrain, the processional topos and its communal connotations disappear in preparation for the increasingly personal orientation in the fifth and sixth stanzas. The plagal cadence itself anticipates the changed style in the fifth stanza, with its conspicuous application of subdominant function and its nonprocessional triple meter, a cappella passages, and key of D major. Contrary to Classical practice, the major mode has been the marked term of the major/minor binary pair in this work, reserved until now for the world of the gods (mm. 36–47 and 69–83).[46]

From the time of the premiere, Brahms's setting of the fifth stanza has been the most enigmatic aspect of *Gesang der Parzen*. The very difference between the stanza and what came before may suggest fundamental shifts in the poem (from past to present and mythic to personal); nevertheless, the musical affect appears to contradict a text concerned with unrelenting vengefulness. Some writers have attributed Brahms's setting of this stanza to his desire to make the situation appear less bleak than it is. Others have suggested that the music cried out for contrast at this point, and still others have seen the poem as referring to the play here.[47] Many years after composing the work, however, Brahms offered a different explanation: "I believe that through the mere entrance of the major mode the hearts of unsuspecting listeners must become soft, their eyes moist because for the first time the utter misery of humanity touches them."[48] He thus attributed his compositional choices to a desire to induce the catharsis associated with performance of a tragedy, an effect that Kretzschmar had implied in an article quoted earlier.

Whether or not Brahms achieved his goal, the affect and musical means in his setting of the stanza are more complicated than his critics appear to recognize.[49] This complexity arises in part from his adroit use of both versions of subdominant–tonic progression: the major-mode progression that relies on the $\hat{4}$–$\hat{3}$ semitone and the minor-mode type based on $\hat{6}$–$\hat{5}$ motion that I described earlier.[50] Since the fifth stanza is in a major key, $\hat{4}$–$\hat{3}$ appears more often. Still, both semitones achieve motivic status, both relate to the $\hat{6}$–$\hat{5}$ motions at the beginning, and, as in previous passages, they contribute to the mournful tone of the composition. Further, as Donald Francis Tovey observed—without distinguishing between major and minor—the subdominant is "an anti-dominant having the opposite effect to the dominant."[51] Without necessarily evoking the marked otherness of semi-autonomous plagal harmony, the effect of subdominant–tonic motion runs contrary to the sense of striving forward of the dominant–tonic motion that supports the tonal system in general. In stanzas 2–4 dominant–tonic motion contributes to the depiction of the mythic conflicts between the gods and the condemned ones. The half-step motives and their plagal setting, in contrast, are basic to Brahms's new approach in the fifth stanza, with its gradual preparation for the shift to still more personal realms of suffering in the sixth.

Reintroducing B♭ (♭$\hat{6}$) at the beginning of stanza 5 clouds D major with minor-subdominant darkness and produces a subtle blurring of functions.[52] In an archetypal example of a diminished seventh with subdominant function, B♭ appears in the treble voices against G ($\hat{4}$) in the bass line in m. 116.[53] After subsequent emphasis on straightforward major subdominant harmony within this first phrase, ♭$\hat{6}$ reappears in an imperfect authentic cadence in m. 121 (Example 5.8) and again, when the phrase is repeated, in m. 127. In these cadences, Brahms suspends the upper three notes of an A dominant seventh chord across the bar line while replacing the inner-voice A with B♭ before resolving the assembled notes to a D-major triad.

Example 5.8. *Gesang der Parzen*, m. 121.

No doubt with the aim of moving listeners to tears, Brahms sets "The once loved / Quietly eloquent features / Of the ancestor" (mm. 134–39 and 148–53) with special tenderness, even though it may at first violate our sense of the stanza as a whole. In these measures, he chooses to stress that the ancestor was once loved, rather than that revenge against his descendants is unending, and Brahms does this by drawing on the capacity of subdominant–tonic motion to suggest retrospection, the past, and other connotations of receding as opposed to progressing. The $\hat{4}$–$\hat{3}$ motion becomes most pronounced in these measures. Functioning as subdominant of C major, an F-major triad initiates the first of several stages of harmonic motion to the A dominant of m. 144 in the first iteration (see the tenor line in mm. 136–43) and then to the D-major tonic of m. 160 in the second (mm. 150–61). Example 5.9 gives the soprano and second bass lines of the latter passage. Here, Brahms dwells on the sopranos' series of descending semitone motions: F–E (mm. 150–53), C–B (m. 155), and G–F♯ (mm. 157–59).

A remarkable clash between the $\hat{4}$–$\hat{3}$ and ♭$\hat{6}$–$\hat{5}$ versions of the half-step motive occurs in the final cadence (mm. 157–59 in Example 5.9). Beginning in m. 156, Brahms embellishes the A dominant with a first-inversion minor subdominant, thus not only injecting the darkness associated with that use of ♭$\hat{6}$ but also placing the B♭–A motion in the bass. In m. 159 G resolves to F♯ as a final iteration of B♭ enters in the bass, producing, as a linear by-product, an augmented triad. When this B♭ definitively moves to A in m. 160, the A "supports" a tonic. Measures 157–60 thus blur surface functions to a greater degree than before. That these measures also create more extended dissonance, after the tenderness of the plagal progressions in mm. 150–55, suggests the present plight of the once-loved one.

The alteration of the refrain's conclusion—the elimination of its processional qualities and the plagal cadence in D major at m. 115—introduced the poetic shift from mythic to personal tragedy in the fifth stanza. In setting the sixth stanza, Brahms more thoroughly reimagined the ritornello's expressive potential. He alluded to one aspect of this transformation in a letter of August 1882, af-

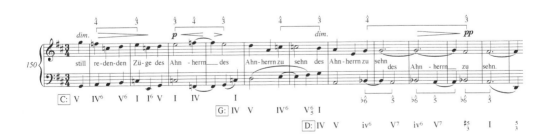

Example 5.9. *Gesang der Parzen,* mm. 150–61, soprano and second bass lines.

Table 5.5. Versions of Motive *y* and Their Resolutions in the Postlude of *Gesang der Parzen*

mm. 162–164.2 Version of *y*: D–C–A–F♯
    164.3–165 Horizontal resolution of 6̂, D, to C♯ followed by other notes in the
                  F♯-minor triad (voices, bassoons, D horns)
    164.3–165 Vertical resolution to C♯ 6̂–5̂, after which inversions of C♯ dominant
                  or E♯ diminished seventh decorate F♯-minor triad

mm. 166–168.2 Version of *y*: F♯–E–C♯–A♯
    168.3–169 Horizontal resolution of 6̂, G♭, to F, followed by other notes in the
                  B♭-minor triad (voices, violas, cellos, bassoons)
    168.3–169 Vertical resolution to F-minor 6̂–5̂, which begins a descending 6̂–5̂
                  sequence

mm. 170–171 Version of *y*: B♭–A♭–F–D
    172.3–174 Horizontal resolution of 6̂, B♭, to A, followed by other notes in the
                  D-minor triad (voices and instruments); the violas' A♭ resolves at the
                  same time, also to A♮, but only implicitly and after a rest
    172.3–174 Vertical resolution: there is no explicit resolution because *y* itself
                  does not appear as a chord

ter Billroth had tentatively objected to the "horrible severity" of mm. 1–2. After requesting that his friend "reflect for a moment on the first F♯-minor chord," Brahms asked Billroth to consider "how ineffective the modulations in the postlude would have been if one had not heard this progression repeatedly and most emphatically right at the beginning!"[54]

In the postlude, Brahms gradually exposes the harmonic meaning of the ritornello's motive *y*, which outlines a dominant seventh that resolves enharmonically as an augmented sixth chord, as it did in the opening measures to the F♯ harmony that Billroth found so troubling. Each of three successive versions of mm. 1–2 that, together, symmetrically divide the D octave through root motion of D–F♯/G♭–B♭–D is now stretched to fill four measures (see Table 5.5).[55] The second version, oriented around the F♯/G♭ dominant (mm. 166–69), softens the longer of the rhythmic figures in the initial *y* motive (mm. 162–65), thus starting a liquidation process: the double-dotted quarter note becomes a less pointed figure, a quarter note tied to an eighth-note triplet. In the third version (mm. 170–74), the figuration disappears altogether to reveal *y*'s basic shape: an ostensible dominant seventh (B♭–A♭–F–D) in the violins, flute, and piccolo.

One consequence of setting the fifth stanza in D major was that it restored the emotional impact of the minor mode; now Brahms invests D minor with a different character. The transformation of the ritornello began as the narrator was revealed ("Thus sang the Fates"). It appears, however, that Brahms wants us to focus not on the narrator but rather on the old exile, the most human figure in the poem, and he expresses the increasing retreat into one person's psyche through increasing reliance on $\hat{6}$ (B♭) as sole leading tone in the natural minor mode. Each apparent dominant seventh/augmented sixth is sustained for two and a half measures, and Brahms progressively minimizes the $\sharp\hat{4}$ in that sonority in favor of ♭$\hat{6}$. During these measures different voices in the chorus repeatedly chant the pitch that is $\hat{6}$ in relation to the minor key/triad to which it will resolve: D in mm. 162–63, F♯/G♭ in mm. 166–67, and B♭ in mm. 170–71 (see Table 5.5). Both the voices and the instrumental bass line also place special stress on the $\hat{6}$–$\hat{5}$ motion—for example, D to C♯ in m. 164—before outlining other notes in the triad of resolution, and dominant function in effect disappears after m. 165.[56] After the basic shape of motive y is laid bare in mm. 170–71, it resolves with the utmost understatement, when $\hat{6}$ moves to $\hat{5}$ of the D-minor tonic on the third beat of m. 172. For each successive iteration of $\hat{6}$, Brahms reserves the moment of resolution for the first stressed syllable in lines 37, 39, and 41—"The exile listens secretly," "The old man, to the songs," and "And shakes his head"—lines that emphasize the poignancy of the man's situation.

In setting this final stanza, Brahms, for the only time in the work, calls for a piccolo, a rare instrument throughout his oeuvre. The D horn plays the x motive (A–D) at the cadence in m. 161, initiating, through linkage, a series of imitative statements first by the trumpets and oboes and then by the violins playing an octave higher and simultaneously by the piccolo yet an octave higher. This expansion in register establishes a musical correlative to the text's narrative distance that is further accentuated when the contrabassoon enters in its lowest register in m. 172 before the final resolution of $\hat{6}$.[57] Still, narrative distance is secondary in importance to the paradoxical psychological closeness that emerges in the final stanza in an all-encompassing effect of almost unmitigated musical desolation. Although brief passages such as the beginning of the refrain and the retransition were based on plagal-modal idioms, the features that evoked the processional topos counteracted the usual tendencies of those idioms, which exaggerate the general receding quality of subdominant–tonic motion. Nothing minimizes those tendencies when they reappear at the very end.

Because of its very difference from the unmarked authentic system, this semi-autonomous plagal harmony "can suggest qualities or states not easily conveyed in tonal music through harmonic means." These conditions include "otherworldliness, distance, timelessness, possibly even alienation"; such harmony can also intimate "something other than, outside of, or prior to tonal music."[58] Here, in a setting that now hinges on transformations of the ritornello, the sense of estrangement from tonal norms gives rise to connotations of estrangement writ large. The increasing importance given to plagal harmony thus conveys the old man's feelings of regret and his state of exile, his position outside the dynamic, self-fulfilling world historically associated with the tonic–dominant axis of the tonal system.

Still, the piece concludes with an expressively ambiguous acoustic effect. In yet another minor plagal gesture, the pitches E, G, and B♭ resolve over a sustained D in the bass to an apparent open fifth, which Brahms nevertheless orchestrates so that a major third will invariably sound in the high winds.[59] Is this spectral Picardy third meant to suggest some hope and solace?

In his review of the premiere, Kalbeck found Brahms's inclusion of the final stanza confusing: "By bringing in a particular, utterly unsupportable [dramatic] situation, the poem's universally valid content is placed into question."[60] The distinction, articulated by Kalbeck and others, between the human particularity of the final stanza and the grandly suprapersonal nature of the poem's first four stanzas has been a consistent thread in discussions of the play as a whole. In these discussions, it is reframed as an opposition between the perceived harshness and fatalism of the world of Euripides's play and Goethe's reinterpretation of Iphigenie in the spirit of the Enlightenment: she must follow her conscience in making a difficult decision.

Goethe's own perspective on *Iphigenie auf Tauris* changed before it was finally performed in 1802, fifteen years after its publication. In a letter to Schiller, he referred to the play as having turned out, contrary to his conscious intentions when he wrote it in the 1770s and 1780s, to be "diabolically humane."[61] Schiller himself called it "astonishingly modern and un-Greek."[62] Almost a century later, Brahms in effect recapitulated Goethe's change of attitude toward his play within his own composition by evoking a severely ritualistic, "ancient Greek" type of tragic expression in the beginning and then revealing a contemporary human focus at the end.

Brahms followed through on his wish to omit any reference to Iphigenie on the title page of his work: a futile act, for, as Kalbeck remarked, "every German knew" the source of the text.[63] Moreover, in setting the final stanza, he included a passage that suggested the play's "diabolically humane" perspective—here, the rueful feelings of an old man about the effect of the past on his children and grandchildren. Out of context, the stanza no longer refers to Iphigenie and Goethe's reinterpretation of Greek myth, but Goethe's worldview remains, as Brahms no doubt realized.

A number of writers have noted not only the changing stance of Goethe and others toward *Iphigenie auf Tauris* but also the problematic nature of its "humanity." Concerning Euripides's drama, Martin Swales writes: "For all its concentration upon the human psychological drama, the gods and goddesses, the demons and furies are ultimately operative," whereas in Goethe's drama "the centre of gravity, the mechanism of arbitration, moves unequivocally from the transcendental plane to the human one." Human beings have been blessed or cursed with the responsibility for making ethical choices: "The darkness, in other words, is still there; indeed, the darkness may be the more profound because of the element of human choice."[64]

It is likely that Brahms would have agreed with this observation. If he believed that his setting of the penultimate, fifth stanza would make "unsuspecting listeners" aware of "the utter misery of humanity"—an effect intensified by his treatment of the final stanza—he would have attributed that misery not to the gods or even fate but rather to human actions. The story of Iphigenie may not qualify as a tragedy according to most critics, and in this sense *Gesang der Parzen* "isn't Goethe's Iphigenie," as Brahms insisted to Billroth. By setting an isolated passage from Goethe's play, Brahms was nevertheless able to evoke tragedy and, by focusing on its "un-Greek" human element but without referring to Goethe's version of the character Iphigenie, to turn it into an even deeper tragedy.

ACKNOWLEDGMENTS

I thank the University of North Texas for a Research and Creativity Enhancement Award, which allowed me to conduct research in Vienna and to write this essay. I thank Clare Carrasco, a doctoral student in musicology at the University of North Texas, for her close and insightful reading of a late draft of the manuscript.

NOTES

1. See, for example, Karl Geiringer, *Brahms: His Life and Work,* 3rd ed. (New York: Da Capo Press, 1981), 322.

2. Brahms to Theodor Billroth, 6 August 1882, in *Billroth und Brahms im Briefwechsel,* ed. Otto Gottlieb-Billroth (Berlin: Urban & Schwarzenberg, 1935), 337: "Ich höre schon Speidel sagen, das sei nicht die Goethesche Iphigenie, und allerdings ist das Parzenlied nicht Iphigenia [*sic*]." Unless otherwise indicated, all translations are by the author.

3. Johann Wolfgang Goethe, *Iphigenie auf Tauris* (Stuttgart: Phillip Reclam Jun., 1984), 50–51, lines 1,726–66. Stanzas and lines are numbered for ease of reference in Table 5.1; the first edition of Brahms's composition presented the poem at the beginning and divided it into six stanzas, as Table 5.1 does.

4. The last type of distance is characteristic of all narratives. There is substantial literature on narrative, with Gérard Genette the seminal theorist in the field. See his *Narrative Discourse: An Essay in Method,* trans. Jane E. Lewin (Ithaca, N.Y.: Cornell University Press, 1980) and *Narrative Discourse Revisited,* trans. Jane E. Lewin (Ithaca, N.Y.: Cornell University Press, 1988). Writing about ancient Greek tragedies, John Gould challenges

Genette's claim (in *Narrative Discourse Revisited*, 41) of a "truly insurmountable opposition between dramatic representation and narrative." Gould bases his arguments in part on the treatment of time in Greek tragedies and, in particular, the frequent, detailed reference to past events within them. See "'. . . And Tell Sad Stories of the Deaths of Kings': Greek Tragic Drama as Narrative," in *Myth, Ritual, Memory, and Exchange: Essays in Greek Literature and Culture* by John Gould (Oxford: Oxford University Press, 2001), 319–34. Carolyn Abbate, the key figure among musicologists, places special emphasis on the distance inherent in narratives. See *Unsung Voices: Opera and Musical Narrative in the Nineteenth Century* (Princeton, N.J.: Princeton University Press, 1991).

5. Günther Müller, "Das Parzenlied der Iphigenie," in *Morphologische Poetik: Gesammelte Aufsätze* by Günther Müller, ed. Elena Müller (Tübingen: Max Niemeier Verlag, 1968), 511: "Es ist nicht Iphigenies Lied, es ist 'Das Lied der Parzen, das sie grausend sangen, / Als Tantalus vom goldnen Stuhle fiel,' und nicht von ihnen hat Iphigenie es gehört, sondern von der Amme, die es ihr und den Geschwistern vorsang."

6. Brahms to Theodor Billroth, 6 August 1882, in Gottlieb-Billroth, *Billroth und Brahms im Briefwechsel*, 337.

7. Theodor Billroth to Brahms, 3 August 1882, in Gottlieb-Billroth, *Billroth und Brahms im Briefwechsel*, 333: "sich unter 'Amme' wohl nur die personifizierte alternde und schon mehr reflektierende Volksphantasie gedacht; Iphigeniens Amme kann unmöglich so gedacht und gesungen haben."

8. In an essay that Brahms scholars seem to have missed, Speidel was expressing his enthusiasm for an actress who had finally broken with this tradition. "Stella Hohenfels als Iphigenie," in *Kritische Schriften*, ed. Julius Rütsch (Zurich: Artemis Verlag, 1963), 304: "das Lied mit der Stärke rezitiert, wie es nach Theaterbegriffen die Parzen mochten gesungen haben." In an obituary for Charlotte Wolter (*Neue freie Presse*, 17 June 1897) reprinted in the same volume, Speidel described an actress who initially lacked every quality the role required but who then grew into it over some two decades. "Charlotte Wolter: 1834–1897," 280–81. On the personal falling-out between Brahms and Speidel, well known to Brahms scholars, see Max Kalbeck, *Johannes Brahms* (Tutzing: Hans Schneider, 1976), 2:427.

9. Kalbeck, *Johannes Brahms*, 3:356: "Der von der modernen Bühne verbannte tragische Chor schien zurückgekehrt."

10. J. F. Reichardt, *Göthe's Lieder Oden, Balladen und Romanzen; zweite Abtheilung: Vermischte Gesänge und Declamationen* (Leipzig: Breitkopf und Härtel, 1804), 42–43. The score is listed in Kurt Hofmann, *Die Bibliothek von Johannes Brahms: Bücher- und Musikalienverzeichnis*, Schriftenreihe zur Musik (Hamburg: Wagner, 1974), 160. Ferdinand Hiller, *"Es fürchtet die Götter das Menschengeschlecht" aus Goethes* Iphigenie (Leipzig: Breitkopf und Härtel, 1881). Hofmann lists this in *Die Bibliothek von Brahms*, 154. This score is hard to find. I thank Randy Kinnett for looking at Brahms's copy in Vienna before I had a chance to do so myself.

11. Reinhold Sietz, *Aus Ferdinand Hillers Briefwechsel, Band IV (1876–1881): Beiträge zu einer Biographie Ferdinand Hillers* (Cologne: Arno Volk-Verlag, 1965), 165: "nicht sogleich gerecht werden"; "Ich habe eben selbst öfter daran laborirt und nun ist es ein eigen unruhiges Gefühl mit dem ich lese und meine besonderen Gedanken nicht los werden kann!" Later letters between Hiller and various correspondents make clear Hiller's bitterness about Brahms's having set Goethe's text so soon after he did.

12. See, for example, Siegfried Kross, *Johannes Brahms: Versuch einer kritischen Dokumentar-Biographie* (Bonn: Bouvier Verlag, 1997), 2:872.

13. Elizabeth Belfiore asks, "Why are modern evaluations of Euripides' play so radically different from that of Aristotle?" See Belfiore, "Aristotle and Iphigenia," in *Essays on Aristotle's Poetics*, ed. Amélie Oksenberg Rorty (Princeton, N.J.: Princeton University Press, 1992), 359–77.

14. Martin Swales, "'Die neue Sitte' and Metaphors of Secular Existence: Reflections on Goethe's *Iphigenie*," *Modern Language Review* 89/4 (1994): 911. Erich Heller wrote an essay about *Iphigenie auf Tauris* and other dramatic works of Goethe entitled "Die Vermeidung der Tragödie," reprinted in Heller, *Essays über Goethe* (Frankfurt am Main: Insel Verlag, 1970), 49–80.

15. Müller, "Das Parzenlied," 511: "wie ein erratischer Block."

16. See, for example, Arthur Henkel, "Die 'verteufelt humane' Iphigenie: Ein Vortrag," *Euphorion* 59 (1965): 14–15, and other writers cited below.

17. Kalbeck gives one account of the question in *Johannes Brahms*, 3:358–59.

18. Brahms was friendly with many highly educated people, among them Gustav Wendt, a polymath who was a renowned scholar of German and Greek literature. Their friendship dated from the time of Brahms's work on the *German Requiem* of 1868. In 1884 Wendt dedicated his translation of Sophocles's tragedies to Brahms.

19. Aristotle's famous words appear in chapters 9–11 and 13–14 of the *Poetics*. See Stephen Halliwell, *The Poetics of Aristotle: Translation and Commentary* (Chapel Hill: University of North Carolina Press, 1987), 42–43, 44–46. Chapter 12 describes the formal sections of a tragedy. Peter H. Smith draws on Aristotle's ideas about tragedy in *Expressive Forms in Brahms's Instrumental Music: Structure and Meaning in His* Werther *Quartet* (Bloomington: Indiana University Press, 2005), chap. 7.

20. Hermann Kretzschmar, "Johannes Brahms" (1884), in *Gesammelte Aufsätze über Musik aus den Grenzboten*, vol. 1 of *Gesammelte Aufsätze über Musik und Anderes* (Leipzig: Breitkopf und Härtel, 1910), 193: "Der Eindruck des Ganzen kommt dem Ideal, daß wir uns von der Wirkung der antiken Musik gebildet haben, so nahe wie möglich. Den Hauptteil des Werkes beherrscht ein düsterer Zug: es beginnt in beklommnem Ton und erhebt sich zu finsterer Größe; am Schlusse, mit dem Eintritt des a cappella-Satzes, löst sich die Furcht und das bange Staunen in eine wehmütige, ergebne Klage." I thank Paul Berry for bringing this passage to my attention.

21. On musical topoi, see Robert S. Hatten in *Interpreting Musical Gestures, Topics, and Tropes: Mozart, Beethoven, Schubert* (Bloomington: Indiana University Press, 2004). In his elaboration of this concept, Hatten follows the work of Leonard Ratner and his students, notably Kofi Agawu and Wye J. Allanbrook.

22. Malcolm MacDonald, *Brahms* (New York: Schirmer Books, 1990), 289; Geiringer, *Brahms*, 323; Christian Martin Schmidt, *Reclams Musikführer Johannes Brahms* (Stuttgart: Philipp Reclam Jun., 1994), 211; and Janina Klassen, "Parzengesang," in *Rezeption als Innovation: Untersuchungen zu einem Grundmodell der europäischen Kompositionsgeschichte—Festschrift für Friedhelm Krummacher zum 65. Geburtstag*, ed. Bernd Sponheuer et al. (Kassel: Bärenreiter, 2001), 330. Klassen gives an overview that construes the form as a series of variations on the first nineteen measures, but see her measured qualification of this interpretation on p. 332.

23. Although the first tonic occurs on the third beat rather than the downbeat and overlaps with the ritornello, it has the force of a structural tonic, unlike the second, severely compromised structural tonic at m. 115.

24. This instance of a recapitulatory overlap resembles Brahms's approach in the first movement of the D-minor Violin Sonata, op. 108, but differs considerably from his approach elsewhere, for example, in the first movement of the B-major Trio, op. 8 (rev. version).

25. For a discussion of this conception of the frame as it applies to one work and references to literature on the topic in film studies, see James A. Hepokoski, "Framing Till Eulenspiegel," *19th-Century Music* 30/1 (2006): 38–40.

26. Richard Bass offers a general theory that accounts for this kind of resolution in "Enharmonic Position Finding and the Resolution of Seventh Chords in Chromatic Music," *Music Theory Spectrum* 29 (2007): 73–100.

27. Harrison, of course, offers many further refinements and embellishments of this basic opposition. See Daniel Harrison, *Harmonic Function in Chromatic Music: A Renewed Dualist Theory and an Account of Its Precedents* (Chicago: University of Chicago Press, 1994), 25–29, summarized in Table 1.1 on p. 27.

28. See Margaret Notley, "Plagal Harmony as Other: Asymmetrical Dualism in Instrumental Music by Brahms," *Journal of Musicology* 22/1 (2005): 90–130.

29. Robert S. Hatten, *Musical Meaning in Beethoven: Markedness, Correlation, and Interpretation* (Bloomington: Indiana University Press, 1994).

30. Nicholas Boyle, *Goethe: The Poet and the Age: Volume I, The Poetry of Desire (1749–1790)* (Oxford: Clarendon Press, 1991), 454, 456. Boyle also notes that Goethe aimed it at a reading public rather than a theatergoing public. (The first prose version had in fact been performed in 1779. Goethe rewrote the play in blank verse only for the fourth, definitive version, which he completed early in 1787. See *Johann Wolfgang Goethe: Iphigenie auf Tauris: Erläuterungen und Dokumente,* ed. Joachim Angst and Fritz Hackert [Stuttgart: Philipp Reclam, 1969], 33.) About the 1787 version Boyle writes: "It *purports* to be a courtly entertainment, a play, and a play in the French classical manner, with operatic features and accommodations to the fashionable Greek style" (*Goethe, Volume I,* 456, emphasis added). Other scholars who have stressed the importance of French precedents include Dieter Borchmeyer, "*Iphigenie auf Tauris,*" in *Goethes Dramen,* ed. Walter Hinderer (Stuttgart: Philipp Reclam, 1992), 117–57; and Hans Heinrich Jauß, "Racines und Goethes *Iphigenie,*" reprinted in *Rezeptionsästhetik: Theorie und Praxis,* ed. Rainer Warning (Munich: Fink, 1975), 353–400.

31. On the early reception of the published play, see Boyle, *Goethe, Volume I,* 456, but also Angst and Hackert, *Erläuterungen und Dokumente,* 57. Boyle does not give a great deal of space to the premiere in *Goethe: The Poet and the Age: Volume II, Revolution and Renunciation (1790–1803)* (Oxford: Clarendon Press, 2000), 724–25.

32. Smith (*Expressive Forms,* chap. 7) traces ramifications of this tradition, which derives above all from Beethoven, in Brahms's instrumental music. He takes as his inspiration James Webster's approach to the idea of theme-as-tragically-flawed-hero in "Brahms's *Tragic Overture*: The Form of Tragedy," in *Brahms: Bibliographic, Documentary, and Analytical Studies,* ed. Robert Pascall (Cambridge: Cambridge University Press, 1983), 99–124.

33. When a stanza given to the chorus has no such complementary part, it is referred to as an epode. The fifth stanza of the *Parzenlied,* lines 29–35, stands alone and in this regard resembles an epode. See William C. Scott, *Musical Design in Sophoclean Theater* (Hanover: University Press of New England, 1996), xiv–xix. Scott gives the first two stanzas of the Ode of Man from Sophocles's *Antigone* as an example of a strophe/antistrophe pair and discusses the unbalanced epode. He suggests that in staging Greek tragedy, "both the music and the dance should make clear, through repetition and rounded units, the basic balanced form of strophe echoed by antistrophe, so that there will be a strong effect at those places where there is no repetition" (xix).

34. Clara Schumann gave Brahms an edition of Sophocles's tragedies in July 1855: *Sophokles Tragödien: Urschrift und Uebersetzung,* 2 vols. in 1 (Halle: Verlag von Richard Mühlmann, 1841, 1842); information in Hofmann, *Die Bibliothek von Brahms,* 108.

35. Hiller, in contrast, respects Goethe's punctuation throughout. Note that the cycles fit within "Phase I" of Table 5.3 and that the intensification of Brahms's setting in Cycle II corresponds to Goethe's intensification of imagery in his antistrophe.

36. On the semantic significance, within a purely instrumental repertory, of overriding expected phrase-endings, see Margaret Notley, "Late-Nineteenth-Century Chamber Music and the Cult of the Classical Adagio," *19th-Century Music* 23/1 (1999): 33–61.

37. Müller, in particular, dwells on the *Zeichenhaftigkeit* of the poem. See "Das Parzenlied," 520–22. Kalbeck elucidates a number of musical images in *Johannes Brahms,*

3:364–65. Kross focuses on the setting of "ein leichtes Gewölke" from the end of stanza 4 (which Kalbeck also notes) and criticizes Brahms because he sees the tone painting here as inconsistent with his approach elsewhere in the piece. Kross takes a surprisingly dim view altogether of this work. See *Brahms*, 2:879.

38. Schoenberg refers to "roving harmony" repeatedly in *Structural Functions of Harmony*, rev. ed., ed. Leonard Stein (New York: W. W. Norton, 1969).

39. Strongly accented imitation at the quarter note between the bass and treble instrumental parts causes rhythmic dissonance in mm. 48–50. This rhythmic conflict is more visible than audible, however, because the vocal parts predominate.

40. For a discussion of abandoned cadences, see William E. Caplin, *Classical Form: A Theory of Formal Functions for the Instrumental Music of Haydn, Mozart, and Beethoven* (New York: Oxford University Press, 1998), 106–107. Although the D♭–C–B motion in mm. 53–54 and 58–59 strongly evokes the Neapolitan–V$^6_4$–$^5_3$ succession, the other voices never rhythmically align so as to complete the Neapolitan triad. Indeed, none of the treble pitches in this succession receives the expected harmonic support in mm. 53–54, measures that might better be interpreted as a linear augmented sixth (or diminished third) chord. See Daniel Harrison's remarks in "Supplement to the Theory of Augmented-Sixth Chords," *Music Theory Spectrum* 17/2 (1995): 192 n. 42. His remarks do not cover this situation, but they are suggestive.

41. Virginia Hancock writes of the work as a whole: "Semitone relations are used almost obsessively in a manner which is unusual in Brahms's choral music." See her *Brahms's Choral Compositions and His Library of Early Music* (Ann Arbor: UMI Research Press, 1983), 130–31. Klassen also remarks on the frequency of the semitone shifts in "Parzengesang," 331 n. 38.

42. In contrast, Webster locates the catastrophe in a passage that he interprets as the coda of Brahms's overture op. 81 in "Brahms's *Tragic Overture*," 116–17. On p. 117 Webster asserts: "Musically and dramatically, the outcome is 'inevitable.' Such inevitability is characteristic of tragic art." It is certainly worth noting that the key of Brahms's self-styled *Tragic Overture*, which he completed in 1880, is the same as that of *Gesang der Parzen*.

43. I discuss certain aspects of Brahms's virtuosity in key articulation in *Lateness and Brahms: Music and Culture in the Twilight of Viennese Liberalism*, AMS Studies in Music (New York: Oxford University Press, 2007), 51–55. In *Gesang der Parzen*, Brahms asserts D-ness in ways that I do not cover in that discussion.

44. That subdominant function in each mode involves a particular half-step motion will become clear. In a recent article, Jeremy Day-O'Connell conflates the two types and does not recognize that 6̂ behaves differently in each mode. See his "Debussy, Pentatonicism, and the Tonal Tradition," *Music Theory Spectrum* 31/2 (2009): 236–37.

45. Jonathan Culler, *Structuralist Poetics: Structuralism, Linguistics, and the Study of Literature* (Ithaca, N.Y.: Cornell University Press, 1975), 165. On the first kind of shifter, see also Émile Benveniste, "The Nature of Pronouns," in *Problems in General Linguistics*, trans. Mary Elizabeth Meek (Coral Gables: University of Miami Press, 1971), 217–22.

46. Hatten introduces the applicability of markedness to music with a discussion of the opposition between the major and minor modes in *Musical Meaning in Beethoven*, 36–37.

47. Schmidt, for example, writes of the composer's inability "to identify with the damning of entire races" (so konnte er sich offenkundig im *Gesang der Parzen* mit der fünften Strophe, mit der Verdammung ganzer Geschlechter, nicht identifizieren). See Schmidt, *Reclams Musikführer Brahms*, 210. Hanslick wrote: "We leave it to others to find profound meanings in Brahms for this surprising change of mood and would like rather to look for the key on the surface, that is, in the musical needs of the composer" (Wir

überlassen es anderen, für diesen überraschenden Stimmungswechsel bei Brahms tiefsinnige Deutungen zu finden, und möchten den Schlüssel eher auf der Oberfläche suchen, nämlich in den musikalischen Bedürfnisse des Tondichters). These he took to be above all contrast. See Eduard Hanslick, *Concerte, Componisten und Virtuosen der letzten fünfzehn Jahre, 1870–1885* (Berlin: Allgemeiner Verein für deutsche Literatur, 1886), 373. Gustav Ophüls considered the poem's place in the play before interpreting the change of mood in light of Brahms's decision to set the final stanza. See Ophüls, "Die fünfte Strophe des 'Gesangs der Parzen' von Goethe in der gleichnamigen Kantate Opus 89," *Zeitschrift für Musik* 92/1 (1925): 8–13. He was defending Brahms's setting against critical remarks by Walter Niemann in the same journal: "Brahms' 'Gesang der Parzen' und Ophüls' Brahms-Erinnerungen," *Zeitschrift für Musik* 89/7 (1922): 156–60.

48. Letter of 13 June 1896 from Brahms, in *Erinnerungen an Johannes Brahms: Ein Beitrag aus dem Kreis seiner rheinischen Freunde* by Gustav Ophüls (1921; repr., Ebenhausen bei München: Langewiesche-Brandt, 1983), 33: "Ich meine, dem arglosen Zuhörer müßte beim bloßen Eintritt des Dur das Herz weich und das Auge feucht werden, da erst faßt ihn der Menschheit ganzer Jammer an." As an example of the marked poignancy that the major mode can express in an overwhelmingly minor-key piece, I offer mm. 121–36 of the "Forlane" of Ravel's *Tombeau de Couperin.*

49. Kross, for example, looks at the "problem" of the fifth stanza from a number of angles but never discusses the music in any detail. *Brahms,* 2:874–76.

50. In *Harmonic Function in Chromatic Music,* Harrison does not acknowledge the power of the descending semitone motion that mm. 150–60 of *Gesang der Parzen* so eloquently illustrate and that depends there on the first inversion of the subdominant.

51. Donald Francis Tovey, "Tonality in Schubert," in *The Main Stream of Music and Other Essays* (Cleveland: Meridian Books, 1949), 134. In the same essay, Tovey referred to the subdominant as "opposite to the dominant in function and effect" (137). On gestures that are "thematized"—or motivic—see Hatten, *Interpreting Musical Gestures,* 123 and elsewhere.

52. Matthew Riley cites Hugo Riemann and Ernst Kurth on this quality of the minor subdominant in "The 'Harmonic Major' Mode in Nineteenth-Century Theory and Practice," *Music Analysis* 23/1 (2004): 11.

53. Although diminished seventh chords frequently communicate a dominant function, Harrison observes that in some cases they may instead function as subdominants. As an example, he analyzes a passage from Richard Strauss's Piano Quartet, op. 13, that is somewhat similar to m. 116 in *Gesang der Parzen,* in that a diminished $\frac{4}{3}$ chord with $\hat{4}$ in the bass progresses to I. See Harrison, *Harmonic Function in Chromatic Music,* 66–69.

54. Brahms to Billroth, 3 August 1882, in Gottlieb-Billroth, *Billroth und Brahms im Briefwechsel,* 333: "die grausliche Härte"; 10 August 1882, 339: "Über den ersten Fis-Moll-Akkord denk eine Augenblick nach; wie die Modulationen im Nachspiel wirkungslos sein würden . . . hätte man dieselbe Fortschreitung nicht öfter gehört und gleich zu Anfang auf das nachdrücklichste!"

55. This recalls both the aborted attempt to divide the D♭ octave in mm. 80–83 and the augmented triad in m. 159.

56. E does resolve upward in m. 169, but it resolves to an F-*minor* triad.

57. See MacDonald on the scoring for the final stanza: "piccolo and muted strings suggesting bleak alpine immensities of distance" (*Brahms,* 290).

58. Notley, "Plagal Harmony as Other," 95, 129.

59. MacDonald, for example, writes of the "hollow, tenebrous conclusion on an archaic-sounding bare fifth on D" (*Brahms,* 290). A doctoral student in composition at the University of North Texas, L. Scott Price, confirmed my different hearing of the ending through an acoustical analysis.

60. Kalbeck, "Feuilleton. Concerte," *Wiener Allgemeine Zeitung*, 20 February 1883, 2: "den allgemein giltigen Inhalt des Gedichtes durch das Hinzuziehen einer besonderen, gänzlich unhaltbaren Situation zuletzt . . . in Frage stellt." Kalbeck recounted his initial reaction and responses by his friends in *Johannes Brahms*, 3:358–59. Critics who mention the stanza as it appears in the play invariably interpret it as a product of Iphigenie's own thoughts. Ingrid Winter thus writes: "The final stanza rounds off the poem only in so far as an absolute standstill is achieved in the figure of the old man. But at the same time the poem stands in a definite place in the dramatic events, that is, in the ongoing action. The last stanza points beyond the poem itself to the speaker, to Iphigenie, who here, so to speak, articulates her own situation." *Wiederholte Spiegelungen: Funktion und Bedeutung der Verseinlage in Goethes* Iphigenie auf Tauris *und* Wilhelm Meisters Lehrjahre (New York: Peter Lang, 1988), 11: "Die letzte Strophe rundet das Gedicht nur insofern ab, als in der Gestalt des Alten ein absoluter Stillstand erreicht ist. Zugleich aber steht das Gedicht an einer bestimmten Stelle im dramatischen Geschehen, d. h. in der fortschreitenden Handlung. Die letzte Strophe weist über das Gedicht selbst auf die Sprecherin, auf Iphigenie, die hier sozusagen in eigener Sache spricht." For Müller, the last stanza "concludes the Fates' Song—'thus sang the Fates'—and then steps out of the realm of impersonal and superhuman rules into the more personal, into the human and epic" (schliesst vielmehr das Parzenlied ab—"so sangen die Parzen"—und dann tritt sie aus dem Raum der unpersönlichen und übermenschlichen Satzung hinüber ins Persönlichere, ins Menschliche und Epische) ("Das Parzenlied," 523).

61. See, for example, Henkel, "Die 'verteufelt humane' Iphigenie." Theodor W. Adorno takes up Henkel's essay and writes about humanity as the "content" rather than the "substance" of the play and about the dialectic between Enlightenment and myth in it. "On the Classicism of Goethe's Iphigenie," in *Notes to Literature*, vol. 2, trans. Shierry Weber Nicholsen (New York: Columbia University Press, 1992), 153–70.

62. This passage (from a letter to Christian Gottlieb Körner) is quoted, for example, in Borchmeyer, "*Iphigenie auf Tauris*," 128: "so erstaunlich modern und ungriechisch."

63. Kalbeck, *Johannes Brahms*, 3:361: "Jeder Deutsche kannte sie."

64. Swales, "'Die neue Sitte," 906–907.

Part Three

6 Sequence as Expressive Culmination in the Chamber Music of Brahms

Ryan McClelland

Sequences permeate tonal music, with patterned motion among chordal roots appearing, at least briefly, in almost any phrase. Even when defined narrowly as coordinated melodic-harmonic motion, sequences are almost never entirely absent from a tonal composition. Sequences, moreover, have characteristic formal and expressive functions, which evolved over the course of the eighteenth and nineteenth centuries. In the Classical style, sequences appear most frequently in developmental passages, such as the start of the continuation of a sentence, the transition of a sonata exposition, and the development of a sonata form. Their primary expressive connotations are motion, transience, instability, and tension. Due perhaps to the nineteenth century's preoccupation with emergent structures and Romantic longing, sequences become increasingly prominent features of principal thematic sections, with a corresponding decrease in the relative proportion of sequences found in developmental passages. In addition, sequences increasingly lead to further sequences rather than to stable tonal goals.

Sequences nevertheless remain central to Brahms's developmental passages, even as they occur in his principal thematic units with some frequency. The topic of this essay, however, is a different deployment of sequential writing. In Brahms's music—especially in his chamber works—sequences often provide an expressive culmination within a final thematic return (in rondo-like forms) or in a coda. These culminating sequences fall into two expressive types. The first includes powerful sequences that maintain tension until the final cadence and thus retain much of their conventional expressive import. When Brahms employs an ascending sequence in his codas, it is inevitably of this expressive type. When powerful culminating sequences are based on descending motion, they remain end-directed but frequently convey an affirmative, even celebratory, affect. The eventual tonal arrival is the structural goal, but the sequence itself provides an expressive high point. Most of these sequences employ a relatively long journey along the circle of fifths and are often decorated with chordal sevenths and/or suspensions. The second expressive type includes sequences that offer a culmination through transcendence rather than vigor. These sequences, which almost invariably involve the descending circle of fifths and the indication *dolce,* use repetition to suggest circularity or stasis, implying a reverie or reflection on the preceding musical arguments. The ensuing illustrations from each category highlight how these contrasting culminating sequences engage earlier thematic content and thereby create large-scale structural processes and expressive meanings.

Type I: Vigorous Culminating Sequences

Vigorous culminating sequences often draw upon a sequential passage from earlier in a movement. When this is the case, the culminating sequence typically expands that earlier sequence, either by durational augmentation or by increasing the number of chords involved in the sequence. Often, the culminating sequence has greater voice-leading fluency: the sequential voice leading is more immediately apparent and conventional and functions to liquidate idiosyncratic or even "labored" characteristics of the original version. In some cases, the culminating sequence incorporates or expands a chromatic pitch or harmony central to the movement's thematic content. Drawing from three chamber works, I analyze vigorous culminating sequences from four movements: the first and third movements of the Piano Quintet in F Minor, op. 34, the finale of the Piano Trio in C Major, op. 87, and the finale of the Clarinet Trio in A Minor, op. 114. The examples proceed from sequences that directly recompose earlier material to sequences in which the elements of recomposition are more abstract.

Brahms's Piano Quintet in F Minor, op. 34, is among his most powerfully tragic works. Unlike in his other multimovement instrumental works in this key—the Piano Sonata, op. 5, and the Clarinet Sonata, op. 120, no. 1—the finale retains its viselike grip on the minor mode to the bitter end. The first movement as well insists on the minor mode at its conclusion, but earlier there are shifts into major; the tragic outcome does not seem as inescapable as in the finale. In fact, the recapitulation in the first movement ends in F major, and the coda lingers in that mode for a considerable time before plunging back into minor. It is in the context of this dramatic turn that the movement's culminating sequence unfolds in m. 286ff. Tracing the history of the sequence's thematic material leads to a fuller appreciation of the sequence's role in the movement's expressive trajectory. The culminating sequence reworks material that enters in the quintet's fifth measure, boldly coming onto the stage after the subdued open octaves of the four-measure prologue. As in several of Brahms's works, the initial passage is not a slow introduction—it is in the main Allegro non troppo tempo and presents the melody that turns out to be central to the first theme—yet its slower rhythms, the subsequent *ritenuto,* and the *fermata* on its goal dominant imbue it with introductory qualities. As a result, one expects the music after the *fermata* to launch a broad thematic statement worthy of this four-measure preparation. Instead, there are short, broken-off gestures, as the foreboding but subdued atmosphere becomes suddenly urgent. Closer inspection of these gestures reveals how de-

Example 6.1. Piano Quintet in F Minor, op. 34, I, mm. 5–11.

Example 6.2. Piano Quintet in F Minor, op. 34, I, chordal reduction of mm. 5–11.

tails of their pitch structure support the more immediately obvious impact of dynamic and rhythmic change.

The initially frustrated gestures eventually cohere into a sequence based on descending fifths, but one with some unusual vertical sonorities (Examples 6.1 and 6.2). In mm. 8–9 the cello articulates the harmonic roots, but the violins add a sixth above the bass in every other chord. The registral separation of the cello from the other instruments, along with the familiarity of the descending-fifths paradigm, renders the sequential model apparent (and thus the harmonic analysis in Example 6.2 shows chords with added sixths rather than $\frac{6}{3}$ chords). The source of these added sixths lies in the aborted gestures in the previous measures (mm. 5–7); the violins preserve the motivic character of the descending stepwise motion when the ensuing sequence begins. Although the bass in the earlier measures moves by fourths, the four-note sonorities do not suggest root-position harmonies; the first arrival (m. 5) provides a diminished seventh chord, a symmetrical construct that cannot be interpreted as a triad with added sixth. Especially in light of this model, the second arrival a third higher suggests the seventh-chord interpretation (i.e., ii°⁷₅) rather than a triadic one with added sixth. Thus, while these aborted gestures explain the origin of the four-note sonorities within the subsequent sequence, their harmonic interpretation is different. As the descending sequence gradually discharges the energetic buildup from the earlier aborted gestures, it also reinterprets their harmonic content in the circle-of-fifths sequence.

At the recapitulation (not shown), this sequence returns without alteration (mm. 166–72 = mm. 5–11). Despite the exactness of the restatement, however,

Example 6.3 *(opposite)*. Piano Quintet in F Minor, op. 34, I, mm. 285–93.

the impact of the unusual sonorities within the sequence is arguably heightened due to an alteration in the context. The passage comprising the sequence—originally the second phrase within the opening theme—launches the recapitulation. A reference to the quasi-introductory first phrase (mm. 1–4) slips into the lowest register of the cello during the final measures of the development (mm. 160–65), lurking beneath *pianissimo* chords in the upper register of the piano, but the burden of the thematic return falls on the sequential passage. As is often the case in Brahms's sonata forms, the moment of recapitulation is not a "double" return; the reassertion of F as *Stufe* arrives only after the sequential passage (m. 172). This tonal delay further enhances the anxious quality inherent in the sequential material.[1]

Brahms recomposes this sequential passage in the lengthy coda. In the first part of the coda (mm. 261–82), the music winds down dynamically and rhythmically (first through the onset of a *poco sostenuto* and then through deceleration from eighth notes to half notes). Combined with the continuation of the major mode from the end of the recapitulation and the piano's long tonic pedal, the movement seems headed for a recessive close. A nontragic outcome seems not only possible but probable. However, just as the rhythmic motion reaches its nadir, material from the end of the development emerges (mm. 273–74 = mm. 162–63). Similar to the boundary between the development and recapitulation, this material leads to a return of the sequential passage from the first theme, launching the coda's second part (mm. 283–99). In this final statement of the sequential passage, the violins invert their melodic step (mm. 286–88), thereby providing pure triadic sonorities throughout the sequence (Examples 6.3 and 6.4). The upper-voice "leading tone" in each of the chords on second and fourth beats now ascends, generating the 10–8 linear intervallic pattern frequently en-

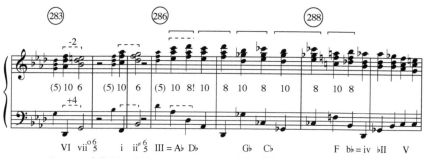

Example 6.4. Piano Quintet in F Minor, op. 34, I, chordal reduction of mm. 283–89.

countered in descending-fifths progressions. Notably, this change in direction gives the sequence's melodic peak to C and D♭, pitches central to the movement's primary melodic material (e.g., mm. 1–2, 12–13, 23–24) and to its tonal structure (i.e., use of the submediant, D♭ major, as the secondary key of the exposition).[2] Brahms highlights the recomposed sequence's greater voice-leading fluency by raising the dynamic level to *fortissimo*, removing the weak-beat *forzati*, and repeating each sequential unit.

The sequence's newfound melodic peak on C–D♭ serves to reverse the descending half step that permeates much of the movement's thematic material, perhaps most notably the *espressivo* sigh figures at the start of the transition (m. 23). In reversing this interval, the local harmony brightens from F minor to D♭ major, and there is a momentary glimpse of hope, even triumph. This affirmative quality is reinforced by the subsequent chromaticism, as the sequence substitutes a G♭-major harmony for G diminished. There is a structural motivation for Brahms's substitution: although a diminished sonority may well occur in root position during a circle-of-fifths sequence, it would not have a good effect when the sequential model involves two iterations of each chord (and when the individual lines are rhythmically unadorned), as is the case here. Nevertheless, the structural necessity of the Neapolitan substitution does not lessen its expressive impact.

The next phrase—and in fact all the remainder of the coda—remains squarely in F minor, without even a single applied seventh harmony. The confines of the minor mode that were briefly transcended in the previous phrase are now inescapable. This diatonicism compensates for the earlier G♭- and C♭-major triads and negates their intimations of a positive expressive outcome, but there is an even more direct connection as well. Although the sequence that begins in m. 290 is arguably not of the descending-fifths type, it still nevertheless progresses through descending stepwise transposition of its chordal pattern (Example 6.5). Moreover, it preserves the 10–8 outer-voice counterpoint of the earlier fifths sequence, only substituting first-inversion sonorities for root-position ones on the strong beats. When the sequence is repeated with an exchange of material between piano and strings, the piano's placement of low bass pitches weakens the pattern's circle-of-fifths basis, but by then the connection has already been forged.

The rhythmic relationships between the coda's sequential passages contribute significantly to the tragic expressive outcome. In the first sequence (mm. 286–88), the sequential unit is two beats long, and the melodic lines move exclusively in quarter notes. Further, each sequential unit is repeated before proceeding downward, delaying the progress of the sequence. In the second sequence and its repetition (mm. 290–95), the sequential unit remains two beats long, but it is

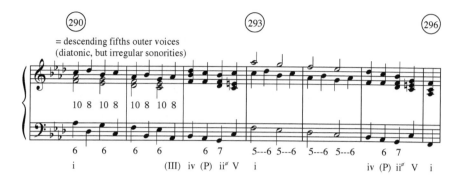

Example 6.5. Piano Quintet in F Minor, op. 34, I, chordal reduction of mm. 290–96.

not repeated. While there exists an important melodic line that moves in quarter notes—the one shown as the structural upper voice at the start of Example 6.5—it is realized in the middle register of the piano part. A salient eighth-note line spins above (and below) the quarter-note one. Thus, the return to "pure" F minor is accompanied by intensification in the rhythmic writing, providing unstoppable momentum that surges headlong into the tonic harmony of m. 296. At this point, all beats are marked with accents alternately in the strings and the piano, the bass line remains planted on F, and within a mere four measures the movement has attained its stormy conclusion. The explosive rhythmic drive of this coda fulfills the need for continuity that so strongly marked the beginning of the sequential passages at the outset of the exposition and recapitulation. What had originally been short outbursts, albeit threatening ones, have become a rhythmically continuous peroration, leading to a terrifyingly crushing result.

In the scherzo, a rather similar, though more radical, structural-expressive sequential recomposition occurs (Example 6.6). The initial sequence in mm. 9–11 has several unusual contrapuntal traits, arising from its canonic design. The leading string melody evolves smoothly from the preceding music, as its sequential cell plainly derives from m. 7 (which is itself an embellished repetition of m. 5). In m. 7 the midmeasure F is a dissonant embellishing tone, and one expects a similar function for the pitch at the middle of each sequential unit in mm. 9–11. Due to the canon, however, the midmeasure pitch forms an octave with the *comes* and is only dissonant against the cello's C pedal (and in m. 9 is not even dissonant against that). The underlying contrapuntal framework of

Example 6.6 (*opposite*). Piano Quintet in F Minor, op. 34, III, mm. 1–14.
Example 6.7 (*opposite*). Piano Quintet in F Minor, op. 34, III, embellishment and displacement within sequential framework of mm. 9–13.

(a) canonic lines as written

(b) tonal embellishments removed

(c) temporal displacements removed

parallel sixths nevertheless becomes apparent through successive removal of the embellishing pitches and normalization of the temporal displacement between the outer voices of the pattern (Example 6.7).

The intricate rhythmic and tonal embellishment of this framework contributes to the suspenseful anxiousness aroused by the tonal and rhythmic context from which the sequence emerges. The opening of the scherzo is tonally destabilized through the conflict between the C-minor tonic implied by the cello's reiterated C and the A♭-major arpeggio of the melodic line in the upper strings.[3] As noted by Peter H. Smith, the placement of the preceding slow movement in the key of A♭ heightens the tonal tension, as does the rhythmic displacement of the melody in relation to the notated meter—a paradigmatic example of what Harald Krebs calls a "displacement dissonance" in the metric dimension.[4]

Before Brahms recomposes this sequence, he returns to it once with minimal alteration other than transposition (mm. 53–56, not shown); it occurs a step higher, and its ending is altered to lead to V/V rather than V. This ascending transposition and its more distant tonal goal join the broader tonal context to heighten the sequence's inherent tension. Although the rhythmically displaced A♭ melody returns at m. 47, this return follows a lengthy standing-on-the-dominant that adumbrates the return of the A♭ idea. The reinterpretation of the A♭ arpeggiation within a dominant span is facilitated by the presence of F♯ in the piano, making the resultant sonority equivalent to an inverted augmented sixth chord. As Smith has noted, this reinterpretation of the A♭ arpeggiation prior to the first recall of the opening at m. 47 further weakens the recall's implied tonic function, especially when the piano reintroduces F♯ in the third measure of the restatement.[5] This passage is a good example of Brahms's general practice in pieces that begin with destabilized thematic material: preliminary returns maintain or increase the instability, leaving the impact of stabilization to the final thematic return.[6]

The *fortissimo* culminating sequence within the scherzo's final thematic return (mm. 150–53, repeated in mm. 154–57) transforms the parallel sixths of the original into a descending-fifths pattern (Example 6.8). The inherent solidity of the circle of fifths is enhanced by the piano's powerful presentation of the bass line. The midmeasure melodic peaks are dissonant against this functional bass, creating 9–8 and 4–3 motions; although appoggiaturas on the surface, they can be viewed as suspensions at a deeper structural level (Example 6.9). Unlike the "opening" gesture of motion to the dominant at the start of the movement (or to V/V at the internal thematic return), the culminating sequence drives to the structural closure for the movement as a whole and unleashes the demonic intensity of the coda. Although there is a strong rhythmic and melodic similarity between the initial and culminating sequences, the actual sequential model is

Example 6.8. Piano Quintet in F Minor, op. 34, III, mm. 144–57 (reduced score).

entirely altered, unlike the situation in the quintet's first movement.[7] The larger tonal and rhythmic context both supports and draws on the sequence's new-found stability. At the final thematic return, the A♭ arpeggiation finally leads to a

Example 6.9. Piano Quintet in F Minor, op. 34, III, embellishment within culminating sequence of mm. 150–53.

root-position C triad (m. 146): the 6–5 tonal displacement resolves, an event that is celebrated by the plain outlining of C-minor harmony in the piano part (in contrast to its sinuous F♯–G–A♭–G material earlier). The rhythmic displacement dissonance also resolves in these measures, making the final thematic return a climactic moment of coordinated tonal and rhythmic-metric resolution, which is then capped off with the recomposed, and now culminating, sequence.

As in the first movement, the culminating sequence brings about an expressive turning point, and of a similar sort. In the thirty-six measures after the culminating sequence (mm. 158–93), the only dynamic indication that appears is *fortissimo*, and this relentlessness is further intensified through the completely uninterrupted barrage of sixteenth notes and, in the scherzo's final measures, through accents on every beat in the strings. Significantly, the closing material is based primarily on the ¾ material that initially functioned as subsidiary thematic

158 *Ryan McClelland*

material (at m. 13; refer back to the end of Example 6.6). On its first appearance (mm. 13–21), this material remained within a shadowy *pianissimo* and was given only by the strings. In the middle of the scherzo, it occurs at length (mm. 57–109) and briefly in *fortissimo* (mm. 57–67 and 100–109) but mainly within a *pianissimo* fugato section. Its *fortissimo* deployment to close the scherzo represents more than a mere change in dynamics; the seemingly subsidiary material has usurped the role of the scherzo's primary theme. Although ending a scherzo in a different meter than the one in which it began is slightly more common than ending in a different key, it is still a remarkable turn of events. The main thematic material—the rhythmically displaced arpeggiated melody—does make two brief appearances (mm. 178–79 and 182–83), but these function as subsidiary interjections. Transposed down a fifth, they introduce $\flat\hat{2}$, and the rhythmic displacement is now a sixteenth note within $\frac{2}{4}$ rather than an eighth note within $\frac{6}{8}$. The tighter displacement intensifies the rhythmic tension, and eventually the D♭–C motion finds its way onto downbeats. The overall effect is of "crushing" the D♭ into the C, resolving the displacement but in a thoroughly violent manner. The transformation from the shadowy, mysterious beginning is complete, resulting in a conclusion that is one of Brahms's most aggressive. An extended slow introduction to the finale provides a necessary reduction in intensity, but the finale never lets go of the minor mode and storms to the tragic outcome anticipated by the angry conclusions set in motion by the culminating sequences in the first and third movements.

Culmination refers to an expressive peak, but the type of expression need not be tragic or violent, as in the quintet. The finale of the Piano Trio in C Major, op. 87, is a jocular movement, but its coda features a sequence that can equally well be considered a culmination. From a structural perspective, this movement's culminating sequence provides a climactic functional resolution of two closely related motivic sonorities, the F♯°7 and F♮°7 harmonies. The movement's opening melody arpeggiates the F♯°7 motive, and its rhythmic design gives agogic emphasis to the chromatic tone (Example 6.10). Brahms further underscores the F♯ by harmonizing it with the fully diminished seventh chord, which receives common-tone, rather than functional, resolution.[8] Particularly notable is Brahms's use of invertible counterpoint in the piano between mm. 1–2, which results in a somewhat unusual $\hat{6}$–$\hat{1}$ leap in the bass between the diminished seventh and the tonic triad in mm. 2–3. When the opening phrase returns in mm. 11–12 (not shown), the original string melody appears in the left hand of the piano, making the bass move entirely by leap. The intervening phrase (mm. 6–10) also gravitates around a common-tone diminished seventh—although one that embellishes dominant harmony—and thus, along with the agogic emphasis and leaping bass, further establishes the motivic role of the sonority.

Example 6.10. Piano Trio in C Major, op. 87, IV, mm. 1–3.

Later events reinforce the importance of F♯°7, especially the connection between the first episode and the return of the rondo refrain. Probing the subsequent role of this sonority requires a brief discussion of the movement's form (Table 6.1). Unlike many analysts, I consider this finale as primarily a rondo, rather than sonata, form; hence my use of "refrain" and "episode" to characterize thematic sections.[9] Besides the jocular nature of the opening theme and its reappearance in the middle and at the end of the movement, the lack of cadential confirmation of a secondary key supports a rondo interpretation. The motion through E minor to G major in mm. 23–58 bears some resemblance to Brahms's three-key expositions, but G major does not receive a strong cadence to provide, in the terminology of James Hepokoski and Warren Darcy, essential expositional closure.[10] In addition, the G-major phrase that begins in m. 47 and that seems destined for a perfect authentic cadence veers back into E minor, thereby circumscribing G major in a way inconsistent with Brahms's treatment of third keys in his three-key expositions.[11] The retreat to E minor is accomplished through the F♯°7 sonority, which functions as vii°7 in G major and ii°7 in E minor and extends across some four measures (mm. 51–54; Example 6.11). Brahms seals the connection to the movement's opening by returning to the melody from m. 1 in mm. 53–54, playfully foreshadowing the imminent return of the refrain. Particularly charming is the dialogue between the strings' ascent in mm. 53–54 and the piano's subsequent descent, which exceeds its expected two-measure length. After the thematic fragmentation and the momentary pause of a humorous rest, the unflappably high-spirited refrain returns in a delightful *pianissimo leggiero* setting.

Table 6.1. Formal outline of Piano Trio in C Major, op. 87, IV

A	T	B	A′	C/Dev
1–17	17–22	23–42, 43–58	59–73	74–87–97 – 116
C	C, V/e	e, V/G G, V/e	C	E, F, V/C, V/e

A	T	B		Coda (A)	
117–33	133–38	139–58, 159–71		171–88	189–224
C	C, V/a	a, V/C C, V/a		F, C	C

In the developmental second episode, F$\sharp^{o7}$ occurs again both as a common-tone embellishment of C-major harmony (mm. 92–93) and as a supertonic harmony in E minor (mm. 94–95). The episode achieves its expected tonal goal: a G pedal underpins mm. 97–112. However, in mm. 114–16 the pedal shifts to B, functioning as dominant of E, thereby preparing the subsequent refrain in a manner similar to the end of the first episode. Although F$\sharp^{o7}$ does not have a harmonic role in the crucial measure that leads the pedal from G to B (m. 113), the melody outlines the motivic sonority.

After beginning far from its destination—with an augmentation of the refrain melody in F major—the coda provides a climactic reinterpretation of both the F$\sharp^{o7}$ and F$\sharp^{o7}$ in a culminating descending-fifths sequence based on the refrain's incipit (Example 6.12).[12] In the last measure of the sequence (m. 217), the incipit

Example 6.11. Piano Trio in C Major, op. 87, IV, mm. 51–58.

Example 6.12. Piano Trio in C Major, op. 87, IV, mm. 214–24.

returns with its original pitch classes, and its terminal G is harmonized by the movement's background dominant. The piano's F#^{o7} in m. 217 resolves functionally as vii^{o7}/V for the first time in the movement. After an expanded cadential $^6_4$ (which includes several vertical statements of F#^{o7} as vii^{o7}/V), the movement closes with the tonal instabilities of its refrain overcome. From a structural perspective, the same was true in the quintet's scherzo: the culminating sequence led to the structural close and to an extended passage hammering on the tonic. Yet from the standpoint of expression, the culmination could hardly be more different. Instead of musical violence there is musical joy, an effect enhanced through temporal features. Since the culminating sequence begins on subdominant harmony (m. 214), its four-measure length provides a unified tonal span that prolongs the motion from the IV of departure to the #IV^{o7} functional reinterpretation of the motivic sonority. This tonal directedness, coordinated precisely with the strongly articulated four-measure hypermeter, renders the functional resolution of the movement's motivic diminished seventh chord a thoroughly glorious moment.[13] The splendor of the close, while not out of character with the finale's gaiety, brings added depth and ensures that the coda is satisfying as a conclusion to the entire work.

Vigorous culminating sequences need not respond to either a chromatic element or recondite aspects of a sequence within an initial theme. They might instead develop a sequential element that remains latent within the primary thematic material. An instance of this strategy occurs in the finale of the Clarinet Trio in A Minor, op. 114 (Example 6.13). This late minor-mode work is considerably more subdued than the piano quintet but is still intense. While lyrical and not thickly scored, the rising sixths of the *forte* opening have a restlessly urgent quality that is momentarily checked by the subsequent descending arpeggios. One of the most fascinating aspects of the opening is its alternation between 6/8 and 2/4 meters. Since the 6/8 meter is heard first and is associated with the more tuneful melodic content (and has harmonic motion!), it emerges as the primary meter. As in the quintet's scherzo, however, the movement ends in 2/4, and a culminating sequence plays a role in that transformation. Also noteworthy is the continuous rhythmic texture; subdivisions are articulated at every moment within both the 2/4 and 6/8 materials, adding to the restlessness of the opening.

Example 6.13. Clarinet Trio in A Minor, op. 114, IV, mm. 1–9.

To understand the origin of the culminating sequence, a close look at the opening phrase is necessary. The movement's second harmony (iv) is realized as a direct transposition of the initial tonic, but this relationship does not initiate a sequence (motive *x* in Example 6.13). In fact, when the phrase is repeated at m. 9, the clarinet's melody disguises the transpositional relationship by embellishing C with the third below and F with the third above. Gradually, the movement investigates the sequential potential of mm. 1–2, a process that reaches its apex in the approach to the final thematic recurrence of this material. Three other aspects of the opening phrase join the i–iv progression to plant the seeds for later sequential developments. First, the cello completes its opening phrase with a purely melodic sequence (motive *y* in Example 6.13). Occurring over a static dominant pedal, this pattern seems to be a "formulaic" diminution of the stepwise E–A descent, but it comes to fruition in the coda as the basis for a second culminating sequence. Second, there is an overlap between the first two phrases as the clarinet enters before the cello reaches its terminal A in m. 9. Phrase overlaps occur frequently in this movement, especially in conjunction with returns of the primary thematic material. Third, although the music remains in A minor (with occasional reference to A major) for over thirty measures, there is no authentic cadence before the modulation to the secondary key of E minor. In particular, m. 29 denies cadential expectation by substituting E for A in the bass. As will become evident, the sequential recomposition of the primary thematic material is closely tied to the long-delayed arrival of A-minor cadential confirmation.

Study of the reworking of the initial thematic material prior to the final refrain and coda reveals a gradual process of recomposition; instead of exact repetitions craftily placed into changing tonal/formal contexts, there is significant reworking of the opening materials. As shown in Table 6.2, I view the movement primarily as a rondo design where the internal returns of the refrain (mm. 66–74 and 116–35) are substantially incomplete.[14] When the refrain first returns (Example 6.14), it slips in a measure before the episode is finished, creating a more extensive phrase overlap than the one at the movement's second phrase. As

Table 6.2. Formal Outline of Clarinet Trio in A Minor, op. 114, IV

A→T	B	A′	C/Dev
1–37	38–58, 58–67	66–74	74–79–93–97–116
a, V/e	e	a	a, F, D♭, A

A″→T	B	A‴	Coda (A)
116–35	136–56 156…168–72		172–93
V/A, V/a	a	a	a

Example 6.14. Clarinet Trio in A Minor, op. 114, IV, mm. 62–81.

Example 6.15. Clarinet Trio in A Minor, op. 114, IV, mm. 161–93.

Example 6.15 *(continued).*

at the opening, the refrain's first phrase is repeated with melodic embellishment, but this time the repetition flows seamlessly into a developmental episode. This episode reveals that the rising sixths of the initial theme can be inverted and realized as a characteristically Brahmsian chain of descending thirds, harmonized along the circle of fifths (m. 77ff.). Thus, the sequential potential latent within m. 1 is activated, but with the substantial alteration of the melodic content from sixths into thirds. The sequence has a recessive dynamic and rhythmic setting, and as the harmonic rhythm progressively slows, the movement reaches its energetic low point. The lessening of dynamics and rhythmic motion induces a moment of calm; the music modulates to F major and then shifts down by major third to D♭ major and finally to A major. The exclusive use of the major mode—especially after the deployment of the minor dominant rather than the relative major during the first episode—combined with these successive shifts to lowered submediants make this central moment a restful oasis. The music remains in $\frac{6}{8}$ meter throughout, and four-measure hypermeter proceeds comfortably (mm. 77–104 consist of seven hypermeasures) with the arrivals on F (m. 81), D♭ (m. 93), and A (m. 97) situated on hyperdownbeats.

After the developmental episode, only the latter portion of the refrain returns, deferring a return of the initial material until after the restatement of the first episode (Example 6.15). As at the end of the original statement of the first episode, this final refrain emerges stealthily. In addition to the exchange of material between piano and clarinet/cello (cf. mm. 64–66 with mm. 162–64), there is an important tonal alteration in the end of the episode. Since the latter episode achieves an F harmony (m. 163) rather than C (m. 65), the refrain incipit enters on the subdominant rather than the tonic. Only after a journey around the circle of fifths does motive x triumphantly proclaim the pitches E and C above tonic harmony (m. 168). Beginning the culminating sequence on the subdominant maximizes the length of the passage: in the descending diatonic circle of fifths, the subdominant is the harmony farthest removed from the tonic. The stunning return of the original pitches E–C, A–F at the end of the sequence is very similar in effect to the C–E–F♯–A incipit's return at the analogous location in the finale of the op. 87 piano trio. Unlike the more languorous transformation of the developmental episode, the melody retains its original contour of ascending sixths, and the passage enters in the midst of a *crescendo* and vigorous running sixteenth notes.

One could argue that the culminating sequence in mm. 164–68 does not, strictly speaking, belong to the final statement of the refrain—that it is instead an extension of the episode designed to lead to the refrain at m. 168. Brahms does indeed mark m. 168 as an arrival by having the piano and clarinet take the leading melodic material, in contrast to the oppositional relationship between the piano and the other instruments earlier in the sequence. However, the seamlessness of the approach to m. 168 makes it difficult to place a sectional division at the end of the preceding measure. Rather, this culminating sequence seems better viewed as the ultimate outgrowth of the movement's propensity for formal overlap. The one-measure overlap that occurred at the end of the first episode now explodes into a five-measure sequence that blurs the boundary between episode and refrain. And, unlike the return after the first episode, the refrain now surrenders its original § identity and is swept away by the sixteenth notes of the $\frac{2}{4}$ meter. Such is the strength of the culminating sequence that the music quickly reaches an authentic cadence (m. 172), providing a powerful tonic closure not attained by earlier refrain statements (e.g., mm. 12–13).

As in the scherzo from the piano quintet, the culminating sequence fuels a dramatic turning point. It drives to the long-awaited structural closure for the refrain, a tonal stability reinforced at the outset of the coda through the tonic pedal in the piano (mm. 172–74 and 176–78). In the quintet, the shift to $\frac{2}{4}$ meter arrives only at the point of structural close, whereas here the metric change occurs during the culminating sequence itself. In both works, it is the subsidiary meter that ultimately prevails, and this rhythmic reversal carries a certain expressive meaning in itself. In both works, though, the impact of that unexpected turn of events is difficult to separate from the increased intensity that results from a shift to a meter in which the subdivisions move more rapidly. In the clarinet trio, the lyrical, albeit restless, sixths of the opening become almost militaristic in the sixteenth-note precision of their $\frac{2}{4}$ instantiation.

A second culminating sequence comprises a large portion of the movement's coda. The coda begins with some of the refrain's closing material (mm. 13–17), here altered to assert tonic rather than dominant harmony (mm. 172–76). In m. 176 a repeat of the preceding four measures begins (with the piano and clarinet/cello exchanging material), but at the end of the third measure (m. 178) a chain of rising parallel § chords takes over. As indicated by the solid brackets in the reduction in Example 6.16, the melodic realization repeats after four beats, and thus this series of § chords (with occasional diminished seventh substitutions) functions as a genuine sequence. Although the sixteenth-note melodic figure most directly derives from the refrain's closing material, it is also identical to motive *y* from the close of the refrain's first phrase (refer back to Example 6.13). As mentioned above, motive *y* draws the opening phrase toward its cadence with a descending melodic, but not harmonic, sequence. In the coda, the material's full sequential potential is unleashed. Rather than providing a "formulaic" melodic descent above a dominant pedal, the material generates sequential harmonies that lead inexorably upward. The sequential energy sweeps the clarinet to its fastest rhythms and highest tessitura in the movement.

Example 6.16. Clarinet Trio in A Minor, op. 114, IV, chordal reduction of mm. 176–88.

The underlying sequential voice leading continues even after the melodic design changes at m. 182, as shown in Example 6.16. The slowing of the ⁶₄ chords to one per measure has a powerful effect and prepares the syncopated break of the sequence in the middle of m. 184. The impact of the rhythmic syncopation is further enhanced by the hypermetric strength of this measure; hyperdownbeats at the four-measure level are strongly projected throughout the coda and the material that precedes it (i.e., mm. 156, 160, 164, 168, 172, 176, 180, and finally 184). When the sequence breaks, the expected first-inversion supertonic harmony is displaced by a root-position ii°⁷, a sonority that has a central motivic role in the trio's first movement.[15] The shattering impact of this sustained harmony suspends the hypermeter until the refrain's incipit returns in augmentation (m. 186) to initiate the work's final cadence. The swift move from the incipit's restatement to the ultimate cadence further cements the solid tonal closure provided at the outset of the coda; the two cadences compensate for the lack of tonic arrivals within the early refrain statements.

It is difficult to hear a prolongational connection between the climactic ii°⁷ and the subdominant harmony of the rhythmic augmentation, since the latter occurs in the middle of the incipit's tonic framework. There is nevertheless a strong melodic association between these two chords (see the line connecting F in two registers in mm. 185 and 188 in Example 6.16). The melodic association heightens the sense that the culminating sequence of ascending ⁶₄ chords leads not just to the augmented incipit but to the concluding cadence itself. In addition, the late melodic emphasis on F reinforces its role in both the first and third measures of the movement (refer to Example 6.13). A beautiful, and slightly hidden, aspect of the refrain is the enlargement of F–E motion: originally, it spans a single beat (mm. 1–2), but then it spans an entire measure (mm. 3–4). The enlargement is exquisitely reharmonized with F-major harmony (submediant as a "plagal" embellishment of tonic). The role of F major as the most substantial key area within the tranquil developmental episode (mm. 79–91) keeps the special status of this pitch alive even in the middle of the movement. Thus, the coda's ascending sequence engages a central aspect of motivic design as it provides the movement with a thrilling culmination.[16]

Type II: Transcendent Culminating Sequences

The second expressive type includes sequences that offer a culmination through transcendence rather than vigor. These sequences, which almost invariably involve descending fifths and the indication *dolce,* use repetition to suggest circularity or stasis, affording the listener a blissful reverie in which to reflect on the preceding musical arguments. Slow movements are perhaps the natural home for such sequences (as in the String Sextet in G Major, op. 36, III, mm. 78–81, and the String Quintet in F Major, op. 88, II, mm. 184–86), but quite often these sequences participate in the recessive endings typical of Brahms's first movements. I will analyze two such sequences, both of which are characterized by a beguilingly self-contained quality. While they are certainly not without connection to key moments earlier in their respective movements, they are much less a "working out" of previous material than an opportunity for profoundly elevated expressive content. Often in these transcendent culminations structural anomalies suggest a turn inward rather than expansion outward; intricate foreground elaborations either permit different interpretations of the underlying sequential pattern or generate apparent surface sonorities to gently camouflage the sequential framework, even as they carry the listener into a moment of self-reflective reverie.

My first example comes from the opening movement of the Piano Quartet in A Major, op. 26. It is a radiant movement with significant indebtedness to the pastoral mode.[17] Nineteenth-century compositions—beginning with Beethoven's later music and especially Schubert's music—expand the established pastoral topic into a pastoral mode that, as Robert Hatten defines it, "begins to shape the main thematic lines and overall dramatic trajectory of works that at the same time may embrace a wider range of topics than strictly pastoral ones."[18] Many of the pastoral markers Hatten identifies appear already in the first phrase of Brahms's piano quartet (Example 6.17). Besides the major mode, these include the frequent support of the melody with parallel thirds, the simple melodic con-

Example 6.17. Piano Quartet in A Major, op. 26, I, mm. 1–4.

tour, and the subtle emphasis on the subdominant in m. 3. Compound meter is a typical feature of the pastoral, and while Brahms notates this movement in $\frac{3}{4}$, there is considerable use of triple subdivision, resulting in an implicit $\frac{9}{8}$ element. The coda's culminating sequence isolates and intensifies these pastoral features from the movement's initial measures.

The movement concludes with a two-part coda (mm. 340–60 and 360–75) launched with a type II culminating sequence. This moment is prepared as something special: the recapitulation ends with almost a full measure of silence, which serves to deny tonic resolution for an extended dominant pedal (since m. 330). So striking is the unfulfilled quest of this dominant that it is the *only* passage of this movement addressed by Donald Francis Tovey in his survey of Brahms's chamber music. Tovey suggests that it is "quite possible" to mistake this buildup "for a crescendo in a Wagner opera" and makes this sweeping inference: "With the exception of Mozart the great masters of sonata form are inhibited from operatic writing not by lack of passion but by excess of concentration in their passion."[19] Brahms's coda is a response to the preceding accumulation of energy, a deliberate stepping away from the possibility of a powerful ending. Although the last two measures of the movement are *forte,* they are but a closing tag to the coda's consistently *piano* dynamic and a nod to the primary triplet subdivisions after the coda's generally slower rhythmic values.

With this perspective on the coda's context in place, consider the culminating sequence, which is based on a *piano dolce* transformation of the first theme (Example 6.18). Its contrapuntal intricacies strongly support the sudden transportation to a magical dream world. Due to the canon at the perfect fifth between piano and strings and the usage of parallel thirds within each stream, an overall descending-fifths sequence emerges. The canon produces sevenths that seem to dissipate before the end of each harmony; the sevenths only exist to the extent that one hears the piano and the string parts as a unified harmonic entity rather than as separate contrapuntal streams. As shown by the dotted slurs in Example 6.18, each tentative seventh is ultimately resolved in the next harmony. In the piano stream in the first phrase (mm. 340–47), the sevenths resolve with the first

Example 6.18. Piano Quartet in A Major, op. 26, I, mm. 340–55 (reduced score).

pitch of the ensuing triplet figure, but in the strings the sevenths do not resolve until the third note of that figure. The sevenths and their resolutions thus have an exquisite delicacy that enhances the dynamic and registral transformation of the theme. When the phrase repeats (m. 348ff.), the piano and strings exchange parts, and the terminal interval in each gesture is expanded into a fifth. This expansion results in a greater clarity of the fifths progression, since all the chords occur in root position. But the sevenths remain tenderly fragile as they only arise through mental retention across the change of harmony; at a surface level, the streams of thirds present chordal roots and thirds (compared to the alternation of chordal fifths and thirds with chordal roots and thirds in the original sequence).

The analytical recomposition as a strictly sequential passage (Example 6.19) highlights the irregular beginning of the sequence: the exactness of Brahms's canon at the perfect fifth causes the subdominant harmony to intrude upon the initial tonic (which does produce a seventh in the musical surface). The recomposition also shows how the latter part of each phrase is based on descending fifths, even as it drops the neighbor-note triplet motive. Harmonic sequence thus permeates the entire passage, leading to an expansion of the subdominant for several measures after the end of the excerpt in Example 6.18.

The prominence of the subdominant at both the beginning and after the sequential phrases forges a relationship with subdominant emphases elsewhere in the movement. These subdominant deflections contribute to the pastoral tone. Even in the opening (refer to Example 6.17), the melodic peak corresponds with the arrival on the subdominant in m. 3, and the underlying harmonic content of mm. 3–4 is an expansion of the subdominant through a 5–6 motion, before the arrival of dominant harmony in mm. 5–8. In the consequent phrase, the subdominant supplants the dominant expected in its fifth measure (m. 13). More to the point is a curious passage in the middle of the lengthy second theme (mm. 53–106). As the theme searches for an authentic cadence in the secondary key of E major, the music turns back to an eighth-note variant of the opening (mm. 86–94). There is not only a thematic reminiscence but a tonal one as well. The neighbor figure expresses A-major harmony (as in m. 1) and also D-major harmony, the harmony within the key of A major that is least likely to help achieve cadential closure in E major. The progression toward essential expositional closure (m. 106), though, is indeed initiated by a D-major chord, functioning as subdominant in A major, at m. 95 (and repeated at m. 99).

Despite the prominence of the subdominant at various moments in the movement and the special role accorded to this harmony in the coda's culminating sequences, these sequences do not principally have the role of working out a problematic detail from earlier. The subdominant emphases do not establish an expectation for recomposition in the way that either chromatic tones or

Example 6.19. Piano Quartet in A Major, op. 26, I, pervasively sequential recomposition of mm. 340–55 (reduced score).

intricacies of counterpoint have in my previous examples. Instead, they are features tied to the quartet's pastoral mode. Given the frequent deployment of the
subdominant in codas, its *non*emphasis in this movement's coda would have
been remarkable, and probably unthinkable. And this delicate sequence with its
fragile sevenths is a beautiful way of stepping back from the powerful surge during the altered closing theme in the recapitulation. The sequence's circle-of-fifths
grounding is a welcome respite after the rising transpositions by major third in
the recomposed and expanded portion of the closing theme (see the A–C♯–F
progression in mm. 323–28).

Perhaps even more crucial than the sequence's subdominant emphasis is its
isolation and intensification of the other and more immediate markers of the
pastoral mode in the movement's opening phrase (refer to Example 6.17). In
mm. 1–4 a majority—but not all—of the melodic notes are shadowed in parallel
thirds, and the bass line moves independently; in the culminating sequence, only
parallel thirds (and their compounds) occur. Melodically, the contour within the
sequence is even simpler than at the opening, as there is continuous stepwise
motion (if not always directly on the musical surface, then at a slightly subsurface
level, involving the tentative sevenths discussed above). Rhythmically, the culminating sequence dispenses with eighth notes. Either there are no subdivisions—
creating a calmer expressive state—or there are triple subdivisions, providing the
gentle rocking motion of the pastoral's characteristic compound meter. The second part of the coda restores the movement's former alternation between eighths
and triplets. While remaining very much within the pastoral mode, this second
part is less exclusively pastoral than the culminating sequence. Besides the return
of eighth notes, the lower register and nagging presence of F♮ as a melodic upper
neighbor temper the transcendent—indeed idealized—pastoral of the sequential
passage.

I draw my final example from the first movement of Brahms's last chamber
work, the Clarinet Sonata in E♭ Major, op. 120, no. 2. Like the opening movement of the Violin Sonata in A Major, op. 100, this compact movement is marked
Allegro amabile, and its notated dynamics do not rise above *forte*. Even more
than in the violin sonata, the clarinet movement is an exceedingly lyrical sonata
form whose expressive effect is enhanced by the numerous returns of the primary theme. The coda (mm. 154–73) begins in the key of the Neapolitan, notated
as E major, with material derived from the transition (which is itself, as is often
the case, based on the primary theme). Example 6.20 provides the opening of
the coda and includes two closely related sequential passages—one in the initial
key of E major (mm. 158–60) and one that restores the E♭ tonic (mm. 162–65).
With its distant key, perpetual drop in dynamics and register, *molto dolce sempre*
indication, and ultimate stasis on V^7/E, this first sequence provides the coda's

Example 6.20. Clarinet Sonata in E♭ Major, op. 120, no. 2, I, mm. 154–66.

Example 6.21. Clarinet Sonata in E♭ Major, op. 120, no. 2, I, mm. 28–31.

central expressive moment. The lack of motion away from E major (i.e., F♭ major) reinforces the Neapolitan's role as the farthest step in this movement's pervasive journeys through "flat-side" keys, begun earlier with emphases on G♭ major and C♭ major (i.e., mm. 93–97 and 117–23). Shifts to ♭II, ♭III, and especially ♭VI often correlate with a shift toward—or, as is the case here, an intensification of—a lyric or transcendent state. The transcendent quality of the coda's E-major sequence is enhanced through striking contrast with the tonal predictability and sharply articulated chord changes in the subsequent sequence, the circle-of-fifths pattern in the home key that follows the magical German augmented sixth enharmonic reinterpretation of m. 161.

A closer look at the first sequence shows how its preparation and foreground details contribute to its exquisite, otherworldly expressive effect. Although the coda begins in a tonally distant key, the underlying voice leading is straightforward: parallel sixths and tenths between the bass line and upper voices occur throughout mm. 155–57, with the rate of harmonic change gently accelerating from once to twice per measure. The harmonic change expected at the entrance of the E-major sequence (downbeat of m. 158) arrives slightly too early; the C♯ and E at the end of m. 157 are two of the anticipated pitches, albeit with the E occurring in the right hand of the piano rather than the clarinet. The third anticipated pitch, A, does not materialize, since the clarinet remains fixed on G♯. The type of rhythmic dislocation produced by the premature harmonic change is new to this material; in the transition, the ascending bass line marches squarely up the scale from tonic to dominant (mm. 11–15), as it did in the original source of this thematic material—the first five measures of the movement.

When the *molto dolce sempre* sequence begins, the A-major harmony denied at the downbeat of m. 158 briefly sounds, as the clarinet's triplet figure wafts from G♯ up to A. This, however, is an illusory harmony consistent with the magical effect of the passage: the A decorates the resolution of the G♯, which has become a dissonant seventh due to the bass motion from C♯ down to A. This interpretation of the outer-voice counterpoint in m. 158 is readily deduced, and memory of the previous appearances of the clarinet melody confirms it. This melody originated in the second theme (mm. 22–40), and there its first pitch was plainly a nonchord tone against the extensively prolonged dominant harmony (see m. 30 in Example 6.21). Paradoxically, in its initial appearance in the consequent phrase of the second theme, this melody was a site of considerable tension. The preceding six-measure antecedent phrase achieved a half cadence in the key of the dominant. The consequent phrase follows the model of the antecedent for two measures but then veers off track at the onset of the *dolce* melody, with its expansion of the dominant harmony and delay of the authentic cadence until the phrase's thirteenth measure.[20] The tension and desire for progression arises from the prolonged *lack* of harmonic motion. In the coda, the situation is altered; the newfound surface harmonic motion renders the sense of delay less palpable, even though one remains aware that the coda needs to find a way back to E♭ major.

The rhythmic canon between the pianist's hands throughout the sequence blurs the harmonic changes and creates a series of illusory harmonies. The idea of canon—and canon involving the specific figure of three eighth notes consisting of a repeated pitch and a descending interval—recalls the start of the second theme, where the clarinet and the left hand of the piano part engage in a canon at the perfect twelfth. In the coda's culminating sequence, there is no exact pitch canon, but the repeated-note beginning of the gestures creates harmonic blurring, especially when combined with the clarinet's long dissonances and their ornamented resolutions. Dissecting the sequence's underpinnings will highlight this harmonic blurring, which contributes centrally to the passage's magical transcendence.

Example 6.22a posits a descending-fifths model for mm. 158–60 with an alternation of first-inversion and root-position seventh chords. Although Brahms's sequence breaks at the start of the third measure, Example 6.22a includes the $\frac{6}{4}$ chord expected at m. 160 because it shares important similarities with the chord that actually ensues at that downbeat. The chord enclosed in brackets provides the next sequential harmony, which differs substantially from the dominant seventh chord that actually occurs (and that is shown after the bracketed chord).

Example 6.22b proceeds from the descending-fifths model of Example 6.22a toward the musical surface by introducing an alternation of 7–6 and 4–3 suspensions. The example notates these suspensions in different voices in order to trace their consonant preparations; in the music, all these suspensions fall within the clarinet melody. When these embellishments infiltrate the sequence's third measure, the sonority at the downbeat is equivalent to the one in Brahms's m.

(a) model of descending fifths sequence for mm. 158–60

(b) descending fifths model embellished with alternating 7–6 and 4–3 suspensions

(c) "illusory" model of mm. 158–60 taking surface elaborations as structural tones

(d) embellished descending fifths model with fragmentation generating pseudo-sequence

Example 6.22. Clarinet Sonata in E♭ Major, op. 120, no. 2, I, sequential framework for E-major culminating sequence.

160: a supertonic seventh chord. This might suggest an alternate model of the sequence, as shown in Example 6.22c. In this model, the chord in the third measure—which is undeniably a supertonic seventh—is taken as part of the preceding sequence, which means that the downbeats of the previous two measures are viewed as root-position rather than first-inversion seventh chords. (Of course, it is necessary to infer a swapping of pitch material between piano and clarinet at the start of m. 160.) This alternate model constitutes a sequence that moves by descending step but that is not a descending-fifths harmonic sequence. This is, in my view, a misreading of the passage's sequential basis, but an excessively literalistic interpretation of the score would actually lead to this model. Due to the ornamented resolutions of the clarinet's 7–6 suspensions, the resolutions actually occur *after* the bass notes change. In m. 158, for example, the clarinet only moves to F♯ on the last triplet eighth of beat 2, whereas the new bass note first sounds on the last eighth note of beat 2. Given the metric strength of the clarinet's long notes and the immediate pitch repetition at the outset of each of the utterances in the bass line, it is straightforward enough to understand eighth-note anticipations of the harmonic changes in the bass line. Nonetheless, it is worth noting that the $\S$ chords shown in the descending-fifths model (Example 6.22a) never actually sound as simultaneities; the simultaneities are the illusory harmonies of Example 6.22c.

What, then, of the supertonic seventh chord at the downbeat of m. 160? As shown in Example 6.22d, this chord arises from fragmentation of the descending-fifths sequence. The last harmony of the preceding measure simply occurs down a third (and then down a fifth). The supertonic seventh of m. 160 is not structurally related to the illusory "IV⁷" and "iii⁷" sonorities in the previous two measures but emerges from the secondary pseudosequence. While this conclusion receives strong corroboration from the fragmentation in the clarinet line in m. 160, the complexity of the diminutions and the possibility that the illusory sequence could lead without break to the supertonic seventh harmony draw one into the compelling glint of these shimmering sonorities.

As noted above, the E-major sequential passage leads to a stasis on that key's dominant seventh, which after some silence is enharmonically reinterpreted as the German augmented sixth chord of E♭ major. A beautiful detail worth noting is the special role of the German sixth chord earlier in the movement. In the exposition, the transition ends on the German sixth in the dominant key—the augmented sixth above G♭ in m. 21—and not on the F dominant of the new key itself. Curiously, in the recapitulation, the transition ends with the very same G♭ harmony, which is resolved as a dominant seventh to allow the second theme to begin in the distant key of C♭ major (m. 120). Had the second theme begun in the home key, the transition presumably would have ended on a C♭ German sixth, paralleling the exposition's transition but transposed down a fifth. Thus, the "missing" German sixth chord from the end of the recapitulation's transition is precisely that sonority lingered upon at the end of the coda's *molto dolce sempre* sequence.

In the Tranquillo section, sequence returns, but it is decidedly more commonplace and "earthbound" than the preceding transcendent one, as noted above. Besides its solid anchoring in E♭ major without even a single applied dominant, the bass line forcefully articulates harmonic changes, and the ornamented suspensions in the melody are absent. Although the three-eighth-note rhythm remains, no longer does it involve pitch repetition. This further enhances the clarity of the harmonic changes, and Brahms's accentuation removes any trace of the tendency toward metric displacement suggested by the harmonic anticipations in the E-major sequence. With its predictable harmonic support and rhythmic pacing, the descent of this melodic line toward structural closure (m. 166) could scarcely be more acceptant.

The expressive strategy in the clarinet sonata is rather similar to the end of the piano quartet movement. In both codas, the culminating sequence presents a fragile, dreamlike state that—while not shattered by the remainder of the coda— is tempered, made more real and human. The structural means of accomplishing these expressive shifts, however, are different. In the piano quartet, the culminating sequence features a simplification of materials to the most identifiably pastoral characteristics, whereas in the clarinet sonata complex relationships among the textural layers create newfound rhythmic and tonal ambiguities. In the earlier work, the culminating sequence occurs twice, and then a change in musical material brings the expressive shift back toward earthly reality, whereas in the later work the sequence is itself transformed tonally and rhythmically. The common element in both works, though, is the presence of sequence at the coda's expressive crux.

* * *

Brahms's culminating sequences reveal expressive meaning both through their idiosyncratic realization of conventional patterns and through their engagement with global processes of thematic and harmonic development. More broadly, they participate in Brahms's reinterpretations of convention with their manipulation of the traditional expressive connotations and formal functions of sequence. This essay has focused on Brahms's chamber music, and while culminating sequences are by no means restricted to this segment of Brahms's oeuvre, they do seem to occur here with somewhat greater frequency than in works for orchestral forces, especially culminating sequences that involve descending motion. In several of Brahms's orchestral works, chromatic ascending sequences do figure prominently in codas; some examples include the finales of the Violin Concerto (mm. 320–24) and Fourth Symphony (mm. 261–72) as well as both outer movements of the Double Concerto (I, mm. 402–408; III, mm. 313–19). To some extent, these sequences appear more conventional, as they prepare powerful conclusions through rising chromaticism and engage less consistently with thematic aspects of their parent movements.

Besides the role of sequences explored in this essay, other aspects of Brahms's rich handling of sequences could serve as the focus for future structural-expressive studies.[21] Although the notion of "labored" sequences was touched on above—in the discussion of the piano quintet—the ways in which Brahms elaborates and hybridizes Classical sequence types could also be viewed through the lens of expressive outcomes. Similarly, the manner in which sequences break off can have expressive implications. Two normative means of ending a sequence—both of which were seen in the examples in this essay—are to arrive squarely at a significant structural goal or to seamlessly deviate from the sequence in the midst of a sequential unit. One particularly Brahmsian ploy, however, is to leave an underlying harmonic sequence intact while shattering the outer-voice counterpoint, often through either an exchange of the outer voices, or a sudden widening of their registral separation, or both.[22]

Although one can contemplate sequences from a strictly structural perspective, this essay has suggested the value in probing them from an expressive standpoint as well. In particular, close readings have demonstrated how central sequences can be to expressive turning points in codas. By their repetitive nature, sequences have unique motional qualities, which can either drive toward a structural-expressive goal or withdraw into a circular reverie. And by recomposing earlier thematic material, additional layers of structural-expressive meaning accrue. Since sequential passages are repetitive, it can be easy to dismiss them as less interesting than nonsequential ones, but doing so only lessens our appreciation of Brahms's artistry and the manifold pleasures it affords.

NOTES

1. Peter H. Smith places the separation of tonal and thematic return in the quintet in the context of Brahms's recapitulatory recompositions in *Expressive Forms in Brahms's Instrumental Music: Structure and Meaning in His* Werther *Quartet* (Bloomington: Indiana University Press, 2005), 73.

2. The centrality of C–D♭ to the movement's tonal design has been frequently noted. In addition to Smith's work cited in note 1, see Walter Frisch, *Brahms and the Principle of Developing Variation* (Berkeley: University of California Press, 1984), 84–86; and Peter H. Smith, "Brahms and Motivic § Chords," *Music Analysis* 16/2 (1997): 182–91.

3. For a thorough discussion of the scherzo from op. 34, see my *Brahms and the Scherzo: Studies in Musical Narrative* (Farnham, England: Ashgate, 2010), 55–67.

4. Smith, "Brahms and Motivic § Chords," 175–82; Harald Krebs, *Fantasy Pieces: Metrical Dissonance in the Music of Robert Schumann* (New York: Oxford University Press, 1999), 33–39.

5. Smith, "Brahms and Motivic § Chords," 180. If tonal structure is interpreted distinctly from formal design, one might plausibly contend that there is no deep-level reart-

iculation of tonic function at the thematic return (i.e., the bass-line C at m. 47 is part of a motion between the preceding dominant and the V/V at m. 57).

6. I pursue this topic at length in "Brahms and the Principle of Destabilised Beginnings," *Music Analysis* 28/1 (2009): 3–61.

7. An interesting similarity to the first movement is Brahms's substitution of the Neapolitan harmony for the diminished supertonic triad in the culminating sequence. As in the first movement, this substitution not only avoids the diminished sonority but also forges motivic links to half-step motions elsewhere. Earlier in the scherzo, the principal half-step motion is between A♭ and G, but in the closing material (mm. 158–93) the arpeggiated melody is transposed down a fifth, thereby highlighting D♭–C. In fact, D♭–C is the scherzo's final melodic utterance, a nod—as Donald Francis Tovey suggested—to the String Quintet, D. 956, of Schubert; see his "Brahms's Chamber Music," in *Essays and Lectures on Music*, ed. H. J. Foss (London: Oxford University Press, 1949), 244.

8. It should be noted that the preceding scherzo also opens with a common-tone diminished seventh chord (to tonic harmony in C minor). The scherzo's shadowy opening material never undergoes substantive recomposition, and thus the opening of the finale continues an important, and never stabilized, thematic element of the scherzo.

9. Due to Brahms's propensity for beginning developments in sonata-form movements with restatements of the main theme in the tonic key, the interplay between sonata and rondo forms is often complex, especially in finales. A seminal treatment of this topic appears in Robert Pascall, "Some Special Uses of Sonata Form by Brahms," *Soundings* 4 (1974): 58–63. Analyses that treat the finale of op. 87 as a sonata form include Smith, *Expressive Forms*, 139; and Roger Graybill, "Brahms's Three-Key Expositions: Their Place within the Classical Tradition" (Ph.D. diss., Yale University, 1983), 75, 179–215. For further discussion of the readiness of analysts to interpret sonata forms in Brahms's finales, see my "Brahms and the Principle of Destabilised Beginnings," 50. A similar sentiment, although argued from a completely different perspective, is expressed in Joel Galand, "Some Eighteenth-Century Ritornello Scripts and Their Nineteenth-Century Revivals," *Music Theory Spectrum* 30/2 (2008): 239–82.

10. James Hepokoski and Warren Darcy, *Elements of Sonata Theory: Norms, Types, and Deformations in the Late-Eighteenth-Century Sonata* (New York: Oxford University Press, 2006), 120–24.

11. It is true that the second episode develops material from the A and B sections. This motivates my qualification that this movement is *primarily* a rondo form, as the developmental quality of the C section does represent some hybridization with sonata form. The transposition of the second B section down a fifth could be viewed as a sonata attribute, but most seven-part rondos in the major mode feature this same transpositional relationship.

12. Edward T. Cone noted the interconnectedness of melody and harmony in this climactic passage; see his "Harmonic Congruence in Brahms," in *Brahms Studies: Analytical and Historical Perspectives*, ed. George Bozarth (Oxford: Clarendon, 1990), 178.

13. For another example of a culminating sequence that composes-out a chromatic pitch from an initial theme, see the treatment of E♭ in mm. 135–37 of the finale of the Cello Sonata in F Major, op. 99.

14. Like the finale of op. 87, some analysts view the last movement of op. 114 as a modified sonata form. Since the refrain in m. 116 picks up more or less where the previous truncated refrain left off, the movement may be interpreted as a "sonata form with displaced development," to use Pascall's phrase ("Some Special Uses of Sonata Form," 59). In that scenario, the recapitulatory impulse begins at the first restatement of the refrain (m. 66) but is temporarily interrupted by the displaced development (mm. 74–115). Since much of the refrain does return immediately after the development, the sonata interpreta-

tion does not involve a reverse thematic recapitulation per se, although it is true that the beginning of the refrain does not recur until near the end of the movement. I favor the rondo interpretation largely due to the distinctly articulated four-measure units throughout the opening theme (and much of the movement) and the sharp contrasts created by the shifts between ¾ and ⅝ meters, but also due to a general discomfort with a lengthy development as an insertion within a thematic recapitulation (even though, of course, one can pursue this model in a handful of Brahms's finales).

15. The importance of the ii°⁷ in the trio's first movement is discussed at length in Peter H. Smith, "Brahms and the Shifting Barline: Metric Displacement and Formal Process in the Trios with Wind Instruments," in *Brahms Studies* 3, ed. David Brodbeck (Lincoln: University of Nebraska Press, 2001), 213–28, and in his "You Reap What You Sow: Some Instances of Rhythmic and Harmonic Ambiguity in Brahms," *Music Theory Spectrum* 28/1 (2006): 77–82.

16. For another example of a powerful ascending sequence in a coda, see the finale of the String Quintet, op. 88, mm. 168–71.

17. For discussion of pastoral features in the scherzo of op. 26, see my *Brahms and the Scherzo*, 136–40. A more extensive treatment of pastoral elements across all the movements appears in Hans Kohlhase, "Konstruktion und Ausdruck: Anmerkungen zu Brahms' *Klavierquartett op. 26*," in *Johannes Brahms: Quellen, Text, Rezeption, Interpretation* (International Brahms Congress, Hamburg, 1997), ed. Friedhelm Krummacher and Michael Struck (Munich: Henle, 1999), 103–26.

18. Robert S. Hatten, *Interpreting Musical Gestures, Topics, and Tropes: Mozart, Beethoven, Schubert* (Bloomington: Indiana University Press, 2004), 53.

19. Tovey, "Brahms's Chamber Music," 242.

20. The contrast between the lengths of the antecedent and consequent phrases is even more extreme than the mere counting of six and thirteen measures suggests. The six-measure antecedent expands an underlying four-measure model through postcadential repetitions.

21. Charles Rosen has highlighted Brahms's creative adaptation of Classical sequences in his "Brahms the Subversive," in Bozarth, *Brahms Studies*, 105–19.

22. One example occurs in m. 33 of the Capriccio, op. 116, no. 7. In mm. 29–32 an ascending stepwise sequence occurs, leading from an A-minor ⁶₄ chord with C in the upper line in m. 29 to a B-minor ⁶₄ chord with D in the upper line in m. 31. At m. 33 one expects a C♯-minor ⁶₄ chord with E in the upper line, but instead the music proceeds to a C♯-minor ⁶₄ chord with G♯ in the upper line. Thus, the outer-voice notes are exchanged, and their registers are shifted outward so that this moment provides the greatest registral dispersion thus far in the piece and a terrifying summit for this portion of the capriccio.

7 "Phantasia subitanea": Temporal Caprice in Brahms's op. 116, nos. 1 and 7

Frank Samarotto

Brahms's Capriccio in D Minor, the first of the op. 116 Fantasies, bursts on us with a volatile mix of tempest and torpor; it just as quickly veers off into music that seems to have drifted in from another intermezzo. The concentrated power of these few moments, reflected in the conspicuous detail of Brahms's performance markings, forces us to confront a paradox with scarcely the time to take it in (Example 7.1).[1] This Presto energico has such explosive force, yet why does it stumble so quickly into metric confusion and harmonic vacillation? Why does such a determined opening settle for such a faltering phrase ending? And why does it seem to forswear its passionate premise to be lost in a protracted tangent?

Not to mention the obvious curiosity of its premise: this music has a serious, driven, almost dramatic character that seems to belie the lightness or triviality implied by the title "Capriccio." To be sure, few prior composers could have been as aware as Brahms of the history behind such a venerable genre. Still— and especially given his own set of variations—the most proximate linkage with Brahms's caprices might appear to be the celebrated set of twenty-four Caprices, op. 1, by Paganini (drawn directly from Locatelli, about which more below). Here, however, in the two capriccios that stand as the first and last numbers of op. 116, I would argue that Brahms is bypassing this sense of capriccio in order to reconstitute an earlier incarnation of the genre. His first look back was in his Klavierstücke, op. 76, where he used the title "Capriccio" four times but seemingly in only a general sense to evoke Baroque keyboard texture—in effect, rewriting preludes in the style of Bach. These capriccios scarcely touch on fugal technique, which is precisely what the capriccio genre originally entailed. Mendelssohn had already revived the fugal capriccio (even as he also wrote these in the new lighter style), but Brahms never linked the term *capriccio* with fugue—and just what his linkage was is hard to divine.[2]

However much he was rooted in the past, Brahms was not satisfied simply to overlay his music with a patina of references to traditional styles and compositional techniques. Anticipating Pound's injunction to "Make it new!," Brahms looked to his predecessors for raw material he could reshape into genuinely novel

Example 7.1. Brahms, Capriccio, op. 116, no. 1, mm. 1–22. Facsimile of the autograph manuscript. Reproduced with the kind permission of Henle Publishers, Munich.

compositions. Here I concur with Kevin Korsyn's characterization of Brahms's relation to his models as that of a composer engaged in a Bloomian "creative misreading," as a struggle with the past, not a naive re-creation of it.[3] And that struggle may indeed be highly multifarious: Brahms may have referenced a particular model and at the same time cross-referenced the many nuances such an open-ended genre had acquired by the time he stood back to survey it.

It is that open-endedness that adds further paradox to our investigation: caprice, by its very nature, resists fixedness. This indeterminacy would seem to belie the otherwise foundational idea that genre is "an implicit and necessary backdrop that functions heuristically . . . like a (Kantian) regulative principle," as James Hepokoski and Warren Darcy articulate it.[4] To be sure, the early instrumental examples were constrained (mostly) by the imitative techniques the genre shared with the fantasy. But caprice has at its core the idea of a whimsical lack of constraint, and this aspect opens the door to an array of realizations that may share nothing but waywardness. The same breadth of possibility that must have attracted Brahms makes analysis difficult; one may have to cast a wide net in pursuit of an appropriate interpretive context for the first and last capriccios of op. 116. Through brief glances at earlier music (and an especially suggestive definition of the genre), a deeper consideration of eighteenth-century models (and even a possible model from the seventeenth), and finally a comparison of the two works from op. 116, I will endeavor not to fix the meaning of the capriccio for Brahms but to open the window of possibilities unique to each work.

Rückblick I

As I have already suggested, the combination of Brahms and caprice immediately brings to mind Brahms's Variations on a Theme by Paganini, op. 35, which, like compositions by Schumann and Liszt, is based on one of the violinist's capriccios. But we learn less from Paganini's virtuosic caprices than from their direct ancestors, those of Pietro Locatelli. As truly remarkable flights of fancy, his capriccios are lengthy and highly virtuosic solo excursions inserted ad libitum into the first and final movements in each of his twelve op. 3 violin concertos (pub. 1733); they are distinguished from cadenzas in that they are sometimes followed by a passage so marked.[5] These twenty-four capriccios are neither imitative in the manner of the older capriccio nor improvisatory in the manner of a free fantasy. They are truly separate pieces of music but of an odd sort not found on their own, existing only as insertions into the discourse of another piece. Thus, their capriciousness is a consequence of the willful juxtaposition of musical materials from different worlds. This compositional technique has a curious correspondence in contemporaneous visual arts: the architectural fantasies found in the etchings of Tiepolo and paintings of Panini. These so-called *capricci* whimsically mixed incongruous people and places, combining the fantastic and the real. Similarly, Locatelli's caprices may hint at material from the concerto proper, but more often they seem to strike off in directions unrelated in all but key. Locatelli's strategy seems that much more whimsical when, as in Example 7.2, the capriccio appears to take up a melodic turn at the close of the orchestral tutti and to twist it into a motivic pattern that is spun out for a considerable stretch, at once superfluous—the tutti has already cadenced in the

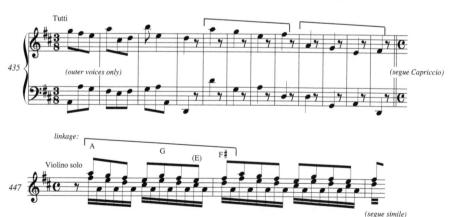

Example 7.2. Locatelli, from op. 3, *L'arte del violino*, Concerto no. 12, *Il labirinto armonico*, passage from final Allegro movement, including opening of Capriccio 24.

tonic—and fortuitous—the change in meter seems to spawn a new piece from an incidental detail. (The resemblance to Brahms's favored *Knüpftechnik,* or linkage technique, to be discussed later, is perhaps significant as well.) Locatelli's interpolations sometimes dwarfed the surrounding concerto movement, in effect, derailing the performance. Much later, Paganini took Locatelli's procedure further and fashioned independent pieces (caprices) that allowed an unaccompanied violin to hold sway on the stage; these free-standing compositions could be thought of as whimsical insertions into the normal concert routine, willful appropriations by a soloist-composer. Heard this way, the capriccio is not an exercise in lightweight virtuosity but an act of forceful creativity. But it is not clear how alive that tradition was for Brahms; the capriciousness of Locatelli may have left only a faint trace.

Arguably more salient to Brahms would have been the ancestral tradition of the capriccio, which he may have known through his studies of Frescobaldi's works.[6] These earlier capriccios mostly follow in the imitative fantasy tradition, but they have a pervasive characteristic that is unexpectedly shared with those much later of a different style. Almost all the capriccios in Frescobaldi's *Il primo libro di capricci fatti sopra diversi soggetti et arie in partitura* of 1624 include changes of meter—indeed, sometimes many such changes—and employ a rich variety of those mensural signs that were available in the evolving practice of the time.[7] Example 7.3 illustrates by providing incipits from some sections of the *Capriccio VII sopra l'aria "Or che noi rimena" in partite.* It is notoriously difficult to reconstruct the nuanced subtleties that these time signatures must have conveyed, but the intent is clear: the combination of signatures and rhythmic durations was meant to create a rich palette of temporal contrasts.[8] This rhythmic diversity is all the more clearly a defining feature of the capriccio for Frescobaldi

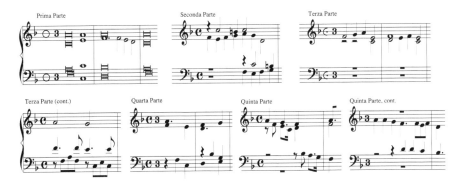

Example 7.3. Frescobaldi, *Capriccio VII sopra l'aria "Or che noi rimena" in partite,* sectional incipits showing meter changes.

in that the Capriccio VII is not imitative but rather a set of variations (*partite*) on a preexisting tune: only the recourse to a series of metric changes is held in common with the other capriccios in the set. It is all the more striking to find this rhythmic strategy as a common element much later, in connection with Locatelli's practice as discussed by Tartini; distinguishing the cadenza from the capriccio, Tartini writes that the capriccio "can be as long as one likes and be made up of different pieces and sentiments, with *varied bar time*."[9] Tartini notwithstanding, Brahms would surely have noticed the array of meter changes in Frescobaldi's capriccios; perhaps he absorbed this metric capriciousness as an essential part of the genre.

Brahms may also have taken specific notice of another source, one that may be the most significant thus far. The extensive dictionary of terms in the third volume of Praetorius's *Syntagma musicum* includes a definition for the capriccio.[10] Brahms might well have encountered it in August Wilhelm Ambros's history of music, where it is quoted in part, as follows:

> Prätorius erklärt den Kunstausdruck "Caprice" in folgender Art: "Capriccio seu Phantasia subitanea, wenn Einer nach seinem eigenen Plesier und Gefallen eine Fugam zu tractiren vor sich nimpt, darinnen aber nicht lange immoriret, sondern bald in eine andere Fugam, wie es ihme in Sinn kömpt, einfället."[11]
> (Praetorius explains the artistic term "Caprice" in the following manner: "The Capriccio or Phantasia subitanea: One takes a subject, but deserts it for another whenever it comes into one's mind so to do.")[12]

Praetorius's original goes on:

> Because, just as in a fugue proper, one never makes use of a text, one is not bound by words, and one is free to add, take away, digress, turn and direct the music as one wishes. In such fantasies and capriccios one may use with all ingenuity and without hesitation anything permissible in music, including suspensions, proportions, etc. Yet one ought not to step too far out of the mode or range [*die Ariam*] but rather remain close by the final.[13]

In part or in whole, this definition is highly suggestive and worthy of scrutiny. "Phantasia subitanea" I take to be Praetorius's invention; one might translate it as "fantasy of suddenness" or even "fantasy of abrupt changes." The second sentence is significant: the definition of the genre explicitly refers to a mental state, referring back to the improvisatory origins of early keyboard works. It describes a train of thought being derailed, the performer-composer in the process of changing his or her mind. Implied but not stated is that one must start with clarity of intention—a mind to change in the first place—and this clarity must be evident to the listener as well. It is also worth noting that all the freedom permitted by this definition is balanced by the compensatory injunction "not to step too far out of the mode."

As a prescription for creation, a composer might find this description liberating, especially when updated to conform to modern style. However tantalizing the possibility, one cannot prove that Brahms knew this language in particular. However, he surely encountered much later works that still embodied the core aspects of the *Syntagma's* definition, pieces from which Brahms could have absorbed a sense of "Phantasia subitanea." It will be useful to study one such work in some detail—Haydn's Fantasy in C Major (Hob. XVII:4)—in order to link Haydn to this Praetorian tradition of the capriccio.

But first, a look back at the threads established by my discussion thus far. Capriccio as a title has at various times suggested (1) a juxtaposition or interpolation of elements not always clearly related; (2) a contrast of temporal states through some combination of changes in meter and rhythm; and (3) a change of mind in the form of an assertion of an idea followed quickly by its desertion for something else. Put this way, the history of the capriccio would seem to place it far from clarity and coherence and instead define it as a trifle not to be taken seriously—hardly characteristics that we normally associate with Brahms's approach to composition.

Rückblick II

Given that the early capriccio was to be guided by a change of mind, I first turn to the question, What constitutes a train of thought in imitative genres? The entrance and reentrance of individual voices, with the apparently necessary restatement of the *soggetto,* is a kind of enactment of logical entailment; there is a satisfying sense of if-this-then-that, a unifying thread we follow in the reappearances of thematic material scattered throughout the polyphonic weave. In the rhetorical style of the eighteenth century, the vertical is replaced by the horizontal: the replication of an initial idea across different voices is replaced by the successive restatement of that idea in the same voice, perhaps symmetrically in a balanced period. This stylistic shift, of course, invokes a whole network of expectations about phrase length and structure, formal design, and even the places where departures from symmetrical norms might be more likely to occur. If one adds the notion of "Phantasia subitanea" to these premises, then the result is a work that may set off in a given direction and then abruptly change its mind, perhaps with great conviction, as if rethinking the whole premise; and it may just as quickly drop that notion and restart as if nothing had happened. When musical logic turns into a zigzag, time's arrow may seem to twist about crazily; one is put in mind of Jonathan Kramer's formulations of multiply directed time, which Praetorius's language seems oddly to prefigure.[14]

As an example of how these attributes play out in a composition, I offer a piece that Haydn labeled a fantasy but that is not actually a fantasy, at least not according to the generic norms of the time. (The eighteenth-century fantasy is all about dream logic, not conscious changes of mind.) Haydn provided confirmation of the true identity of his Fantasy in C Major when, a year after publishing his Capriccio in G Major (Hob. XVII:1), he wrote to Artaria concerning his newly composed C-major work: "In a moment of most excellent good humor, I have written a quite new Capriccio for the fortepiano, whose tastefulness, originality and special construction must win applause from connoisseurs and amateurs alike."[15] Subsequent letters suggest that the new title "Fantasia" was not Haydn's idea; one can guess the publisher made the change to better distinguish it from the earlier G-major capriccio and perhaps sell more copies.[16] The "special construction" Haydn hints at is not obvious; the piece is not quite a rondo or even a sonata-rondo. It is something resistant to generic form, and a clue to that resistance is planted in the opening phrase.

About that opening phrase, the editor of the Wiener Urtext edition, Franz Eibner (who happened to be a student of the Schenkerian Oswald Jonas), makes a subtle critical note on performance, and his insight helps lead us to the heart of the matter. He suggests that one should not bring out the phrase's downbeat pitches but rather the ascending notes C–D–E, notwithstanding their fleeting presentation.[17] This idea is fruitful, and I incorporate it as an instance of reaching over in Example 7.4, a sketch of the opening. Eibner does not comment on what follows: that this ascending third is immediately twisted to a downward turn of a sixth (and beyond), a hint that this piece may point one way and then swerve elsewhere. The close of the first period in m. 16 brings a contrasting but related phrase; we expect to hear the first four bars of this contrasting phrase repeated, but instead the music gets lost in arpeggios and hypermetric expansion—on the tonic, no less. As it comes to rest on a low G (m. 28), we recognize a huge enlargement of the descending sixth E–G, in effect, a change of mind projected in an even grander manner (see the analysis in Example 7.4).

We have two sorts of capricious behavior here: changing one's mind, of course, but also insisting by exaggeration that one really meant it—hyperbole in the service of capriciousness.[18] Haydn overexaggerates his gestures, and he does so too early in the piece, before we have had time even to grasp the opening phrase's general direction. Notice that the G–A–G neighbor figure never gets its expected repetition (see the bracket in Example 7.4, mm. 18–20). Once past the swerve, Haydn sets off to make up for it, but with a change of key and texture, and beset by hypermetric confusion. He sets off to lock in the dominant of G major

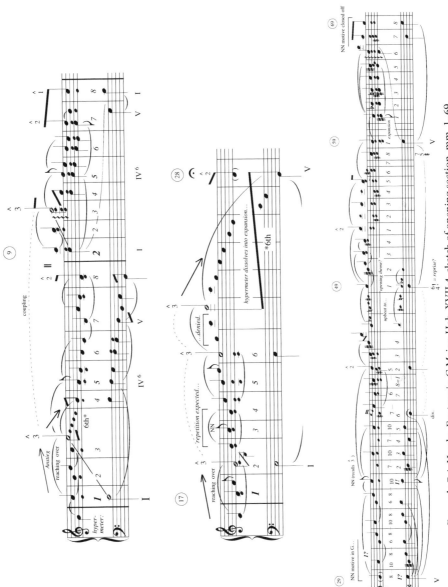

Example 7.4. Haydn, Fantasy in C Major, Hob. XVII:4, sketch of opening section, mm. 1–69.

with a traditionally effective pedal point (mm. 39–58), but the door is stuck, the pedal point will not relent, and it stays in place beneath a restatement of the opening theme (see the bottom system of Example 7.4). The overly insistent pedal point also suggests a form of hyperbole, and even more of it follows the perfunctory cadence in G (which belatedly completes the G–A–G motive). A sort of second theme—a pastorale—floats in, drifts down to another dominant pedal, and takes much, much too long to fade away, with a newly insistent pedal in tow. Lulled into complacency, we find the piece has changed its mind again: B♭-major arpeggios burst in like boisterous revelers, comically arrayed in three-bar groups (mm. 88–99). They take us on a trip through the omnibus progression to show us that the goal is really an E-major chord, sounding locally as V of A minor—thus, the intention is changed once again. Example 7.5a shows my reading; the arpeggios, registral spread, and hypermetric anomaly lead me to connect the B♭ major with the opening C tonic, leading to another, far more lengthy trip down a sixth, the grand gesture drawn out in the bass. It seems that Haydn has finally made up his mind: E as dominant really is the goal of all this wayward activity (mm. 106–16). But the implied A tonic is not forthcoming: a brief transition takes us back to the C tonic instead (m. 124), so we can start the whole process again (see the end of Example 7.5a).

The focus on III♯ is not in itself so unusual; III♯ occurs frequently as a middleground goal for sonata developments, for instance.[19] There, however, a structural dominant is already in place (the V *Stufe* of the second key area); here, the middleground C–E bass motion seems somehow unfulfilled. In fact, Haydn is not done with being capricious, and his game for the remainder of this lengthy piece involves that as-of-yet-incomplete bass motion and its eventual path to V. But how to complete it? Haydn will present one alternative after another, changing his mind and trying another option, until only a structural cadence can bring the process to an end. A quick tour of the main harmonic events will demonstrate; the structural bass notes in Example 7.5 tell much of the story.

The return to the opening feels like a rondo in progress (see Example 7.5b), but its theme is diverted midstream to D minor (m. 142) and then by fifths to F major; flats and enharmonic sleight of hand take us again to E-as-dominant (m. 192). This goal seems secure: Haydn gives the extraordinary directive to hold the E until the sound fades away (*tenuto intanto, finchè non si sente più il suono*).[20] With silence, the E is supplanted by F—the correct ascending trajectory at least for a bass line—but it is the wrong sort of F: rather than functioning as a tonic, this F provides a dominant pedal for a recollection of the pastoral B♭ music, heard as if from a distance. When this passage of recollection drifts off, we make it back to E in the bass—$\hat{3}$ again—but with a difference: it is now E♭ (m.

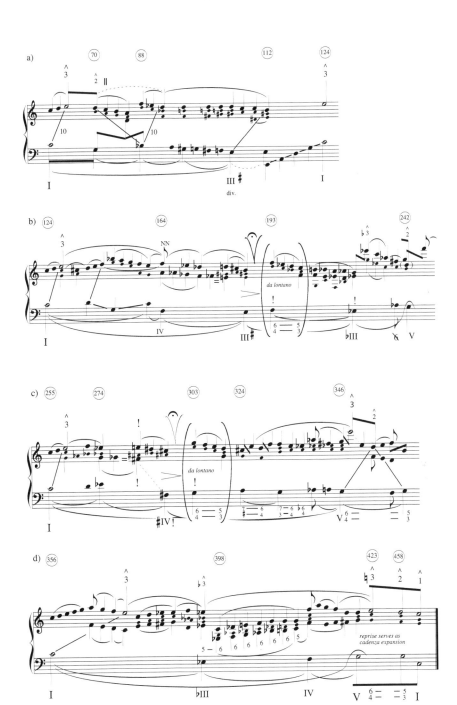

Example 7.5. Haydn, Fantasy in C Major, Hob. XVII:4, middleground sketches of whole piece.

223). But this ♭III suffices to get us to V of the home key and the "rondo" theme again (m. 255).

Following on the heels of the thematic restatement, Haydn quickly deflects to E♭ again (m. 274), but now the chosen path is to an unrelated F♯ (Example 7.5c); as before, this passage is directed to fade to nothing, and then the F♯ proceeds directly to G as dominant, with the distant pastoral music as a faint halo (mm. 303–307). This G nevertheless seems parenthetical and not yet the goal we want (which finally comes later). It is only with the last attempt, Example 7.5d, that the capriciousness finally relents: this time the bass ascent is conventional, albeit still with the aberrant E♭. Although I present the close only in summary fashion in Example 7.5d, it should be noted: Haydn feels the need to compensate for his vacillation with an elaborately worked out and witty resolution, perhaps creating a conclusive effect functionally analogous to the modal unity required by Praetorius to keep the capriccio ultimately under control.

Brahms I

Haydn's capriccio-fantasy forgoes imitation in favor of a broad landscape in which open-ended phrases are repeatedly followed by capricious reversals. At least in the case of op. 116, no. 1 (and every case may be different), Brahms's re-reading of this genre may indeed take note of eighteenth-century models and may also include a significant linkage with even earlier models (and from an unexpected source). One thing seems clear: Brahms, like Haydn, plants the seed of reversal within the opening phrase. Brahms, though, employs a subtle temporal instability to send the music off course and finally to a crisis of resolution. Temporal play is much more at issue here, and close study of its details is required.[21]

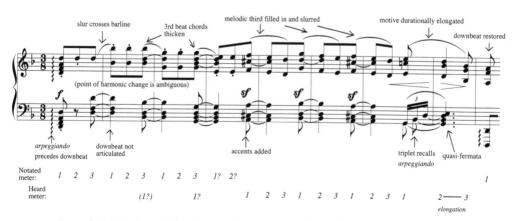

Example 7.6. Brahms, Capriccio, op. 116, no. 1, evolution of displacement in the opening phrase.

Op. 116, no. 1, manifests Brahms's resumption of piano writing after a long hiatus, and the powerful downbeat chord seems to inaugurate this return to keyboard composition with proud certainty. It is only in retrospect that we realize that even the opening *arpeggiando* acts to undermine metric clarity, and these disturbances to the temporal order will only become more intense. I detail the factors that gradually displace the heard meter one beat back from the notated meter in Example 7.6. Note that Brahms's use of harmonies by descending thirds, together with careful voicing, allows him to blur the harmonic rhythm and thus the bar line as well. Metric counting of "heard meter" under Example 7.6 suggests one possible listener response, and the addition of *sf* accents in m. 4 allows this potential metrical dissonance to prevail, leaving the notated meter a subliminal dissonance in the back of one's mind.[22] But not just accents derail this phrase: the dominant arrives with these *sforzandi* but is curiously at odds with the melodic third ($\hat{3}$–$\hat{2}$–$\hat{1}$) slurred above it. Right here this phrase is thrown off course and must make up its mind what to do. To understand this moment of indecision, we must imagine what it might have done.

Example 7.7. Brahms, Capriccio, op. 116, no. 1, rhythmic analysis of the opening phrase.

Brahms might have structured the harmonies as in Example 7.7a, which hypothesizes an even distribution of tonic, subdominant, and dominant functions, each with hypermetric emphasis. We can elaborate this schematic hypothetical by extending the subdominant with a passing $^6_4$, as shown in Example 7.7b; the later arrival of dominant seems more typical, but the cadential $^6_4$ is poorly placed. More characteristic would be another passing $^6_4$, which would extend the subdominant and displace the dominant into the next hypermetric unit, as illustrated in Example 7.7c. This alternative is almost what Brahms does, though his actual dominant is far longer in coming. But he does feint at the dominant; Example 7.7d shows that just where the displacement takes hold, the conflict of melody and harmony provides just enough friction to negate that apparent V chord, forcing its resolution to a $^6_4$ and rendering it passing despite its stronger hypermetric position.[23] The result of all this complexity is that the V chord, toward which the descending third progression is so strongly directed, has vanished; in midstream, the phrase stalls on the subdominant and gives up. The music has changed its intention, or perhaps metric dissonance has forced a change of mind. In either case, the phrase ends with a weak plagal cadence, which suffices only because the elongated motive stretches to fill an extra beat, in the manner of a written-out *ritardando,* as shown at the end of Example 7.6. This *ritardando* corresponds with a melodic downturn, a far cry from the vigorous opening leap upward. The capricious reversal is not just rhythmic but affective, a turn from blustering certainty to resigned regret.

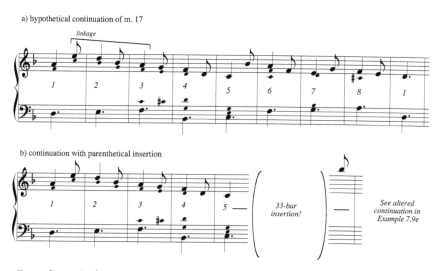

a) hypothetical continuation of m. 17

b) continuation with parenthetical insertion

Example 7.8. Brahms, Capriccio, op. 116, no. 1, hypothetical and actual continuation from m. 17ff.

Example 7.9. Brahms, Capriccio, op. 116, no. 1, rhythmic analysis of first parenthetical digression.

The first phrase elides with its own repetition, but perhaps regret weakens the upper voice and forces the melody into the bass. Or, more prosaically, this invertible counterpoint could be Brahms's nod to the distant historical origins of the capriccio style. Regardless of potential motivation, both phrases end the same way, and, sixteen bars into the piece, they need an answer. Measure 17 is ready to supply it by picking up where the previous phrases left off, an example of Brahms's ubiquitous *Knüpftechnik*.[24] Linkage technique is a thread of continuity across a formal divide. It is a train of thought made audible in music. We expect that train of thought to reach some reasonable conclusion; a hypothetical continuation is given in simplified form in Example 7.8a, which sequences the linked motive just as Brahms does. But that sequence seems to do us in. Brahms seems to get lost in thought as he veers off midphrase, never to return to the four bars we just heard. This is Brahms abruptly changing his mind, not just about this phrase but about the piece as a whole. We seem to have drifted into another piece, some intermezzo perhaps, different in every way but one: after a moment's thought, it seems to recall the motivic linkage from before (see the G–F–D in mm. 27–28 of Example 7.9b), the linkage in the sequenced form, that set Brahms on this drift.

And what a drift it is. The music stalls on the dominant of F and remains mired on that harmony for thirty-four measures—hyperbole indeed! This extended pedal dwarfs the preceding music, and it seems temporally dilated too; Example 7.9 (a–e) illustrates progressively how I hear this music as slowed down from the prior pacing, a point highlighted through comparison of the hypothetical Example 7.9a with the more literal 7.9b (which simply omits the displaced hemiola of the right hand). There is even a further effect of written-out *ritardando* in m. 37ff.; see the hypermetric interpretation in Examples 7.9c and d, where the harmonic rhythm is syncopated. The drawn-out descending thirds in the upper voice are distant counterparts to the frenetic thirds of the first phrase. We snap back to that distant world quite suddenly. What this endless dominant leads to is a single F-major chord (m. 55), immediately contradicted by a hypermetrically syncopated II$^6_5$/D (see Example 7.9e). Returning to Example 7.8b, I show this entire passage as a parenthetic insertion, a capricious interpolation that can be heard as a vast expansion of a single moment. Although there is a kinship with Locatelli's capriccios, the effect here is not so much public display as private musing: the train of thought has been suspended, and for that long moment, we are brought inside that thought.

The syncopated II$^6_5$ signals the return of the opening metrical dissonance (m. 59), now an abrupt intrusion of that change of mind. Finally, after the seemingly endless parenthesis, we arrive at the dominant denied in the opening phrases. But caprice continues: in another hyperbolic reversal, the opening phrase returns but is recast to focus entirely on dominant prolongation (indeed, it elides with the attainment of V).[25] Though we clearly hear V of D minor, no resolution is forthcoming; instead, the paired phrase that follows continues to prolong A but as its own minor tonic. It is not like the opening, though. The metrical dissonance is recast, the melody seems absent, and the whole is quieter, thinner. A bit of melody emerges from within block chords, and the phrase spins out to fourteen measures, stumbling onto the V of A minor (see mm. 67–80). Every

a) hypothetical transposed opening phrase without expansion

a) reduction of mm. 83–103; hypothetical model is abandoned after four bars

Example 7.10. Brahms, Capriccio, op. 116, no. 1, rhythmic analysis of mm. 83–103.

restatement of the opening phrase takes a wrong turn, not stabilizing the outer form but instead burrowing deeper into the inner form. The most striking turn comes with the oddly nonfunctional transition (mm. 81–82) to C♯ minor, which sequences the hollow version just heard. The opening phrase is now a disembodied remnant—Example 7.10 fleshes out the expansion—and the music is at a loss for closure, at a genuine impasse.

Rückblick III

Whence comes this darkness? Observe the presence of the capriccio characteristics already discussed: whimsical interpolation, temporal contrast, and, most of all, change of mind. Here, however, the capriccio elements are charged with an intensity that hints at a motivation lying beneath the surface. Perhaps a hidden influence is at work. Brahms's models can be elusive—it seems clear that he did not in all cases want them recognized—but the search for clues may be revealing on its own.

In January 1864 Brahms conducted his second concert at his new post at the Vienna Singakademie. Like many of his programs, it featured early music, but it stood out for other reasons. For one, he lavished special attention on the preparation of Heinrich Schütz's now celebrated "Saul, Saul, was verfolgst du mich?"[26]

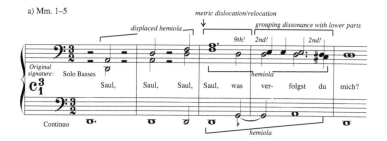

a) Mm. 1–5

b) Mm. 17–22, simplfied score

Example 7.11. Heinrich Schütz, "Saul, Saul, was verfolgst du mich?," SWV 415, simplified excerpts with annotations.

For another, the concert was a dismal failure. Though the then-unknown Schütz piece was the most appreciated, the whole concert prompted Clara Schumann to accuse Brahms of forcing too arcane a repertoire on the Viennese audience: one scarcely doubts that her criticism stung.[27] A much older Brahms was to encounter the "Saul" setting again in a volume of the ongoing complete works edition, a volume he received just a few months before the composition of op. 116.[28] Did a fresh encounter with this powerful score bring forth composerly admiration or conflicted feelings—or both? Can we hear a Bloomian misreading at work?

The opening of the Schütz is given in short score with annotations in Example 7.11a.[29] The extraordinary representation of the echoing voice of God

c) Mm. 24–28; opening of new section

d) Mm. 45–53, simplified score

e) Mm. 79–80, final bars

Example 7.11 *(continued)*.

takes the form of a displaced hemiola that is immediately dislocated metrically;
this shift relocates the top voice to the downbeat, but now the lower voices articulate a hemiola that is dissonant with the top voice.[30] Though the opening
hemiola resembles rhythmic effects in the middle of Brahms's capriccio, a more
subtle and cogent connection arises with the midphrase metric shift, as striking in the Schütz as in the Brahms. The downward melodic turn at the end of
Brahms's opening phrase has a model also: the skip down from Schütz's high A
is marked rhetorically by the unresolved ninth, a *syncopatio catachrestica,* that
leaps into the cadential dissonance, painting the word "verfolgst" (forsaken).
That the metric shift is important to Schütz is confirmed by the intensified version of the opening that he presents in m. 17, as shown in Example 7.11b. The
displaced hemiola is overlaid by its echo a beat later (thus twice displaced). The
fluidity of metric placement continues in the next two measures (mm. 20–21),

where the longer note emphasizing the second beat is shifted forward. (This long note will eventually be resolved to the downbeat in m. 36 and onward.)

These repeated cadences bring a new line of text and also something remarkable. This music seems new. Even the meter changes, but something remains: Example 7.11b shows the use of *Knüpftechnik* to connect these contrasting sections, made more salient by the preceding metric flux. Brahms could not have failed to notice his favored technique; the melodic shape even resembles the linked motives in the piano piece (see Example 7.11c). The biblical text does suggest Schütz's sectional contrast: "Saul, Saul, why do you persecute me? / It will be hard for you to kick against the pricks." If Brahms was indeed sensitized to Schütz's moment of contrast and linkage, he may have heard these lines at more than face value. There is a curious change in tone between the challenging question to Saul and the more thoughtful, internal contemplation of the future, perhaps even a moment of contemplation with special resonance for Brahms's past experience with this piece. Could this change in tone be a kind of reversal, one that Brahms composed into the strange swerve in op. 116, no. 1?

Schütz's "Saul" has still further affinities with the piano work. Example 7.11c shows the rhythmic fluidity with which Schütz treats the linking third motive (compare Example 7.9). Later in the piece, Schütz takes that motive on an excursion that successively introduces flats by fifth to attain a point of farthest remove from the modal final D, as shown in Example 7.11d. Is this remove to flats reversed by Brahms in his dark turn to C♯ minor?

Brahms II

We need a way out of Brahms's excursion to C♯ minor, and for that we need some context. Example 7.12 provides voice-leading sketches of most of the capriccio. Example 7.12a provides a middleground overview of the first phase of the piece, up to the dominant-prolonging return of the opening. Example 7.12b picks up with this transformed opening. As noted, the phrase wanders into an expansion; the moment of this digression coincides with the reinterpretation of the previous G♯ as A♭, which sets off a sequence suddenly broken at V of A. That same digression takes a fantastic course through what follows. The turn to C♯ minor draws the *Kopfton* A down to G♯ (m. 83). The restatement in this key gets mired midway and struggles to escape through enharmonic transformation to flats. The enharmonic reinterpretation is functionally real, and when the top voice brings in A♭ as focal pitch, we recognize that G♯/A♭ is again the trigger for diversion.

This diversion is more extravagant: the key of E♭ is implied, but only its dominant is finally attained (m. 99ff.). B♭ as V/♭II is a wrong turn, and its status as dominant is immediately gainsaid by its inflection to minor. This reversal coincides

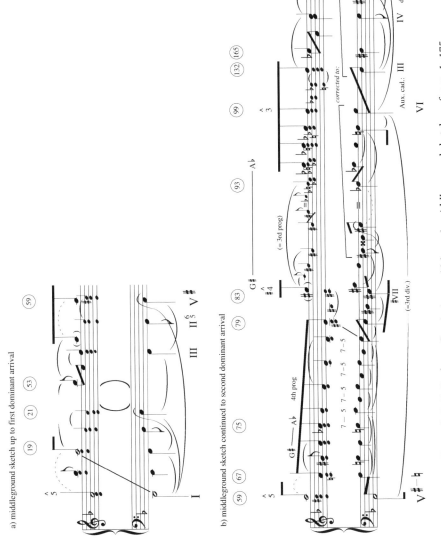

Example 7.12. Brahms, Capriccio, op. 116, no. 1, middleground sketches of mm. 1–175.

Example 7.13. Brahms, Capriccio, op. 116, no. 1, rhythmic analysis and sketch of m. 176 to end.

with the return of the parenthetical music, to be greatly extended here to sixty-two measures. The return from this parenthetical passage seems a bit more deliberate this time, but much is changed, and curiously so. The order is reversed from its first appearance, and the upper voice that was harmonized as a major $\frac{6}{4}$ above a dominant pedal now reappears as a plaintive B♭-minor melody above its apparent tonic bass. Lacking direction, the B♭ minor dissolves into hollow arpeggios of a diminished seventh, yielding finally in m. 132 to a V of B♭. Now we can restore the proper order of the parenthetical music, though it appears that we had given up the parenthesis a long time ago: this is now the main action. We snap awake from this dream when the dominant moves to a deceptive resolution and to a jarringly voiced diminished tenth chord (m. 167). The subsequent arrival at a structural dominant corrects the previous aberrant arrival on VI and resets the path of the bass; see the lower brackets in Example 7.12b, indicating not so much a motivic parallelism as a middleground course correction, a large-scale change of mind.

It seems that we are prepared for a reprise of the opening. However, we should not mistake that intention for an adherence to a standard form; nothing about the arrangement of events has followed a prescribed routine. Most notably, the opening music has never been given proper closure (even the A-minor half cadence in m. 79 quickly slips away), nor has the parenthetical music been closed off either (as if it had any capacity to do so!). In fact, these two passages have been vying to derail the train of thought for the piece thus far, and it is time they confronted each other. Example 7.13a, a rhythmic analysis of this ending, shows the opening idea spinning out of control as it seeks closure. The gradually broader pacing leads to an augmentation of the thirds just heard, and we recognize the slower time scale of the parenthetical music just as it is seizing control of this closing. (I have fancifully adapted the proportional time signature Brahms saw in Schütz to suggest the revaluing of the $\frac{3}{8}$ bars as a proportional division of a duple meter.) The conflict only intensifies, with fast metrical dissonance surging from the lowest register and the slow metrical consonance quashing it from above. Ironically, as Example 7.13b shows, the previously parenthetical slower time has wrested control of the structural voice leading, rendering its adversary superfluous. (The low-register echoes of the opening are shown only as parentheses that do not participate in the structure.) Note finally in Example 7.13a that the hypermetric structure is completed outside the bounds of the score (by counting through the *fermata*). Once again, there may be another echo of Schütz's "Saul": quite remarkably for its time, that piece ends not just quietly but with an entire measure of rest (perhaps an unprecedented notation). Brahms's capriccio reverses Schütz's dynamic scheme, but the implied final hyperbeat echoes Schütz's empty bar in a subtle and transformed way.[31]

Rückblick IV

The claim here is not that I have uncovered Brahms's definition of capriccio as used in his own music; indeed, it may be that his use of the title "Capriccio" has a somewhat different meaning in the context of each individual work. Recall the idea of genre as a regulative force. From the array of historical influences available to him, Brahms may have distilled the more general notion of nonregulation, of capriciousness itself, as a compositional principle, one that does not submit to genre but rather evades the very notion of genre. Even in works with an apparently conventional form, caprice as a guiding premise may allow true uniqueness to be realized.

Example 7.14. Brahms, Capriccio, op. 116, no. 7, rhythmic analysis and sketch of A section, mm. 1–20.

Brahms III

The D-minor capriccio ends firmly but somehow inconclusively, as if the musical issues it raises have not been fully resolved. The last of the op. 116

208 *Frank Samarotto*

Fantasies, also a Capriccio in D minor, seems to pick up on that sense of irresolution, almost too obviously: such overt similarities between the endpoints of this sort of collection are not Brahms's usual modus operandi.[32] It will be worth a very brief overview of the final number for comparison's sake; I will let the analytical examples fill in most of the details.

Op. 116, no. 7, begins with a clear and definite downbeat assertion, but conflict sets in almost immediately. The tonic chord is, at best, only implied, and the two hands toss the opening idea back and forth in metrically contradictory ways (see the score and Example 7.14). The phrase can end, but not in the tonic; it must repeat. Still, its repetition curiously loses force: the broken-chord motive is offset to a metrically dissonant position. It is as if there is a drag on this music, and it shows itself in the displaced hemiola of the middle section of mm. 21–44 (arrived at through motivic linkage). This is not a conventional contrasting middle section, however. The piece seems to change its mind about what it wants to do; the opening *agitato* does not accomplish anything—it just gives up. As suggested in the rhythmic reduction and voice-leading sketch of Examples 7.15a and b, the middle part is not just in another meter; rather, the pacing of events is such as to suggest an Andante character, a sort of dark minuet, hidden by the veil of the eighth-note accompaniment (but revealed by the undisplaced simplification shown in Example 7.15a). This middle section has a conventional form, but its second ending deliberately stifles closure. What follows is functionally transitional but is effectively trying to reanimate the opening music, backing into it through the metrically displaced version; this process is sorted out in Examples 7.16a and b, again through a combination of rhythmic and voice-leading analysis.[33] This transition can be heard as a vast expansion of the unsatisfactory third with which the middle section ended (see the brackets in 7.16b), meaning that the very element that weakened the middle section's integrity now leads us back for a second attempt. It is a kind of repudiation, if not a change of mind.

The return of the opening, however, retains its character of instability. There is genuine frustration in the way the repeat falters. The drag on this music is made palpable in the written-out *rubato* elongation of mm. 74–75 that swings into a lumbering ⅜. With this change of signature we are truly in capriccio territory and seem even closer to the concerns of the opening capriccio of op. 116. And this last piece engages in a similar struggle to achieve its closing cadence; as Example 7.17 shows, its pathway re-creates the top-voice thirds of the transition section (compare Example 7.16b), but the top-voice resolution is delayed by a restatement of the opening on a restless tonic pedal. No further dominant is forthcoming; instead, a weak plagal ending finally gives way to the major tonic. Now we recall the odd turn taken by the first op. 116 capriccio, the capricious di-

a) rhythmic analysis of B section, mm. 21-46

Example 7.15. Brahms, Capriccio, op. 116, no. 7, rhythmic analysis and sketch of B section, mm. 21–46.

vergence from resolution at the end of the first phrase, as if this final piece cannot achieve real closure but can finally only yield to capricious diversion.

Rückblick V

There is at least one more issue worth considering, but not, however, the problem of the supposed triviality of the capriccio as a genre. The musical complexity analyzed here clearly belies any such charge in the case of Brahms's conception of the genre.[34] The problem is rather one of arbitrariness. If Brahms is composing a series of willful changes of mind, how can the result be coherent? The problem is similar to the issue of free will articulated by Hegel in his *Philosophy of Right,* which includes specific mention of the dilemma of the artist:

> This is the contradiction contained in caprice. . . . When I will the rational, I do not act as a particular individual but according to the conception of ethical life

b) sketch of B section, mm. 21-46

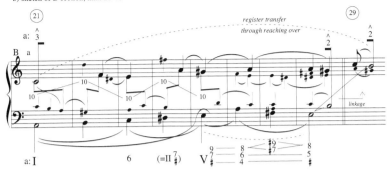

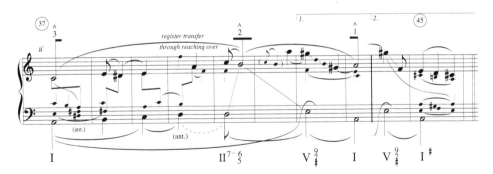

Example 7.15 *(continued).*

in general. . . . The rational is the highway on which every one travels, and no one is specially marked. When a great artist finishes a work we say: "It must be so." The particularity of the artist has wholly disappeared and the work shows no mannerism. . . . But the poorer is the artist, the more easily we discern himself, his particularity all caprice.[35]

The problem can be restated in terms of genre. If a genre has no regulative force, is the resultant music merely a depiction of individual whim? The question

a) rhythmic analysis of transition, mm. 47–54

b) sketch of end of B section and transition, mm. 45–61

Example 7.16. Brahms, Capriccio, op. 116, no. 7, rhythmic analysis and sketch of transition section, mm. 47–61.

has no easy answer—the piece itself is the answer—but I can imagine Brahms relishing the capriccio as an opportunity to reconsider the roles of freedom and constraint in the artwork, to show that, in the guise of a look backward, he could uncover meaning by looking inside.

a) rhythmic analysis of A' section, mm. 62–92

b) sketch of A' section, mm. 62–92

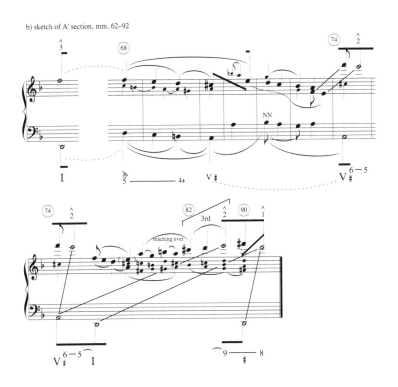

Example 7.17. Brahms, Capriccio, op. 116, no. 7, rhythmic analysis and sketch of A' section, mm. 62–92.

"Phantasia subitanea" 213

Notes

1. The facsimile reproduced in Example 7.1 is from Johannes Brahms, *Fantasien für Klavier opus 116: Faksimile nach dem Autograph im Besitz der Staats- und Universitätsbibliothek Hamburg* (Munich: Henle, 1997).

2. See, for instance, the third of Mendelssohn's Four Pieces for String Quartet, op. 81, labeled "Capriccio" and in the form of a prelude and fugue.

3. Kevin Korsyn, "Towards a New Poetics of Musical Influence," *Music Analysis* 10/1–2 (1991): 3–72.

4. James Hepokoski and Warren Darcy, *Elements of Sonata Theory: Norms, Types, and Deformations in the Late Eighteenth Century Sonata* (New York: Oxford University Press, 2006), 605.

5. The salient differences are discussed and summarized in Philip Whitmore, "Towards an Understanding of the Capriccio," *Journal of the Royal Musical Association* 113/1 (1988): 47–56.

6. Brahms studied a variety of seventeenth- and eighteenth-century Italian compositions, including works by Frescobaldi. Karl Geiringer, "Brahms the Collector of Books and Music," (1933), repr. in *On Brahms and His Circle: Essays and Documentary Studies*, rev. and enl. George S. Bozarth (Sterling Heights, Mich.: Harmonie Park Press in Association with the American Brahms Society, 2006), 17.

7. Ten out of the twelve capriccios have signature changes; the remaining two are the shortest in the set. This publication was also included in a 1626 collection with other types of pieces. By comparison, none of the ricercars have meter changes, and the canzonas have fewer changes with less variety.

8. For an accessible treatment of these unusual time signatures, see George Houle, *Meter in Music 1600–1800: Performance, Perception, and Notation* (Bloomington: Indiana University Press, 1987).

9. Tartini, *Traité des agréments de la musique* (Paris, 1771), 117–18, emphasis added, quoted in Whitmore, "Towards an Understanding," 52. It is worth noting that some of Paganini's caprices also juxtapose sections of differing meter and tempo.

10. Praetorius's *Syntagma musicum, Termini musici* (Wolfenbüttel, 1619), 21. This volume is mostly in German, despite the Latin title.

11. August Wilhelm Ambros, *Geschichte der Musik* (Leipzig: Leuckart, 1881), 4:457. Though it seems Brahms did not own this volume, Ambros's work was well known in Vienna. Remarkably, most of Praetorius's definition is also quoted in Koch's *Musikalisches Lexikon* (Frankfurt am Main: Hermann, 1802), 144, which reveals a continued awareness of the genre's oldest connotations.

12. Hans Lampl, "A Translation of *Syntagma musicum III* by Michael Praetorius" (D.M.A. diss., University of Southern California, 1957), 60. Quoted in Paul Collins, *The Stylus Phantasticus and Free Keyboard Music of the North German Baroque* (Aldershot: Ashgate Publishing, 2005), 34.

13. Praetorius, *Syntagma musicum, Termini musici*, 21, translation by the author. The complete original is as follows: "Capriccio seu Phantasia subitanea: Wenn einer nach seinem eignem plesier und gefallen eine Fugam zu tractiren vor sich nimpt / darinnen aber nicht lang immoriret, sondern bald in eine andere fugam / wie es ihme in Sinn kömpt / einfället: Denn weil ebener massen / wie in den rechten Fugen kein Text darunter gelegt werden darff / so ist man auch nicht an die Wörter gebunden / man mache viel oder wenig / man digredire, addire, detrahire, kehrer und wende es wie man wolle. Und kann einer in solchen Fantasien und Capriccien seine Kunst und artificium eben so wol sehen lassen: Sintemal er sich alles dessen / was in der Music tollerabile ist / mit bindungen der Discordanten, proportionibus &c. ohn einigs bedencken gebrauchen

darff; Doch dass er den Modum und die Ariam nicht gar zu sehr überschreite / sondern in terminis bleibe."

14. Jonathan Kramer, *The Time of Music: New Meanings, New Temporalities, New Listening Strategies* (New York: Schirmer, 1988).

15. Quoted by Franz Eibner in his preface to *Joseph Haydn: Klavierstücke* (Vienna: Schott, 1975), ix. Although we cannot be certain that Brahms knew these works, there is evidence that suggests that at the very least he would have known about them. Carl Ferdinand Pohl, the early Haydn scholar, was among Brahms's closest friends in Vienna. Brahms was quite familiar with Pohl's work on Haydn (he owned the first two volumes of Pohl's monograph on the Classical composer), and on a number of occasions Pohl introduced Brahms to works by Haydn. In the second volume of his monograph, Pohl mentions both the C-major fantasy and the G-major capriccio, and he quotes Haydn's comment that I give in the text. *Joseph Haydn* (Leipzig: Breitkopf & Härtel, 1882; repr., Wiesbaden: Sändig, 1971), 2:236.

16. See the follow-up letter, where Haydn complains of mistakes in the edition, which went to print without his review or approval. The same lack of approval is presumably true of the title change. Translated in H. C. Robbins-Landon, *Haydn: Chronicle and Works* (Bloomington: Indiana University Press, 1978), 2:724.

17. Eibner, preface to *Joseph Haydn: Klavierstücke*, xi: "The head motive of Haydn's *Fantasia*, whose meaning is rooted in absolute music, is a diminution of a 'rising' basic progression from c^2 via d^2 to e^2 [example omitted] but if one accentuates on the *bar* here, the notes c^2–b^1–c^2 are stressed and all the refinement of Haydn's declamation goes to the wall."

18. To be sure, surprising continuations, reversals, and exaggeration, along with interruptions and stalling on a harmony, are all elements of Haydn's humor that recur in many of his other genres. For two of the more detailed explorations of these techniques, see Gretchen Wheelock, *Haydn's Ingenious Jesting with Art: Contexts of Musical Wit and Humor* (New York: Schirmer, 1992), and L. Poundie Burstein, "Comedy and Structure in Haydn's Symphonies," in *Schenker Studies* 2, ed. Carl Schachter and Hedi Siegel (Cambridge: Cambridge University Press, 1999), 67–81.

19. As discussed by, among others, David Beach, "A Recurring Pattern in Mozart's Music," *Journal of Music Theory* 27/1 (1983): 1–29; Charles Rosen, *Sonata Forms* (New York: Norton, 1988), 262–75; and James Webster, *Haydn's "Farewell" Symphony and the Idea of Classical Style: Through-Composition and Cyclic Integration in His Instrumental Music* (Cambridge: Cambridge University Press, 1991), 135–38, 142–44.

20. Elaine Sisman describes this passage, and its subsequent reiteration, as a combination of a reference to the *wie aus der Ferne* topic, common in the nineteenth century, with a quality of "dying away." She considers these passages as "strikingly similar" to the end of Schumann's *Papillons*, op. 2. Sisman, "Rhetorical Truth in Haydn's Chamber Music: Genre, Tertiary Rhetoric, and the Opus 76 Quartets," in *Haydn and the Performance of Rhetoric*, ed. Tom Beghin and Sander M. Goldberg (Chicago: University of Chicago Press, 2007), 294–95 n. 15. Schumann's knowledge of Haydn's Fantasy, which Sisman implies, bolsters the hypothesis that Brahms also knew the Haydn work.

21. For an analysis concerned more with tonal issues, see Murray Dineen, "Schoenberg's Logic and Motor: Harmony and Motive in the 'Capriccio,' no. 1 of *Fantasien* op. 116, by Johannes Brahms," *GAMUT* 10 (2001): 3–26.

22. The terminology here is that of Harald Krebs, *Fantasy Pieces: Metrical Dissonance in the Music of Robert Schumann* (New York: Oxford University Press, 1999).

23. That is, because the upper voice outlines F–D (mimicking the previous leap, G–E), the inner voice C♯ at the end of m. 4 is to be thought of as a nonchord tone that resolves to D (as shown in Example 7.7d); to be sure, the persistence of that C♯ confuses the harmony, which is precisely what undermines its clarity as V.

24. This motivic linkage is quite striking: Brahms echoes the end of m. 15 by freely introducing the simultaneity E–C as a dissonance above tonic harmony. For a recent study on this type of compositional technique, see Peter H. Smith, "New Perspectives on Brahms's Linkage Technique," *Intégral* 21 (2007): 109–54.

25. Specifically, dominant chords now replace tonic as frames for this phrase, and the descending thirds in the left hand now outline dominant seventh harmony.

26. Brahms came to know the piece from Carl von Winterfeld's *Johannes Gabrieli und sein Zeitalter* (Berlin: Herrmann, 1834), 3:92–98. His careful annotations are discussed in Virginia Hancock, "Brahms's Performances of Early Choral Music," *19th-Century Music* 8/2 (1984): 125–41.

27. Virginia Hancock discusses this performance and the subsequent reaction. See "The Growth of Brahms's Interest in Early Choral Music, and Its Effect on His Own Choral Compositions," in *Brahms: Biographical, Documentary and Analytical Studies,* ed. Robert Pascall (Cambridge: Cambridge University Press, 1983), 33–34.

28. Brahms to Eusebius Mandyczewski, 26 May 1892. This letter is given in the English version of Karl Geiringer's 1933 article, "Johannes Brahms im Briefwechsel mit Eusebius Mandyczewski," in Bozarth, *On Brahms and His Circle,* 253. Geiringer's footnote identifies the volume Brahms mentions as that containing the "Saul" setting.

29. The work is scored for six soloists, two choirs, two violins, and continuo. The connection with a solo piano piece seems unlikely until one thinks of a piano reading of this score, whose fully textured passages would result in thick chords similar to the capriccio.

30. Manfred Bukofzer speaks of its "impetuously accelerated rhythm" in *Music in the Baroque Era* (New York: Norton, 1947), 93.

31. Curiously, the Winterfeld edition omits the final empty bar; however, Hancock, "Brahms's Performances," 131, makes it clear that Brahms studied the original parts in preparing his performance and would have been able to notice Schütz's unusual notation.

32. The unity of the collection is fully explored in Jonathan Dunsby, "The Multi-piece in Brahms: Fantasien, Op. 116," in Pascall, *Brahms,* 167–89.

33. There is a discrepancy with the autograph in m. 49 that has been pointed out by Camilla Cai (see below). I agree with her argument that Brahms missed an error in the first proofs (as he did many others!) and that this is a printer's error. Thus, in m. 49, the last two notes should be D–C♯ instead of C–B♭. This correction has an effect on the shape of the passage, which can be observed in Example 7.16. See Camilla Cai, "Brahms' Short, Late Piano Pieces—Opus Numbers 116–119: A Source Study, an Analysis and Performance Practice" (Ph.D. diss., Boston University, 1986), esp. 193. I am also grateful to Channan Willner for helping to confirm the contents of proof sheets.

34. Indeed, as late as 1807 the philosopher Christian Friedrich Michaelis characterized the capriccio as "serious and sublime." He is quoted more fully in Annette Richards, *The Free Fantasia and the Musical Picturesque* (Cambridge: Cambridge University Press, 2001), 135.

35. *Grundlinien der Philosophie des Rechts* (Berlin, 1821), Eng. trans. S. W. Dyde, *Philosophy of Right* (London: Bell, 1896), 26.

8 Monumentality and Formal Processes in the First Movement of Brahms's Piano Concerto No. 1 in D Minor, op. 15

James Hepokoski

Does the epic, sprawling character of the opening movement of Brahms's First Piano Concerto present its listeners with uncommonly daunting formal and hermeneutic problems? Such was the claim of Giselher Schubert in 1994: "The massive first movement of the Piano Concerto, op. 15, remained unique in Brahms's *œuvre:* never again did he compose an instrumental movement of such length. . . . In the first movement . . . Brahms considerably increased the number of theme groups, with the result that the movement is almost impossible to grasp as a whole."[1] Was Schubert registering a generally shared impression? What is required of us to experience a coherent succession of events in this movement? Following an overview of some historical and methodological considerations, this essay proposes the outlines of a Sonata-Theory–based reading of the movement as a whole.[2]

In the past several decades discussions of Brahms's op. 15 have focused largely on one or both of two interrelated issues.[3] The first seeks to lay out the remaining traces of its troubled, still somewhat mysterious compositional history from 1854 through 1859—from two-piano sonata to symphony to concerto, a history mediated by reactions and advice provided by Julius Otto Grimm, Clara Schumann, and Joseph Joachim—sometimes extending to its initial publication in a solo-piano arrangement in early 1861.[4] The second issue, often intertwined with the first, centers around deciphering the presumed allusions and connotations of a few of its themes—the crisis-ridden opening page, the "Benedictus" text-underlay at the onset of the D-major Adagio, and so on—with particular attention given to their potential biographical implications. Here, Brahms's intimacy and psychological identification with the Schumann family loom large.

Such exercises in decoding are inquiries into what I call the *vertical* implications of an isolated thematic module: a single passage's connotative significance considered apart from the role of its placement(s) within a composition. Vertical connotations comprise such things as programmatic representations, quotations of or allusions to specific moments of esteemed earlier works, and the deployment of standardized theme, gesture, topic, tempo, or texture types associable with culturally constructed, subjective moods or actions. These last include the stock-in-trade affective postures circulating within nineteenth-century Austro-Germanic music: heroic, celebratory, marchlike, hymnic, folklike, introspective, reverential, aspirational, melancholic, funereal, stormy, combative, menacing, demonic, "purely musical" (self-referential images of the music-technical, as with, say, imitative/fugal practice or conventional developmental procedures), and so on. Vertical resonances are historical through and through. Among other things, they situate an individual work within a specific cultural tradition. This presupposes a network of shared expectations within a community of listeners themselves shaped by institutions devoted to sustaining that tradition.

With regard to at least the first movement, less attention has been paid to providing an adequate account of what additional connotations accrue to those modules by virtue of their assignments within the movement's formal processes.[5] These constitute what I call their *horizontal* aspect, the work's events considered as participants in the ongoing, linear-temporal flow, with particular attention paid to the manner in which they are placed into a dialogue with the generic action spaces of, in this case, a sonata-form–based structure. What does it mean to have *this* musical module situated *there* (as opposed to elsewhere)—*and* following, say, *that* module? Within any composition each module has both a vertical and a horizontal aspect. Any text-adequate discussion needs to be concerned with both.

The Quest for Monumentality

An important component of Brahms's concerto was its enormous size. Its durational expanse challenged any listener who wished to follow its overarching musical argument, as opposed to merely basking in selected individual moments. The 484 bars of its first movement alone span around twenty-two minutes, the concerto as a whole around forty-eight—much to the distress of Eduard Bernsdorf, its bewildered and hostile critic in the *Signale für die musikalische Welt*.[6] This made the work longer than its only significant rivals, Beethoven's Violin Concerto and Fifth Piano Concerto. In contrast, Mendelssohn's and Schumann's concertos had been more modestly sized, while Liszt's two piano concertos were veritable miniatures, requiring only about twenty minutes each.[7] As Brahms supporter Adolf Schubring put it in 1862, "The first movement is more gigantic than that of any other concerto known to me. Gigantic works demand gigantic proportions."[8]

But neither the tallying of bar numbers nor the clocking of absolute durations tells the full story. The composer also enhanced the movement's impression of uncommon magnitude through his choice of an unusual meter: a broadly sweeping, Maestoso $\frac{6}{4}$. (With its opportunities for strategically placed, "Brahmsian" $\frac{3}{2}$ hemiolas, $\frac{6}{4}$ would reappear in several of his later works, among them the Third Symphony and the Second Piano Concerto.) From one perspective, the $\frac{6}{4}$ can strike us as a joining together of two bars of $\frac{3}{4}$, as if notating a hypermeter that could invite those who read the notation to perceive the work—an aspect of which is the notation itself—as coursing onward in oversized metric strides. From another, it can be perceived as a notationally fortified $\frac{6}{8}$, a heftier, weightier alternative, plunging ever forward like a sturdy ship through wide seas.[9] How might readers of the score perceive this movement differently had it been notated in $\frac{3}{4}$—the meter of Mozart's C-Minor Piano Concerto, K. 491, or Beethoven's "Eroica"—or in the typically lighter $\frac{6}{8}$?[10]

For all these reasons and more (including thematic content and orchestration) the colossal impression of Brahms's concerto, recalling the proportions of Beethoven's and Schubert's Ninth Symphonies, is anything but culturally neutral. Its commanding bulk and resounding earnestness suggest its viability as a cultural monument on behalf of the Austro-Germanic tradition within which it is so self-consciously situated. Brahms's concerto was a contemporary yet historicizing work. As such it participated in the midcentury drive toward grand-scale feats of commemoration and monumentalism, topics treated recently by Alexander Rehding. Any such monument—musical, sculptural, or architectural—is charged with the connotation of cultural depth and seriousness of purpose. It "accords privileged importance to heritage and traditions . . . [and thereby] approaches the fundamental question of who we are by telling us where we come from." Above all—as is the case in Brahms's first concerto—it seeks to provide its listeners with

> the sense of being a self-sufficient musical object that radiates greatness as though out of itself; and it piggybacks on the newly minted work-concept that had bestowed new prestige on the art of music and that only made this monolithic, self-reliant impression possible. The work that the nineteenth-century musical monument was to perform effectively consists in bringing together two distinct types of magnitude: one component, historical greatness, can be summarized under the modern keywords of collective memory and identity formation, while its other component, physical size, shows a marked tendency toward dramatic proportions (or even lack of any proportionality) that would elicit astonishment from its audience . . . an aesthetics of wonderment.[11]

Metaphorical Hermeneutics and Dialogic Form

Any search for a cogent pathway through this monumental first movement needs to pursue questions of its thematic-modular succession. That succession cannot be suspected of being arbitrary: one must presume that Brahms intended it to "make sense" within the contexts of its cultural traditions. Steering clear of vapid trumpetings on behalf of "unity" or "perfection," my concern is only to inquire into the composer's staging of a dramatized musical narrative appropriate to concerns within the state of composition in Germany in the 1850s.[12] While that narrative may be read as one founded on an exclusively musical logic—motives, chords, keys, contrapuntal lines, formal patterns—its linear ordering of contrasting affective states also invites its listeners heuristically to attach to it any number of external metaphors of response, action, and striving.

None of what follows should be taken as a bluntly programmatic reading. Any claim of programmaticism would imply the presence of a privileged reading intended by the composer in which this or that theme is to be conceptually associated with only this or that poetic idea, person, or activity. That is not the argument of this essay. One needs to distinguish between overtly or covertly illustrative music and the capacity of abstract instrumental music to be synchronized with a wide range of metaphorical analogues, none of which can claim exclusivity. Such music harbors multiple strata of potential meanings. These are differing registers of metaphor that may be activated through close analysis and responsible hermeneutics. None of these registers discloses any supposed single meaning—the *proper* meaning—once and for all.[13] One of my aims, though, will be to explore the metaphorical analogue that situates this piece within a much-conflicted historical situation. Whatever other connotations it might have sought to convey, Brahms's concerto also spoke, as a manifesto by example, to the strained and polemical context of Austro-Germanic art music at that time. But any such manifesto involves more than size. It must also be discernible in the musical processes themselves, not only in the choice of the concerto's ideologically charged materials but also in their disposition within a minor-mode, sonata-oriented work.

The commentary that follows is grounded in the concept of *dialogic form:* interpreting a work as participating in a dialogue with established traditions, one that the listener or analyst can seek to recover.[14] Its premise is that the meaning of a work's succession of details is not to be sought exclusively in its acoustic surface —what it audibly presents to us. No work is a self-sufficient statement capable of defining its own terms from ground zero. Instead, every work plugs into the power systems of genres that are already there as foundational elements within the contemporarily accepted norms of musical discourse. An essential aspect of a work's meaning is to be located in the details of how it realizes—or refrains from realizing—the set of expectations of the genre within which it participates. No genre (such as any type of sonata form) is to be construed as a rigid, ahistorical template. Not only do genres comprise generous and flexible arrays of compositional options for the realization of any expected action space within them, but they are also historically situated, bearing cultural connotations and aesthetic ideologies that change with time. Brahms's midcentury sonata form started from premises that had changed since the era of Mozart and Beethoven, premises that led to different inflections of historicized consciousness.

While one aspect of a work is *immanent,* or specific to the content of that work alone (Brahms's concerto is distinguishable from Beethoven's "Emperor" concerto, not merely reducible to the genre that they share), another aspect is *relational*—how it interacts dialogically with the historically situated norms of the genre, which provide interpretive guidelines for what happens immanently within the piece. In this case Brahms composed the first movement in dialogue with the concerto-sonata format of an earlier generation—that which, like Mozart's and Beethoven's, begins with a substantial orchestral tutti (or ritornello) preceding the onset of the solo exposition proper.[15] Sonata Theory calls this the Type 5 sonata.[16] By the 1850s there was a more efficient alternative. Mendelssohn's concertos, Schumann's piano and cello concertos, and others had omitted this opening tutti, producing trim, Type 3 sonata forms without any expositional repeat.[17] Thus at midcentury one could compose the first movement of a concerto either in the older Type 5 format (in the case at hand, subjected to a number of midmovement modifications) or in the leaner, more modern Type 3 abridgment or variant thereof. While it would be overdrawn to conclude that Brahms's retention of an initial, Type 5 ritornello was an anachronism, it is possible to read it as ideologically significant: a proclamation of solidarity with the Beethovenian concerto tradition in all its architectural splendor and gravitas, a tradition that he and Joachim were coming to regard as aesthetically compromised in their own times. Merely by deploying such an opening tutti, Brahms not only demonstrated that his work was emphatically a concerto (as its title promised) and not a symphony (however symphonic its materials and treatment might strike its listeners) but also proposed another set of solutions (as opposed to, say, Liszt's) as the truest successors to the Beethoven legacy.[18]

Equally significant for our charting of the narrative of the work is that this is a movement in D minor. As is the situation with most minor-mode sonatas, animating that narrative is the procedure of composing the successive action zones as event spaces through which an initially negative state (represented by the minor mode and certain styles of thematic material) is reacted to in an attempt to overcome it, to transform it permanently into a positive one (the major mode). None of this should be approached simplistically: obviously, major and minor modes carry wide ranges of expressive tints and topoi depending on the manner in which they are realized. Positive or negative connotations are less in the modes themselves than they are historical tropes of signification accepted culturally as community-shared features of musical communication.[19] By the 1850s the major-minor modal dichotomy and its historically accrued connotations had long been crystallized into an absolute binary, an essential feature of any composer's palette of colors. At the heart of this movement is the customary minor-major premise: the deploying of Type 5 sonata processes to generate a drama of starkly contrasting feelings that seeks to emancipate the initial D-minor situation into D major. Every recurrence of D minor (or minor-mode proxy) suggests the persistence of a state of threat, sorrow, weariness, or potential defeat; every D-major gleam (or major-mode proxy), however underdetermined or fleeting, suggests a vision of escape or overcoming.

This leads us into an overview of the individual details of the first movement, which Brahms constructed upon the varying appearances of seven separate modules—the movement's basic musical ideas, some of which are motivically interrelated. For purposes of reference these are provided in Examples 8.1–8.7. (Example 8.3a sprouts an important variant in the development, m. 278, labeled here as Example 8.3b.) I have also provided the relevant Sonata Theory designation for each of them. The symbol R1:\ means that the module is first presented in the opening ritornello (or tutti), mm. 1–90.[20] Subsequent, varied versions of that module will also be labeled with the R1:\ identifier to remind us where it had originally appeared. The symbol S1:\ refers to the two modules (Examples 8.6 and 8.7) introduced only in the solo exposition, a space that includes its sololed preface at m. 91 (Example 8.6). The P, TR, S, and C labels are standard within Sonata Theory (primary theme, transition, secondary thematic zone, closing zone, each construed as a generic action space to be decked out with appropriate content). TM³ (Example 8.7) refers to the third member of a trimodular block, which term will be addressed as it arises below.

In any sonata analysis the most pressing requirement is to explore the implications of its musical materials as they are initially presented at the opening of the piece. As a result, much of what follows will concentrate on the initial *Anlage* (layout) of modules presented in the orchestral tutti (R1) and their reappearance and expansion within the subsequent solo exposition (S1). Once the implications of R1 and S1 are grasped, the remainder of the movement can be dealt with more efficiently.

The Opening Tutti (Ritornello, R1, mm. 1–90): Overview

The presence of a broad and thematically differentiated opening orchestral tutti aligns this movement with formalized "Classical" practice. An opening tutti has three structural functions.[21] The first is an *introductory/anticipatory function*: preparing for the soloist's entry, which in turn must be planned to be

Examples 8.1–8.7. Brahms, Piano Concerto No. 1 in D Minor, op. 15, themes.

Example 8.1. R1:\P, mm. 1–12.

Example 8.2. R1:\TR, mm. 26–36.

Example 8.3a. R1:\S, mm. 45–51.

Example 8.3b. Development, variant of R1:\S, mm. 278–80.

Example 8.4. R1:\C$^{1.2}$, mm. 76–80.

Example 8.5. R1:\C$^{1.3}$, mm. 82–86.

Example 8.6. S1:\P^{pref}, mm. 91–96.

Example 8.7. S1:\TM^3, mm. 157–64.

engagingly responsive to what has just preceded it. The second is an *expositional-rhetoric function*: laying out a succession of modules that, regardless of the contrasting keys they may (or may not) visit, topically suggest the action zones of a sonata exposition, P TR ' S / C.[22] The third is a *referential-layout function*: the establishing of a succession of modules that will be recycled, in this order, in later rotations. Brahms's initial tutti carries out all these functions.[23] This is not to say that mm. 1–90 (R1) are merely normative. On the contrary, they abound with provocative content.

One of R1's notable features is its tonal/modal course. The Classical precedents had begun and ended in the same key and normally in the same mode, with declarative security at both ends, regardless of any tonal diversions that might have been placed into their interiors. Brahms alluded to this precedent as a conceptual norm but realized it in a dramatically unconventional way. In this D-minor concerto R1 concludes in D *major* (mm. 82–90)—easily assimilated to the norm—but, as all commentators have noted, the eruptive opening, R1:\P, with its first chord of $B\flat^6$ (mm. 2–3, soon turned into a $B\flat^6_5$, mm. 4–10), is tonally underdetermined. Considered only vertically, in isolation and without regard to the key signature, the turbulent opening page does not suggest D minor. As Joseph Dubiel put it, what we encounter at the outset is a "characteristic Brahmsian gambit," that of starting a composition with the postponement of any "clear presentation of . . . [the] tonic triad."[24] (Retrospectively, one might suppose that "D minor" batters the work open in an alarming variant, inflected with a $\hat{5}$–$\hat{6}$ shift [$B\flat^6$] that ratchets up its urgency—or one might construe the opening chord as suggesting a dark D-minor triad altered via the *Leittonwechsel* [L] operation. However we derive it theoretically, it is as if any pure D minor—fatalistic enough on its own—is blown apart, as though a mere D-minor chord is unable to contain its explosive distress.)[25] This invites us to grasp the succession of modules comprising R1 as a process that, by degrees and through various tonal digressions, eventually produces—or is unable to evade—the stark inevitability of a D-minor PAC (perfect authentic cadence, m. 66, R1:\EEC [the first tutti's analogous point of "essential expositional closure"], even though the tonic is represented only by octave Ds).[26] But even while the brute fact of D minor is confirmed at m. 66, the process does not end here. This seemingly no-exit moment reignites the initial "$B\flat^6$" music full force (m. 67). This time, through an effort of will (mm. 76–81), that passage is crafted to break through to a concluding stage, its emancipation into D major (mm. 82–90)—a proleptic vision of the desired outcome of the sonata activity to follow: exorcising the D-minor threat by converting it into D major.

But this is only a description of the obvious. The larger questions are ones of purpose and implication: how might we frame this R1 music as a whole? It is clear that the opening tutti subdivides into two complementary sections (mm. 1–66, 66–90), each of which is launched by the "symphonic" opening module R1:\P. Within the tradition this explosive eruption could be read as an unforeseen intrusion "coming out of nowhere"—bursting into our awareness from the blankness of silence and suggesting an immediate and extreme existential crisis. Each R1 section responds to R1:\P with different material: the first, groping, mourning, spectral, tonally insecure (Examples 8.2 and 8.3a); the second, pushing through to a short-lived *forte* celebration of major-mode attainment (Examples 8.4 and 8.5). This is the fundamental expressive structure of R1.

Thus the opening tutti stages contrasting responses to the anguished crisis implied by R1:\P. The generically inevitable reintrusions of R1:\P (sometimes varied) also dominate all that follows, each appearance beginning a new cycle of response. On the broadest level the movement is "about" responding to the recurring challenge of whatever calamitous upheaval R1:\P might be imagined to represent. From this perspective the movement calls upon the action spaces of the Type 5 format first (in R1) to conjure up the extremity of the crisis and to suggest two modes of response to it, and second (in the remainder of the movement) to deploy the genre as a goal-driven medium through which the trajectory of reactions to the initial module can be dramatized.

R1:\P (mm. 1–25): Connotations

R1:\P (Example 8.1) is not only the determinative module for the entire composition, but it is also the richest in connotations. It can be explored from three different vantage points: programmatic implication and its broader resonances of metaphor; intertextual allusions; and musical processes. With regard to the first, no commentator fails to associate R1:\P's turbulence with Brahms's alarm at learning the news of Robert Schumann's suicide attempt—his leap into the Rhine—on 27 February 1854, an association conveyed many decades later to Max Kalbeck by Joseph Joachim. In response to a request from Kalbeck, Joachim had replied that it had been originally composed in its aftermath as "a kind of powerful shiver" (*eine Art mächtiger Schüttelfrost*)—doubtless referring to that module's brandishing of strident trills. Kalbeck, then, was able to declare that it had arisen from a representation (*Vorstellung*) of the catastrophe and as such conveyed Brahms's shuddering, sympathetically experienced "soul-image" (*Seelenbild*) of the event.[27] The compositional facts line up with this claim. Within about two months after this "most devastating day of Brahms's life" (as Styra Avins characterized it), Brahms had drafted three movements of a D-minor sonata for two pianos (provisionally orchestrated to become a projected symphony by June and July 1854).[28] The opening of the first movement of this sonata is usually agreed, on the basis of remarks by Joachim and Albert Dietrich, to have been an early version of the music that now begins the concerto.[29] Complementarily, Brahms's refashioning of earlier conceptions of the work into a piano concerto (with newly composed second and third movements) was undertaken in earnest two years later, around October 1856, only a few months after Schumann's death on 29 July.[30] It is not difficult to presume that the monumental concerto—largely drafted in the ensuing three months—figured in Brahms's mind as an act of commemoration and solidarity.

What are we to make of such information? Does R1:\P (mm. 1–25) point toward the interiority of Brahms's shock in 1854 or, more literally, toward a hyperdramatized portrayal of Schumann's fateful "Sprung in den Rhein" as an objective event? Is it "mehr Ausdruck der Empfindung als Malerei"? Or the reverse? Or both? Crude as it might seem to absolute-music partisans, it is certainly possible to construe the module as realistically pictorial, with the terrifying event translated into graphic musical analogues. Beyond the portentous ultimacy of the moment we find a determined ascent to a trilling madness high above the (pedal-point) river (m. 8: notice the demonic-tritone anacrusis to the high point) followed by an impetuous downward plunge (mm. 8–11).[31] (Dare one go so far as to suggest the proto-Straussian image of the resultant splash in the second half of m. 11?)

Of course one need not reduce the potential R1:\P connotations to this image alone. Indeed, some might prefer that any all-too-literal depiction of the delusion-driven leap be sidelined altogether as a trivialization of R1:\P's more elevated resonances within a venerated tradition of "pure music." It is often held, for instance, that the power of abstract instrumental music—its ability, particularly in the era of subjectivity, to stir us at more primordially affective levels—lies in its normative refusal to demand any such referential attachment, conveying instead, in Roger W. H. Savage's recent characterization (grounded in concepts of Heidegger and Ricoeur), a precognitive "ontological vehemence" that "touches the fundamental element of our mortal dwelling," opening us to "dimensions of experience that precede the objectification of reality" in a way that "refigures our inherence in the world."[32] Within the conceptual world of nineteenth-century Germanic Romanticism, such poetic qualities within music were claimed to access soul states (*Seelenzustände,* as both Robert Schumann and A. B. Marx had put it), expressing feelings beyond words or reductions to prosaic images or rule-of-thumb analyses.[33] This was a conception of music's expressive value that young Brahms, in all likelihood, would have shared. R1:\P is a *Seelenzustand* of explosive alarm, the onset of an unspecified catastrophe that must now be faced.

Yet we have every reason to think that the distress conveyed by this opening was linked in Brahms's mind, even if not pictorially, with the memory of

Schumann's 1854 misfortune and (by 1856) death. From this perspective one aspect of the concerto is "about" Brahms's relation to Schumann (along with Clara and the Schumann family). But the Schumanns were not merely individuals whom Brahms happened to know. On the contrary, they embodied an artistic position lobbying on behalf of the presumed sanctity and weightier purposes of art, as opposed to current compositional styles that they regarded as trading in publicity or ego-inflated virtuosity. Schumann's decline and death could be taken as a symbol for the state of that aesthetic position within Austro-Germanic art music, threatened with eclipse by cultic and progressive trends. On these terms the concerto could be construed as both a monument to all that Schumann had represented and a demonstration that young Brahms, as his de facto chosen successor, was now up to the task of carrying on the enterprise in the grandest possible formats.

As mediated by Brahms, then, the Schumann crisis was also a crisis of continuation. Under these lights the concerto is "about" the challenges of its own musical present in the wake of a tragic and enormous loss, just as the processes of this first movement can be read as seeking at the outset to reenact the crisis of that critical situation, whose urgency can be heard to cry out in the gripping *Angst* of R1:\P. Can the Austro-Germanic tradition be renewed in the hands of a young, rising master, committed to remaining true to the highest aspirations of Mozart, Beethoven, and Schumann? This political aspect of the work's implication is buttressed not only by its interest in self-promotion as a public-display piece (initially with the composer as soloist) but also by the processes of the piece's execution as one works one's way through it. As an aesthetic manifesto the concerto is "about" the obligations of composing a "symphonic" concerto worthy of that description under the burden of the seemingly unsurpassable achievements of the past. The first movement posits a recurring, in extremis question in R1:\P and then stages a reply to it in the bar-by-bar moments of its performance, taking us through the heavy friction of a Type 5 sonata. The piece, in short, demonstrates itself.

That the tradition was somehow at stake in imperiled times is suggested by R1:\P's apparent pointings to specific passages from classic repertory pieces. R1:\P propels the concerto forward through a purposeful act of backward-looking recall. It participates in the aesthetics of the secret: those with knowledge of the repertory can hear one register of its meaning in terms of the similar music that it calls up to memory. Identifying the specific passage alluded to is less important than the invitation to open such an inquiry—to hear (or to believe that one hears) the coexisting presence of esteemed tokens from the past in the presentness of the concerto's opening bars. While the game of allusion spotting in Brahms encourages unconfirmable speculation (those insisting on absolute verification may frown on the practice altogether), this may well have been its point: to invite the listener to connect current, audible presence to a historical, newly canonical past.

In the case of R1:\P three such allusions might be proposed, and together these three invoke the three masters whose achievements most clearly represented the tradition with which Brahms was seeking to align himself: Beethoven, Mozart, and Schumann. The *fortissimo*, apocalyptic ferocity of the onset, initially a $B\flat^6$ (mm. 2–3), seems to point toward the blazing D^6 moment of recapitulation in the first movement of Beethoven's Ninth Symphony (m. 301), just as it may also evoke in its "B-flatness" the D-minor/B♭-major conflict (i and VI) in that earlier work. Apart from the biographical context typically noted by commentators—that Brahms had experienced his first hearing of a live performance of Beethoven's Ninth in Cologne in late March 1854, about a month after Schumann's suicide attempt—one need only recall that since its premiere the Ninth had been often regarded as a work that had exhausted the limits of the old formats.[34] Through this allusion Brahms takes up the challenge of meeting the problem head-on. Equally provocative, though, are R1:\P's similarities to certain features of the (much quieter) opening of Mozart's C-Minor Piano Concerto, K. 491. These could hardly be coincidental: the triple meter, the early displacement of $\hat{5}$ by $\hat{6}$ in the top voice, the upward leap on the two strongly pronounced quarter notes, and the negatively connotative descending chromatic line. Finally, while the eruptive opening of Brahms's concerto might recall that of Schumann's Third Symphony (both texturally and in its melodic leaps), a case has also been made on behalf of R1:\P's intertextuality with the first movement of Schumann's Fourth. Richard Taruskin reads that module as "constructed almost entirely out of 'classical' allusions. The most immediate one is to Schumann's own D-minor symphony, composed in 1841 as his Second, but revised in 1851 and published posthumously as his Fourth. It, too, begins by 'allowing the timpani and the drums to resound' in a lengthy roll . . . and its first Allegro theme (alluded to thereafter in all the other movements) is also marked by a surprising leap that lands on the very same notes [D and F] as does Brahms's intensified version."[35]

In purely musical terms the opening $B\flat^6$ (mm. 2–3; $B\flat^6_5$, mm. 4–10) and its displacement of an expected D minor have been commented upon so often that little more needs to be added here. What we encounter more broadly within R1:\P is a wide-ranging, eleven-bar module elided with its much-intensified variant (mm. 11–21, A^6_5, now suggesting D minor). This leads to an elided continuation (mm. 21–25) that is cut short on the V^6_4 chord of D minor, leaving its resolution hanging in the air. Holding the entire paragraph in place is the chromatically sinking bass from D (as conceptual tonic, despite what occurs above it) to A (as dominant) in ever-shortening durations: D (mm. 1–10), C♯ (11–20), C♮

(21–22), B♮ (23–24¹), B♭ (24²), and A (25). In other words, we have the traditionally negative symbol of the chromatically descending tetrachord, and it is that fatalistic emblem that controls the course of R1:\P as a whole.

R1:\TR and S (mm. 26–66): Bleak Aftermath

The drop from an aggressive *forte* to a soul-weary *piano* at m. 26 is the first of many stark contrasts offered by this movement: the opening assault lifts to reveal a crushed presence only beginning to emerge from under the onslaught (Example 8.2). This is the kind of abrupt shift that the exasperated Eduard Bernsdorf singled out for criticism in the *Signale für die musikalische Welt* in his 3 February 1859 review of the Leipzig premiere: "The musical ideas either crawl forward in a feeble and sickly manner or they rear up into the heights in a feverish frenzy, only in order to collapse even more exhaustedly. In a word, the whole emotional tone and invention in the piece is unhealthy. . . . Only very rarely can one speak of an organic process of development and a logical spinning-forth."[36]

Here Bernsdorf may have reduced the concept of *Fortspinnung* (or, alternatively, what we might call developing variation) to one of a smoothly progressive causation, in which one module seemingly generates another "logically," while moving ever forward into the piece. This is defensible so far as it goes: each of any piece's moments is obviously vectored forward in terms of temporal duration, reaching outward to create and consolidate a future. But even as any moment is to be oriented forward (by the text-adequate listener) to play its role in the realization of a generic goal to come, it is also to be referenced backward, under the presumption that it responds to its immediate predecessor or to the state of affairs produced thus far in the piece. This latter quality is a module's reactive aspect. From that point of view we may speak of *reactive modules*. This first movement consists of an accumulating set of reactive modules, successively responding to the traumatic state of affairs implied by R1:\P and also, by extension, to the cumulative chain of reactive modules that has preceded each of them. While the concept of causality implies an irreversible linearity, the reactive aspect of modules involves a retrospective dimension. Or, to draw upon phenomenological perspectives, all streaming moments of acoustic presentness have aspects of both retention (a consciousness of what is just past) and protention (anticipating the not yet). Each present moment is heavy with the burdens of both the past and the future.

In terms of their proto-expositional function, mm. 26–45 are transitional (R1:\TR), serving as a linking passage to a secondary thematic zone (R1:\S) that begins in m. 46. Here the rhetorically transitional function is also modulatory, moving from a residue-husk of D minor (m. 26, over V) to a sequential reiteration up a fifth on A minor (m. 35) and finally dissolving into a much-clouded preparation for the B♭-minor coloration characterizing R1:\S. Particularly notable is Brahms's choking-down of dynamics for the entirety of R1:\TR. It had been the almost invariable Classical norm to sound R1:\TR with an elided burst of *forte* vigor that continues to gain energy up to the medial caesura (MC).[37] Here Brahms reversed the norm. An overwhelming R1:\P, ending with clubbed force (m. 25), is succeeded by a TR from which the normative energy has been drained. It is as if the act of continuation were unthinkable. And yet the task of proceeding onward must be faced if the piece, along with the tradition, is not to be shut down altogether. All the more significant, then, is that the A-minor sequence (m. 36) reduces the dynamics from the original *piano* (m. 26) to *pianissimo* (with *diminuendo* in m. 40), mutes the upper strings (*con sordino*), finds itself unable to reproduce the entirety of its model intact (crumbling into a common-tone diminished seventh chord, m. 41), and is capable of only slouching its way toward a weakly articulated MC effect in m. 45 (the gap on beat 1). We are faced with a cluster of counternormative, entropic images.

The reactive status of R1:\TR is clear. Its bass consists of lingering reverberations of the incipit of R1:\P (mm. 2–3) with two modifications: the initial B♭ has been settled back to A, clarifying its D-minor orientation (here implicitly over V); and that incipit has been rhythmically altered into single-bar-length reiterations. R1:\TR floats above these bobbing shock-wavelets, with whose triple-time, rocking pulsations its own are allied. At the same time, setting out from a D-minor reality, R1:\TR's upper voice is aspirational, prayerlike, as if descrying the possibility of a D-major emancipation far down the road, not yet graspable in its current present. Brahms arrayed the thematic model, mm. 27–34, as a sentence: two complementary hoists (the presentation, mm. 27–28, 29–30), prepare one for a yearning, upward glance (the continuation, mm. 31–35), projecting a fleeting vision of "D major" (a V^6_4 of hopeful expectation, *crescendo*, with upper-voice intervals recalling those of R1:\P), decaying at once to V^6_4 of D minor (m. 32, *diminuendo*, a weary sigh—the thrust of the entire movement *in nuce*) and thence to the $\frac{5}{3}$ resolution, an A-major chord completing a half cadence in D minor. (This $\frac{5}{3}$ chord also furnishes the "missing" resolution of the V^6_4 in m. 25, whose dominant is prolonged in the bass through m. 34.) When the A-major chord darkens to A minor (m. 35), echoing the D-major/D-minor "lights-out" decay in m. 32, the model begins to be replicated sequentially, and more softly, a fifth higher, a spectral sequence suggestive of loss. This time, the music stalls on the corresponding major-minor decay (A–a, m. 40), disintegrating into the mists of a diminished seventh, out of which materializes the dominant of an unexpected key, B♭ minor. At the moment of the R1:\MC (m. 45, beat 1), almost all sense of forward motion, and the will to continue, has been lost.

What is launched at m. 46 must be regarded as R1:\S (Example 8.3a), although nearly everything about it is estranged from customary practice. Within nineteenth-century, minor-mode Type 5s, the norm at this point was to provide a major-mode S that started either in the relative major (III) or, less often, in the tonic major (I).[38] In this case not only is the major mode absent, suggesting the inaccessibility of consolation or relief, but for fourteen bars the key evoked, over its prolonged dominant, is B♭ minor, the minor submediant of D minor. From one perspective B♭ minor might respond to the implied "B-flatness" of the opening upheaval, mm. 2–3, now dimmed into a grieving minor. From another, one might regard B♭ minor as the bleak, maximally distant hexatonic pole of the longed-for D-major sonority ephemerally glimpsed only a few bars before.[39] However one interprets it, from the standpoint of any normative procedure the impression conveyed is that of having wandered into foreign tonal territory—a zone of utter darkness.

Led by quiet winds, R1:\S struck Joachim as a "wonderfully beautiful, first minor-mode song."[40] In context, it issues forth as a desolate *Grablied,* or funereal grave song—a site of mourning. Melodically, it continues the gently rocking figures heard in R1:\TR, perhaps recalling its descending fourths (from mm. 28–29, 30–31). As Dubiel noted, R1:\S is also "the movement's most mobile theme . . . the one theme to change in character, and, in most performances, tempo, from its original form."[41] Here in R1 the theme begins with an antecedent-like gesture (mm. 46–51, though entirely over V), whose consequent, begun in m. 52, stalls in mm. 55–59, *diminuendo,* and, through downward slippages in the bass, drifts into the hazy murk of C♯^{o7} (mm. 62–63)—again suggesting, as with R1:\TR, an inability to complete or continue.

And then everything changes. This C♯^{o7} in mm. 62–63, vii^{o7} of D minor, precipitates a moment of decision. The gears clench; frozen grief gives way to determination; the calamity is to be faced and overcome; the tradition must continue. The violins remove their mourning mutes, and a dissonantly explosive, *forte* rush (mm. 64–66) swerves into D minor, bringing R1:\S to an end with a firmly stamped i:PAC that seizes the challenge of what that global tonic represents.[42] The perfect authentic cadence in m. 66 may be construed as R1:\EEC, simultaneously opening the way to a subsequent closing zone. That closing material starts by reigniting R1:\P in m. 67, which unsettles the just-confirmed D minor with its *Leittonwechsel* "B♭6" and brings us back to the situation initially set forth at the beginning.[43] This time, the response to it will be different.

R1:\C (mm. 66–90):
Confrontation and Prediction of Victory

Notwithstanding its sense of rebeginning, the return of R1:\P in m. 67—now recast as R1:\C—is less formally idiosyncratic than it might initially appear. Here Brahms may have had in mind what had become an "alternative" option within the concerto practice of the preceding several decades. In those Type 5, minor-mode concertos, in which R1:\S had begun in a nontonic key, it had become conventional to provide a stormy, often *forte* return to the original minor tonic toward the end of R1, either before or shortly after the PAC that marked the attainment of R1:\EEC. Occasionally (as in John Field's Piano Concerto No. 7 in C Minor), the shift back into the tonic was ushered in with a return of R1:\P, as occurs here, creating something of a "ternary" impression.[44] (Instances in which the secondary key persisted and attained satisfactory closure at the end of R1 seem to have been rare.)[45] Apart from any possible precedent in Field's works or in now-little-known works of others, two obvious minor-mode models would also have been Mozart's Piano Concerto in C Minor, K. 491/i (m. 63, *forte*—although in this case R1:\S, m. 44, had also been in the tonic) and Schumann's Violin Concerto in D Minor, WoO 23 (m. 42, merging, *crescendo*, into D minor after an R1:\S, m. 31, like Brahms's, also largely over the dominant).[46] Brahms's difference from these last two precedents lies in the caesura-gap impression of m. 66 (octave Ds corresponding to m. 1, now *crescendo*). This produces an effect of nonelision, facilitating an inexorable thrust into the convulsive thematic content of m. 67, reerupting in high relief (R1:\P = R1:\C[1.1]).

This briefer, second cycle is one of action. Measures 66–75 replicate mm. 1–9 with enhanced orchestration, including new leaps in the horns. Upon reaching the downbeat of m. 76 (= m. 10, now reconceived as iv of D minor), these correspondence measures are swept away in favor of an athletic intervention springing forward with a new, eighth-note-driven propulsion, R1:\C[1.2], mm. 76–82 (Example 8.4). This passage is structured as a three-bar unit repeated in slightly altered invertible counterpoint, thus creating the presentation modules of a new sentence. R1:\C[1.2] signals the fictive protagonist's "musically active" determination to take up the R1:\P challenge.[47] And to conquer it: R1:\C[1.2] steers into a full-orchestra shout of major-mode triumph—a *Jubelruf* ("shout of jubilation," Example 8.5, R1:\C[1.3], mm. 82–90), envisioning the hoped-for victory down the road: the overturning of D minor into D major.[48] Simultaneously, in the bass the "threat" intervals of R1:\P (or the bass of R1:\TR) are turned into a sunny dance of joy. Such early visions cannot last: this D major fades to *piano* (and *pianissimo* in the trumpets) by m. 90, the end of the opening tutti. As a whole, R1 has been preparatory. It has outlined a recurring crisis, two responses to it, and an imagined outcome. The larger journey—that of seeking a sonata-oriented realization of all this on a broader scale—is about to begin.

Solo Exposition, Part 1:
Preface and Onset of S1 Proper (mm. 91–141)

The entry of the soloist at m. 91 introduces a more personalized intervention into the discourse (particularly evident when Brahms himself was the pianist), setting out into the open seas of Solo 1 and all that follows. The final sonic item is now activated: the piano itself, in dialogue with all that has preceded it. This is a dramatic moment in all Type 5 sonata forms. Here the shift of attention to the piano is coupled with a shift from R1's concluding D major back to D minor ("lights out"), resetting the modal situation back to its status quo ante. All this is spliced smoothly into the proceedings. The broad, D-major *diminuendo* of the previous bars had suggested a receding of the tutti to prepare for this quiet entrance, which picks up and continues those measures' reiterative triple groups in the bass. Similarly, the piano's "new" melody at this point (Example 8.6) spins out the rhythms and contours of the vigorous R1:\C$^{1.2}$ (Example 8.4).[49] Pushed onward into each succeeding bar with recurring, oar-stroke anacruses, it allows elements from R1:\C$^{1.2}$ to flower into a lyricism more expansive than anything heard thus far. Starting out from a subdued D minor, the theme conveys a hypnotic, antique flavor, marked by undulating thirds and sixths in gentle descents. We might hear in it something set apart, reverentially ceremonial: a *Requiem*-inflected entry cloaked in black, mindful of the sober circumstances that have given rise to the will to construct this musical monument. Donald Francis Tovey's suggestion might not be far from the mark: "a touching theme worthy of Bach's ariosos in the *Matthew Passion*."[50]

While the piano entry signals the textural start of Solo 1, what it provides is a corridor to the onset of the solo exposition proper (the point at which material from R1:\P returns to start another rotation of material—here, m. 110). This commonly encountered feature is what Sonata Theory calls a "preface," labeled as S1:\P^{pref}. Its length and content vary from one work to another.[51] In this case the entry is somber and understated, antivirtuosic, calling attention to the "symphonic" intent of the concerto in its initial avoidance of technical display.[52] In the harried context of all that has preceded it this module seems leisurely, precisely measured. A primly contained, four-bar antecedent (mm. 91–94) leads to what starts as an expanded consequent (m. 95) but that, after some harmonic blossoming, returns only to another half cadence (V/D, m. 101). As the figuration starts to climb upward (m. 101), the orchestral strings swell dynamically, soon suggesting the return of a postponed but inexorable threat. Registering the increasing tension, the soloist's 3 + 3 subdivisions of the $\frac{6}{4}$ bars split into 2 + 2 + 2 hemiolas (mm. 107–108, *molto crescendo*), and the theme's initial security comes undone with the *forte* C♯[07] in m. 109, hurling once again into shuddering crisis-material from R1:\P (m. 110), now rattled forth, *fortissimo*, by the soloist. The appearance of that module announces the onset of the solo exposition proper.

Or does it? Matters are not that simple. The return of R1:\P material in the piano, m. 110, does not start at the beginning of that theme but rather at the point corresponding to m. 18—midway through that module's convulsions (mm. 110–17 = 18–25). Here one recalls that the preceding entrance of R1:\P at m. 66/67 (positioned as R1:\C$^{1.1}$) had provided only mm. 1–10 of the theme. In short, m. 110 continues the R1:\P material that had been interrupted (by R1:\C$^{1.2}$) at m. 76; or, from another perspective, mm. 76–109 can be construed as an interpolation replacing the "missing" mm. 11–17 of R1:\P. Did the "exposition" actually begin much earlier? If the return of mm. 1 and 2 of R1:\P is taken to mark the initiation of a new, large-scale rotation, that would indicate that the rotation had begun in m. 66/67. Such an initiation is typical of the onset of the solo exposition, not of the closing zone of R1. On the other hand, the obviously concluding gestures of mm. 76–90, along with the suppression of the soloist until m. 91, demonstrate that ultimately they are to be regarded as the end of the opening tutti. Here we experience an ambiguity of structural boundary points.[53] Rotation 2 does start at m. 66, but the solo exposition proper—led into by the lyrical S1:\P^{pref}—is not fully released until the resumption of R1:\P material at m. 110. It is as if the attempt to start a solo exposition at m. 66/67 had been derailed with the intervention of R1:\C$^{1.2}$ at m. 76 and is only permitted to rebegin (shorn of its "used-up" initial modules) at m. 110.

Measures 117–23 provide a brief but strenuous, quasi-canonic working out of R1:\P's incipit.[54] In this final version the turmoil is cut short by an abrupt half cadence (V/d, m. 123) and, following the rotational ordering of the opening tutti, a slightly altered, now piano-led, R1:\TR—personalized broodings on that "aspirational" module. Sounded a fifth higher than its version in the opening tutti, this passage proceeds, *diminuendo*, to an MC effect in m. 141, suggesting the arrival of F minor, in order to prepare the way for secondary-theme space.

Solo Exposition, Part 2: The Trimodular Block (TMB) and S1–R2 Closing Zone (mm. 142–225, 226–30)

While the practice is not invariable, it is typical of Type 5 sonatas to interpolate a new theme at some point within Solo 1's S space. One of the ways that this could be handled was to resound R1:\S as an opening module leading to a *second* apparent MC and the new theme (in the proper secondary key or mode), introduced by the soloist. In such cases Solo 1 displays apparent double medial caesuras, the situation producing a trimodular block (TM^1, TM^2, TM^3, in which TM^1 and TM^3 are thematic, and, between them, TM^2 is a transitional passage setting up the second caesura).[55] In this case R1:\S = S1:\$TM^1$ (m. 142, in F minor over V), merging into S1:\$TM^2$ at m. 150, altering the module with a modal shift to F major and leading to a second MC (expressing III:HC, m. 156), and thence to the pianist's new, hymnic theme, S1:\$TM^3$ (m. 157, in F major, Example 8.7). The aim is to lift the minor-mode pall that has been dominating most of the movement in order to open an expansive zone of radiant, major-mode promise.[56] As with all minor-mode sonatas that move to the major mediant for their secondary theme, that thematic module bears the hope (not always realized) of reappearing in the tonic major in the recapitulation, thereby, through the mechanisms prebuilt into the sonata process, emancipating the original tonic minor into tonic major.

To grasp the logic of this portion of the solo exposition, one needs to consider how it responds to and furthers the comparable passage in the opening tutti. There, stasis, grief, and mourning (R1:\TR, R1:\S) had given way to a determination to reconfront and conquer the initial crisis, imagining the eventual victory with the tutti's concluding, D-major *Jubelruf,* R1:\$C^{1.3}$. While the sequence of events remains much the same here, the expositional pathway to that modal success is broadened into an expansive major mode and a new, confidently hopeful theme. Initially, the soloist murmurs the cold *Grablied* (R1:\S = S1:\$TM^1$), but before long it is led in a different direction. There is no need to repeat the blunt, cadential decision heard in m. 66 of R1. That choice has already been made, and as the movement proceeds, every new bar displays its accumulating results. This time, the *Grablied* is made to turn the corner, lightening into the major mode with a warm breeze of strings, *crescendo* (S1:\$TM^2$). The III:HC MC at m. 156 is the rotational analogue to the earlier i:PAC (m. 66). It opens the gateway to the thematic goal of the exposition, the lyrical S1:\$TM^3$ (Example 8.7), *poco più moderato,* an extended, major-mode passage for unaccompanied soloist. Within the still operative rotation its opening ten bars replace R1:\$C^{1.2}$ (which, as a consequence, never reappears in this movement).

This sentential theme subdivides into two parts: presentation (S1:\$TM^{3.1}$, mm. 157–66, sounded as two antecedents) and continuation (S1:\$TM^{3.2}$, mm. 166–99).[57] The expressive role of S1:\$TM^{3.1}$ within the movement is so obvious as to need little additional comment here. (Tovey noted its "vein of noble consolation"; Dubiel characterized it as an "anthem"; Roger Moseley likened it to an eloquent soliloquy "embodying the protagonist's true character.")[58] Every listener senses that its upward-rising motion (imitated in the left hand) reverses the mournful droops of the preceding *Grablied*. Perhaps less apparent is its incipit's adoption (mm. 157, 158) of the rhythm of the negatively bobbing bass of R1:\TR (m. 25/26ff.; see Example 8.2), finally reconfiguring the aftershocks of the initial crisis into a positive theme of mellifluous promise. The continuation, m. 166, is the theme's telos— the now lyrically absorbed *Jubelruf* (m. 166, R1:\C[1.3] = S1:\TM[3.2]), completing the rotational succession laid out in the opening tutti. The soloist lingers on this *dolce* module as a moment of cherished attainment—prolongs its vision and drifts into a nearly static reverie, deflecting away chromatically from F onto the warm shadow of a D♭ chord (m. 176). The soloist appears to be so deeply lost in introspection as to be unable to continue, and the completion of the module is handed over to supportive woodwinds. Within a few bars the winds lead the theme back to F major for a first point of rest with the III:PAC at m. 184; the cadence is elided with a varied restatement of the entire S1:\TM[3], led by the strings.

The cadence at m. 184 represents a point of achievement, but the exposition's work is not finished. The positive response to the initial crisis, it seems, needs confirmation. The string-led reiteration of S1:\TM[3.1] at m. 184, enriched by the soloist's accompanying figuration, begins as that confirmation, but it soon swells into an urgent call to action, imagining, perhaps, a more declarative expositional conclusion. The orchestra rears up to sound four statements of the *Jubelruf* on descending fifths—the major-minor sevenths, A[7], D[7], G[7], and C[7] (mm. 192–95)—as if summoning reinforcements from the four corners of the earth. To no avail: the rapt soloist defuses the energy with a gentle drift downward to a *pianissimo* III:IAC at m. 199.

While m. 199 is not a moment of full cadential closure, the remainder of the exposition has the character of a prolonged and static epilogue, settling into an even deeper, richer serenity. As the bass winds down to near motionlessness, soft reverberations of the *Jubelruf*—now as misty evocations in the horn—are intermixed with fragmentary recollections of the incipit of S1:\TM[1] and TM[2]. The expositional close proceeds in two phases. The first, mm. 199– 210, seeks to provide a fuller closure with a PAC in F major. Its initial glide toward that cadence is evaded in m. 204 with a bass slippage to A♭, momentarily darkening onto an F-minor chord immediately shaded with dominant evocations of D♭ (mm. 205–206; cf. m. 176) before reaching an F:PAC in m. 210.[59] This is the moment best regarded as S1:\EEC, even as the same motives, in the exposition's final moments, continue to linger in the air for the next several bars: subdominant-tinted memories of accomplishment over a pedal-point F bass.[60] Its final touch is the fading away, in the orchestra alone, of R1:\S (S1:\ TM[1]) in mm. 216–26: a wistful, memorial recall of the *Grablied,* beyond whose initial mourning the work's advancement has, at least, brought us this far into the movement.[61]

The state of supreme calm reached at the end of the exposition (m. 226) is one of achievement, stretched out on a broad plain of satisfaction. It stands as the polar opposite to the frenzied shock of the opening. The structural problem that it brings, though, is that its *pianissimo* stillness reverses the nearly invariable generic norm within earlier concertos. The expected procedure was to conclude the solo exposition with an extended round of bravura: a display episode concluding with a trill cadence elided with the *forte* onset of the second tutti (or ritornello, R2). This is not what happens here. Instead, we have been lulled into a state of countergeneric tranquility—precisely where "the concerto" qua concerto ought not to be at this point. And indeed, some eleven bars before the end of the broader exposition the piano had faded away into silence, relinquishing the final settling of accounts to the orchestra. Since the soloist is no longer playing, we might construe this subdued close, mm. 216–26, as the second tutti (R2)—or at least as in dialogue with the concept of that traditional structural pillar, whose normally brilliant energy is fully suppressed here.

Brahms's antiexhibitionistic stance could not be clearer. Such a conclusion repudiates this aspect of the virtuoso concerto. But in terms of compositional accomplishment, have we been beguiled into a narcotized stasis at the "wrong" generic moment, when so much more remains to be accomplished? The heroism of the mission—like Odysseus's or Aeneas's or Rinaldo's—requires the sustaining of a multistaged linear journey toward a clear goal: the completion of the concerto, the carrying on of the endangered tradition. Bewitchment into an eroticized tarrying can lead one, however momentarily, to forget the duties of the larger task at hand. The unexpected *fortissimo* alarm in the piano at m. 226 registers a sudden awakening out of the dream, a panicked jolt of awareness. Turning the *Jubelruf* into a strident call to action, the soloist is hurled headlong into the developmental fray—and into the return of the original problem, the R1:\P module, the start of the development proper.

Development (mm. 231–310)

The return of R1:\P at m. 231, along with its "B$\flat^6$," restores to memory, with a vengeance, the original crisis.[62] As a whole, the development (as was the norm) cycles through its materials in rotational order, proceeding only as far, though, as R1:\S. Thus we have, in succession, R1:\P at m. 231, the "aspirational" R1:\TR at m. 255/259, and the important transformation of R1:\S (Example 8.3b) at m. 278. The development stops short of attaining the next modules in line, the emancipatory modules, R1:\C$^{1.2}$, S1:\TM$^{3.1}$, or the *Jubelruf*. In other words, it is dominated by the negative modules, not the positive ones.

The R1:\P segment, mm. 231–55, locks the soloist and orchestra in a char-acteristically stormy, *forte* struggle: the descending bass line recurs—D–C♯–C♮–B♮–A (omitting B♭)—but is thereupon wrenched into a plummeting sequence of descending fifths (m. 245), doubling its speed at m. 248 and emptying onto a high-tension G♯^{o7} at m. 251. Dropping to *piano* at m. 255, the modulatory R1:\ TR, with its major-minor decays further enhanced, is turned into a chiaroscuro dialogue between the orchestra and the piano in a model (mm. 259–67) and varied sequence (mm. 267–73, touching on the crucial B♭^{6} in m. 271). Heard here for the last time in the movement, R1:\TR fades into empty wisps, mm. 274–77, with the final bar retracing R1:\MC, now on V of B minor—preparing the arrival of R1:\S, the module next in line.[63]

This time Brahms recasts that module, originally so haunted and spectral, as an agent of determination (m. 278), setting out forcefully in B minor (still over the dominant). This is a transformative moment. Now with the key signature temporarily altered to a more hopeful two sharps, the soloist seizes the R1:\S *Grablied* and converts its formerly mournful stasis into a commanding vector rushing forward in impatient cross-rhythms (mm. 283–85) toward a decisive cadence. Surprisingly, that cadence arrives with a Picardy-third B-major chord (m. 287) and a simultaneous drop to *piano*. Registering a premature delight in this initial success of the motivic transformation, the B-chord opens the door to a playful and *leggiero* modulatory model (mm. 287–91) and sequence (mm. 291–95), as if all were well. But this is not the case: the end of the sequence falls into the clutches of a half cadence in the fateful key of D minor (V$^{4–3}$, mm. 295–96). Measure 295 is the onset of a prolonged dominant lock in that key, laid down even more resolutely in m. 297, as the two-sharp signature relapses back to one flat. Above the swelling A dominant, preparing for the recapitulation, the premature hopes of the transformed R1:\S (Example 8.3b) can be heard dissolv-ing away.

The entry into the recapitulation could not be more shattering (mm. 306–10, again, with the parallel moment of the first movement of Beethoven's Ninth Symphony obviously in mind). With maximal force the *fortissimo* or-chestra sweeps up the futile resistance of the soloist with a cadential vortex of sound. Hammered forth rhythmically with triplet upbeats, the four-bar drive to cadence accrues weight and inescapability with each beat, pointing at the D-minor resolution to come with a plunging inner voice descending from 8̂ to 1̂ and a hastening split into hemiola subdivisions in mm. 308–309. The cadence onto octave Ds (i:PAC, m. 310; cf. m. 66) is so potent as to overwhelm any hope of escape.[64] The gravitational force of D minor is too strong. We are looking into the abyss.

Recapitulation (mm. 310–443)

No commentator fails to mention the grand coup at the outset of the recapitulation—Solo 3—and its extraordinary treatment of the return of R1:\P. Instead of allowing the music to burst into the customary B♭⁶ crisis (followed at once by B♭⁶₅), the soloist jams a *fortissimo,* fully packed E-major chord above the D bass (also played by the left hand). This creates the E♮ shock in m. 311, rivaling the analogous passage in Beethoven's Ninth. Summoning unanticipated resources at the piece's darkest hour, the soloist trumps the blackness of the moment with a blaze of light. The musical ultimacy of this sonic moment (vertically) is enhanced by its placement (horizontally) at one of the most crucial points in any minor-mode sonata: the triggering of the recapitulatory rotation, within which the expositional materials must be reconfronted and, by its end, resolved in either victory (major mode) or defeat (minor mode). Moreover, although the onset of the recapitulation is often the site of the vestigial third tutti in the orchestra (R3), its role is usurped here by this pianistic intervention. Straining to seize control over R1:\P, the soloist has elbowed R3 out of the way. One cannot improve upon Dubiel's remarks: at the moment of recapitulation "the specter of the B♭ chord arises again. . . . The piano's E six-four-two in m. 311 . . . works for the [D] tonic, even as it pushes the tonic aside, because it finally breaks the spell of the B♭ chord."[65] And it is the soloist who now commands the thematic material of R1:\P, full force, for the next several measures.

But that module is not so readily overtaken. The E♮ sets off a struggle, with the R1:\P material, now in the piano, sounded in extenso, replete with perilous, mocking trills and downward-cascading leaps. Not only is the theme's initial portion harmonically reconceived, but it also features two vertiginous tritone leaps in the bass (D–G♯ in m. 317; G–C♯ in m. 327)—sonic images of a disorienting madness or howling malevolence, of the *diabolus in musica.* Measures 310–27 are referential measures, recomposing mm. 1–18 bar for bar. R1:\P regains its original harmonic footing in the center of m. 327, and mm. 328–34 are more literal correspondence measures with mm. 19–25 (at the original pitch level but reorchestrated), finally completing the remainder of the chromatic-tetrachord descent (C♯–C♮–B♮–B♭–A) begun with the D in mm. 310–16.

The correspondence measures are left behind at m. 334, the start of the recapitulation's recomposed transition zone; the original transition (Example 8.2) is abandoned. The struggle with R1:\P continues into the next several bars, intensifying toward the *fortissimo* V₄⁶ at m. 341. With the arrival of that ₄⁶ the impassioned, full orchestra pours forth S1:\P^pref, a theme associated more properly with the soloist (and here, with its newly charged verve, sounding quasi-"Hungarian"). In the context of such intense conflict, that module seems impulsively grabbed onto, orchestrally blurted as a gesture of desperation (perhaps trying also to discharge its postponed, pent-up R3 pressure). Adding to this impression, its placement is dislocated. In normative rotational order, if it were to reappear at all, it would have been presented before R1:\P, not after it. All this suggests a culminating frenzy of disorientation.[66]

This revised passage moves through a series of stepwise-ascending tonalities, D minor (the movement's tonic), E minor, and F♯ minor, which winds up preparing for the return of S1:\TM^1 (= R1:\S) in that unexpected key in m. 366. The revision proceeds in three discrete blocks, the first of which is the modulatory model, mm. 341–48. This model starts out with a fierce *fortissimo* in D minor (S1:\P^{pref}, initially over V) that is almost immediately choked back to *piano* to produce a "Picardy" D-major cadence at m. 345. Again we experience a glimpse of the larger tonal vision of the concerto: D minor giving way to D major (above which a smiling, major-mode fragment of R1:\P is briefly heard in the horn, mm. 345–46). But that D major is only short-lived: with the soloist's rippling entry at m. 345 (F♯^{o7}), it evaporates and is led into E minor at m. 348. Measures 348–55 sound a dynamically subdued sequence of the model: E minor to E major (m. 352, with the R1:\P fragment now sounded in the cellos) and thence to F♯ minor, m. 355. At this point the soloist picks up its own melody, S1:\P^{pref}, with what initially seems to be the start of another sequence but is instead a transposition of a chordal succession associated with that module at its first sounding (mm. 355–61 = 95–101, up a major third); the pianist thus refashions the theme more closely to its original presentation. This generates a half cadence in F♯ minor at m. 361, which is then made to function as a medial caesura ushering in five bars of caesura fill and the onset of S1:\TM^1 in that remote key.

Bringing back S1:\TM^1 in ♯iii carries a number of implications. First and most important, that module is not to be resolved into the tonic at this point: within sonata space the *Grablied* will remain alienated from the tonic, incapable of being assimilated into it.[67] Second, that module relapses to its original, limpid version (Example 8.3a), not to its energized transformation sounded in the development (Example 8.3b). Third, its F♯ minor counterbalances the opening tutti's presentation of the theme in B♭ minor: both are a major third away from the D tonic; both are in the minor mode; and both belong to the same hexatonic system.[68] Fourth, hexatonically (via a simple *Leittonwechsel* operation), F♯ minor can suggest a deflated alternative to the tonic, D major. F♯ minor is readily re-inflated back to D major through a maximally smooth $\hat{5}$–$\hat{6}$ shift. Hexatonically construed, its remoteness instead turns out to be very close. One needs only to supply a tonal adjustment around the TM^2 area to accomplish the transformation into D major, and this happens in mm. 374–75. While mm. 366–74 are referential measures to mm. 142–50, m. 375 (A^7) is more literally what Sonata Theory calls the crux—the point at which, for the most part, this portion of the recapitulation begins to be a transposition of the analogous bars of the exposition with only small variants (m. 375 = 151, 376 = 152, and so on, in similar correspondence measures)—in this case preparing for the tonal resolution to be provided by S1:\ TM³, now in D major. At this crux point, principles of symmetrical balance—a broad stretch of near-literal restatement, now in the tonic—supersede those of compositional invention.

Most of the tonal resolution, from S1:\TM³ onward, needs no extended commentary. The issues that it retraces are those of the expositional model, now transposed to the tonic, wherein any cadence or major-minor fluctuation takes on added significance. The articulation of the S3:\ESC ("essential structural closure") is of consummate importance: this is the goal of the entire sonata trajectory, carrying with it the hopes for the cadential resolution of the original D-minor premise into its parallel major. Tracking through the dozens of correspondence measures, one expects this to occur at m. 434, the major-mode, authentic-cadential moment parallel with the S1:\EEC at m. 210. And perhaps m. 434 should be understood in this way, although a small alteration in the right hand of the piano (suppressing the tonic pitch on its second note) renders this PAC slightly more attenuated than the one at m. 210. The main point, though, is that by the initial bars of the recapitulation's closing zone, mm. 434–37, the minor-mode problem of the movement appears to have been overcome. D minor has been transformed into an extended stretch of D major (m. 381ff.) and confirmed by major-mode authentic cadences (mm. 408, 423, 434). The apparatus of the sonata has done its work and provided us with what promises to be a successful outcome. By m. 437 (= m. 213), four bars into the cozy, subdominant-leaning fade-out (and some thirteen bars short of a complete retracing of the expositional model's concluding music), all seems secure.

Then the illusion collapses. In m. 438 ominous timpani strokes intrude: dominant and tonic, *piano* and *marcato*. Suddenly the soloist's reverie-like arpeggiations shift from D major to D minor. With a chill, we enter a region of loss. Everything so far gained through the sonata process slips through our grasp. Here, near the end of the recapitulation, the sonata is shown to have modally failed. It has proven unable to overturn the original situation, D minor, into a permanent D major. With the unexpected darkening into D minor—the return of the repressed—the soloist's arpeggiations, *pianissimo* and *diminuendo*, shrivel away, marked with falling lines in both right and left hands like musical tears or images of expiration. Particularly notable is that the left hand, mm. 440–42, reinscribes most of the descending chromatic tetrachord (from tonic to dominant, D–C♯–C♮–B♭–A) that had provided the bass underpinning for R1:\P at the movement's beginning. In this case, however, the half cadence on the dominant of D minor (mm. 442–43) produces an unexpected medial-caesura effect (i:HC MC), whose subsequent upbeat fill, m. 443, recalls that of mm. 45, 141, and 277. What is being prepared is a return of the *Grablied,* which has yet to be sounded in the tonic.

Merger: End of Recapitulation and Coda (mm. 444–50, 451–84)

But to sound the *Grablied* in its original, mournful version (Example 8.3a) would be only to return to the original condition of static grieving. This could suggest an inability to continue to pursue the task of modal overcoming in subsequent movements. Instead, at m. 444 the soloist bolts forward with the resolute version of that module (Example 8.3b), originally introduced in the development and regrasped here in D minor (over V), with even more energetic determination (*Tempo 1 poco più animat*o, even, by bar 446, *più agitato*). Is m. 444 the beginning of the coda, following an open end to recapitulatory space? Although opinion on this matter is not unanimous, Tovey, Böttinger, and Dubiel all think so.[69] Intuitively, one might suppose that the sudden change of tempo and texture argues in its favor, and within a few bars, with the frenzied return of the major-minor struggles associated with R1:\P (m. 451), a new rotation of materials has begun, obviously infused with coda rhetoric. But we also recall that at the m. 443 fade-out, the equivalent of mm. 216–26 had not yet been sounded (the exposition's final bars, valedictory memories of the R1:\S *Grablied*). In other words, at m. 443 the recapitulatory rotation of expositional materials is not complete. Thus the tonic return of Example 8.3b at this point, even while suggesting coda rhetoric, alludes to the calmer, earlier recall of Example 8.3a, in III, at the end of the exposition. It is doubtless for this reason that some analysts—notably Carl Dahlhaus and Renate Ulm—have deferred the onset of the coda to the return of R1:\P at m. 451.[70] The plunge forward of mm. 444–50 serves both as a reference to the conclusion of the expositional rotation and as the onset of contrasting coda rhetoric, although perhaps not yet, strictly considered, the coda proper. Instead, it is a solo-led *crescendo* link into the more explicit coda that follows in m. 451, a *fortissimo* tutti that is also a recrafting of the R4 expectation, even as the soloist continues to be heard. The traditional cadenza is suppressed: another indication of Brahms's "symphonic," not virtuosic, intention.

The tumultuous coda enacts a struggle to avoid—but ultimately to be overwhelmed by—the gravitational force of a concluding, negative cadence in D minor.[71] The electrifying D-major (D^6) onset of R1:\P at m. 451 cannot be sustained. It leads, through G-minor coloration, to an emphatic A-major cadence in m. 461, but this is only V of D minor, as the roaring octaves in the piano above it immediately show. By m. 466 the soloist wails out variants of S1:\P^{pref} in desperate attempts to forestall any D-minor cadence. In vain. After two swirling windups (mm. 474–75, 476–77) D minor asserts itself once and for all, slamming the iron door shut with a final i:PAC and resounding bars of confirmation, mm. 481–84.

*   *   *

In sum: the moment-to-moment processes of this movement (along with the whole concerto) intervened into the heated aesthetic and cultural issues of mid-century Germany. The work was a monumental manifesto, allying itself with a more classicizing tradition of which young Brahms saw himself as the emerging champion. This aspect of the movement was evident in two conspicuous ways: in its full-blown presentation of a bulky, Type 5 sonata, pointing back toward a re-vered Austro-Germanic tradition (with Beethoven as the foremost model); and in the aspiration to write a movement that is more symphonic than virtuosic—a movement that displays its suppression of technical bravura at the telling points in the form where they would have been most expected.

In terms of structure, the movement stages a "purely musical" drama that initially lays down the image of a catastrophic D-minor situation and then seeks to overcome it through the D-minor-to-D-major potential of the sonata process. The resulting Type 5 sonata is organized around seven contrasting musical mod-ules whose successions may be construed by the listener as laying out a quest narrative in search of a lasting D major. The initial crisis (R1:\P) invites inter-pretation via differing levels of metaphorical connotation, although in one way or another the evocation of Robert Schumann, or, more generally, the aesthetic position that he held, hovers over the entire conception. Ultimately, Brahms constructed this first-movement sonata as failing, as being unable to sustain the seemingly secure D-major reverie outcome that fills most of the recapitulation's second half, until the decay near its end. The disintegration back to D minor, and thus to the condition of the original problem, is enhanced in the coda, whose in-escapable currents sweep away any apparent gains made in individual moments in the preceding sonata.

But this is only the first act of a three-act drama. The D-major vision will glow again in the "Benedictus" movement that follows (Adagio and also in $\frac{6}{4}$): the "gentle portrait" of Clara Schumann—a radiantly contemplative offering whose thematic materials, however much they contrast with those of the first, may be heard as transformations of some of that earlier movement's modules.[72] And while the Type 4 finale (sonata-rondo) will recollapse the Adagio's D ma-jor to D minor, it will, in the end, push through to a more permanent D major. Here too, as is always pointed out, the finale's rondo theme is a fast-tempo, minor-mode transformation of the first movement's hymnic S1:\TM³, as if the process initiated earlier is regenerated under new terms. Even as the conclusion of the first movement is a representation of bitter defeat, the drama is by no means over.

NOTES

1. Giselher Schubert, "Themes and Double Themes: The Problem of the Symphonic in Brahms," *19th-Century Music* 18/1 (1994): 10–23 (quotation from p. 13).

2. James Hepokoski and Warren Darcy, *Elements of Sonata Theory: Norms, Types, and Deformations in the Late-Eighteenth-Century Sonata* (New York: Oxford University Press, 2006).

3. English-language summaries of these two issues may be found in George S. Bozarth, "Brahms's First Piano Concerto op. 15: Genesis and Meaning," in *Beiträge zur Geschichte des Konzerts: Festschrift Siegfried Kross zum 60. Geburtstag*, ed. Reinmar Emans and Matthias Wendt (Bonn: Gudrun Schröder Verlag, 1990), 211–47. See also Siegfried Kross, "Brahms and E. T. A. Hoffmann," *19th-Century Music* 5/3 (1982): 193–200; Christopher Reynolds, "A Choral Symphony by Brahms?," *19th-Century Music* 9/1 (1985): 3–25.

4. A summary of the stages of the compositional process is provided in Juan Martin Koch, *Das Klavierkonzert des 19. Jahrhunderts und die Kategorie des Symphonischen: Zur Kompositions- und Rezeptionsgeschichte der Gattung von Mozart bis Brahms* (Sinzig: Studio, 2001), 305–25. Among other things, Koch clarifies and provides dates for three different layers of the final autograph score.

5. The principal exception here is Joseph Dubiel's "Contradictory Criteria in a Work of Brahms," in *Brahms Studies* 1, ed. David Brodbeck (Lincoln: University of Nebraska Press, 1994), 81–110. Germanic discussions—including Giselher Schubert's and Juan Martin Koch's (nn. 1 and 4 above)—tend to stem from Carl Dahlhaus's overview in *Johannes Brahms: Klavierkonzert Nr. 1 D-Moll, op. 15* (Munich: Wilhelm Fink, 1965). A more casual reading of the concerto had been provided decades earlier by Donald Francis Tovey, "Brahms: Pianoforte Concerto in D Minor, op. 15," in *Concertos*, vol. 3 of *Essays in Musical Analysis* (London: Oxford University Press, 1936), 114–20.

6. 3 February 1859, repr. in Dahlhaus, *Johannes Brahms*, 30: "Und dieses Würgen und Wühlen, dieses Zerren und Ziehen, diesen Zusammenflicken und wieder Auseinanderreissen von Phrasen und Floskeln muß man über Dreiviertelstunde lang ertragen!" (And this throttling and rummaging about, this tugging and pulling, this patching up and tearing apart again of phrases and clichés—one must put up with it over three-quarters of an hour!) Translation by the author.

7. Chopin's Piano Concerto No. 1 in E Minor, op. 11, is also an extended work: a first movement of around twenty minutes, with the whole concerto requiring just under forty.

8. "Adolf Schubring: Five Early Works by Brahms (1862)," trans. Walter Frisch, in *Brahms and His World*, rev. ed., ed. Frisch and Kevin C. Karnes (Princeton, N.J.: Princeton University Press, 2009), 212. Joachim's D-Minor Violin Concerto (*Konzert in ungarischer Weise*), op. 11, from the late 1850s—a sibling work by one of Brahms's closest friends of the time and one that was dedicated to him—similarly features a twenty-minute initial movement within a complete-work duration of about forty minutes. On the complementarity of the two concertos, see Malcolm MacDonald, "'Veiled Symphonies'?: The Concertos,"

in *The Cambridge Companion to Brahms,* ed. Michael Musgrave (Cambridge: Cambridge University Press, 1999), 160–61.

9. The simile is only fanciful, stressing the forward-vectored yet triple-time "rocking" motion. Still, within a different tradition, compare the § in, say, the sea-voyage first movement of Rimsky-Korsakov's *Sheherazade* (1888), whose principal theme also sports two clipped, downbeat quarter notes.

10. Is it relevant to note that, according to a 1914 report by Charles Villiers Stanford, when in the later nineteenth century Brahms himself conducted the First Piano Concerto he did so in a way that brought out the movement's "rhythmical swing," namely, "in an uneven four," with alternating strong and weak beats on counts 1, 3, 4, and 6? See Bernard D. Sherman, "How Different Was Brahms's Playing Style from Our Own?," in *Performing Brahms: Early Evidence of Performance Style,* ed. Michael Musgrave and Sherman (Cambridge: Cambridge University Press, 2003), 6.

11. Alexander Rehding, *Music and Monumentality: Commemoration and Wonderment in Nineteenth-Century Germany* (New York: Oxford University Press, 2009), 26–27.

12. For our purposes narrative can be taken to imply a planned succession of contrasting (and recurring) affective or connotational states that invite us to interpret them metaphorically within a cultural tradition of generic norms.

13. See the broader discussion of metaphor and narrative in Hepokoski and Darcy, *Elements of Sonata Theory,* 251–54.

14. James Hepokoski, "Sonata Theory and Dialogic Form," in *Musical Form, Forms & Formenlehre,* by William E. Caplin, James Hepokoski, and James Webster, ed. Pieter Bergé (Leuven: Leuven University Press, 2009), 71–89; and Hepokoski and Darcy, *Elements of Sonata Theory,* e.g., 9–11, 340–42, 614–18.

15. By the 1850s, and probably even several decades before, the term *tutti* is preferable to *ritornello,* which in this context can seem fussily archaic. For concertos of the Mozart-Beethoven era, Darcy and I use the terms *ritornello* and *tutti* interchangeably— as they were used in the late eighteenth century (*Elements of Sonata Theory,* 445–47). Ritornello reminds one of the classical concerto's origins in earlier concerto formats; tutti is a more neutral label.

16. Hepokoski and Darcy, *Elements of Sonata Theory,* 345, 431–33, 469–95.

17. The Type 3 sonata is that of the standard, textbook format: exposition, development, recapitulation. A Type 3 sonata without expositional repeat—increasingly an option in modern symphonies and sonatas from the 1830s onward—reduced the grand-scale symphonic or sonata-oriented format to that of the overture, which generically lacked an expositional repeat.

18. The issue of the "symphonic concerto" or the "Sinfonie mit obligatem Klavier" has swirled around Brahms's concerto ever since its 1859 premiere. Juan Martin Koch has recently provided a study of such concertos in *Das Klavierkonzert des 19. Jahrhunderts* (see n. 4 above). Koch (319) essentially agrees with Peter Böttinger, who sought to locate symphonic aspects of Brahms's op. 15 in its polyphonic and contrapuntal moments—particularly with regard to the first theme of the opening tutti—and in its treatment of orchestral sound considered apart from thematic materials. Böttinger, "Jahre der Krise, Krise der Form: Beobachtungen am 1. Satz des Klavierkonzertes op. 15 von Johannes Brahms," in *Aimez-vous Brahms "the Progressive"?,* ed. H.-K. Metzger and R. Riehn (Munich: Fritz Kriechbaumer, 1989), 41–68.

19. A more nuanced discussion of the minor-mode sonata and its implications may be found in Hepokoski and Darcy, *Elements of Sonata Theory,* 306–17. See also Hepokoski, "Approaching the First Movement of Beethoven's *Tempest* Sonata through Sonata Theory," in *Beethoven's Tempest Sonata: Perspectives of Analysis and Performance,* ed. Pieter Bergé,

Jeroen D'hoe, and William E. Caplin, Analysis in Context: Leuven Studies in Musicology, vol. 2 (Leuven, Belgium, and Dudley, Mass.: Peeters, 2009), 181–212.

20. On the terms *tutti* and *ritornello,* see n. 15 above. To avoid a revision of shorthand labeling in this essay, I have retained the first part of Sonata Theory's label for ritornello or tutti themes: R1:\. The alternative T1:\, however, referring to the first tutti, is also possible. The Type 5 labeling system is laid out in Hepokoski and Darcy, *Elements of Sonata Theory,* 451–53.

21. Hepokoski and Darcy, *Elements of Sonata Theory,* 447–51.

22. Explicating the action zones and their symbols is the burden of much of Hepokoski and Darcy, *Elements of Sonata Theory.* For an expository summary, see 14–22.

23. For more on the referential-layout function vis-à-vis subsequent rotations, see Hepokoski and Darcy, *Elements of Sonata Theory,* 469, 470–75.

24. Dubiel, "Contradictory Criteria," 81.

25. Robert S. Hatten interprets the "annunciatory force" of this chord as deriving from the same "recitative chord" at the opening to the recapitulation in the first movement of Beethoven's Ninth Symphony (another monumental work). *Musical Meaning in Beethoven: Markedness, Correlation, and Interpretation* (Bloomington: Indiana University Press, 1994), 183–84.

26. The bare octaves make this a case of an "attenuated" PAC. See Hepokoski and Darcy, *Elements of Sonata Theory,* 170.

27. Both comments are cited in Bozarth, "Brahms's First Piano Concerto," 213. Original German and translation also in Reynolds, "A Choral Symphony by Brahms?," 4, 24 n. 8.

28. Styra Avins, *Johannes Brahms: Life and Letters,* trans. Josef Eisinger and Styra Avins (New York: Oxford University Press, 1997), 36.

29. Bozarth, "Brahms's First Piano Concerto," 211–15, 222; Koch, *Das Klavierkonzert des 19. Jahrhunderts,* 305–309; Dahlhaus, *Johannes Brahms,* 3; Reynolds, "A Choral Symphony by Brahms?," 5.

30. The dating here follows Koch, *Das Klavierkonzert des 19. Jahrhunderts,* 309.

31. Such, more or less (though our descriptions differ slightly), is the view of Richard Taruskin, *The Nineteenth Century,* vol. 3 of *The Oxford History of Western Music* (New York: Oxford University Press, 2006), 686–88. Taruskin's larger point is to call attention to Brahms's subsequent suppression of the pictorial realism in favor of other, aesthetically ideological purposes.

32. Roger W. H. Savage, *Hermeneutics and Music Criticism* (New York: Routledge, 2010): "ontological vehemence," x, 5, 84, 87, 93, 123, 138; "fundamental element," 110; "dimensions of experience," 102; "refigures our inherence," 109 and elsewhere. Savage links his assertion regarding the affective content of music with the "state of mind" or "attunement" suggested in Heidegger's existential *Stimmungen,* or moods, background manners or colorations "in which we inhabit the world" (93–95, 101–102, 104). Heidegger's objectless *Stimmungen,* attributes of *Dasein,* are also appealed to (via Heinrich Besseler) by Karol Berger in *A Theory of Art* (New York: Oxford University Press, 2000), 200–201.

33. On Marx, Schumann, and *Seelenzustände,* see Scott Burnham, "Criticism, Faith, and the 'Idee': A. B. Marx's Early Reception of Beethoven," *19th-Century Music* 13/3 (1990): 188 n. 26, 191; Leon B. Plantinga, *Schumann as Critic* (New Haven, Conn.: Yale University Press, 1967), 120; and Beate Perrey, *Schumann's Dichterliebe and Early Romantic Poetics: Fragmentation of Desire* (Cambridge: Cambridge University Press, 2002), 19 ("'rare' and 'secret states of the soul'"), 36, 64, 113, 137–39.

34. James Hepokoski, "Beethoven Reception: The Symphonic Tradition," in *The Cambridge History of Nineteenth-Century Music,* ed. Jim Samson (Cambridge: Cambridge University Press, 2002), 424–59, esp. 426–30.

35. Taruskin, *The Nineteenth Century*, 688. Further D-minor relationships with Schumann's music—beyond the fourth symphony—are suggested in Reynolds, "A Choral Symphony by Brahms?," 7–8.

36. Repr. in Dahlhaus, *Johannes Brahms*, 29–30: "Die Gedanken schleichen entweder matt und siechhaft dahin, oder sie bäumen sich in fieberkranker Aufgeregtheit in die Höhe, um desto erschöpfter zusammenzubrechen; ungesund mit einem Worte ist das ganze Empfinden und Erfinden in dem Stucke. . . . Von einer organischen Entwicklung und einem logischen Fortspinnen ist gar selten die Rede."

37. Hepokoski and Darcy, *Elements of Sonata Theory*, 483–84. As noted in that discussion, it had been common to compose the spirited R1:\TR in such a way as to allow its opening portion to serve as the elided onset of R2, following the normative trill cadence at the end of S1.

38. Issues of key-choice for R1:\S are central to all conceptions of Type 5 concerto structure. As noted in Hepokoski and Darcy, *Elements of Sonata Theory*, 488–90, the late eighteenth-century (Mozartian) norm for *major-mode* concertos, with only a few notable exceptions, was to sound R1:\S in the tonic, thus retaining the tonic key throughout an essentially nonmodulatory opening tutti. Julian Horton has pointed out, however, that by the 1790s some composers—such as John Field—moved to V (within major-mode concertos) for the whole of R1:\S and typically returned to the tonic toward the end of R1 in preparation for the soloist's entry. See Horton, "John Field and the Alternative History of Concerto First-Movement Form," *Music & Letters* 92 (2011): 43–82, esp. 56–60. "The modulating R1" (an option that also occurs, at least as a modulatory "feint," in Beethoven's first three piano concertos) is "a practice that gained currency in London in the 1790s and was sustained throughout the nineteenth century in concerti from Hummel to Brahms" (56).

In the first half of the nineteenth century minor-mode concertos written in the Type 5 format often moved to III to begin R1:\S—like a sonata exposition, opening up an alternative space of light—although that relative-major key normally collapsed back to the tonic minor at some point before the end of R1 (see n. 44 below; for some exceptions, see n. 45). Less frequently, a minor-mode Type 5 could present the opening of its R1:\S in the tonic major, as in Chopin's Piano Concerto No. 1 in E Minor, op. 11, whose R1:\S starts in E major before being reclaimed by E minor. See also the discussion of concerto form in Claudia Macdonald, *Robert Schumann and the Piano Concerto* (New York: Routledge, 2005).

39. On hexatonic poles, along with an interpretation of them in terms of the *unheimlich*, see Richard Cohn, "Uncanny Resemblances: Tonal Signification in the Freudian Age," *Journal of the American Musicological Society* 57/2 (2004): 285–323.

40. Joachim to Brahms, 4 December 1856 ("wunderbar schönen ersten Moll-Gesang"), commenting on the (now-lost) first version of this movement—one that apparently lacked any major-mode alternative theme in its solo exposition. See, e.g., Koch, *Das Klavierkonzert des 19. Jahrhunderts*, 313, who associates Joachim's comment with both R1:\TR and R1:\S. Compare n. 56 below.

41. Dubiel, "Contradictory Criteria," 105.

42. On the attenuated PAC (octaves, m. 66), see n. 26 above.

43. Dubiel, "Contradictory Criteria," 84, suggests a different reading of the cadence at m. 66 followed at once by that "B♭⁶": "The qualification of D [m. 66] consists in its immediate reorientation back toward the B♭ chord that initially delayed it—as though the resolution of this chord somehow did not take and the process must be attempted all over again." To the extent that one emphasizes the cadence on D minor as "not taking," one might propose that this unsettling undoes the R1:\EEC effect at m. 66—thereby construing the remaining modules of R1 as extensions of S space. While remaining open to this option, my preference is to regard m. 66 as R1:\EEC, in part because the return of R1:\P is a more characteristic C than S gesture.

44. Examples of modulatory R1s that bring back the minor-tonic key (but not R1:\P) toward the end of R1 abound in the first decades of the nineteenth century. To cite only a sample: Hummel, Piano Concerto No. 2 in A Minor, op. 85/i (a–C–a) and No. 3 in B Minor, op. 89/i (b–D–b); Moscheles, Piano Concerto No. 3 in G Minor, op. 60/i (g–B♭–g); Ries, Piano Concerto No. 3 in C♯ Minor, op. 55/i (c♯–E–c♯) and No. 4 in C Minor, op. 115/i (c–E♭–c); Kalkbrenner, Piano Concerto No. 1 in D Minor, op. 61/i (d–F–d) and No. 2 in E Minor, op. 80 [86]/i (e–G–e). Compare Mozart, Piano Concerto No. 20 in D Minor, K. 466/i, in which R1:\S leads off in an F major that it cannot sustain; and Beethoven, Piano Concerto No. 3 in C Minor, op. 37/i, in which R1:\S begins in E♭.

Four examples of both major-mode and minor-mode concertos that return to the tonic with a second sounding of R1:\P are cited in Horton, "John Field and the Alternative History," 56–60. "Field composed a modulating R1 for five of his seven [piano] concerti, nos. 1 (1799), 2 (1810), 3 (published 1816; date of completion uncertain), 4 (1812–15), and 7 (1832, although the first movement was completed in 1822). He adopts two basic variants: either A [our R1:\P] is reprised in the tonic before the soloist enters [the "ternary" option]; or the non-tonic end of B [essentially our R1:\S, perhaps extending in some cases into R1:\C] is linked to the tonic solo entry via a modulating retransition" (57). Of the seven concertos, no. 7 (in C minor) is the only minor-mode work. See also n. 38 above.

45. The example perhaps best known to Brahms was the companion piece to his own piano concerto, Joachim's Violin Concerto in D Minor, op. 11/i, "Hungarian," which introduces R1:\S in an F major that persists to the end of the opening tutti. (A solo bridge cadenza leads back to D minor and Solo 1.) Similarly, in Brahms's Piano Concerto No. 2 in B♭, op. 83/i, the key of R1:\S (D minor, iii) persists to the end of R1 (m. 65, although three bars of aftermath fill return us to V/B♭, m. 69). See also the examples of Field's piano concertos (surely also known to Brahms), cited in nn. 38 and 44 above.

46. While Schumann's Violin Concerto was not published until 1937, it was composed in 1853—the period in which he first became acquainted with Brahms. The concerto was certainly known to Joachim and thus probably to Brahms as well, since the former had been involved with a private reading of the concerto in Hanover in January 1854.

47. Note the coincidence(?) of the rhythmic configuration of R1:\C$^{1.2}$ with a not-dissimilar module in the first movement of Schumann's third symphony, mm. 25–30, 77–82 (in between whose appearances one also encounters a full-throated return of P at m. 56).

48. On Jubelrufe in the nineteenth-century repertory, see Constantin Floros, Gustav Mahler (Wiesbaden: Breitkopf & Härtel, 1977), 2:211–14, 392. Renate Ulm interprets this initial sounding of R1:\C$^{1.3}$ as "a kind of 'Hunt-motive.'" "'Lässt er noch keine Pauken und Drommeten erschallen?': 1. Klavierkonzert D-Moll, op. 15," in Johannes Brahms: Das symphonische Werk: Entstehung, Deutung, Wirkung, ed. Ulm (Kassel: Bärenreiter, 1996), 130.

49. Those who had heard intertextual allusions of R1:\P to portions of Schumann's fourth symphony might also imagine that this new melody at m. 91, S1:\P^{pref}, in its sinuous working around the intervals between F and C♯, is not dissimilar to another generative motive of that symphony, for example, mm. 2–4, 5–7. On the other hand, its rhythm, based on that of R1:\C$^{1.2}$, also recalls the rhythm from Schumann's third, mentioned in n. 47 above.

50. Tovey, "Brahms: Pianoforte Concerto," 116.

51. Hepokoski and Darcy, Elements of Sonata Theory, 498, 511–12, 516–20.

52. Immediately following the 1859 premiere of Brahms's concerto, his assailant in the Signale für die musikalische Welt, Eduard Bernsdorf (nn. 6 and 36 above), remarked acidly that "the composer has deliberately made the principal part of this concerto as uninteresting as possible" (repr. in Dahlhaus, Johannes Brahms, 30; also quoted in Roger Moseley, "Between Work and Play: Brahms as Performer of His Own Music," in Frisch and Karnes, Brahms and His World, rev. ed., 139).

53. Apart from the special problem addressed in this work, ambiguities in the boundary point of S1 are common in concertos whose initial entry is a newly thematic S1:\P^{pref} (Hepokoski and Darcy, *Elements of Sonata Theory,* 519). Concertos that feature a S1:\P^{pref} typically lead to a restatement of R1:\P in the orchestra, unlike the situation here (511).

54. In an earlier (now lost) version of this movement, this passage, along with its analogue in the recapitulation, was apparently longer and even more blustery before Brahms's revisions of either November–December 1857 or February 1858; these were among the last compositional retouchings that he made in this movement. Koch, *Das Klavierkonzert des 19. Jahrhunderts,* 314–18. See n. 4 above.

55. Hepokoski and Darcy, *Elements of Sonata Theory,* 170–77, explicates the concept of the trimodular block; 535–42 discuss the trimodular block in the context of the Type 5 sonata. The latter section explores Mozartian treatments of the trimodular block in Type 5 sonatas; Mozart, more typically, revisited R1:\S as the third module of the trimodular block, TM^3, the reverse of the procedure found here in Brahms's concerto.

56. It is likely that Brahms's (no longer available) first draft of this movement, from late summer and early autumn 1856, lacked the major-mode theme that now starts at m. 157. On 4 December 1856, after reviewing that initial draft, Joachim suggested that to the "wonderfully beautiful minor-mode song" (n. 40 above) he add "something correspondingly elevated and beautiful . . . in major" (cited in Dahlhaus, *Johannes Brahms,* 5; Koch, *Das Klavierkonzert des 19. Jahrhunderts,* 313).

57. Hearing mm. 157–60, an obvious antecedent, one expects that m. 161 will begin a parallel consequent. That pseudo-consequent, however, leads to another III:HC at m. 166 and moves onward to a new idea at that point. This converts the "two antecedents" into the presentation of a large-scale sentence. See Hepokoski and Darcy, *Elements of Sonata Theory,* 125–28, which discusses a parallel case in Beethoven's First Symphony.

58. Tovey, "Brahms: Pianoforte Concerto," 116; Dubiel, "Contradictory Criteria," 99; Roger Moseley, "Brief Immortality: Recasting History in the Music of Brahms" (Ph.D. diss., University of California, Berkeley, 2004), 131.

59. The PAC is slightly attenuated at m. 210, since the right hand of the piano does not sound F on the downbeat of that bar. While the closure may not be completely full, I nonetheless regard it as the effective point of closure for S1's secondary-theme space.

Retrospectively, we may construe the double sounding of the horn call (mm. 199, 210) as a valedictory gesture belonging "naturally" in C space. The III:IAC in m. 199 provides an impression so close to full closure that it is as if the horn misunderstands the situation and releases itself prematurely (with preplanned C material). Within two bars, however, Brahms stages the narrative as if "realizing" that a full-closure III:PAC (S1:\EEC) has not yet been attained. Consequently, as a recovery move, the bass moves downward to $\hat{3}$, the typical I^6 onset of an expanded cadential progression, seeking to initiate the characteristic motion toward producing the PAC not achieved at m. 199. Along the way, that cadence is evaded (mm. 203–204), the expected A bass darkens to A♭, and so on. The PAC (S1:\EEC) is finally attained at m. 210, whereupon the horn call is rereleased, now situated in the proper place and heard over a tonic pedal that confirms C-space.

60. Compare "C as S-aftermath," in Hepokoski and Darcy, *Elements of Sonata Theory,* 182–83.

61. Measures 216–26 are constructed on two cycles of an $\hat{8}$–♭$\hat{7}$–$\hat{6}$–♭$\hat{7}$–$\hat{8}$ module, circling around an attained tonic usually held in the bass as a pedal point. This is a common procedure within the tradition, often found within closing zones (Hepokoski and Darcy, *Elements of Sonata Theory,* 184). Its presence helps to support the interpretation of mm. 210–26 as S1:\C (post-EEC).

62. Alternatively, if one had decided not to construe mm. 216–26 as R2, one might suppose that this R1:\P at mm. 231–32 represents a vestigial memory of the traditionally *forte* R2 gesture (the second tutti), merging immediately into Solo 2 at m. 233.

63. Dubiel, "Contradictory Criteria," 106–107, makes much of this R1:\TR passage, and particularly of its rising bass-line succession C (m. 259), C♯ (m. 263), D (m. 271), reversing (or undoing) the "abnorm" of the D–C♯–C succession first heard in mm. 1–22 and thus providing a strong corrective action on the way to further assimilations in the recapitulation.

64. This is one of the few development sections in the repertory to end with an explicit perfect authentic cadence in the tonic (as opposed to being interrupted on V). The absolutism of this cadential moment seems to have impressed Mahler, who composed an analogous, though further radicalized, reentry into the recapitulation in the first movement of his Symphony No. 2 in C Minor, "Resurrection."

65. Dubiel, "Contradictory Criteria," 85.

66. Along with the coda, mm. 451–84, this entire transitional passage, mm. 339–62, was an April 1857 replacement for whatever had originally been in Brahms's second draft of the movement from December 1856 and very early January 1857—an improvement, wrote Brahms to Joachim on 22 April, of one of the earlier version's "weak spots." Koch, *Das Klavierkonzert des 19. Jahrhundert,* 314.

67. On the concept of tonal alienation within S or TMB modules, see Hepokoski and Darcy, *Elements of Sonata Theory,* 245–47, 277–78. Thus far, R1:\S and its Example 8.3b variant have appeared in B♭ minor (m. 46), F minor (m. 142), B minor (m. 278), and F♯ minor (m. 366).

68. In this instance, this is what Richard Cohn dubbed the "southern" hexatonic system, incorporating major and minor triads on D, B♭, and F♯. See Cohn, "Maximally Smooth Cycles, Hexatonic Systems, and the Analysis of Late-Romantic Triadic Progressions," *Music Analysis* 15/1 (1996): 9–40; and "As Wonderful as Star Clusters: Instruments for Gazing at Tonality in Schubert," *19th-Century Music* 22/3 (1999): 213–32.

69. Tovey, "Brahms: Pianoforte Concerto," 117; Böttinger, "Jahre der Krise," 63; Dubiel, "Contradictory Criteria," 105.

70. Dahlhaus, *Johannes Brahms,* 10; Ulm, "'Lässt er noch keine Pauken,'" 128.

71. Measures 451–84 comprise a second-thought recomposition from April 1857; what was originally there is unknown. See Koch, *Das Klavierkonzert des 19. Jahrhunderts,* 316.

72. Reynolds, "A Choral Symphony by Brahms?," 6; Koch, *Das Klavierkonzert des 19. Jahrhunderts,* 326–31.

9   The Drama of Tonal Pairing in Chamber Music of Schumann and Brahms

Peter H. Smith

If it is reasonable to assume that musical meaning emanates from a composition's technical characteristics, then there is perhaps no more basic a source for expressivity in tonal music than the centripetal force of the tonic. The overarching control of a tonal center that is established at the outset and reaffirmed at the close provides one means to create the archetypal musical drama of departure and return. That the tonic may remain implicitly present despite its absence from the musical surface affords the possibility for a composition to project a sense of distance in the journey, which, through the further influence of monotonality, may be characterized by either clearly directed motion or delays and detours on the way to the goal of closure.[1]

The highly developed formal patterns of the eighteenth century, with their tendency to dramatize large-scale tonal relationships, are especially conducive to these basic forms of musical expression. In the nineteenth century, the situation becomes more complicated, as a penchant for decisive articulation of large-scale tonal relationships gradually loses sway as a stylistic hallmark. Composers instead tend increasingly to favor a seamless musical fabric marked by heightened degrees of continuity and formal ambiguity. These composers further complicate the picture by expanding the tonal resources for the key areas of their forms, while they also manifest a keen interest in alternatives to the unambiguously centered monotonality of the eighteenth century. The degree to which these alternatives may have come to replace or merely to supplement univalent tonal centricity remains open to debate. There seems to be no question, however, that nineteenth-century form exhibits techniques of tonal organization that challenge, even if only temporarily, the transparency of the monotonal ideal.

One such challenge to monotonality arises from the practice of *tonal pairing,* in which two keys—usually third related—intertwine throughout a composition.[2] In the most robust examples of tonal pairing, it is often not clear, for considerable spans of music, which of the two tonics might function as the overarching tonal center. But even in circumstances in which the challenge to tonal hierarchy is less extreme, the ambiguities of tonal pairing may serve to expand the expressive resources for the tonal drama of musical form. Rather than arise from the particular *way* in which a tonic asserts its function as tonal nexus, the question of the very *perspective* from which we are to hear tonal relationships becomes an issue that composers may pursue to various expressive ends.

Much has been written about tonal pairing and the related topics of the double-tonic complex and directional tonality in Schubert's and Wolf's songs, Chopin's piano works, Wagner's music dramas, and the fin de siècle symphonic practice of Bruckner and Mahler.[3] The technique also has been associated with Schumann's songs and piano music, where it has long been recognized as an important compositional resource. Not as much attention has been paid, however, to Brahms's engagement with tonal pairing and how this engagement might relate to Schumann's practice of tonal dialectics.[4] Nor have there been many attempts to suggest possible expressive correlations for dialectical tonal processes in the "absolute" music of these composers, above all in their chamber music. Although it is likely that Schubert also influenced Brahms's development of dialectical tonal strategies, his general importance as a precursor for Brahms has been explored more fully than Schumann's. Given the more sympathetic treatment Schumann's traditional instrumental forms have received of late (in contrast to the long-standing tendency to denigrate these forms), the time appears ripe to study areas beyond rhythmic invention in which Schumann may have served as a model for Brahms.[5]

I propose to explore Schumann's and Brahms's approaches to tonal pairing, with attention to the musical meanings that might arise as the interaction between two tonal centers develops over the course of an instrumental movement. This exploration includes (1) an *analytical perspective:* a close reading of structural characteristics; (2) an *intertextual perspective:* an examination of one facet of the relationship between Schumann's and Brahms's approaches to composition; and (3) a *dramatic perspective:* speculation about the musical expression that emanates from the tension between the unitary demands of tonal centricity and the seemingly contradictory claims for a decentered harmonic rhetoric of tonal pairing. Rather than construct explicit extramusical narratives, my approach to expressive interpretation reads technical processes as forms of dramatic development to which various types of expression may correlate. Although I do not wish to make absolutist claims about the privileged role of technical analysis in musical hermeneutics, my approach here rests on the assumption that works of Schumann and Brahms may be interpreted productively as essays in shared compositional strategies and that comparison of the nuances of these strategies forms a legitimate site for expressive interpretation.[6]

I begin with an introductory analysis of a passage of tonal pairing in the first movement of Brahms's String Sextet in B♭ Major, op. 18, before moving on

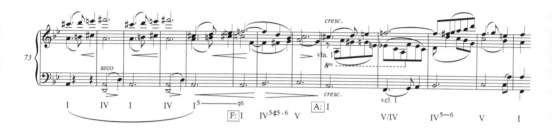

Example 9.1. Brahms, String Sextet in B♭ Major, op. 18, I, second theme (simplified).

to the more detailed analyses of the essay's core repertory: the middle movements of Schumann's Violin Sonata in A Minor, op. 105, Brahms's Violin Sonata
in A Major, op. 100, and Brahms's String Quintet in F Major, op. 88. The sextet
provides a straightforward example of tonal pairing, illustrates how pairing may
interact with form, underscores the role of musical topics as components of expression, and provides a context to draw all these facets together in the service
of expressive interpretation. Tonal pairing moves to the forefront in the middle
key area of the first movement's three-key exposition, as annotations indicate in
the short score of Example 9.1. Observe that the harmonic language is marked
by more than the persistence of a subsidiary motivic chord (F, tonicized in mm.
66–68 and 78–80) within a progression otherwise centered on A. Rather, the circular motions around A and F call into question which of these harmonies might
function as overriding tonic within the section. Although F may be heard as ♯VI
of A, A may also be heard as III♯ of F, reflecting the ambiguity of perspective that
stands at the heart of tonal pairing.[7]

The result is a temporary suspension of the larger tonal trajectory of sonata
form. The transition of mm. 43–60 arrives on the conventional goal of II♮ (V/F),
but the motion lacks the tonal-textural intensification—in short, the articulative
force—customary for a sonata-style modulation to the dominant. The middleground analysis of Example 9.2 instead suggests a relatively shallow structural
significance for this weakly articulated II♮: its C bass functions as part of a motion
to an inner voice above an overriding B♭–A bass descent. The absence of a deci-

254 *Peter H. Smith*

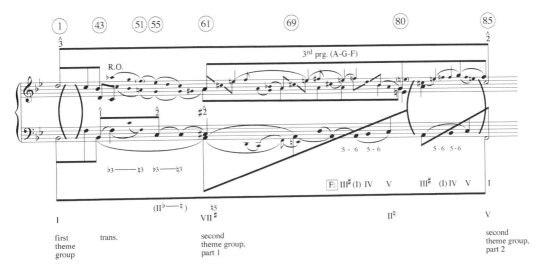

Example 9.2. Brahms, String Sextet in B♭ Major, op. 18, I, graph of mm. 1–85.

sive transitional V/F is one of the characteristics that prevents the subsequent A harmony from fulfilling a clearly subsidiary function in relation to the F tonicizations of the transition and A/F theme. Rather, A and F both receive emphasis as local tonics, but neither steps forward as an unequivocal tonal center in relation to the other. The ambivalence of the pairing resolves only with the emergence of the main II♮ (m. 80) toward the end of the A/F area, and even there it takes two attempts for the auxiliary cadence to lead—finally—to the arrival of F as univalent center for the exposition's third part.

The topical orientation of the sextet's thematic material allows for refinement of the expressive interpretation we might draw from these technical observations. One possible interpretation for the tonal-formal interaction is that of a consciousness marked by two sharply differentiated planes of awareness. Sonata convention, as reflected by the tonal centricity of the tonic and dominant areas, establishes a primary level of consciousness in the manner of the experience of everyday "reality." This primary train of thought, however, is interrupted by a tonal/mental digression to an alternative state of awareness during the A/F pairing.

A dichotomy with the surrounding key areas arises from additional factors beyond the shift to a decentered harmonic rhetoric. The stasis of the second theme's A/F pairing joins the theme's *Ländler* topic to suggest the idealized world of an Arcadian reverie. Overall, the movement falls into a pastoral expressive genre, characterized in part by the serenade-like character of the tonic and dominant themes.[8] Brahms evokes the pastoral through key (especially the F major of both parts of the two-part second group), $^6_4$ hypermeter, a relatively uncompli-

cated harmonic vocabulary, moderately paced harmonic rhythm, clearly articulated phrases, patterns of small and midscale thematic repetition, melodic motions in parallel thirds and sixths, and recourse to pedal points. The specifically
serenade-like tone arises additionally from the congenial and lyrical character of
the themes and the sextet scoring.[9]

A dancelike character is not exclusive to the A/F section; the F-major material also has a dancelike lilt. But the combination of the brightness of A major
(especially as set off against its mellower F pair), the dreamy stasis of the pairing itself, the shift to a hushed *pianissimo* and *dolce,* the *pizzicato* accompaniment, and the more overtly dancelike topic of the material—its tonal and topical
markedness, in other words—endows the second theme with the character of
a dream (or perhaps daydream), in contrast to the more earthly reality of the
formally grounded tonic and dominant sections.[10] Tonal pairing works in the
service of an evocatively coloristic passage that manifests a detour from the main
path of the sonata argument. From the perspective of expressive interpretation,
the weakness of the transition's motion to II♮ acquires a positive connotation: it
correlates with a gradual drift from full consciousness to a magical dream state.
The vigor of the dominant theme in turn receives justification as a psychological
call to order following this Arcadian reverie.

Although the otherworldly character of Brahms's A/F theme constitutes an
expressive high point, it is important to recognize that the theme's tonal pairing
remains a relatively circumscribed phenomenon. (It is also important to note
that a fuller interpretation of the expressive significance of the A/F theme would
require detailed analysis of the entire movement—a task that falls beyond the
scope of this introductory discussion.) Viewed locally, monotonality temporarily relaxes in favor of a decentered alternation between third-related keys. But
from a broader perspective, the local circularity poses no challenge to the conventional tonal order. B♭ and F function as the unambiguous centers for their
respective sections, and these large-scale harmonic pillars frame the A/F pairing
and clarify its function as a transient passage. Similarly, on a still deeper level, F
functions as (tonicized) dominant and thus as a subsidiary harmony in relation
to the B♭ tonic.

Recognizing these limits of scope is crucial for differentiating manifestations of tonal pairing in Brahms from the more thoroughgoing manner in which
tonal dialectics might pervade, say, a Wagnerian music drama or multiple pieces
within a Schumann cycle of character pieces. In Brahms's and Schumann's chamber music, pairings inevitably fall within a larger monotonal context, and even
the temporary functional ambiguities in a case like the sextet are the exception
rather than the rule. As we will see, these local interactions between emphasized
harmonies will tend to fall within *locally* monotonal frameworks. Tonal relation-

ships may shift back and forth from phrase to phrase or section to section, per-haps resulting in brief moments of ambiguity as the adjustments take place. It is in this sense that Schumann and Brahms go beyond mere emphasis on subsid-iary motivic harmonies to engage a practice related to the more robust strategies of pairing that were to emerge in other genres and composers of the nineteenth century. But one should not expect, nor do I mean to attribute to Schumann's or Brahms's chamber music, the kind of long-range irresolution that scholars have associated with tonal pairing in Wagner and others.

A Promissory Note, Tonal Pairing, and Tragic Expression in Schumann's Violin Sonata in A Minor, op. 105

The middle movements of Schumann's Violin Sonata in A Minor, op. 105, and Brahms's in A Major, op. 100, provide a forum to explore relation-ships between the composers' engagement with this qualified approach to tonal pairing. Michael Struck considers Brahms's movement to be closely related to Schumann's, and the similarities begin with each interior movement's position within a cycle of three rather than four movements, where it fulfills both slow and scherzo functions.[11] The blend of slow and fast movement types is more transparent in the Brahms, with its straightforward alternation of Andante and Vivace sections. The Schumann nevertheless embeds a scherzando idea within its refrain (mm. 9–12) that contrasts with both the movement's more leisurely main theme and still more overtly slow-movement–like first episode (mm. 16–25). Moreover, the scherzando material blossoms into a second episode (mm. 41–56), where Schumann intensifies the scherzando character via a *Bewegter* indication.

The similarities do not end with the movements' mutual hybrid character, as Struck notes. Both are rondo forms that manifest a shift from both sonatas' over-arching A tonality to an F major in which the key of D minor receives emphasis. F and D intertwine in the manner of a tonal pair, and cross-references to these keys serve as a means to link the sections of the rondo forms. The interaction of slow and scherzo movement types thus finds a parallelism in the F/D interac-tions.[12]

There is nevertheless at least one crucial difference, notwithstanding these similarities. The key of D in the Schumann makes its presence felt through ar-ticulation of its A dominant rather than a structural D tonic. In the Brahms, D appears as both key and tonicized *Stufe*. So in the Schumann, it is A in its capac-ity as V/D, rather than D itself, that interacts with F on the musical surface. D nevertheless forms an important component of the pairing through its implicit presence as a key on the tonal horizon.[13] In both movements, moreover, the keys intertwine partly through emphasis on A as III♯ in F-major contexts. Indeed, the

III♯ function is central to tonal pairing in all my examples from Schumann and Brahms, including the B♭ sextet, where, as we have seen, A also functions, both locally and on the middleground, as III♯.[14]

Schumann's tonal dialectics are also somewhat more complex in their recourse to a second pairing between F and C. These multiple pairings serve as a means to integrate the harmonic language of the interior rondo with idiosyncrasies of tonal organization in the first and last movements. The emphasis on A major in particular resonates with the A tonic of the outer movements and especially with those movements' recapitulation of secondary material in the major tonic. A similar contribution to cyclical unification also characterizes tonal pairing in Brahms's String Quintet in F Major, op. 88—another important analogue in these composers' engagement with harmonic dualism. In the Schumann sonata, we will eventually see that tonal relationships spanning the three movements contribute to a powerful expression of musical tragedy in which the promise of transcendence offered by passages in the major tonic is ultimately dashed by the negative force of the minor mode.

A tendency for tonal dialectics emerges at the outset of the sonata's middle movement, where, as Example 9.3 indicates, the refrain references the aforementioned F/C interaction, even as it clearly prolongs a C *Stufe*. Is this an F-major theme that makes a hasty move to the dominant, or is it a C-major theme with a strong subdominant coloration? At this stage of the movement, interactions with the A dominant merely hint at the alternative F/D pairing that will emerge more

Example 9.3. Schumann, Violin Sonata in A Minor, op. 105, II, mm. 1–3.

fully in the second episode. The motivic A harmony is marked for consciousness as a striking substitute for the cadential C of the opening antecedent phrase (m. 3), at the parallel cadence in the consequent (m. 8). Although this III♯ chord has a surface V/D function, it participates in a circle-of-fifths motion back to F. A structural D tonic fails to emerge, although the hint of an F/D interaction does intensify ever so slightly with the juxtaposition of V/F and V/D at the turn of mm. 9–10.

The juxtaposition is significant because it has the effect of pitting the two dominants against each other, thus suggesting a tonal pairing rather than a more straightforward articulation of III♯. After an initial attempt at a return to F in m. 9, the A dominant stubbornly interrupts the progression and reasserts D tonicity. Schumann underscores the disruptive character of A in both of its appearances through *fermata* and *tenuto* indications, respectively. It is only upon a second attempt that the circle-of-fifths motion is able to overcome D-minor gravity and lead to closure in F. This detail notwithstanding, it is clear that Schumann's tonal dialectics here are not nearly as robust as Brahms's in the sextet, where there is a somewhat more extended competition between A and F within the second theme.

In contrast to the Arcadian reverie I have suggested as a correlation for Brahms's tonal stasis, meaning in the Schumann may begin to be accessed through the metaphor of a promissory note.[15] Scholars have tended to associate the notion that initial tonal idiosyncrasies may have long-term consequences with the acknowledged nineteenth-century masters of traditional instrumental forms—Beethoven and Brahms—and, in the case of a promissory note in particular, Schubert. But here we find Schumann engaged in a similar practice with no apparent lack of compositional foresight.

The A dominant enters as a chromatic intruder within an otherwise whimsical refrain, and the D-minor debt it incurs remains unpaid in the immediate context. Indeed, the promissory obligation intensifies through the repetition of the refrain in mm. 26–40, where the lack of recomposition insures that A's path to D remains blocked. The unfulfilled tonal implications reach fruition only in the D-minor second episode (mm. 41–56), where A finally blossoms into a structural harmony and D emerges as governing key. Note, in Example 9.4, that the F/D pairing remains palpable on the foreground via cross-references to the refrain's F tonic in m. 47. Here the A *Stufe* and D key move into the forefront; it is the lingering influence of F that colors the progression, in tonal pairing's characteristic reversal of harmonic perspective. Observe also that the development of the refrain's scherzando material in the episode links the passages and therefore encourages an interpretation in which the newfound prominence of A fulfills a harmonic urge that remains repressed within the two refrain statements. The

Example 9.4. Schumann, Violin Sonata in A Minor, op. 105, II, mm. 45–50.

forte and *sforzato* indications in the episode (mm. 45–48 and 54–56) also strategically mark the A harmony, similar to the *fermatas* and *tenutos* of the refrain.

The turbulence the episode unleashes, as the promissory note comes due,
is never fully reconciled with the quiet charms of the refrain, despite other elements of resolution in the final statement of the A material (mm. 57–79). Among
the most prominent of these elements of resolution is the shift from F/C interactions in the opening phrase to F/B♭ interactions as Schumann recomposes
the final refrain (cf. the F/C duality of mm. 1–8 with the F/B♭ emphasis of mm.
63–79). The tense dominant leanings of the opening thus shift to more relaxed
subdominant colorations appropriate for impending closure. The A dominant,
by contrast, eschews a final appearance and any nod toward reconciliation. One
could argue perhaps that the repetitions of the thirty-second-note motive in mm.
64–67 represent a local taming of the previous outbursts: the passage references
the material of the C episode in a context in which the material's tonally disruptive features have been neutralized. The final refrain nevertheless makes no
specific recall of either the A harmony or the D-minor key. On the contrary, the
emphasis on $\hat{3}$ in the closing measures hints at A's life beyond the movement
through both the flickers of energy provided by the trills in m. 75—note also
here the thirty-second-note motive—and the prominence of A in the top voice
of the final F tonic expansion (mm. 76–79). Ultimately the tensions of the F/D
pairing function as part of a larger drama of tonal dialectics spanning all three
movements. Although a thorough analysis of these cyclical relationships extends
beyond the purview of this essay, some summary observations should suffice to
suggest this tonal pairing's globally integrative function and the manner in which
it contributes to the sonata's overarching tragic expression.[16]

Example 9.5. Schumann, Violin Sonata in A Minor, op. 105, I, tonic-submediant interactions.

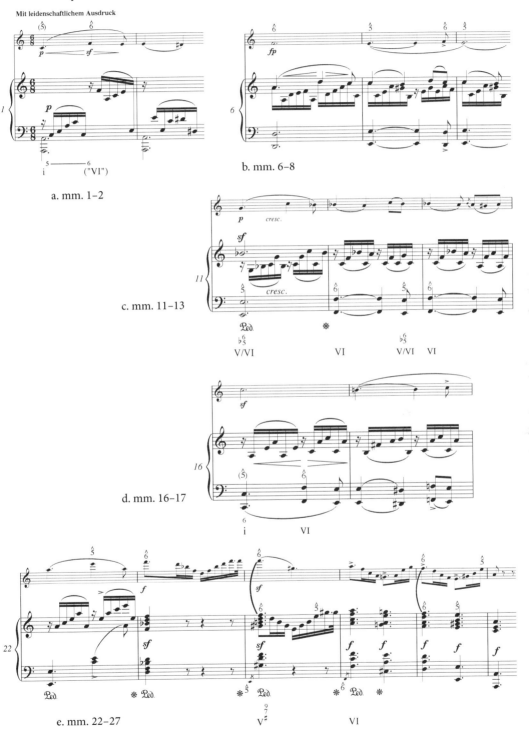

Example 9.6. Schumann, Violin
Sonata in A Minor, op. 105, I,
deceptive cadences.

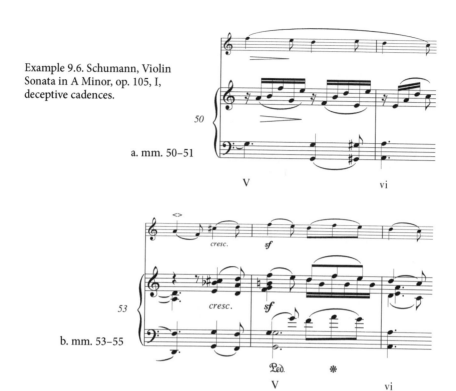

a. mm. 50–51

V   vi

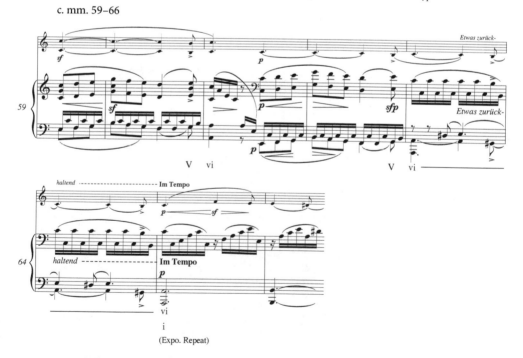

b. mm. 53–55

V   vi

c. mm. 59–66

V   vi   V   vi

vi

i

(Expo. Repeat)

The sonata-form outer movements are noteworthy for Schumann's recourse to tonal pairing, rather than polarity, as he develops his expository key relations. In the first movement, a motivic role for A/F relationships emerges through the tonic area's emphasis on the submediant and $\hat{5}$–$\hat{6}$ interactions. Example 9.5 summarizes these dual forms of F emphasis. The secondary area (mm. 35–64) becomes the site for an alternative interaction between A and C: the expansion section of this continuous exposition refuses to cadence in C and instead recalls the A tonic through the multiple V–vi deceptive progressions highlighted in Example 9.6. Although the A/F pairing we have observed in Brahms's sextet arises in the context of an avowedly Schubertian three-key exposition, Brahms's strategy also relates to Schumann's approach here. In the sextet, Brahms intertwines A and F before F emerges for the dominant area, while Schumann intertwines C and A before A emerges for either the exposition repeat or the transition to the development. Indeed, the last of Schumann's deceptive progressions (m. 63) reintroduces the specific foreground A harmony that becomes the tonic point of departure for both the expository repeat and developmental transition. Schumann's tonic and mediant key areas thus establish the same tonal pairing—or "tripling," to be more precise—of A, F, and C that colors the harmonic language of the middle movement.[17]

The tonic area of the finale similarly highlights F through $\hat{5}$–$\hat{6}$ interactions and submediant emphasis, as seen in Example 9.7. Here, however, the F emphasis foreshadows a move to the submediant itself for the secondary material (mm. 31–57), which instantiates a more overt A/F pairing. As Example 9.8 highlights, Schumann introduces F abruptly, and before the secondary material is able to settle more comfortably into F, it steers back onto an A-minor path at m. 36 (not shown). The second theme subsequently returns to F at m. 43, but it fails to close strongly in F before A reemerges for both the exposition repeat and the transition to the development, in a back-and-forth between third-related keys that could have easily served as a model for Brahms's approach in the sextet.[18] Just as Schumann's first movement intertwines A and C as the basis for its secondary material, so too does the secondary area in the finale intertwine A and F. The second movement's F, C, and A (V/D) interactions thus resonate with the idiosyncratic harmonic organization of the framing sonata forms.

The tragic consequences of this harmonic organization hinge in part on the tonal reinterpretation of secondary material in the recapitulations. In both recapitulations, Schumann transposes the secondary material to A major (mm. 149–76 and 147–67, respectively), a characteristic that strengthens the connection with the second movement, where A appears exclusively as a major sonority. Yet neither recapitulation is able to sustain the major mode's promise of a positive expressive outcome, a failure that is largely a consequence of the material's

Example 9.7. Schumann, Violin Sonata in A Minor, op. 105, III, tonic-submediant interactions.

a. mm. 1–5

b. mm. 9–17

Example 9.8. Schumann, Violin Sonata in A Minor, op. 105, III, mm. 25–32.

tonal pairing. Restated in terms of Byron Almén's theory of musical narrative, the specifically tragic trajectory arises through "the defeat of a transgression"—here the secondary material's major mode and concurrent positive expressive character—"by an order-imposing hierarchy"—the governing force of the minor tonic and negative intensity of the primary thematic complex.[19]

In the first movement, the failure to cadence in C and, in particular, the shadow cast by the articulations of A-minor vi chords allow the (minor) tonic to maintain an upper hand. In technical terms, A remains the controlling *Stufe* at levels closer to the foreground than is typically the case in sonata form. The most the secondary material is able to muster is expansion of V/C (♭VII), and even this unstable *Stufe* functions as a middleground neighbor to the tragic A minor of the tonic area, as Example 9.9 suggests. Similarly in the finale, the abrupt transition to F, the subsequent circular motions around F and A, and the weak closure in F prevent the major-mode material from mounting a forceful challenge to A's predominance. Neither exposition succeeds in its attempts to overcome the gravity of the tonic area's minor mode.

One possible expressive corollary for these expository tonal failures is the suggestion of a preordained pessimism regarding the possibility for either movement to transcend the negative expression—restless and haunting in the first, agitated and perhaps even obsessive in the third—established by the main themes. Indeed, the dramatic buildup to A-minor closure at the end of the primary area in the first movement marks A minor with signs of tragic foreboding (mm. 19–27). The inability of the secondary material to shake A's influence sug-

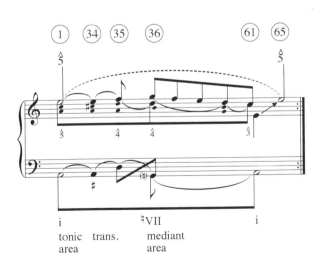

Example 9.9. Schumann, Violin Sonata in A Minor, op. 105, I, graph of exposition.

gests the inevitability of a negative outcome, as a correlation to classical notions of tragic fate. To carry the analogy further, we might even think of the secondary material's tonal idiosyncrasy in both movements as a tragic flaw: one of the most aesthetically compelling characteristics of these beguiling sections—their failure to reach tonal closure in favor of tonal dualism—is also what will lead to their dramatic undoing.

When the second themes return in A major, the expressive tension increases: now it is the promise of the major tonic itself that is dashed by the materials' original inability to reach closure. The second movement similarly partakes in A's failed utopian aspirations. The sharp-side *Stufe* glows brightly in the F-major context, but here, too, the harmony ultimately remains ineffectual. Although it resonates brightly, it is unstable as dominant and specifically as dominant of a turbulent D *minor* episode. Moreover, in the outer movements, it is the return of the haunting main theme from the first movement in both cases, with its submediant shading of the A tonic, that participates in a final V–♯VI (E–F♯) cadential evasion, as the secondary material collapses into the tragic A-minor intensity of the coda (mm. 177 and 168, respectively). The A/F pairing thus moves center stage at these two pivotal moments of defeat, as it does also in the first movement's closing cadence of mm. 205–209. There the grim final chords express A minor's tragic force even more powerfully than the brusque cadential harmonies at the end of the tonic area. Schumann uses similar A-minor hammer blows to conclude the finale of this extraordinary and expressively devastating tonal tragedy.

Suspense and Wit in a Brahms Andante-Vivace

Despite tonal pairing's global influence, interactions among Schumann's motivic harmonies never achieve the equilibrium necessary to create ambiguity regarding which tonic functions as nexus for each of the individual movements. F's predominance is clear throughout the middle movement (with the possible exception of the opening measures, where C competes for control), as is A's in the outer movements. The middle movement of Brahms's Violin Sonata in A Major, op. 100, by contrast, culminates in a passage of genuine suspense about this basic question, in a moment of tonal equivocation that intensifies the strategy of pairing inherited from Schumann, with far-reaching consequences for expressive interpretation.

The movement alternates its refrain with two statements of a contrasting episode to create the rondo form outlined in Table 9.1. A contrast of pastoral subtopics complements both the rondo's F/D tonal interactions and hybridization of slow and scherzo functions—an extension of the strategy of pairing into the topical realm that we will also observe in the middle movement of Brahms's

Table 9.1. Brahms, Violin Sonata in A Major, op. 100, II, formal overview

Measure Numbers	Formal Function	Harmonic Orientation
1–15	**A Section or Refrain**	I with solid closure at m. 13
	B Section or Episode	
	rounded binary	
16–31	a	Begins in D minor (vi) but continues to prolong F *Stufe* until arrival of D *Stufe* at m. 24
31–48	b	Begins in F (III/D but also reference to global I!) and leads back to D via vii^{o7}
49–71	a′	D: i to V
72–93	**A′ or First Refrain Restatement**	Begins with D-major tonic expansion with shift back to F at m. 79 and solid closure in F at m. 92
	B′ Section or Episode Restatement (variation)	
	rounded binary	
94–109	a	Begins in D minor (vi) but continues to prolong F *Stufe* until arrival of D *Stufe* at m. 102
109–26	b	Begins in F (III/D but also reference to global I!) and leads back to D via vii^{o7}
127–49	a′	D: i to V
150–61	**A″ or Second Refrain Restatement**	Begins with D-major tonic expansion that includes reference to global F tonic via passing $^6_4$ (mm. 152–53); shifts back to F at m. 155 and closes in F at m. 157
162–68	**Coda**	I with references to D as subsidiary vi in standard cadential progression

String Quintet in F Major, op. 88.[20] The refrain evokes the pastoral through its F tonality, melodic motions in parallel thirds, $\hat{5}$–$\hat{6}$–$\hat{5}$ neighbor figures, slow harmonic rhythm, and tonic and dominant pedals. The character of the material, however, is hardly rustic but rather is elevated, and the movement thus begins in a mood of Elysian transcendence. The dance rhythms and folk character of the episode, by contrast, have the lower character of an Arcadian tableau.

The episode remains fundamentally unchanged in its repeat, although Brahms treats the material to surface variation. The first restatement of the refrain, however, provides an opportunity for an intensely expressive passage of expansion (mm. 85–91), while the second presents much of the refrain in recomposed form. In both cases, the changes further elevate the tone of the mate-

Example 9.10. Brahms, Violin Sonata in A Major, op. 100, II, expansion and recomposition in refrain.

a. mm. 89–93

b. mm. 150–56

rial—and thus intensify the contrast with the folklike episode—through motion into the violin's upper register, whose soaring Olympian character Brahms underscores through his performance indications (*espressivo* and *crescendo* to *forte* in mm. 85–89; *dolce, molto dolce,* and *sempre più dolce* in m. 150ff.). Not incidentally, both of these passages also develop the F/D pairing. The first does so in an avowedly F-major context through motion to III♯ in its characteristic function as V/vi (Example 9.10a). This, of course, is the same treatment of III♯ that characterizes the refrain of the middle movement of the Schumann sonata, and it similarly creates associative links to the D minor of the episodes. The second of Brahms's passages intensifies the interaction between the keys through juxtaposition of F and D tonics before it settles into closure on F (Example 9.10b).[21]

The global F/D interactions reflected in these passages flow across the sections of the rondo form and eventually culminate in a moment of doubt regarding the predominance of either structural harmony. In this way, Brahms extends Schumann's strategy of pairing in the context of a hybrid movement to create a degree of tension comparable to the ambiguities that Schumann sustains across greater spans in his character pieces and songs. Ultimately, the pairing and its resolution serve a comic expressive function: the last-minute victory of the heretofore Elysian F arrives with a final flourish based on the rustic dance that wittily punctures the refrain's high seriousness. Theorized in relation to Almén's narrative archetypes, the comic trajectory arises through a combination of emergence and synthesis as discursive strategies.[22] The transgressive element—the episode's tonal challenge to the control of the refrain's F tonic and, along with it, the challenge of the Olympian by the vernacular—begins at a very low level of intensity and emerges gradually over the course of the movement. The aspect of synthesis arises through the resolution of the resulting conflict by means of a coda that combines previously distinct musical elements: the refrain's F tonality comes to govern the close of the movement but only as the previously elevated F is overtaken by the episode's rustic dance.

The initial statement of the refrain foretells the inevitability of F's eventual triumph. The material gives no hint of competition from D, and it is not until the B section that the two harmonies begin to intertwine. Significantly, even at the entrance of the B section, F continues to dominate. It not only provides a rock-solid foundation for the primary thematic material of the refrain but also delays the arrival of the apparently subsidiary D *Stufe* through the melodic-harmonic linkage outlined in Example 9.11a. Note the similarity with the introduction of F as a harmony paired with A in Schumann's violin sonata (Example 9.11b). There, too, a contrapuntal 5–6 motion in the main theme expands the tonic even as it gives rise to an F sonority that anticipates the submediant's motivic function. Even after D emerges as a structural harmony in the Brahms, F continues to

Example 9.11. Tonic-submediant linkage via the 5–6 technique.

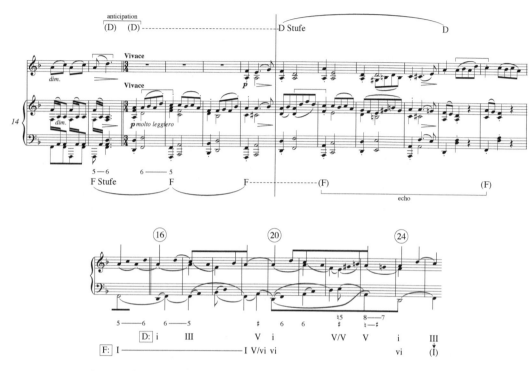

a. Brahms, Violin Sonata in A Major, op. 100, II, mm. 14–25.

b. Schumann, Violin Sonata in A Minor, op. 105, I, mm. 1–2.

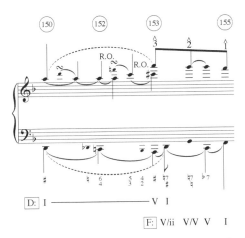

Example 9.12. Brahms, Violin Sonata in A Major, op. 100, II, graph of mm. 150–55.

shadow it in the form of a subsidiary tonicization at the beginning of the tripartite episode's b section of mm. 31–48.[23]

D's challenge to F emerges more fully only later in the movement, as the ends of the two episodes overlap tonally with the returns of the refrain. In each instance, the refrain provides the D tonic resolution for the episode's final A dominant. D thus comes to control the return of the primary thematic material, just as F remains active across the emergence of both statements of the secondary material. The idea of a competition between these tonics becomes most acute at the second B statement. Not only does Brahms float back and forth between D and F orientations, but he initially evokes F through a $\frac{6}{4}$ chord that is subsidiary to the larger D-major expansion graphed in Example 9.12. The straightforward formal-tonal overlap at the first return of the refrain thus blossoms into a more forthright intermingling of motivic harmonies, with the apparently subsidiary D momentarily gaining the upper hand.

Yet despite the refrain restatements' gradual shift to somewhat increased D prominence, each iteration of the A and B sections eventually settles into its "proper" tonal orientation. F eventually yields to D in the episodes as D does to F in the refrains. This would appear to provide further support for the inference drawn from the refrain's initial statement: that F functions as overriding tonic throughout, notwithstanding the importance of its motivic interactions with D. F not only governs the entire initial statement of the primary thematic material; it also governs the motions to closure in each repetition of that material.

At the end of the final refrain, however, Brahms leads to one last statement of the motivic 5–6 motion (mm. 160–61). In all previous occurrences, this 5–6 motion initiates a transition to (eventual) D control. The close of the refrain thus becomes the site for a moment of tonal drama: might the 5–6 motion again lead to D—here as a closing harmony in a coda—and thus overturn previous perceptions that signaled F's supremacy? And therefore might the prominence of D at the beginning of each refrain restatement be understood retrospectively to function as part of the gradual emergence of D as overriding tonic rather than as off-tonic returns that reflect Brahms's more general proclivity for tonal-formal overlap?

The wit of the coda arises out of the sudden and emphatic "No!" it answers in response to this moment of suspenseful questioning. F major comes to govern the close of the movement, but, as mentioned previously, it does so only through its synthesis with the coda's final statement of the dance theme. Brahms, moreover, absorbs the submediant into the final F expansion as part of a conventional cadential progression. On the one hand, this cadence maintains a trace of the F/D pairing, thus providing another element of synthesis in the harmonic dimension. On the other hand, it does indeed forthrightly resolve the tonal dialectic by including D as an unambiguously embellishing harmony.

Although Brahms is not a composer we typically associate with compositional jesting, here his comic timing is impeccable. The final 5–6 motion generates suspense precisely because the possibility for D closure seems so unlikely in the face of the clear signals of F's predominance in all that has come before. The abrupt shift in character that arrives with the coda's punch line provides the appropriately brusque temporal complement, as the frozen moment of the 5–6 motion yields to the highly measured rhythmic activity of the coda. The triumph of F, moreover, comes at the expense of the high seriousness of the refrain. Previously, it has been the refrain that has drawn the D of the rustic dance up to its Olympian heights in a contrasting form of synthesis, and the brightness of D major has likewise added luster to the main theme. But it is the rustic dance that has the last word, as it pulls the F tonic down to *its* level and playfully refuses to accede to the refrain's pretense of superiority.

Monotonality and the Paradox of a Plagal Cadence in Brahms's String Quintet in F Major, op. 88

The expressive character of the C♯-minor middle movement of Brahms's String Quintet in F Major, op. 88, could hardly provide a sharper contrast, despite the many compositional strategies it shares with the violin sonata's rondo.[24] Brahms again alternates a refrain with a twice-stated episode in the slow-scherzo hybrid form outlined in Table 9.2. The emphasis similarly falls on third-related tonics, and the harmonies here also forge links across the sections of the form. Tonal continuity is most obvious at the returns of the refrain. At the first return

Table 9.2. Brahms, String Quintet in F Major, op. 88, II, formal overview

Measure Numbers	Formal Function	Harmonic Orientation
1–31	**A Section or Refrain**	i with solid closure at m. 28 within codetta (mm. 26–31)
	B Section or Episode	
	rounded binary	
32–41	a	VI (tonicized) with local A: I–V progression
42–52	b	Expansion of A: ii
53–74	a′	A: IV (tonicized with A as V⁷/D) to V–I
74–79	retransition	A tonic becomes V⁷/D again but then reinterpreted as German $\frac{6}{5}$ in C♯
80–116	**A′ or First Refrain Restatement**	Begins on V but eventually leads to solid closure in C♯ at m. 111 within codetta (mm. 110–16)
	B′ Section or Episode Restatement (variation)	
	rounded binary	
117–26	a	VI (tonicized) with local A: I–V progression
127–44	b	Expansion of A: ii
145–63	a′	A: IV (tonicized with A as V⁷/D) and no closure on A
164–200	**A″ or Second Refrain Restatement**	Begins with A reinterpreted as local tonic again but returns to C♯ key and *Stufe* via auxiliary cadence in mm. 175–76; closure in C♯ at m. 189 and again in codetta of mm. 196–200
200–208	**Coda**	i–VI alternation culminates in A: iv–I plagal cadence

(m. 80), the conclusive A dominant of the episode resolves as an augmented sixth chord, in the familiar enharmonic reinterpretation, to create the formal-tonal overlap into C♯ minor graphed in Example 9.13. At the second return (m. 164), the main theme reenters in A rather than C♯ in a strategy similar to the off-tonic restatements in the violin sonata.

The quintet's thematic materials, like those of the sonata, project a dichotomy of topical orientations as a complement to the binary interactions of third relations and slow/scherzo formal functions. The three refrain statements present variously expanded versions of what was originally an A-minor/major sarabande that Brahms had composed in the mid-1850s, while the two episodes rework an

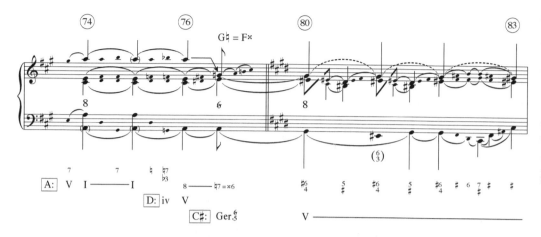

Example 9.13. Brahms, String Quintet in F Major, op. 88, II, V⁷/German § reinterpretation.

A-major gavotte also from that time.[25] A link perhaps exists between the origins of these themes and the relationship with Schumann I have asserted based on the more all-encompassing technique of tonal pairing. The mid-1850s were, of course, the time of Brahms's greatest personal intimacy with the Schumanns, and scholars have placed dance movements composed by both Schumann and Brahms (including Brahms's sarabande and gavotte) in the context of their renewed interest in piano and orchestral suites, which occurred at that time.[26] It is also the case that Clara performed a sarabande and gavotte by Brahms—possibly the very dances later to be adapted for the quintet—in her London concert of 1856. In the quintet of 1883 (composed in 1882), Brahms may have returned to dances with a strong personal association with the Schumanns and meshed them with a form—the slow-fast hybrid of Schumann's A-minor sonata—and a compositional technique—tonal pairing—both loosely inspired by Robert. Historical evidence suggests that the middle movement of Brahms's violin sonata in A major (1886) originated in 1883, further supporting the thesis that *both* movements may have followed Schumann's precedent.[27]

The contrasting affective associations of the sarabande and gavotte derivatives roughly parallel the expressive dichotomy of high and low postures in Brahms's A-major violin sonata. Here, however, the elevated seriousness of the refrain is darkly shaded by the sarabande's minor mode—indeed, the "difficult" minor mode of C♯—in contrast to the sunny and accessible F major of the sonata's refrain. The contrast grows further from the specific manifestations of these tonalities: diatonic and relatively simple in the sonata versus chromatic and complex in the quintet. In the quintet, Brahms uses the major mode differently: to underscore the contrasting sprightly character of the B sections' dance rhythms, even as this material, like the episodes in the sonata, projects its own shift to a more vernacular tone. (Note in particular the rustic foot stomping of the synco-pated *forte* passages of mm. 122–23, 127–28, 131–32, and 150–57 and the folklike lilt of the siciliano rhythms and elfin eighths of the softer phrases.) The major mode also provides slivers of C♯-major light that nevertheless serve to underscore the chiaroscuro darkness of the refrain's elegiac minor-mode material.[28]

The basic distinction, then, is between a slow-scherzo hybrid movement that builds to a witty conclusion and a similar hybrid form in which an intensely sol-emn (Grave ed appassionato) sarabande assumes the primary position, with con-trast provided by the fast tempo and major mode of dancelike sections of a de-cidedly lighter character. The tonal interactions between the refrain and episodes also come to a head in the quintet's coda, but in this case the closing measures fail to provide a straightforward denouement. The abrupt shift to A at the coda's final plagal cadence (mm. 204–208) has led scholars to different interpretations of the movement's C♯/A pairing. Most commentators hear the C♯/A interactions from the perspective of directional tonality in which the movement progresses from its C♯ beginnings (or balanced C♯/A interactions) to a conclusion in A. In a distinctly minority view, Robert Morgan argues instead for C♯'s predominance and an analysis in which the A cadence functions as part of a postclosural tran-sition to the finale. Still other analysts acknowledge the possibility for diverse interpretations but otherwise place the weight of emphasis on connections the C♯/A pairing forges with tonal processes in the outer movements.[29]

I find an attribution of directional tonality unconvincing and instead favor the minority view—C♯ predominance—while also acknowledging the broader cy-clical function of the movement's third relations. In expressive terms, the move-ment is, for me, fundamentally an elegy in which the mournful C♯ minor of the sarabande governs not only the body of the movement but also its close. The last-minute "amen" of the coda's plagal cadence on A serves a dual expressive function. On the one hand, it transfigures the corporality of the deceased, as represented by the reality of C♯ as overarching tonic, into the heavenly in the form of a conclusive A harmony that transcends the earthly bounds of C♯ structural closure. It also, however, creates a structural-expressive transition to a finale that, along with the first movement, draws this elegy into a larger pastoral whole with an affirmative cyclical conclusion that at least one commentator has described as comic.[30]

Morgan's critique of a directional tonal interpretation is sagacious yet brief due to its presence in a book review; he focuses only on factors in the final refrain that point to C♯'s predominance. I wish to extend his argument through attention to characteristics that signal C♯ centricity throughout the movement. It is not a matter of a balanced interaction between C♯ and A that is decided, one way or the other, by one's interpretation of the closing plagal cadence, as the principle of directional tonality suggests. Rather, from the outset, Brahms forecasts the

Example 9.14. Brahms, String Quintet in F Major, op. 88, II.

V/♮II and augmented sixth functions for A in refrain.

a. mm. 11–12

b. mm. 24–31

c. mm. 182–89

d. mm. 196–200

Example 9.14 *(continued)*.

V/♭II and augmented sixth functions in episode.

e. mm. 52–57

f. mm. 61–65

g. mm. 73–79

inevitability of C♯'s tonic function and along with it the elegiac expressive corollary, notwithstanding A's undeniable importance as a contrasting secondary key. The crux of my interpretation is that it is precisely the norms of monotonality—which govern Brahms's and Schumann's instrumental movements generally and which, I submit, remain strongly in effect here—that lend the final A cadence its expressive intensity, as a contradiction of those very monotonal norms projected by all that has transpired previously. It is this paradox that allows the A cadence to close a movement otherwise in C♯ and thus to express the transfiguration that I hear in these final measures.

All the movements studied in this essay thus illustrate the inevitability of monotonality in Brahms's and Schumann's chamber music despite—or perhaps because of—their interest in tonal pairing. Brahms's sonata does so through jocular confirmation of the seemingly inevitable: the coda's F closure confirms the centricity of the F tonic affirmed by the opening refrain and eventually reaffirmed by the refrain's two returns. The quintet, by contrast, expresses the mystery of death and spiritual transcendence through the irony of its final gesture: the profound structural ambivalence of the A cadence, notwithstanding that cadence's ultimate temporal location, *confirms* rather than denies the predominance that C♯ projects throughout the movement.[31] The contrast of this structural ambivalence with the normative aspects of C♯ centricity allows for an expressive correlation in which the final bright A-major sonority floats away from the earthly reality of the intense grief of the C♯ tonal world. One might even suggest that the rising arpeggiation of the first violin across the plagal cadence embodies this transfiguration: the low register of the C♯ chord expanded in mm. 196–203 corresponds with the image of low earthly reality and the violin's final sustained A in the higher register with the image of the spiritual realm above.

All these expressive speculations ultimately hinge on a technical argument for C♯ centricity, and here my interpretation grows from the most basic of formal considerations. The refrain—the material that clearly functions as the primary theme—is solidly in C♯, as is the first restatement of that material.[32] A major, by contrast, is associated with the secondary material of the episode, with the exception of the second return of the refrain, about which I will comment shortly. In addition, the primary material draws attention specifically to A's subsidiary status through internal emphasis on A in its dual role as V/♭II and augmented sixth chord. Significantly, these subsidiary functions also come to color the large-scale A *Stufe* when A moves to the forefront as tonic for the episodes, as Example 9.14 illustrates. The associative relationships that link the harmonies across the formal sections thus betray A's subsidiary status, even when A purportedly begins to assert itself as a possible rival tonic in a pattern of directional tonality.[33]

Example 9.15. Brahms, String Quintet in F Major, op. 88, II, D-minor tonicization at end of episode.

A's ancillary status grows further from the way in which these alternative harmonic functions interact with the episodes' form. Although both episodes begin in A, neither closes in A, in contrast to the clear control C♯ asserts across the refrain. They instead turn toward D in their a′ sections (mm. 53 and 145) and thus present A in a less stable form as surface dominant. It is true that the first episode eventually leads to an authentic cadence in A at m. 74, but the articulation is light. Moreover, the cadence overlaps with a retransition that transforms this A back into V⁷/D, which in turn ushers in the C♯ return of the refrain, as described above (Example 9.13, p. 274).

The second episode likewise arrives on a prolongation of A as dominant and does not even include the first episode's qualified A closure. One consequence is that, although the final refrain begins with the main theme transposed to A, this tonal articulation is less than definitive: a vii°⁴₃/V–V progression in D straddles the formal hinge, as Example 9.15 indicates. It is only *after* the refrain restatement gets under way that it becomes clear that the prolonged A *Stufe* has returned to the surface tonic function it has lost over the course of the episode. Thus, even at a formal juncture in which A might be felt to move into the forefront, its stability is less than secure, especially compared to the unambiguous tonal control C♯ exerts throughout the first two refrain statements.[34]

The remainder of the final refrain serves to confirm these doubts about A's status as a possible rival tonic. The A tonicization dissolves into a C♯ key orientation immediately after the half cadence that closes the opening phrase (mm. 164–72). Although a C♯ tonic *Stufe* emerges only later, at m. 176, this type of dissociation of formal signals is characteristic of Brahms's overlapped reprises.[35]

The Drama of Tonal Pairing 279

Both the specific way that the tonic *Stufe* reemerges and its conclusive prolongation further confirm C♯'s priority. The material is new to the final refrain and simultaneously works both to solidify C♯'s status and to sublimate A. Note, in Example 9.14c, the dramatic buildup to the G♯ V^6_4 of mm. 182–83, the preparation for this G♯ by A in one of its subsidiary guises as augmented sixth chord, and the resolution to C♯, here sumptuously expanded by an understated yet expressively climactic circle-of-fifths sequence.[36] The culmination of the sequence further emphasizes C♯ through a pattern of cadential evasion and fulfillment in mm. 186–89, and this pattern in turn highlights A's alternate subsidiary function as V/♭II. The entire passage thus not only confirms C♯ as overriding tonic but also recapitulates both the augmented sixth and V/D♮ functions that previously have signaled A's ancillary status. The same is true for the final statement of the refrain's codetta phrase of Example 9.14d, with its clear C♯ orientation and unambiguous articulations of A as V/♭II.[37]

All these different forms of C♯ emphasis indicate why I hear substantially less, if indeed any, possible challenge to tonal centricity compared to the violin sonata, where there exists at least a moment of suspense just prior to the coda's definitive clarification. The character of the quintet's final A cadence further supports this paradox: the violin sonata resolves in favor of the expected tonic even despite the indecision raised by its final 5–6 motion, whereas the quintet does in fact end—though it perhaps does not close—on the harmony that otherwise has so clearly remained subsidiary up through the final measures. I write "end" rather than "close" and "harmony" rather than "tonic" because the final progression lacks the specific characteristics of structural closure as defined by either conventional or Schenkerian analysis. In Schenkerian terms, there is no dominant *Stufe* to provide harmonic support for an *Urlinie* descent in A.[38] Rather, this form of structural closure occurs only in C♯, as Example 9.16 illustrates.[39] The resulting background perspective leads us to hear the final A progression beyond the frame of the main tonal action of the movement. Put more simply, the final refrain provides multiple authentic cadences in C♯ (some with Picardy third), while the final progression to A forms the type of plagal motion—albeit to the "wrong" harmony—typically associated with postcadential tonic expansion.[40]

The problem, of course, is that the arrival on A is the *last* progression we hear, and there is thus a dissociation between harmonic identity—nontonic—and temporal location—final—even though the cadence type is appropriate to the formal location. And it is this paradox that lends the final measures their profoundly spiritual character: that they mysteriously float free from the earthly reality of C♯ that the movement has otherwise unambiguously affirmed. The intensity of expression in this remarkable passage depends centrally on the movement's avowed monotonality and not on notions of directional tonality, notwith-

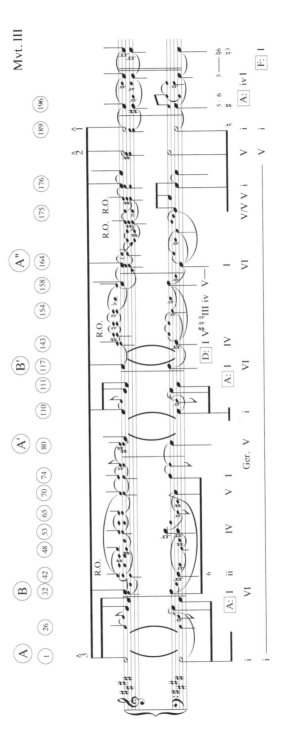

Example 9.16. Brahms, String Quintet in F Major, op. 88, II, C♯ predominance.

standing A's crucial formal-motivic role. The high seriousness of the somber sarabande dominates both the movement and its close, in striking contrast to the witty reversal of tone at the end of the violin sonata movement. The religious overtones of the plagal cadence with minor subdominant—but on the wrong "tonic"—only serve to raise the elegiac expression to a still higher level: that of a transfiguration extending beyond the reality of C♯ monotonality.

Previously, I have suggested an additional function for this unusual close: the final cadence's striking violation of tonal norms might raise the possibility that the movement remains in some sense unresolved and therefore open to tonal interconnection with the surrounding movements. There are indeed a number of striking local and large-scale links across the cycle. Morgan has suggested that the final A cadence forms a transition from closure in C♯ to the F major of the finale. The $\frac{6}{4}$ position of the finale's opening F tonic bolsters this interpretation: a continuity of A as bass forms a connection across the movements as the C♯–A–F chain of major thirds reaches completion, as suggested in Example 9.16.[41] The finale also modulates to A major for its secondary area in a further cyclical link.

Wayne Petty goes even further to offer an interpretation in which the C♯/A third relations participate in a process spanning the three-movement cycle. He demonstrates a three-stage progression by which the first movement retains, yet downplays, fifth relations in favor of third relations, including the C♯/A pair; the second movement intensifies the tertiary focus through its orientation around C♯ and A as key areas; and the finale "corrects" this drift from tonal convention through emphasis on tonic and dominant in their traditional roles as formal tonal pillars.[42] The interactions of C♯ and A with the F major of the outer movements provide an additional link with Schumann's A-minor sonata, where we have also observed the function of tonal tripling as a basis for cyclical integration. The specific III♯ function for A in these F-major outer movements suggests still another connection, as was the case for the middle movement of Brahms's A-major violin sonata. The difference is that Schumann marshals his patterns of tonal tripling in the service of a tragic expressive trajectory, whereas Brahms provides a larger consolatory frame in the quintet in the form of pastoral outer movements with a decidedly affirmative character.[43]

* * *

The quintet, like all the compositions explored in this chapter, demonstrates the impact tonal pairing may exert at the intersection of musical structure and expression, even in the context of an unambiguously monotonal framework. That pairings may work hand in hand with dualities of form, topic, and movement type is a sign of their foundational role in Schumann's and Brahms's musical thought. It is nevertheless the force of monotonality itself—perhaps challenged only for brief spans, if at all—that allows for tension to develop and meaning to emerge. By the same token, monotonality's predominance should not be reason to minimize either the importance of tonal pairing or the relationships manifest with broader dialectical trends in other composers and genres of nineteenth-century music. My point, rather, is to highlight the need for analytical caution in order to avoid either attribution of tonal ambiguities where none exist or precipitous recourse to concepts of directional tonality and "second practices." The illusion of tonal inevitability remains a primordial source of expression for Schumann and Brahms not despite the presence of tonal pairing but indeed in the very face of such pairings.

The similarities among the works analyzed in this chapter bring us back to an issue I have raised at various points throughout: the question of influence—whether Brahms may have based his compositional approach partly on Schumann's precedent, either in the case of specific modeling or more generally in terms of the broad development of his compositional voice. The issue is complex, of course, and thorough treatment of it extends well beyond the purview of this essay. I nevertheless have chosen my examples and tailored my analyses to suggest a strong connection between Schumann and Brahms and thus to provide some close technical scrutiny of a compositional relationship that all too often has been downplayed or even ignored. There is no doubt that the works of Beethoven and Schubert loomed large for Brahms as models for instrumental composition. It is nevertheless high time for us to follow the lead of more recent Schumann scholarship and put aside the long-standing negative judgments of the composer's traditional instrumental forms in order to explore the success these works achieve both on their own terms and as models for later composers.

To date, the study of Schumann's influence on Brahms has emphasized not his chamber music but his early poetic/programmatic works for piano, such as the Kreisler-inspired Variations on a Theme by Robert Schumann, op. 9. More recently, scholars have similarly linked Brahms's Variations on a Theme by Robert Schumann, op. 23, to Schumann's variation techniques. There also exists discussion of Schumann's influence on Brahms's First and Third Symphonies and the D-minor Piano Concerto. Yet many of these studies hinge on Brahms's allusions to Schumann's themes and compare only a small number of compositional characteristics, at times in a less than thoroughgoing manner.[44] I believe a fuller understanding of the Schumann-Brahms relationship will first require more systematic analyses of Schumann's instrumental works. Moreover, it is perhaps time to move beyond the methodology of these studies to engage a comparative approach focused on the ways a compositional technique like tonal pairing plays out across works in the same or related genres, with the comparison expansive enough to include consideration of the ways Schumann and Brahms employed the shared technique for a variety of expressive purposes.

Such an endeavor nevertheless will be best served not merely through comparison of isolated works or passages, with attention to similarities of compositional strategy. Although this may be a necessary first step, it will also be important to explore how both of these composers participated in larger compositional traditions. Such an approach has been standard practice in Brahms studies, of course, but in the case of Schumann's traditional forms, the tendency, until recently, has been to contextualize in order to denigrate. Although the movements I have analyzed share some striking points of contact, it is also the case that techniques such as 5–6 motions, emphasis on III♯, the tight interconnection of motives, harmonies, key schemes, and form, the compositional development of seemingly anomalous details, the basis of form in the alternation of slow and fast sections set in third-related keys, binary contrasts among topical orientations, and the unification of movements within a multimovement cycle are all part of the basic grammar of the tonal language that Schumann and Brahms both spoke fluently.

The task, then, will be to draw connections between works, to be sure, but also to heighten our appreciation of Schumann's and Brahms's compositions through interpretation of the expressivity of their tonal language in the context of the broader tonal language they shared with Bach, Haydn, Mozart, Beethoven, Schubert, Mendelssohn, Chopin, and others. I like to imagine that Brahms may very well have understood Schumann on these terms—as *a part* of, rather than *apart* from, the instrumental tradition both composers revered—and, moreover, that he would be pleased to see Schumann's music celebrated and his influence explored in an essay collection otherwise devoted to himself.

ACKNOWLEDGMENTS

The author wishes to thank Robert S. Hatten and Heather Platt for the numerous helpful suggestions and constructive criticisms they offered during the preparation of this essay.

NOTES

1. My focus here and throughout this essay on the foundational role of tonal centricity reflects the influence of Schenker, of course, but also the more recent ideas on the hermeneutic potential of Schenkerian concepts of monotonality developed by Carl Schachter, "The Triad as Place and Action," *Music Theory Spectrum* 17/2 (1995): 149–69.

2. Robert Bailey coined the term *tonal pairing* and the related term *double-tonic complex*. For a representative discussion of these concepts, see his "An Analytical Study of the Sketches and Drafts," in *Prelude and Transfiguration from Tristan and Isolde,* ed. Robert Bailey (New York: Norton, 1985), 113–46.

3. For some representative analytical applications and an extensive bibliography of additional sources, see William Kinderman and Harald Krebs, eds., *The Second Practice of Nineteenth-Century Tonality* (Lincoln: University of Nebraska Press, 1996).

4. One noteworthy exception with respect to pairing in Schumann's chamber music is Julie Hedges Brown, "'A Higher Echo of the Past': Schumann's 1842 Chamber Music and the Rethinking of Classical Form" (Ph.D. diss., Yale University, 2000).

5. For a representative statement summarizing the negative reception of Schumann's traditional forms, see Charles Rosen, *The Romantic Generation* (Cambridge, Mass.: Harvard University Press, 1995), 699–710. Rosen offers similarly negative conclusions in *The Classical Style: Haydn, Mozart, Beethoven* (New York: Norton, 1972), 451–60, and *Sonata Forms,* rev. ed. (New York: Norton, 1980), 365–408. Studies that question this received wisdom include John Daverio, *Robert Schumann: Herald of a "New Poetic Age"* (Oxford: Oxford University Press, 1997) and *Crossing Paths: Schubert, Schumann, and Brahms* (Oxford: Oxford University Press, 2002); Joel Lester, "Robert Schumann and Sonata Forms," *19th-Century Music* 18/3 (1995): 189–210; Hedges Brown, "'A Higher Echo of the Past'" and "Higher Echoes of the Past in the Finale of Schumann's 1842 Piano Quartet," *Journal of the American Musicological Society* 57/3 (2004): 511–64. On the possible influence of Schumann's rhythmic procedures on Brahms, see Walter Frisch, "The Shifting Bar Line: Metrical Displacement in Brahms," in *Brahms Studies: Analytical and Historical Perspectives,* ed. George Bozarth (Oxford: Clarendon Press, 1990), 139–63.

6. My approach here, as in my book *Expressive Forms in Brahms's Instrumental Music: Structure and Meaning in His* Werther *Quartet* (Bloomington: Indiana University Press, 2005), thus falls into a category of expressive interpretation that Nicholas Cook labels "formalist" ("Theorizing Musical Meaning," *Music Theory Spectrum* 23/2 [2001]: 170–95). Although this so-called (and perhaps misnamed) formalist school embraces a diversity of analytical method, Robert S. Hatten's *Musical Meaning in Beethoven: Markedness, Correlation, and Interpretation* (Bloomington: Indiana University Press, 1994) articulates a clear vision for its underlying principles. Hatten has continued to develop his theories in ways that intersect with my methodology in *Interpreting Musical Gestures, Topics, and Tropes: Mozart, Beethoven, Schubert* (Bloomington: Indiana University Press, 2004). More recently, Kofi Agawu has argued the merits of a formalist approach to expressive interpretation in *Music as Discourse: Semiotic Adventures in Romantic Music* (Oxford: Oxford University Press, 2009).

7. Both the three-key organization of the exposition and the tonal ambivalence of the A/F section reflect Schubert's influence on Brahms's sonata practice, as argued persuasively by James Webster, "Schubert's Sonata Form and Brahms's First Maturity," *19th-Century Music* 2/1 (1978): 18–35, and 3/1 (1979): 52–71. I suggest an alternative relationship between Brahms's two-part second groups and older sonata traditions in *Expressive Forms,* 122–80. In the present essay, I also offer the possibility that Schumann may well have influenced Brahms's recourse to tonal dialectics in both his sonata forms and other movement types in his chamber music.

8. For discussion of the pastoral as an expressive genre, see Hatten, *Musical Meaning in Beethoven,* 67–111; Hatten, *Interpreting Musical Gestures,* 53–67; and Raymond Monelle, *The Musical Topic: Hunt, Military and Pastoral* (Bloomington: Indiana University Press, 2006), 185–273.

9. Passages in which the melody appears in parallel thirds or sixths include the transition theme (mm. 43–46 and 51–54) and the A/F theme at m. 61. The extensive delay

of closure following the evaded cadence at m. 103 of the dominant key area (mm. 107–37) presents a striking combination of both local- and phrase-level repetition, a dominant pedal, and a long *crescendo* and *decrescendo*, all reminiscent of Beethoven's tonal language in the "Pastoral" Symphony. Straightforward phrase repetition also characterizes the exposition's other main thematic units: the main theme, the transition theme, the A/F theme, and the dominant theme are all stated and repeated, with minimal variation beyond reinstrumentation.

10. On the significance of markedness for musical expression, see Hatten, *Musical Meaning in Beethoven*, 29–66.

11. Michael Struck, "Beziehungs-Probleme: Zum Verhältnis der Komponisten Schumann und Brahms, dargestellt am Beispiel von Violinsonaten," in *"Neue Bahnen": Robert Schumann und seine musikalischen Zeitgenossen: Bericht über das 6. Internationale Schumann-Symposion am 5. und 6. Juni 1997 im Rahmen des 6. Schumann-Festes, Düsseldorf,* ed. Bernhard R. Appel (Mainz: Schott, 2002), 294–347. My discussion extends Struck's insights through more thoroughgoing technical analysis and engagement with questions of meaning, a topic that falls beyond the scope of his study.

12. As Margaret Notley discusses insightfully in the Brahms movement in "Brahms's Chamber-Music Summer of 1886: A Study of Opera 99, 100, 101, and 108" (Ph.D. diss., Yale University, 1992), 82–107, and "Discourse and Allusion: The Chamber Music of Brahms," in *Nineteenth-Century Chamber Music,* ed. Stephen E. Hefling (New York: Schirmer, 1998), 262–64. In her dissertation, Notley cites, as precedents for Brahms's alternation of slow and fast sections, movements by Mozart and Beethoven, but she does not mention Schumann's hybrid form in the A-minor violin sonata, nor does she draw a connection between Brahms's F/D pairing and Schumann's tonal dialectics. Her excellent study nevertheless stands as an important foundation for my work here.

13. The situation is thus similar to tonal interactions in one of Schumann's most famous instances of pairing, "Im wunderschönen Monat Mai," where the keys of A major and F♯ minor intertwine, but through emphasis on A-tonic and C♯-dominant *Stufen.*

14. In their recourse to III♯ as a salient chromatic harmony, Schumann and Brahms participate in a broader compositional tradition that extends at least as far back as the Baroque era (with, for instance, the practice of ending a slow movement with a Phrygian half cadence and then launching the subsequent Allegro from the tonic a major third down) and continues in sonata and other contexts in the later eighteenth century, as discussed by, among others, David Beach, "A Recurring Pattern in Mozart's Music," *Journal of Music Theory* 27/1 (1983): 1–29; Rosen, *Sonata Forms,* 262–75; and James Webster, *Haydn's "Farewell" Symphony and the Idea of Classical Style: Through-Composition and Cyclic Integration in His Instrumental Music* (Cambridge: Cambridge University Press, 1991), 135–38, 142–44.

15. I borrow the promissory metaphor from Edward Cone, "Schubert's Promissory Note: An Exercise in Musical Hermeneutics," in *Schubert: Critical and Analytical Studies,* ed. Walter Frisch (Lincoln: University of Nebraska Press, 1986), 13–30.

16. I undertake a more thorough exploration of the sonata's technical attributes in "Harmonies Heard from Afar: Tonal Pairing, Formal Design, and Cyclical Integration in Schumann's A-minor Violin Sonata, op. 105," *Theory and Practice* 34 (2009): 47–86. A more concise discussion appears in Linda Correll Roesner, "The Chamber Music," in *The Cambridge Companion to Schumann,* ed. Beate Perrey (Cambridge: Cambridge University Press, 2007), 123–47.

17. An additional connection arises in the emphasis the second movement places on $\hat{5}$–$\hat{6}$ interactions. The F-major refrain repeatedly returns to a D–C neighbor (mm. 2–3, 3–4, 4–5, etc.), the first episode emphasizes the minor-mode version of this motivic dyad

(mm. 20, 22–23, etc.), and the D-minor second episode highlights both the original E–F form of the first movement and a transposed A–B♭ version (Example 9.4, bass of mm. 45–47).

18. The lightness of F closure results partly from the arrival on $\hat{3}$ rather than $\hat{1}$ in the structural top voice at m. 52, in perhaps another reflection of the A/F pairing. (Recall the similar emphasis on A in the top voice in the F-major close of the middle movement.) It is also a consequence of the textural continuity across this cadence point and the absence of a codetta confirming the (qualified) closure. Instead, a 5–6 motion immediately destabilizes the F harmony and reinterprets it as pivot (iv⁶) for the modulation back to A.

19. Byron Almén, *A Theory of Musical Narrative* (Bloomington: Indiana University Press, 2008), 66.

20. Donald Francis Tovey describes the movement from the violin sonata as a "pastoral comedy" but characteristically fails to flesh out his suggestive insight. "Brahms's Chamber Music," in *Essays and Lectures on Music* (London: Oxford University Press, 1949), 262. My analysis pursues the implications of both aspects—the pastoral and the comic—of his characterization. An attribution of humor to the movement dates to the sonata's early reception, as exemplified by the critic Theodor Helm's description of it as a "humorous middle movement, an interesting exhibition of that singular combination of *Andante . . .* and *Scherzo . . .* that Brahms first realized in his F-major Quintet," in the *Deutsche Zeitung* of 11 December 1886 (quoted and translated by Notley, "Brahms's Chamber-Music Summer," 103).

21. Notley ("Brahms's Chamber-Music Summer," 98–99) draws attention to these passages of expansion and recomposition as sites for development of the F/D dialectic. She also notes the motivic origin of the D–C bass motion of the second passage (m. 150ff.) in the $\hat{5}$–$\hat{6}$ interactions that create linkage across the emergence of the episodes.

22. Almén, *A Theory of Musical Narrative*, 195–221.

23. Daverio draws attention to Schumann's and Brahms's shared proclivity for tonic-submediant interactions via the 5–6 technique in *Crossing Paths,* 162–68. He focuses on the similar recapitulatory consequences the technique motivates in Schumann's A-minor violin sonata and Brahms's String Quartet in C Minor, op. 51, no. 1. As Notley demonstrates ("Brahms's Chamber-Music Summer," 93–97, and "Discourse and Allusion," 262–64), historical evidence strongly suggests that Brahms modeled both the basic idea of the episode and its third-related harmonic progressions on a similar theme in the second movement of Grieg's Violin Sonata in G Major, op. 13. That the sonata simultaneously references works by Schumann and Grieg (and perhaps others) should come as no surprise, given Brahms's well-known penchant for "allusive webs."

24. Indeed, Margaret Notley goes so far as to suggest that, as a culmination for the movement's C♯/A pairing, the final measures convey "a psychological drama unprecedented in instrumental music." *Lateness and Brahms: Music and Culture in the Twilight of Viennese Liberalism* (New York: Oxford University Press, 2007), 3.

25. For discussions of these earlier dance movements, see Robert Pascall, "Unknown Gavottes by Brahms," *Music and Letters* 57/4 (1976): 404–11; and William Horne, "Brahms's Düsseldorf Suite Study and His Intermezzo, Opus 116, No. 2," *Musical Quarterly* 73/2 (1989): 249–83. Notley ("Brahms's Chamber-Music Summer," 82–87) and Hans Gál (*Johannes Brahms: His Work and Personality,* trans. Joseph Stein [New York: Knopf, 1963], 163–68) both provide descriptions of how Brahms adapted the earlier dance pieces for the quintet. Within these adaptations, the second B section (B', m. 117) remains somewhat more faithful to the gavotte idea: it retains the original's duple meter, eighth-note streams, and dotted-rhythm syncopations but forgoes the dance type's characteristic anacrusis phrase beginning. The first B section (m. 32) more thoroughly recomposes the material through transformation into a § version characterized by siciliano-like dotted rhythms.

26. Klaus Wolfgang Niemöller, "Suitenbildung mit alten und neuen Tänzen in der Klaviermusik von Schumann und Brahms 1853–1855," in Appel, *Neue Bahnen,* 328–39. See also Horne, "Brahms's Düsseldorf Suite Study."

27. That Brahms knew all Schumann's music intimately is without doubt, and he may have had the op. 105 sonata fresh in his ear as a consequence of the survey of the violin sonata literature that he undertook during the summer of 1883 in Wiesbaden with the amateur violinist Rudolf von Beckerath. Margaret Notley ("Brahms's Chamber-Music Summer," 8–12) persuasively demonstrates that the second movement of Brahms's sonata traces its origins back to the summer of 1883 and these *Hausmusik* performances with Beckerath. Alas, Beckerath's wife's diary, which lists music that Brahms and her husband performed, does not include Schumann's A-minor sonata. The diary is published in Kurt Stephenson, *Johannes Brahms und die Familie von Beckerath. Mit unveröffentlichten Brahmsbriefen und den Bildern und Skizzen von Willy von Beckerath* (Hamburg: Christians Verlag, 1979), 29–39.

28. The play between C♯ minor and major is an important contributing factor to the overall complexity of the refrain. The minor mode nevertheless clearly predominates, as the closing cadence and codetta of the first two refrain statements—not to mention the key signature—clearly indicate. The final turn to C♯ major at the end of the movement results from a Picardy third, that is, a final surface inflection of an overriding minor tonic.

29. Morgan makes his case specifically in response to Kevin Korsyn's interpretation of the movement as an example of directional tonality in his "Are There Two Tonal Practices in Nineteenth-Century Music?," article/review of *The Second Practice of Nineteenth-Century Tonality,* ed. William Kinderman and Harald Krebs, *Journal of Music Theory* 43/1 (1999): 135–63. (Korsyn's essay is titled "Directional Tonality and Intertextuality: Brahms's Quintet op. 88 and Chopin's Ballade op. 38," 45–83.) In an earlier interpretation, I also—mistakenly, I now believe—describe A major as emerging as closing tonic following a decentered interaction with C♯. "Brahms and Motivic § Chords," *Music Analysis* 16/2 (1997): 208. Margaret Notley ("Brahms's Chamber-Music Summer," 87) similarly asserts that with the final D–A progression "it becomes clear that A major, the key of the quicker interludes, is the key of the movement as a whole." In her later analysis in "Discourse and Allusion," however, she notes that "the eventual triumph of A major raises the possibility of arbitrariness . . . since most of the harmonic and formal signals point to C♯ (minor or major) as the overall tonal center of the work" (266). Wayne Petty traces connections between the C♯/A interactions and tonal processes involving these motivic harmonies in the outer movements in "Brahms, Adolf Jensen and the Problem of the Multi-Movement Work," *Music Analysis* 22/1–2 (2003): 105–37. Yet even as Petty remains open to the possibility that the A cadence forms part of a transition following a C♯ close, he suggests that "real features of the music make [the] matter undecidable" (128). Moreover, echoing Korsyn, he asserts that the coda's C♯ and A cadences "do indeed create the effect that neither key is primary" and adds that "the hovering between the C♯ major and A major triads near the end can certainly be taken as a way to insist on the equality, or at least a continuing autonomy, of the two keys" (126).

30. Victor Ravizza, "Möglichkeiten des Komischen in der Musik: Der letzte Satz des Streichquintetts in F dur, op. 88 von Johannes Brahms," *Archiv für Musikwissenschaft* 31/2 (1974): 137–50.

31. Here again I take my inspiration from Tovey ("Brahms's Chamber Music," 262), who describes the movement as a "sublime mystery."

32. This C♯ orientation is unambiguous both from the perspective of traditional harmonic analysis and from a Schenkerian perspective, as Korsyn's graph ("Directional Tonality and Intertextuality," 63–64, Example 10) of the refrain demonstrates.

33. Korsyn ("Directional Tonality and Intertextuality," 53) notes the emphasis on A harmonies within the refrain. He hears this emphasis, however, solely as preparation for the second key and not as part of a strategy that signals A's subsidiary status.

34. Notley ("Brahms's Chamber-Music Summer," 85) stresses the tonicization of D across the formal articulation, whereas Korsyn ("Directional Tonality and Intertextuality," 74) mistakenly asserts that the second episode "remains in A major, thus setting up the reprise of the first theme in A major/minor."

35. As Morgan notes in "Are There Two Tonal Practices?," 144. A similar delay characterizes the first return of the refrain. There the augmented sixth chord on A resolves to the dominant of C♯ at the thematic return, as previously noted (Example 9.13). The theme returns in the home key, to be sure, but the tonic *Stufe* reemerges only later. Note the difference with the delayed return of the tonic in the final refrain of the violin sonata (m. 150). Recall that there the off-tonic return in D receives preparation from its own dominant. Moreover, the first reference to F enters as part of an unstable ⁶₄ chord within an expansion of D (m. 152), so that D momentarily gains the upper hand. It is only after that temporary reversal that F reemerges as structural tonic.

36. See Ryan McClelland's essay in the current volume for discussion of this type of recessive yet expressively intense sequence as one of several categories of cumulative sequence that Brahms favored toward the ends of movements of his chamber works.

37. An additional element of tonic grounding arises in the recomposition of other material from the refrain. The passage that prolongs the vii⁰⁷ chord in mm. 13–16 returns at m. 176, but Brahms recomposes the phrase so that it articulates the C♯ tonic at its moment of entry. This idea also returns at m. 194, but Brahms again adjusts it to emphasize C♯.

38. Unless one is willing to argue for a connection from the E dominant of m. 172 to the closing A harmony, an exceedingly improbable interpretation in light of the enormous emphasis the intervening material places on C♯.

39. My graph is intended primarily to illustrate the predominance of C♯ on the large scale and, as a consequence, omits many beautiful intricacies of tonal organization within each of the formal sections. The first two statements of the refrain, in particular, only appear in their barest outlines, since I take for granted their unambiguous internal focus on C♯ as governing *Stufe*.

40. Further ambiguity arises from the relationship of the final cadence to the V/♯II–♯II motions in the immediately preceding C♯ cadential progressions, as Morgan ("Are There Two Tonal Practices?," 144) has suggested. The progression from D minor, rather than D major, in the final cadence raises the possibility of a i–V orientation rather than iv–I, especially given the previous emphasis on A as dominant of the Neapolitan and, more broadly, on the D tonicizations in the a′ sections of the episodes. Interestingly, a similar ambiguity arises in the arrival on the C♯-major version of the tonic in mm. 192–94. This material transposes the half-cadential arrival on G♯ from mm. 8–9 of the original version of the refrain, and its return on the C♯ level retains the half-cadential shading: is C♯ tonic or V/iv here?

41. I discuss this connection in the context of a broader study of Brahms's special treatment of ⁶₄ chords in "Brahms and Motivic ⁶₄ Chords," 208–209. Schenker's unpublished sketch of the passage (Oster Collection, file 34, item 153) also suggests a connection of A in the bass across the movements, as Petty points out. Petty transcribes Schenker's sketch as his Example 8 in "Brahms, Adolf Jensen and the Problem," 128.

42. Petty, "Brahms, Adolf Jensen and the Problem," 128–30.

43. Expressive interpretation of the entire quintet falls beyond the scope of this essay, but the combination of my engagement with the second movement here, the insightful structural analysis of the outer movements provided by Petty, and Ravizza's reflections on

the finale should provide the interested reader with a substantial foundation on which to build.

44. Discussions of the op. 9 variations include Hermann Danuser, "Aspekte einer Hommage-Komposition: Zu Brahms' Schumann Variationen op. 9," in *Brahms-Analysen: Referate der Kieler Tagung 1983*, ed. Friedhelm Krummacher and Wolfram Steinbeck (Kassel: Bärenreiter, 1984), 91–106; and Oliver Neighbour, "Brahms and Schumann: Two Opus Nines and Beyond," *19th-Century Music* 7/3 (1984): 266–70. George Bozarth likewise surveys Schumann's influence on Brahms's op. 9 and explores the relationship between Brahms's op. 23 Variations and Schumann's Andante and Variations, op. 46, in "Brahms und Schumann: Erinnerungen in Musik," in Appel, *"Neue Bahnen,"* 259–78. On the mutual use of mottos in the composers' symphonies, see Akio Mayeda, "Schumanns Motto und Brahms's Erste Symphonie: Motivanalyse und Versuch einer Deutung," in Appel, *"Neue Bahnen,"* 279–93. David Brodbeck identifies allusions to Schumann in his *Brahms: Symphony No. 1* (Cambridge: Cambridge University Press, 1997), as does Robert Bailey for the Third Symphony in "Musical Language and Structure in the Third Symphony," in Bozarth, *Brahms Studies*, 405–21. For discussion of the concerto, see George Bozarth, "Brahms's First Piano Concerto op. 15: Genesis and Meaning," in *Beiträge zur Geschichte des Konzerts: Festschrift Siegfried Kross zum 60. Geburtstag*, ed. Reinmar Emans and Matthias Wendt (Bonn: Gudrun Schröder Verlag, 1990), 211–47.

Selected Bibliography

Agawu, Kofi. *Music as Discourse: Semiotic Adventures in Romantic Music.* Oxford: Oxford University Press, 2009.

Almén, Byron. *A Theory of Musical Narrative.* Bloomington: Indiana University Press, 2008.

Bailey, Robert. "An Analytical Study of the Sketches and Drafts." In *Prelude and Transfiguration from Tristan and Isolde,* ed. Robert Bailey, 113–46. New York: Norton, 1985.

———. "Musical Language and Structure in the Third Symphony." In *Brahms Studies: Analytical and Historical Perspectives,* ed. George S. Bozarth, 405–21. Oxford: Clarendon Press, 1990.

Beller-McKenna, Daniel. *Brahms and the German Spirit.* Cambridge, Mass.: Harvard University Press, 2004.

———. "Reminiscence in Brahms's Late Intermezzi." *American Brahms Society Newsletter* 22/2 (2004): 6–9.

Berry, Paul. "Old Love: Johannes Brahms, Clara Schumann, and the Poetics of Musical Memory." *Journal of Musicology* 24/1 (2007): 72–111.

[Billroth, Theodor, and Johannes Brahms.] *Billroth und Brahms im Briefwechsel,* ed. Otto Gottlieb-Billroth. Berlin and Vienna: Urban & Schwarzenberg, 1935.

Bottge, Karen. "Brahms's 'Wiegenlied' and the Maternal Voice." *19th-Century Music* 28/3 (2005): 185–213.

Bozarth, George. "Brahms's First Piano Concerto op. 15: Genesis and Meaning." In *Beiträge zur Geschichte des Konzerts: Festschrift Siegfried Kross zum 60. Geburtstag,* ed. Reinmar Emans and Matthias Wendt, 211–47. Bonn: Gudrun Schröder Verlag, 1990.

———. "Brahms's *Lieder ohne Worte:* The 'Poetic' Andantes of the Piano Sonatas." In *Brahms Studies: Analytical and Historical Perspectives,* ed. George S. Bozarth, 345–78. Oxford: Clarendon Press, 1990.

Brachmann, Jan. *"Ins Ungewisse hinauf . . . ": Johannes Brahms und Max Klinger im Zwiespalt von Kunst und Kommunikation.* Kassel: Bärenreiter, 1999.

———. *Kunst, Religion, Krise: Der Fall Brahms.* Kassel: Bärenreiter, 2003.

[Brahms, Johannes.] *Johannes Brahms in Briefwechsel mit Heinrich und Elisabet von Herzogenberg,* ed. Max Kalbeck. Berlin: Deutschen Brahms-Gesellschaft, 1921.

[Brahms, Johannes.] *Johannes Brahms: The Herzogenberg Correspondence,* ed. Max Kalbeck, trans. Hannah Bryant. New York: E. P. Dutton, 1909. Repr., with an introduction by Walter Frisch. New York: Da Capo, 1987.

Brinkmann, Reinhold. *Late Idyll: The Second Symphony of Johannes Brahms,* trans. Peter Palmer. Cambridge, Mass.: Harvard University Press, 1995.

Cadwallader, Allen. "Foreground Motivic Ambiguity: Its Clarification at Middleground Levels in Selected Late Piano Pieces of Johannes Brahms." *Music Analysis* 7/1 (1988): 59–91.

Cadwallader, Allen, and William Pastille. "Schenker's Unpublished Work with the Music of Johannes Brahms." In *Schenker Studies* 2, ed. Carl Schachter and Hedi Siegel, 26–46. Cambridge: Cambridge University Press, 1999.

Cohn, Richard. "As Wonderful as Star Clusters: Instruments for Gazing at Tonality in Schubert." *19th-Century Music* 22/3 (1999): 213–32.

———. "Complex Hemiolas, Ski-Hill Graphs and Metric Spaces." *Music Analysis* 20/3 (2001): 295–326.

———. "Maximally Smooth Cycles, Hexatonic Systems, and the Analysis of Late-Romantic Triadic Progressions." *Music Analysis* 15/1 (1996): 9–40.

———. "Uncanny Resemblances: Tonal Signification in the Freudian Age." *Journal of the American Musicological Society* 57/2 (2004): 285–323.

Cone, Edward T. "Harmonic Congruence in Brahms." In *Brahms Studies: Analytical and Historical Perspectives*, ed. George Bozarth, 165–88. Oxford: Clarendon, 1990.

Cook, Nicholas. "Theorizing Musical Meaning." *Music Theory Spectrum* 23/2 (2001): 170–95.

Dahlhaus, Carl. *Johannes Brahms: Klavierkonzert Nr. 1 D-Moll, op. 15.* Munich: Wilhelm Fink, 1965.

Dubiel, Joseph. "Contradictory Criteria in a Work of Brahms." In *Brahms Studies 1*, ed. David Brodbeck, 81–110. Lincoln: University of Nebraska Press, 1994.

Ehrenpreis, David. "Beyond the Femme Fatale: Female Types in Wilhelmine Visual Culture." Ph.D. diss., Boston University, 1998.

Frisch, Walter. *Brahms and the Principle of Developing Variation.* Berkeley: University of California Press, 1984.

———. *German Modernism: Music and the Arts.* Berkeley: University of California Press, 2005.

———. "The Shifting Bar Line: Metrical Displacement in Brahms." In *Brahms Studies: Analytical and Historical Perspectives*, ed. George S. Bozarth, 139–63. Oxford: Clarendon, 1990.

Gadamer, Hans-Georg. *Truth and Method.* New York: Seabury, 1975.

[Geiringer, Karl.] *On Brahms and His Circle: Essays and Documentary Studies.* Rev. and enl. George S. Bozarth. Sterling Heights, Mich.: Harmonie Park Press in Association with the American Brahms Society, 2006.

Hancock, Virginia. *Brahms's Choral Compositions and His Library of Early Music.* Ann Arbor, Mich.: UMI Research Press, 1983.

Hanslick, Eduard. *Aus meinem Leben.* 1894. Repr., Farnborough: Gregg, 1971.

———. *Fünf Jahre Musik [1891–1895].* Berlin: Allgemeiner Verein für deutschen Literatur, 1896.

Hatten, Robert S. *Interpreting Musical Gestures, Topics, and Tropes: Mozart, Beethoven, Schubert.* Bloomington: Indiana University Press, 2004.

———. *Musical Meaning in Beethoven: Markedness, Correlation, and Interpretation.* Bloomington: Indiana University Press, 1994.

———. "The Troping of Temporality in Music." In *Approaches to Meaning in Music*, ed. Byron Almén and Edward Pearsall, 62–75. Bloomington: Indiana University Press, 2006.

Hepokoski, James. "Approaching the First Movement of Beethoven's *Tempest* Sonata through Sonata Theory." In *Beethoven's* Tempest *Sonata: Perspectives of Analysis and Performance*, ed. Pieter Bergé, Jeroen D'hoe, and William E. Caplin, 181–212. Analysis in Context: Leuven Studies in Musicology, vol. 2. Leuven, Belgium, and Dudley, Mass.: Peeters, 2009.

———. "Beethoven Reception: The Symphonic Tradition." In *The Cambridge History of Nineteenth-Century Music*, ed. Jim Samson, 424–59. Cambridge: Cambridge University Press, 2002.

———. "Sonata Theory and Dialogic Form." In *Musical Form, Forms & Formenlehre*, by William E. Caplin, James Hepokoski, and James Webster, ed. Pieter Bergé, 71–89. Leuven: Leuven University Press, 2009.

Hepokoski, James, and Warren Darcy. *Elements of Sonata Theory: Norms, Types, and Deformations in the Late-Eighteenth-Century Sonata*. Oxford: Oxford University Press, 2006.

Hofmann, Kurt. *Die Bibliothek von Johannes Brahms*. Hamburg: Wagner, 1974.

Jenner, Gustav. "Johannes Brahms as Man, Teacher, and Artist." In *Brahms and His World*, ed. Walter Frisch, 185–204. Princeton, N.J.: Princeton University Press, 1990.

Kalbeck, Max. *Johannes Brahms*. 4 vols. Berlin: Deutsche Brahms-Gesellschaft mbH, 1910–14. Repr., Tutzing: Hans Schneider, 1976.

Karnes, Kevin C. "Brahms, Max Klinger, and the Promise of the *Gesamtkunstwerk*: Revisiting the *Brahms-Phantasie* (1894)." In *Brahms and His World*, 2nd ed., ed. Walter Frisch and Kevin C. Karnes, 167–91. Princeton, N.J.: Princeton University Press, 2009.

Kersten, Ursula. *Max Klinger und die Musik*. Frankfurt am Main: Lang, 1993.

Kinderman, William, and Harald Krebs, eds. *The Second Practice of Nineteenth-Century Tonality*. Lincoln: University of Nebraska Press, 1996.

Klassen, Janina. "Parzengesang." In *Rezeption als Innovation: Untersuchungen zu einem Grundmodell der europäischen Kompositionsgeschichte—Festschrift für Friedhelm Krummacher zum 65. Geburtstag*, ed. Bernd Sponheuer et al., 323–35. Kassel: Bärenreiter, 2001.

Klein, Michael L. *Intertextuality in Western Art Music*. Bloomington: Indiana University Press, 2005.

Koch, Juan Martin. *Das Klavierkonzert des 19. Jahrhunderts und die Kategorie des Symphonischen: zur Kompositions- und Rezeptionsgeschichte der Gattung von Mozart bis Brahms*. Sinzig: Studio, 2001.

Kohlhase, Hans. "Konstruktion und Ausdruck: Anmerkungen zu Brahms' Klavierquartett op. 26." In *Johannes Brahms: Quellen, Text, Rezeption, Interpretation*, ed. Friedhelm Krummacher and Michael Struck, 103–26. Munich: Henle, 1999.

Krebs, Harald. *Fantasy Pieces: Metrical Dissonance in the Music of Robert Schumann*. New York: Oxford University Press, 1999.

———. "Some Early Examples of Tonal Pairing: Schubert's 'Meeres Stille' and 'Der Wanderer.'" In *The Second Practice of Nineteenth-Century Tonality*, ed. William Kinderman and Harald Krebs, 17–33. Lincoln: University of Nebraska Press, 1996.

Kretzschmar, Hermann. "Johannes Brahms" (1884). In *Gesammelte Aufsätze über Musik aus den Grenzboten*, 151–207. Vol. 1 of *Gesammelte Aufsätze über Musik und Anderes*. Leipzig: Breitkopf und Härtel, 1910.

Kross, Siegfried. "Die Terzenkette bei Brahms und ihre Konnotationen." In *Die Sprache der Musik: Festschrift Klaus Wolfgang Niemöller zum 60. Geburtstag am 21. Juli 1989*, ed. Jobst Peter Fricke, 335–46. Regensburg: Gustav Bosse, 1989.

———. *Johannes Brahms: Versuch einer kritischen Dokumentar-Biographie*. 2 vols. Bonn: Bouvier Verlag, 1997.

Lewin, David. "On Harmony and Meter in Brahms's Opus 76, No. 8." *19th-Century Music* 4/3 (1981): 261–65.

Litzmann, Berthold. *Clara Schumann: Ein Künstlerleben*. 3 vols. Leipzig: Breitkopf und Härtel, 1923.

———, ed. *Letters of Clara Schumann and Johannes Brahms, 1853–1896*. 2 vols. London: Edward Arnold, 1927.

MacDonald, Malcolm. *Brahms*. New York: Schirmer, 1990.

———. "'Veiled Symphonies'?: The Concertos." In *The Cambridge Companion to Brahms*, ed. Michael Musgrave, 156–70. Cambridge: Cambridge University Press, 1999.

Malin, Yonatan. "Metric Displacement Dissonance and Romantic Longing in the German Lied." *Music Analysis* 25/3 (2006): 251–88.

————. "Metric Dissonance and Music-Text Relations in the German Lied." Ph.D. diss., University of Chicago, 2003.

————. *Songs in Motion: Rhythm and Meter in the German Lied.* New York: Oxford University Press, 2010.

Mayer-Pasinski, Karin. *Max Klingers* Brahmsphantasie. Frankfurt: Rita G. Fischer, 1982.

McClelland, Ryan. "Brahms and the Principle of Destabilised Beginnings." *Music Analysis* 28/1 (2009): 3–61.

————. *Brahms and the Scherzo: Studies in Musical Narrative.* Farnham, England: Ashgate, 2010.

————. "Discontinuity and Performance: The Allegro appassionato from Brahms's Sonata Op. 120, no. 2." *Dutch Journal of Music Theory/Tijdschrift voor Muziektheorie* 12/2 (2007): 200–214.

————. "Metric Dissonance in Brahms's Piano Trio in C Minor, Op. 101." *Intégral* 20 (2006): 1–42.

————. "Tonal and Rhythmic-Metric Process in Brahms's Early C-Minor Scherzos." *Intersections: Canadian Journal of Music* 26/1 (2005): 123–47.

McCreless, Patrick. "Contemporary Music Theory and the New Musicology: An Introduction." *Journal of Musicology* 15/3 (1997): 291–96.

Monelle, Raymond. *The Musical Topic: Hunt, Military and Pastoral.* Bloomington: Indiana University Press, 2006.

————. *The Sense of Music: Semiotic Essays.* Princeton, N.J.: Princeton University Press, 2000.

Murphy, Scott. "On Metre in the Rondo of Brahms's Op. 25." *Music Analysis* 26/3 (2007): 323–53.

Nelson, Thomas. "Brahms in Accorde with Klinger, Part II." *American Brahms Society Newsletter* 18/2 (2000): 4–7.

————. "Brahms's Fantasies: In Accorde with Max Klinger, Part I." *American Brahms Society Newsletter* 18/1 (2000): 1–5.

————. "Klinger's *Brahmsphantasie* and the Cultural Politics of Absolute Music." *Art History* 19/1 (1996): 26–43.

Ng, Samuel. "The Hemiolic Cycle and Metric Dissonance in the First Movement of Brahms's Cello Sonata in F Major, Op. 99." *Theory and Practice* 31 (2006): 65–95.

Notley, Margaret. "Brahms's Chamber-Music Summer of 1886: A Study of Opera 99, 100, 101, and 108." Ph.D. diss., Yale University, 1992.

————. "Discourse and Allusion: The Chamber Music of Brahms." In *Nineteenth-Century Chamber Music,* ed. Stephen E. Hefling, 242–86. 2nd ed. New York: Routledge, 2004. First published 1998 by Schirmer Books.

————. *Lateness and Brahms: Music and Culture in the Twilight of Viennese Liberalism.* Oxford: Oxford University Press, 2007.

————. "Plagal Harmony as Other: Asymmetrical Dualism and Instrumental Music by Brahms." *Journal of Musicology* 22/1 (2005): 90–130.

Parmer, Dillon. "Brahms and the Poetic Motto: A Hermeneutic Aid?" *Journal of Musicology* 15/3 (1997): 353–89.

Petty, Wayne. "Brahms, Adolf Jensen and the Problem of the Multi-Movement Work." *Music Analysis* 22/1–2 (2003): 105–37.

Platt, Heather. "'Anklänge' as Brahms's Lied Manifesto." *American Brahms Society Newsletter* 28/1 (2010): 6–9.

————. "Dramatic Turning Points in Brahms Lieder." *Indiana Theory Review* 15/1 (1994): 69–104.

————. "Hugo Wolf and the Reception of Brahms's Lieder." *Brahms Studies* 2, ed. David Brodbeck, 91–111. Lincoln: University of Nebraska Press, 1998.

———. "Jenner versus Wolf: The Critical Reception of Brahms's Songs." *Journal of Musicology* 13/3 (1995): 377–403.

———. "Unrequited Love and Unrealized Dominants." *Intégral* 7 (1993): 119–48.

Reynolds, Christopher. "A Choral Symphony by Brahms?" *19th-Century Music* 9/1 (1985): 3–25.

Riley, Matthew. "The 'Harmonic Major' Mode in Nineteenth-Century Theory and Practice." *Music Analysis* 23/1 (2004): 1–26.

Rings, Steven. *Tonality and Transformation.* New York: Oxford University Press, 2011.

Rohr, Deborah Adams. "Brahms's Metrical Dramas: Rhythm, Text Expression, and Form in the Solo Lieder." Ph.D. diss., University of Rochester, 1997.

Rosen, Charles. "Brahms the Subversive." In *Brahms Studies: Analytical and Historical Perspectives,* ed. George Bozarth, 105–19. Oxford: Clarendon, 1990.

Samarotto, Frank. "Against Nature: Interval Cycles and Prolongational Conflict in Brahms's Rhapsody, op. 79, no. 1." In *A Composition as a Problem III: Proceedings of the 3rd International Conference on Music Theory, Tallinn, March 9–10, 2001,* ed. Mart Humal, 93–108. Tallinn: Estonian Academy of Music, 2003.

———. "Determinism, Prediction, and Inevitability in Brahms's Rhapsody in E-flat Major op. 119, no. 4." *Theory and Practice* 32 (2007): 69–99.

———. "Fluidities of Phrase and Form in the 'Intermezzo' of Brahms's First Symphony." *Intégral* 22 (2008): 117–43.

Sams, Eric. *The Songs of Johannes Brahms.* New Haven, Conn.: Yale University Press, 2000.

Schmidt, Christian Martin. *Johannes Brahms und seine Zeit.* Laaber: Laaber-Verlag, 1983.

Schoenberg, Arnold. "Brahms the Progressive" (1947). In *Style and Idea,* ed. Leonard Stein, 398–441. New York: St. Martin's Press, 1975.

Schubring, Adolf. "Adolf Schubring: Five Early Works by Brahms" (1862). Trans. Walter Frisch. In *Brahms and His World,* ed. Walter Frisch and Kevin C. Karnes, 195–215. Rev. ed. Princeton, N.J.: Princeton University Press, 2009.

Smith, Peter H. "Brahms and Motivic § Chords." *Music Analysis* 16/2 (1997): 175–217.

———. "Brahms and the Shifting Barline: Metric Displacement and Formal Process in the Trios with Wind Instruments." In *Brahms Studies* 3, ed. David Brodbeck, 191–229. Lincoln: University of Nebraska Press, 2001.

———. "Brahms's Motivic Harmonies and Contemporary Tonal Theory: Three Case Studies from the Chamber Music." *Music Analysis* 28/1 (2009): 63–110.

———. *Expressive Forms in Brahms's Instrumental Music: Structure and Meaning in His Werther Quartet.* Bloomington: Indiana University Press, 2005.

———. "New Perspectives on Brahms's Linkage Technique." *Intégral* 21 (2007): 109–54.

———. "You Reap What You Sow: Some Instances of Rhythmic and Harmonic Ambiguity in Brahms." *Music Theory Spectrum* 28/1 (2006): 57–97.

Stark, Lucien. *A Guide to the Solo Songs of Johannes Brahms.* Bloomington: Indiana University Press, 1995.

Struck, Michael. "Beziehungs-Probleme: Zum Verhältnis der Komponisten Schumann und Brahms, dargestellt am Beispiel von Violinsonaten." In *"Neue Bahnen": Robert Schumann und seine musikalischen Zeitgenossen: Bericht über das 6. Internationale Schumann-Symposion am 5. und 6. Juni 1997 im Rahmen des 6. Schumann-Festes, Düsseldorf,* ed. Bernhard R. Appel, 294–347. Mainz: Schott, 2002.

Tovey, Donald Francis. "Brahms: Pianoforte Concerto in D minor, op. 15." In *Essays in Musical Analysis, Vol. 3, Concertos,* 114–20. London: Oxford University Press, 1936.

———. "Brahms's Chamber Music." In *Essays and Lectures on Music,* ed. H. J. Foss, 220–70. London: Oxford University Press, 1949.

Ulm, Renate, ed. *Johannes Brahms: Das symphonische Werk: Entstehung, Deutung, Wirkung.* Kassel: Bärenreiter, 1996.

Van Rij, Inge. *Brahms's Song Collections*. Cambridge: Cambridge University Press, 2006.

Webster, James. "Brahms's *Tragic Overture:* The Form of Tragedy." In *Brahms: Bibliographic, Documentary, and Analytical Studies,* ed. Robert Pascall, 99–124. Cambridge: Cambridge University Press, 1983.

———. "Schubert's Sonata Form and Brahms's First Maturity." *19th-Century Music* 2/1 (1978): 18–35, and 3/1 (1979): 52–71.

Youens, Susan. *Heinrich Heine and the Lied*. Cambridge: Cambridge University Press, 2007.

Contributors

James Hepokoski is professor of music history at Yale University. He has written numerous books, including *Music, Structure, Thought: Selected Essays; Sibelius: Symphony No. 5; Giuseppe Verdi:* Otello; *Giuseppe Verdi:* Falstaff; and (with William E. Caplin and James Webster) *Musical Form, Form & Formenlehre: Three Methodological Reflections.* His work coauthored with Warren Darcy, *Elements of Sonata Theory: Norms, Types, and Deformations in the Late-Eighteenth-Century Sonata,* was awarded the Wallace Berry Prize from the Society for Music Theory in 2008. His articles on topics in nineteenth-century music and sonata form have appeared in *19th-Century Music, Journal of the American Musicological Society,* and the edited volume *Beethoven's* Tempest *Sonata: Perspectives of Analysis and Performance.*

Yonatan Malin is associate professor of music at Wesleyan University. He is the author of *Songs in Motion: Rhythm and Meter in the Lied.* His articles concerning music-text relations and theories of rhythm and meter have appeared in *Music Theory Spectrum* and *Music Analysis.*

Ryan McClelland is associate professor of music theory at the University of Toronto. He is the author of *Brahms and the Scherzo: Studies in Musical Narrative.* His articles concerning Brahms, Schenkerian analysis, rhythmic-metric theory, and performance studies have appeared in *Music Analysis, Music Theory Spectrum, Theory and Practice, Intégral, Journal of Music Theory Pedagogy, Intersections: Canadian Journal of Music,* and *Indiana Theory Review.*

Margaret Notley is professor of music at the University of North Texas. She is the author of *Lateness and Brahms: Music and Culture in the Twilight of Viennese Liberalism.* Her work has appeared in the *Journal of the American Musicological Society, 19th-Century Music, Journal of Musicology, Brahms Studies,* and a number of anthologies. For the article "Late-Nineteenth-Century Chamber Music and the Cult of the Classical Adagio," she received the American Musicological Society's Alfred Einstein Award in 2000. Most of her recent publications and current projects are on twentieth-century topics, with particular emphasis on Alban Berg and twentieth-century opera in general.

Heather Platt is professor of music history at Ball State University. She is the author of *Johannes Brahms: A Research and Information Guide*. Her articles concerning Brahms's lieder have appeared in *Brahms Studies, Journal of Musicology, The Cambridge Companion to the Lied*, and *Intégral*. She has also published review essays concerning theoretical approaches to Brahms's music in *19th-Century Music Review* and the *Journal of Music Theory*.

Steven Rings is assistant professor of music and the humanities at the University of Chicago. His monograph *Tonality and Transformation* includes analyses of a number of compositions by Brahms. His diverse research interests include the exploration of intersections between theoretical and cultural questions in music from Bach to Bob Dylan. His articles have appeared in *19th-Century Music, Journal of Music Theory*, and *Journal of Schenkerian Studies*.

Frank Samarotto is associate professor of music theory at Indiana University. He has published articles on the music of Brahms in *Intégral, Theory and Practice*, and *A Composition as a Problem III: Proceedings of the 3rd International Conference on Music Theory, Tallinn, March 9–10, 2001*. Other articles and reviews exploring issues in Schenkerian theory and analysis, some of which also reference Brahms, have appeared in *Music Theory Online, Schenker Studies 2, Theory and Practice, Beethoven Forum, Music Theory Spectrum*, and a festschrift for Carl Schachter.

Peter H. Smith is professor of music and director of undergraduate studies in the Department of Music at the University of Notre Dame. He is the author of *Expressive Forms in Brahms's Instrumental Music: Structure and Meaning in His Werther Quartet*. He has published articles on the instrumental music of Brahms and related composers, Schenkerian approaches to analysis, and theories of musical form in *Music Theory Spectrum, 19th-Century Music, Journal of Music Theory, Music Analysis, Intégral, Theory and Practice, Brahms Studies*, and the essay collection *Rethinking Schumann*.

Index of Brahms's Compositions

Page numbers in italics indicate musical examples.

General Index

Page numbers in italics indicate musical examples and illustrations.

Abbate, Carolyn, 15n14, 17n19, 46, 50n49, 138n4
absolute music, 4, 12, 14n1, 65, 227, 253
Adorno, Theodor W., 143n61
Agawu, Kofi, 5, 8, 11, 285n6
Almén, Byron, 13, 18n29, 265, 269
ambiguity, formal (blurring boundary points), 169, 235, 250n53, 252; tonal, 182, 18n27, 254, 256–57, 266, 283, 289n40
Ambros, August Wilhelm, 190, 214n11
Aristotle, 8, 117, 118, 139n19
Auerbach, Brent, 14n3
augmented sixth chord, 74, 122, 128, 134, 135, 141n40, 156, 178, 181, 273, 276, 277, 278, 280, 289n35
Austro-Germanic musical tradition, 12, 218, 219, 220, 228, 244
auxiliary cadence, 86, 106n17, 255

Bach, Johann Sebastian, 186, 234
Backfisch, 88, 89–90, 92, 104, 107n24, 107n27, 108n35
Bailey, Robert, 17n26, 18n27, 106n13, 285n2
Baroque, 118, 120, 186, 286n14
Barthes, Roland, 80, 105n4
Beckerath, Rudolf von, 288n27
Beethoven, Ludwig van, 15n11, 53, 106n12, 140n32, 171, 218, 219, 221, 228, 229, 244, 248n38, 249n44, 250n57, 259, 283, 285n9, 285n12; Symphony no. 9, 219, 229, 239, 240, 247n25
Beller, Steven, 47n10
Beller-McKenna, Daniel, 34, 48n16
Bernsdorf, Eduard, 218, 230, 249n52
Berry, Paul, 15n8, 66
Bierbaum, Otto Julius, 90, 107n27
Billroth, Theodor, 81, 105n5, 111, 113, 115, 117, 134, 137
Bizet, Georges, 27
Blake, William, 110n56
Bloom, Harold, 187, 202
Böcklin, Arnold, 90, 92, 98, 104, 108n33, 109n45, *Plate 4.1*
Bottge, Karen, 33, 48n39
Böttinger, Peter, 243, 246n18
Boyer, John, 47n10
Boyle, Nicholas, 123, 140n30, 143n31
Bozarth, George, 49n36, 245n3, 290n44
Brachmann, Jan, 48n16, 72, 76

Brahms, Johannes: allusions to other composers, 5, 15n8, 66, 217, 226, 228–29, 249n49, 283, 290n44; autobiographical implications of works, 17n21, 48n12, 104, 107n20, 110n56, 217, 226–28, 229; chamber works, 12, 27; influenced by other composers, 186–89, 190, 196, 201, 203, 204, 207; influenced by Schumann, 226, 249n49, 253, 257, 263, 274, 283–84, 286n12, 287n23, 290n44; intermezzi, 8, 24, 27, 45, 46, 48n16; late style, 8, 10, 24; lieder, 13, 80, 85–86, 97, 103, 105n5, 107n28, 108n40, 109n42, 110n52, 110n56; the performer, 48n18, 246n10; performing music by, 8, 24, 27–30, 31, 40–41, 43, 45–46, 49n26, 50n41; reception history of works, 5, 8–9, 25–31, 41, 47n10, 47nn18–19, 53, 54, 103, 111, 115–16, 117, 118, 131–32, 136, 141n47, 143n60, 218, 246n10, 249n52; and women, 66, 80, 105n1, 110n56. *See also* Index of Brahms's Compositions
Brinkman, Reinhold, 48n16
Bruckner, Anton, 11, 24, 253

Cadwallader, Allen, 18n28
Cai, Camilla, 216n33
Candidus, Karl, 55, 65
canon, 14, 19, 33–36, 38, 39, 40, 43, 45, 50n41, 154, 172, 174, 179, 235
Caplin, William, 7, 141n40
capriccio, 11, 48n11, 186, 187, 188, 189, 190–92, 196, 199, 201, 207, 209–12, 213n2, 216n34
Chamisso, Adelbert, 90
Chopin, Fryderyk, 245n7, 248n38, 253
circle of fifths, 147, 148, 150, 153, 156, 161, 168, 171, 174, 176, 178, 179–81, 237, 239, 259, 280
Classical style, 147, 183, 185n21, 222, 225, 231, 246n15, 248n38
coda, 10, 141n42, 147, 148, 152–54, 156–59, 161, 163, 164, 169–71, 172–83, 185n16, 243–44, 272, 275, 278, 280, 288n29
Coester, Mathilde, 88, 94
Cohn, Richard, 7, 14n3, 16n16, 18n28, 78n20, 107n20, 248n39, 251n68
concerto, 221, 228, 231, 238, 246n15, 246n18. *See also* sonata form, in concerto first movements

Cornelius, Peter, 92
counterpoint, 26, 39, 129, 153, 154, 159, 176, 179, 183, 191, 246n18. *See also* canon; invertible counterpoint
Culler, Jonathan, 131
cyclical works, 71, 79n32, 209, 216n32, 244, 245, 258, 260, 275, 282. *See also* Klinger, Max, *Brahms Fantasy* cyclical relations

Dahlhaus, Carl, 14n1, 26, 27, 243, 245n5
dance types and topics, 87, 233, 256, 267, 269, 272, 275; *Ländler,* 255; sarabande and gavotte, 274, 287n25; waltz, 39
Daverio, John, 79n32, 287n23
Day-O'Connell, Jeremy, 141n44
declamatory rhythm, 57, 58, 63, 73, 79n39, 100
Deiters, Hermann, 7
Dessoff, Otto, 100
dialogic relationship, 6, 12, 13, 17n21, 218, 219–21, 234, 238, 239
Dietrich, Albert, 227
directional tonality, 253, 275, 278, 280, 283
distance, 31, 34, 50n41, 59, 65, 66, 72, 96, 99, 101, 102, 113, 125, 135, 138n4, 142n57, 194
drama, musical, 12, 13–14, 58, 59, 95, 96, 99, 104, 148, 169, 171, 186, 220, 222, 226, 234, 244, 245; tonal, 225, 250, 252, 253, 260, 265, 266, 272, 280, 287n24
Dubiel, Joseph, 225, 232, 236, 240, 243, 245n5, 248n43, 251n63

Eibner, Franz, 192, 215n17
enharmonic reinterpretation, 74, 85, 134, 178, 181, 194, 204, 273
Euripides, 112, 117, 123, 136
Everett, Walter, 102, 106n19

fantasy, 187, 188, 189, 190, 192, 196
Ferris, David, 71
Feuerbach, Anselm, 90, 91, 92, 108n33
Field, John, 233, 248n38, 249nn44–45
folk style, 9, 13, 32, 33, 34, 80, 81, 82, 88, 92, 93, 96, 97, 100, 103, 104, 106n14, 108n35, 110n52, 267, 269, 275
form, 10, 118–20, 128, 139n22, 191. *See also* rondo form; sonata form
Forte, Allen, 4
frame, harmonic, 57, 75, 102–103, 120, 139n25, 216n25, 256, 280, 282
Frescobaldi, Girolamo, 189–90, *189,* 214n6
Friedrich, Caspar David, 94

Gadamer, Hans-Georg, 6
Gál, Hans, 287n25
Geiringer, Karl, 118
Genette, Gérard, 137n4

genre, 6, 10, 11, 48n11, 186, 187, 190, 191, 196, 207, 210, 211, 214n11, 218, 220, 221, 226, 230, 238
German, 19th-century culture and society, 5, 12, 33, 82, 88–93, 136, 244
Glaser, Hermann, 89, 107n28
Goethe, Johann Wolfgang von, 8, 10, 89, 110n56, 111, 112, 113, 115, 117, 118, 123, 124, 125, 126, 136, 137, 138n11, 140n30, 140n35
Gould, John, 137n4
Greek, ancient tragedy, 8, 108n33, 113, 117–18, 120, 123, 136, 137n4, 140n33; choric ode, 113, 123, 124
Gretchen, Goethe's, 89, 103, 107nn27–28
Grieg, Edvard, 287n23
Grimm, Julius Otto, 217
Groth, Klaus, 75

Hancock, Virginia, 141n41, 216nn26–27, 216n31
Hanslick, Eduard, 5, 14nn6–7, 25–26, 30–31, 48n18, 78n31, 81, 141n47
Harrison, Daniel, 122, 142n50, 142n53
Hatten, Robert, 5, 6, 11, 13, 14n6, 15n11, 40, 108n39, 109n50, 122, 139n21, 141n46, 142n51, 171, 247n25, 285n6, 285n8, 286n10
Haydn, Franz Joseph, 11, 215nn15–18, 215n20; Fantasy in C Major (Hob. XVII:4), 191–96, *193, 195*
Hegel, Georg, 210–11
Heldburg, Helene Freifau von, 78n31
Helm, Clementine, 89, 90, 94, 107n26
Helm, Theodor, 287n20
hemiola. *See* rhythm
Henkel, Arthur, 143n61
Hensel, Wilhelm, 94
Hepokoski, James, 11–12, 16n16, 17n21, 139n25. *See also* Sonata Theory (Hepokoski & Darcy)
Hepokoski & Darcy. *See* Sonata Theory (Hepokoski & Darcy)
Herder, Johann Gottfried von, 33, 36
hermeneutics, 6, 7, 9, 10, 11, 13, 15n12, 15n14, 219–22, 253
Herzogenberg, Elisabet von, 7, 15n14, 28–31, 46, 48n11, 49n28, 49n32, 80, 105n1
Heyse, Paul, 73, 81, 82, 88, 105n10, 106n11, 108n28
Hiller, Ferdinand, 116, 118, 138n11, 140n35
Himmel, Friedrich Heinrich, 92
Hock, Lisbeth, 86, 96
Hoeckner, Berthold, 49n34, 71, 79n33
Horne, William, 287n25
Horton, Julian, 248n38, 249n44
Hummel, Johann Nepomuk, 248n38, 249n44

humor, 159, 160, 192, 194, 196, 215n18, 269, 272, 275, 278, 282, 287n20
Huschke, Konrad, 105n1
hypermeter, 85, 162, 168, 170, 192, 194, 196–201, 206, 207, 209–10, 219, 255

innig, 10, 23, 27, 46
introspection, 10, 11, 30, 90, 98, 171, 237
inversion, 19, 20, 21, 22, 23, 27, 39, 40, 41, 43, 46n1, 47n7, 129
invertible counterpoint, 129, 159, 199, 233
Iphigenie, 108n33, 111, 113, 115, 117, 131, 136, 137, 143nn60–61

Jankélévitch, Vladimir, 46
Jenner, Gustav, 77n7
Joachim, Joseph, 15n11, 26, 27, 217, 221, 226, 227, 232, 245n8, 248n40, 249nn45–46, 250n56, 251n66

Kalbeck, Max, 100, 105n5, 116, 117, 125, 136, 140n37, 143n60, 226
Kalkbrenner, Friedrich, 249n44
Kapper, Siegfried, 81
Kinderman, William, 17n26
Klassen, Janina, 118, 139n22, 141n41
Klein, Michael, 5, 13, 40
Klinger, Max, 9, 15n14, 53–56, 59–60, *60*, 61, 62, 65, 66–67, 68, 69, *70*, 77n2, 77n4, 77n6, 77nn8–9, 78n16, 78nn25–26, 78n31, 79n35, 90; *Brahms Fantasy* cyclical relations, 56, 67, 70, 71–76
Knapp, Raymond, 106n12
Koch, Juan Mart, 245n4, 246n18, 248n40
Kopp, David, 17n27
Korsyn, Kevin, 187, 288n29, 288n32, 289nn33–34
Kramer, Jonathan, 192
Kramer, Lawrence, 86
Krebs, Harald, 7, 78n20, 106n13, 109n43, 156
Kretzschmar, Hermann, 7, 118, 132
Kross, Siegfried, 140n37, 142n49, 245n3

Le Guin, Elizabeth, 50n47
Lewin, David, 7, 14n3, 16n16
linkage technique (*Knüpftechnik*), 189, 196, 200, 204, 209, 216n24, 269, 287n21
Liszt, Franz, 11, 12, 188, 218, 221
Locatelli, Pietro, 11, 186, 188–89, *188*, 190, 200
Loewe, Carl, 90
Luft, David S., 47n10
lullaby, 33–34, 36, 49n36, 50n43

MacAuslan, John, 104
MacDonald, Malcolm, 118, 142n57, 142n59, 245n8
Mahler, Gustav, 251n64, 253

major/minor contrasts, 23, 40, 47n7, 57, 58, 63, 67, 69, 75, 84, 96–97, 122, 126–27, 128, 131, 134–35, 141n46, 142n48, 148, 153, 221–22, 225, 231, 234, 236, 239, 241, 242, 243, 244, 258, 265, 266, 274, 275, 288n28
Malin, Yonatan, 8, 9, 13, 108n36
markedness, 6, 95, 119, 122, 131, 132, 135, 141n46, 142n48, 154, 203, 229, 233, 234, 242, 252, 254, 255, 256, 259, 286n10
Marx, A. B., 227
McClelland, Ryan, 5, 10–11, 12, 289n36
McCreless, Patrick, 14n4
McEwan, Ian, 3
melancholy, 25, 48n16, 49n27, 70, 84, 85
Mendelssohn, Felix, 186, 214n2, 218, 221
meter, 163, 169, 172, 184n14, 189–90, 191, 207, 218–19, 246nn9–10; metric dissonance, 23, 40, 63–65, 78nn19–20, 83, 182, 196–98, 200, 203, 209. *See also* rhythm
Meyer, Leonard, 49n26
modal harmonies, 93, 101, 102, 112, 194, 204
Monelle, Raymond, 109n50, 285n8
monotonality, 252, 256, 278, 280, 282, 283, 284n1
monumentalism, 12, 217, 219, 244
Morgan, Robert, 275, 282, 289n40
Moscheles, Ignaz, 249n44
Moseley, Roger, 39, 236
Mozart, Wolfgang Amadeus, 49n32, 172, 219, 221, 228, 229, 233, 249n44, 250n55, 286n12
Müchler, Karl Friedrich, 92
Müller, Günther, 115, 117, 140n37, 143n60
Murphy, Scott, 14n3
Musgrave, Michael, 110n52

narrative, 137n4; musical, 12, 13, 18n29, 220, 221, 244, 246nn12–13, 250n59, 265, 269
Neapolitan harmony, 63, 65, 68, 71, 72, 73, 74, 75, 79n32, 79n35, 126, 128, 141n40, 153, 159, 176, 178, 184n7
Neo-Riemannian analysis, 7, 16n16, 18n28, 127, 128, 225, 232, 241, 251n68
Newman, Ernest, 103
Ng, Samuel, 14n3
Niemann, Walter, 141n47
Nietzsche, Friedrich, 26, 27, 48n22
Notley, Margaret, 8–9, 10, 12, 13, 17n21, 24, 27, 48n11, 102, 286n12, 287n21, 287nn23–25, 288n27, 288n29, 289n34

Ophüls, Gustav, 141n47, 142n48

Paganini, Nicolò, 186, 188, 189, 214n9
Parmer, Dillon, 36, 49n36
Pascall, Robert, 184n9, 184n14, 287n25

pastoral, 32, 34, 35, 36, 50n41, 85, 171–72, 174, 176, 182, 185n17, 194, 255–56, 266, 267, 275, 282, 285nn8–9, 287n20

Perrey, Beate Julia, 71

Petty, Wayne, 282, 288n29, 289n41, 289n43

phrase structure, 14, 40, 57, 62, 73, 79n39, 81, 83, 85, 94–95, 120, 122, 125, 140n36, 164, 174, 179, 185n20, 191, 192, 196–200, 204, 209, 232, 233, 234, 236, 250n57

plagal cadence, 73, 76, 79n44, 100, 102, 106n12, 106n14, 109n41, 122, 130, 131, 132, 133, 135, 198, 209, 272, 275, 278, 280, 282

Platt, Heather, 8, 9, 12, 18n28, 79n44

Pohl, Carl Ferdinand, 215n15

Polko, Elise, 89

Praetorius, Michael, 190, 191, 192, 196, 214n11

promissory note, 259–60

recapitulary overlap, 119, 139n24, 150, 152, 279

Rehding, Alexander, 219

Reichardt, Friedrich, 116

Reynolds, Christopher, 245n3

rhythm, 7, 8, 9, 13–14, 14n3, 58, 59, 72, 78n21, 99–100, 102, 108n40, 134, 152, 153–54, 163, 168, 169, 170, 172, 176, 181–82, 191, 239, 287n25; rhythmic dissonances (including hemiolas), 34, 76, 81, 85, 95, 106n12, 108n36, 141n39, 156, 158–59, 178, 203, 209, 219, 235. *See also* meter

Richter, Adrian Ludwig, 88

Ries, Ferdinand, 249n44

Riley, Matthew, 106n12, 142n52

Rimsky-Korsakov, Nikolay, 246n9

Rings, Steven, 8, 15n14, 16n16, 17n21, 18n28, 46n1, 88

ritornello, 118, 119, 120–23, 128, 129, 133, 134, 221, 222, 225–26, 246n15, 247n20. *See also* sonata form, in concerto first movements

Rohr, Deborah Adams, 79n39

rondo form, 109n43, 109n50, 118, 147, 160–61, 164, 168, 192, 194, 196, 257, 258, 266, 267, 269, 272–73, 278–79

Rosen, Charles, 20, 185n21, 285n5

Rothstein, William, 7

Samarotto, Frank, 5, 10, 11, 108n40

Savage, Roger W. H., 227

Schachter, Carl, 7, 284n1

Schenker, Heinrich, 16n16, 40, 47nn2–3, 284n1, 289n41

Schenkerian analysis, 7, 11, 16n16, 18n28, 47n6, 280, 284n1, 288n32

Schiller, Friedrich von, 136

Schmidt, Christian Martin, 24, 118, 141n47

Schmidt, Matthias, 103–104

Schoenberg, Arnold, 14n3, 40, 141n38

Schorske, Carl, 47n10

Schubert, Franz, 7, 89, 103, 106n13, 108n39, 109n43, 171, 184n7, 219, 253, 259, 263, 283, 285n7

Schubert, Giselher, 217

Schubring, Adolf, 218

Schumann, Clara, 7, 24–25, 26, 28, 31, 39, 41, 46, 48n12, 49n27, 50n44, 78n31, 80, 104, 140n34, 202, 217, 228, 244, 274

Schumann, Robert, 12, 15n14, 53, 71, 97, 104, 109n41, 188, 215n20, 218, 221, 226, 227, 228, 229, 233, 244, 248n35, 249nn46–47, 249n49, 253, 256, 257, 283, 284, 285n5, 286nn13–14; *Frauenliebe und Leben,* 90, 92; Violin Sonata in A Minor, Op. 105, 266, 282, 287n23, 288n27; Violin Sonata in A Minor, Op. 105, first movement, *261, 262, 263, 265, 269, 270;* Violin Sonata in A Minor, Op. 105, second movement, 254, 257–60, 263, *258, 260,* 269, 278; Violin Sonata in A Minor, Op. 105, third movement, 263, *264, 265. See also* Brahms, Johannes, influenced by Schumann

Schütz, Heinrich, 207; "Saul, Saul was verfolgst du mich?," 201–204, *202–203,* 207, 216n31

Scott, William C., 140n33

semitone motives (especially descending motives such as ♭$\hat{6}$–$\hat{5}$), 58, 60–61, 62, 111, 112, 122, 128, 129, 132, 133, 135, 141n41, 141n44, 142n50, 153, 159, 171, 184n7, 263, 286n17

sequence, 10–11, 12, 39, 62, 63, 126, 128, 147–83, 184n7, 185n16, 185n22, 200, 201, 204, 231, 239, 241, 280, 289n36

Shelley, Percy, 110n56

Siebold, Agathe von, 94, 103–104, 108n38, 110n54

Simrock, Fritz, 81, 105n5

Singer, Hans Wolfgang, 69, 73

Sisman, Elaine, 215n20

Smith, Peter H., 5, 10, 12–13, 16n16, 17n27, 18n28, 78n20, 97, 139n19, 140n32, 156, 183n1, 185n15, 216n24

Solie, Ruth, 92

sonata form, 118, 147, 152, 172, 176, 184n9, 194, 200, 218, 263, 265; in concerto first movements, 12, 220–44, 248n38, 249n44, 250n53; minor mode sonata forms, 148, 221–22, 232, 233, 236, 240, 246n19, 248n38; sonata versus rondo form, 160, 184n9, 184n11, 184n14; three-key exposition, 160, 254–56, 263, 285n7. *See also* recapitulatory overlap; Sonata Theory (Hepokoski & Darcy)

Sonata Theory (Hepokoski & Darcy), 11, 160, 187, 217, 221, 222, 234, 241, 247n20,

MUSICAL MEANING AND INTERPRETATION
Robert S. Hatten, editor